Knowledge of one or more high-level symbolic mathematics programs is rapidly becoming a necessity for mathematics users from all fields of science. The aim of this book is to provide a solid grounding in Maple, one of the best known of these programs. The authors have sought to combine efficiency and economy of exposition with a full coverage of Maple.

The book has twelve chapters, of which eight are completely accessible to anyone who has completed the usual calculus and linear algebra sequences as taught in American universities. There are three chapters on Maple programming. These can be read without prior programming experience, but a knowledge of a high-level programming language (Basic, Fortran, C, etc.) will be helpful. There is also a chapter on some relevant aspects of abstract algebra.

Although complete in its coverage of Maple, there is no "fat" in the book. Above all, the book is designed to enable the reader to extract value from Maple without wasting time and effort in the learning process. It provides a fast track to Maple expertise.

Contents

To Amir and Zahra and to Linda

Published by the Press Syndicate of the University of Cambridge
The Pitt Building, Trumpington Street, Cambridge CB2 1RP
40 West 20th Street, New York, NY 10011-4211, USA
10 Stamford Road, Oakleigh, Melbourne 3166, Australia

First published 1996

Printed in the United States of America

Library of Congress Cataloging-in-Publication Data

Nicolaides, Roy A.
    Maple : a comprehensive introduction / Roy Nicolaides, Noel
Walkington.
        p.   cm.
    ISBN 0-521-56230-9 (hardcover)
    1. Maple (Computer file)   I. Walkington, Noel.   II. Title.
QA76.95.N53   1996
510′.285′53 – – dc20   95-47895
                                                          CIP

A catalog record for this book is available from the British Library.

ISBN 0-521-56230-9 Hardback

MAPLE
A comprehensive introduction

Roy Nicolaides
Carnegie Mellon University

Noel Walkington
Carnegie Mellon University

CAMBRIDGE
UNIVERSITY PRESS

MAPLE
A Comprehensive Introduction

Preface

This book is a complete course in the use of the symbolic mathematics program called Maple. It is based on courses we have taught at Carnegie Mellon during the past several years. From this book you can acquire a sound knowledge of Maple sufficient for almost any normal purpose. In the process you will get a feeling for how the whole Maple system is constructed and what it is capable of doing.

For the most part, the level of mathematical sophistication of the book is that of a person who has taken (or is taking) the standard calculus and linear algebra sequence as taught in North American universities. Some familiarity with numerical methods will be helpful. In addition, the chapters on programming (Chapters 10–12) will be easier to follow if you have some basic programming experience. Such a background is sufficient to follow all but Chapter 7, which deals with additional topics in abstract algebra.

Foremost in our minds while we were writing the book was a desire to make the learning process as efficient as we could. We have tried to point out common errors and misconceptions (there are many) and to write concisely and avoid unnecessary detours. The first chapter of the book deals with Maple itself; how it is organized, how it structures data, and how it works. The next four chapters run parallel to the usual precalculus, calculus, linear algebra, and numerical methods sequence as taught in American universities. Chapter 6 covers graphics, and Chapter 7 covers algebra. Chapter 8 discusses utilities, both mathematical and nonmathematical. Chapter 9 discusses Maple packages, which are collections of functions for specific applications; much of Maple's capability resides in these packages. Chapters 10–12 concern writing Maple programs. Exercises are provided for the first four chapters and for Chapters 11 and 12. Most of these exercises are not simple, and some are quite demanding.

Chapters 1 and 2 provide a necessary foundation for the remainder of the book. As far as Maple (as opposed to mathematics) is concerned Chapters 3–9 are independent and can be read in any order, while Chapters 10–12 form a logical sequence.

Symbolic mathematics programs such as Maple have been widely available since the late 1980s. As professional mathematicians, we have found these programs to be extremely valuable tools for performing mundane computational tasks and for assisting our research. In our teaching, we have found that students greatly enjoy using the power (but not the frustrations) that Maple places at their fingertips. We firmly believe that everyone who performs mathematical computations needs to know how to use one or more of these programs and we will be very happy if our book helps spread to the word. Incidentally, Maple is an ideal program for learning because it has a simpler structure than some competing products but is just as capable.

Finally, although they are too numerous to mention individually, we would like to thank all of our friends and colleagues who, knowingly or not, contributed ideas and suggestions for the book. We would also like to thank the several generations of students who took our courses and who, through their questions and suggestions, improved our understanding of Maple. We wish to thank Doug Meade of the University of South Carolina for his comments on the book and Dave Pintur of Waterloo Maple Software for his help with getting an early copy of Maple V.4 up and running. Alan Harvey of Cambridge University Press also deserves our thanks for his untiring efforts and suggestions for improving the quality of the book. Last of all, a big thank you to our families for their support during the long process of putting this book together.

Roy Nicolaides
Noel Walkington
Pittsburgh.
September 1995

1 Planting the seeds: Introducing Maple

This chapter begins with a short section designed to introduce absolute beginners to entering instructions and finding their way around in Maple.

The second section covers a number of key ideas about the inner workings of Maple. For many purposes, it is not essential to know the material in this section. However, as you get more familiar with Maple it will be useful to understand the ideas presented here. We recommend that to you skim this section first and return to it later when the need arises.

The goal of the third section is to introduce some practical tools for working with Maple. This covers Maple's definition of terms such as set, list, and array as well as the difference between an equation and an assignment and other topics. This section can also be used for reference after a quick reading.

The fourth section provides a concise introduction to Maple's two- and three-dimensional graphics features. This material will enable you to graph some of the functions encountered in the first few chapters of the book. Chapter 6 provides a full treatment of graphics. The final section contains reference lists for the functions and Maple terms found in this chapter.

1.1 The basics

This section covers the most basic aspects of using Maple. The topics here are

- Interfaces to Maple
- Simple Input and Output
- Assignments and Expressions
- Functions and Their Arguments
- Online Help
- How Maple is Organized

Interfaces to Maple

Maple is a program that runs in many different operating environments that range from supercomputers to personal computers. Various versions may differ in their interfaces although the tendency is toward creating uniform interface capabilities. The interface is regarded as separate from the Maple program itself. This book only briefly discusses particular interfaces.

You may encounter different versions of the Maple program. This can happen because the latest versions of the program tend to get disseminated first for the most widely used platforms. New versions may appear later for other platforms. This book is based on the current version of Maple called Maple V, Release 4; however, much of the presentation applies just as well to the earlier versions of Maple.

To proceed from this point, you need to know how to start Maple and how to use your local interface. You also need to know how to exit from Maple (for example, by typing `quit`). It may also help to know how to interrupt a calculation that seems to be going on for too long. Although this is interface dependent, it is usually easy to find out what to do.

Simple input and output

The basic method for using Maple is "conversational." You input a computation and Maple immediately starts to work on it. There are no separate steps for compilation and linking. By way of illustration:

```
>2+2;
```

$$4$$

When the *enter* or *return* key is pressed after the semicolon, Maple responds with the result. The semicolon terminates the statement between it and the prompt ">." You should not omit the semicolon because it signifies the end of the input statement. However, it is permissible to put more than one statement on a line:

```
>1+1; 2+2;
```

$$2$$

$$4$$

Conversely, a single statement may occupy several lines as shown by the next (somewhat extreme) example:

```
>1
>+
>1
>;
```

$$2$$

If you want a result to be computed but not printed, you can type a colon in place of the semicolon. Typing the semicolon or colon soon becomes automatic even though at first it is easy to forget.

Assignments and expressions

Usually, you will need to give names to your results. This is done through an assignment statement. The typical assignment statement has a name on the left side and some other expression on the right side of the assignment operator ": =". The following example assigns the name e to an expression:

```
>e:=x^2-y^2;
```

$$e := x^2 - y^2$$

Notice that here Maple has simply returned what you typed in. This contrasts with the previous examples, in which the returned expressions were not the same as the input expressions. In fact, Maple tried to do something with the previous expression but found that it didn't know anything about its subexpressions. It is a general rule that Maple will apply whatever information it has about the elements of an expression before returning the value of the expression. Two important related ideas called *automatic simplification* and *immediate evaluation* are explained in Section 1.2.

Functions and their arguments

Much of your communication with Maple will consist of asking Maple to evaluate functions (also called commands, procedures, or routines). For example, the following command asks that the factoring function called factor() be evaluated on the expression e, which we just defined:

```
>factor(e);
```

$$(x - y) \ (x + y)$$

Maple responds by computing the factors of e. Here, e is the argument of the function `factor()`. Currently, Maple has between 2,000 and 3,000 functions for many different kinds of work. These functions usually take several arguments, some of which may be optional. There is some variability in how arguments are presented to functions. For example, they may be explicit expressions or the results of evaluating other functions. In fact, functions can be nested as deeply as you like.

One example of a function that performs nonmathematical work is `interface()`, and we will use it to illustrate some additional ideas. The `interface()` function allows you to control many aspects of your Maple working environment. For example, the original definition of the expression e was returned in a slightly different form from its input. It was passed through a Maple facility called the "prettyprinter" which produces a form of output closer to standard mathematical notation. You can turn off the prettyprinter using `interface()`. You can also decide what symbol you wish to use as a prompt, how wide you want the output screen to be, and several other things.

To change something using `interface()` you call it with the appropriate arguments. For example, in the MS-DOS environment the following changes the number of output columns to fifty-five and changes the prompt:

```
>interface(screenwidth=55,prompt=`Ready:`);
```

If you want to know the current setting of a parameter you omit the equals sign. For example, the number of lines defining the screen can be found as follows:

```
Ready:interface(screenheight);
```

$$25$$

The expressions appearing in the first call to `interface()` used equals signs and not assignment symbols. These expressions are called equations, as you might expect, and they are different from assignments. The difference is discussed in Section 1.3. Note also that the symbol for the new prompt is enclosed in backward-sloping quote symbols (also called "back quotes" or "string quotes" as distinct from "forward quotes", also called apostrophes) to inform Maple that it is dealing with a string. (Strings are discussed in Sections 1.2 and 1.3.)

Online help

Even when you have considerable experience with Maple, it is difficult to remember all of the possible arguments for the functions. Fortunately, Maple has an easy-to-use help system containing the arguments and other information. To see the help file for a particular function, type a question mark followed by the name of the function. For example, here is a part of the help file for `interface()`:

```
>?interface


FUNCTION: interface - set or inquire user interface
            variables


CALLING SEQUENCE:
    interface( arg1, arg2, ... )
    where the arguments are either equations or names


PARAMETERS:
    name=val - specifies the setting for the named
               variable
    name      - retrieves the current value of the named
               variable


SYNOPSIS:
- The function interface is provided as a unique
mechanism of communication between Maple and the user
interface (called Iris). Specifically, this function is
used to set and inquire about all variables that affect
the format of  the output but do not affect the
computation.
```

The file goes on to list the allowed arguments and their values and concludes with a set of examples, part of which is reproduced here:

```
EXAMPLES:
interface( plotdevice=postscript, plotoutput=myfile );
oldquiet := interface( quiet, quiet=true );
interface( echo=2, prompt=`#-->`);
```

To begin the help system at the highest level you type a lone "?" (no ";" is needed). From there on, enough online assistance is provided to find your way around. In addition to information about functions, the help system contains descriptions of other Maple entities including, for example, arrays, data types, and procedures. The help system also includes a multilevel "browser," which provides assistance for selecting functions for a specific task and a tutorial. The browser can usually be accessed through an interface "help" button.

There are four functions that can be used to access specific headings from the help file. These are `info()`, `usage()`, `example()`, and `related()`. Type `?info` to see the help file on these functions.

In this book, we will present the main arguments of Maple functions, often leaving the optional arguments to the online help system. We hope that you agree with this approach as it avoids a lot of minutiæ and allows us to emphasize an overall view of Maple, which is one of the keys to using it efficiently. We would like to encourage you to get into the excellent habit of routinely using online help. Maple's online help system is very easy to use and offers a wealth of useful information.

How Maple is organized

Maple's functions, mathematical and otherwise, are stored in what is called the Maple library of which there are four parts. The most basic part of the library is called the kernel. The functions in the kernel are referred to as "built-in" functions. Typically, built-in functions manipulate the internal representation of their arguments in a more direct way than other functions do. The kernel is always present in your Maple session in the sense that the functions it contains can be called on directly without having to be "loaded" from another source. The functions in the kernel are the foundation for the rest of Maple.

Functions in the next part of the library are also accessed directly. However, they are not as directly available as the built-in functions. Instead, before using one of these "demand-loaded" functions, Maple automatically retrieves it from the library. Usually, you will be unaware of this operation, and the demand-loaded functions appear similar in use to built-in functions. However, there is an important distinction between the two functions: You can read the code that defines a demand-loaded function. The code is a standard Maple procedure, which consists of a list of Maple commands combined with various programming constructs (covered in Chapters 10, 11, and 12 of this book). This very valuable feature of Maple applies to all parts of the library except the kernel.

The third part of the library contains functions that you have to load manually before you can use them. Loading is easily performed using a Maple command called `readlib()` whose single argument is the function you want to use. Once this command has been executed, the function is available for use. The first three levels of the library contain several hundred functions in all.

The fourth, and by far the largest part of the library, contains what are called packages. Basically, a package is a collection of functions grouped around a well-defined mathematical topic. For example, one of the most important packages is called `linalg[]` and contains most of Maple's facilities for doing linear algebra, including solving equations and finding eigenvalues (the `linalg[]` package is the main topic of Chapter 4). There are packages for topics such as combinatorics, statistics, differential forms, projective geometry, and many others. (Chapter 9 describes these packages.) Functions in packages can and often do use functions from other packages. Ultimately however, everything is built on the functions in the kernel. You load a package by using the command `with()`, where the name of the package is the argument. Following the loading step, the functions in the package are available for use as usual. It is also possible to access a function in a package without loading the entire package first. The `plots[]` package subsection in Section 1.4 illustrates how to do this.

Take the tour!

If you are a new Maple user, this would be a good time to scan the practical illustrations of Maple found throughout this book. The illustrations should give you a feel for the kinds of things you can do with Maple and will illustrate the material in the rest of this chapter.

1.2   Behind the scenes

It is helpful to have a general knowledge of how Maple is designed and how it operates. Section 1.2 provides some of the necessary background. This material is also useful for understanding the terminology in Maple's online help system and documentation. The subsection titles are

- Expressions and Types
- Full Evaluation
- Automatic Simplification
- More on Types and Type Conversions

Expressions and types

The online help system and other Maple literature often mention expressions. In this section we discuss this term and its significance in Maple. The concept of an expression is one of the cornerstones of the modern theory of programming languages. Generally, the expressions in a language are defined operationally as an explicit list of allowed expressions (which make extensive use of placeholders for operations and data). You do not usually need to learn the abstract definitions of the allowable expressions. However, the *Maple V Language Reference Manual*[1] does present these definitions for Maple. More information on expressions and their role in programming languages can be found in almost any basic computer science text.

Most of what you type into Maple contains expressions. By way of illustration, we present four expressions. In each case, the outputs are suppressed because they are not of immediate interest:

```
>x:
```

```
>print(evalf(x*y*z,9)):
```

```
>(D@@42*D@@2+1)(z)=0:
```

```
>series((exp(t)-1)^(2),t=0,9):
```

These examples imply that an expression may contain subexpressions that are themselves expressions. Thus expressions may be generated recursively. The simplest examples of expressions are numbers and names. At the other end of the scale, the collection of statements making up a function is also an expression.

Expressions are represented internally by a "tree" (also called directed acyclic graph) data structure. When Maple is presented with an expression, the expression is "parsed" (analyzed) and a tree is made that represents it. The "nodes" of this expression tree correspond to various defined entities called types, which are discussed below. Figure 1.1 depicts an expression tree for the polynomial (expression) (x-1)^2-y^2+2.

Each node represents a Maple type. For this example the types are +, *, ^, integer and string. In this case, the nodes of the tree contain the symbols +, ^, *, x, y, and some integers. Each of these symbols is an example of a Maple type. The "variables" x and y are of a type called string and the integers are of type integer. The arithmetic operator symbols themselves are used to represent types. For example, there is a type called + that stands for a summation of terms. For further information about types see the More on Types and Type Conversions subsection. Right now, we want to emphasize that regardless of how complicated an expression may appear, it is always represented as a tree in the way sketched in Figure 1.1. This tree is Maple's way of representing the expression, and subsequent calculations involving the expression start from the tree form.

---

[1]B. W. Char et al., Springer Verlag, 1990.

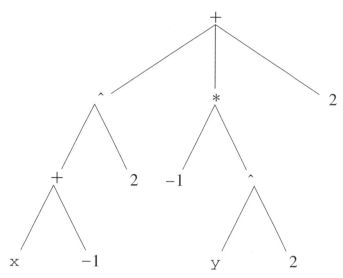

Figure 1.1: An expression tree for $(x-1)^2 - y^2 + 2$.

It is the fate of expressions to be "evaluated." The way evaluation occurs in Maple is highly important, and we will discuss it again in the next subsection. For now, we mention that initiating evaluation of the polynomial expression given above leads to a definite sequence of events: first, any numerical values that might be assigned to x and y are substituted for their names and second, starting from the "leaves" of the tree containing the numerical data, the arithmetic operations in the tree are applied. The evaluation concludes at the topmost node of the tree with the value of the expression.

If the expression tree contains variables without assigned numerical values, the expression can still be evaluated to a result that contains those variables as literals. In that way, both symbolic and numeric evaluations can occur. In more complicated expressions than the simple polynomial above, the variables in the expression tree may themselves be the names of arbitrary expressions. In Maple, these names are "pointers" to (that is, addresses of) the corresponding expressions. When such a name is encountered in an evaluation process, the pointer tells Maple where to look to find the corresponding expression.

Not everything that you input to Maple is an expression. One example is an assignment statement. For example, the following is not an expression:

```
>x:=1:
```

Although the assignment statement is not an expression, both of the items on the left and right sides of the assignment symbol are expressions. The left side is represented internally by Maple as a type called name, and the right side, here an integer expression, in general may be any expression.

Sometimes you may wish to know how a particular expression is represented in its tree. That means knowing what its nodes are and what links exist between them. Three of the Maple functions for finding this out are `nops()`, `op()`, and `whattype()`. The following example illustrates the use of these functions:

```
>e:=x*(x+y);
```

$$e := x (x + y)$$

```
>whattype(e);
```

$$*$$

```
>nops(e);
```

$$2$$

This means that the topmost node of the tree for e is a * and that this node has two "branches" emanating from it. To find out what is at the end of the branches, you use `op()` as follows:

```
>o1:=op(1,e); o2:=op(2,e);
```

$$o1 := x$$

$$o2 := x + y$$

Each of these expressions can be dissected in a similar way:

```
>nops(o1); nops(o2);
```

$$1$$

$$2$$

When you find an argument, say arg, for which `nops()` returns the value 1 and such that `nops(op(1,arg))` also returns 1, you have gone as far as possible on that branch of the tree and only finding the type of the operand remains. The function whattype() can also be used for this:

```
>whattype(o1);
```

$$string$$

Note that obtaining a string type for an expression does not necessarily mean that no further reduction is possible (for example, a proc (that is, a procedure) has a string type); you must also perform the test given above.

Any expression tree in Maple can be analyzed in a similar way, at least in theory. In practice, this approach can be rather tedious if the tree is at all complex. The functions seq() and map() can be used to reduce the work. Chapter 12 contains a programming example that automates the entire process of finding expression trees. In addition, the readlib() defined function dismantle() can often give detailed information on how an expression is recorded.

It is possible to selectively change one or more operands of an expression with a function called subsop(). (See the example in the Working with Structured Data subsection. There is additional information on types in More on Types and Type Conversions below and also in Section 11.1, Type Checking and Procedure Arguments.)

Full evaluation

In this subsection, we will look more closely at how evaluation works in Maple. Some understanding of this topic is necessary in order to use Maple effectively. We will begin with the polynomial used to illustrate expressions in the previous subsection. First, we assign it the name e:

```
>e:=(x-1)^2-y^2+2;
```

$$e := (x - 1)^2 - y^2 + 2$$

Maple has now parsed the expression on the right of the assignment and made the corresponding tree structure. Now make another assignment:

```
>x:=3;
```

$$x := 3$$

To have e evaluated, you can simply enter its name. Here is the result:

```
>e;
```

$$6 - y^2$$

Each time Maple encounters the name x in the evaluation of e, it substitutes the expression to which x points, in this case the integer 3, and uses it in the evaluation in place of x.

What if x had already been assigned before e was assigned? The answer is that Maple explicitly incorporates the value 3 into the expression tree:

```
>x:=3;
```

$$x := 3$$

```
>e:=(x-1)^2-y^2+2;
```

$$e := 6 - y^2$$

In this instance, the expression tree does not contain x. You can check this by removing the assignment of x and then evaluating e. We will see again later that you unassign a variable by enclosing it in forward quote symbols like the following:

```
>x:='x';
```

$$x := x$$

The variable x now is just a name, which is what the previous result shows.
Evaluating e again gives:

```
>e;
```

$$6 - y^2$$

The point here is that it is 3 and not x that is in the expression tree for e.

What if the evaluation tree contains the names of more complex subexpressions than integers? The answer is that nothing essentially different happens. Maple goes off and evaluates these subexpressions and their subexpressions and so on. Evaluation proceeds in this way until the top of the tree is reached. No matter how complex the expression tree, the evaluation starts at the lowest levels and proceeds to successively higher levels evaluating (recursively) whatever subexpressions appear in a path. Eventually, there is nothing left to compute and the evaluation is complete. Note the following important point: The expression tree itself is not changed by evaluation. The tree (and the trees of all the subexpressions) look the same after evaluation as they did before evaluation.

The technical name for this automatic evaluation scheme is "full recursive evaluation" or just "full evaluation." Full evaluation is a basic operating principle of Maple. With few exceptions, which will be mentioned as they occur, full evaluation of an expression takes place automatically whenever the expression appears in a statement as a function argument or on the right-hand side of an assignment. This can have surprising consequences, and we will see many examples as we proceed. The essential point to bear in mind is that expressions are evaluated using everything that is currently known about their subexpressions before they are used for (just about) any purpose.

It is easy to underestimate the full evaluation property. For example, the "number of operands" function `nops()`, which is used for dissecting expressions, might be applied to the expression `int(x^2,x)` (which asks for the integral of x^2 with respect to x). You might easily believe that the next command is telling you the number of operands of the expression `int(x^2,x)`:

```
>nops(int(x^2,x));
```

$$2$$

but unfortunately that is wrong. We have here an expression in which the argument to the function is a subexpression. Because of full evaluation of the argument, what has been returned is not the number of operands of the expression `int(x^2,x)` but the number of operands of the expression `x^3/3` representing $x^3/3$. If you realized this you're ahead of the game!

The next example is a standard one that illustrates how full evaluation propagates its results:

```
>a:=b;  b:=c;  c:=1;
```

$$a := b$$

$$b := c$$

$$c := 1$$

```
>a;
```

$$1$$

When you asked for a, Maple evaluated the expression and found b. Then it evaluated b and found c, and then it evaluated c and found 1. No more evaluations are possible, so the process stops and the value 1 is returned.

There is another aspect of full evaluation that needs to be mentioned. Its simplest form occurs in a legal Maple assignment such as e:=e+1 when e has no assigned value. When you attempt to evaluate e, the assignment causes an infinite recursion to be attempted. This happens because in the full-evaluation setting the statement is self-referential. It is a variation of the propagating evaluations illustrated in the previous paragraph. Maple will warn you when it detects this problem:

```
>e:=e+1;
```

```
Warning: Recursive definition of name
             e := e + 1
```

Anything that causes e to be evaluated (for example typing e;) will now cause a "stack overflow" error (jargon for a situation in which Maple has run out of space for tracking the evaluations of e). This may result in a system crash or just an error message. In more complicated expressions, a recursive definition of a name can occur without a warning from Maple. Even though there is no warning, attempting evaluation will inevitably result in a stack overflow.

It is often necessary to prevent Maple from evaluating an expression. For example, recalling the earlier example, you may really want to know the number of operands in the expression int(x^2,x) and not the number of operands in the result of this integration. Maple provides a mechanism for letting you do this. For example, we first define an expression u to be a simple derivative: before printing the result, Maple evaluates the expressions (diff() is covered in Chapter 3):

```
>u:=diff(x^2,x);
```

$$u := 2 x$$

Now suppose that you want u to be the expression diff(x^2,x) rather than the result of an evaluation of it. You would do the following:

```
>u:='diff(x^2,x)';
```

$$u := \frac{d}{dx}\, x^2$$

The difference lies in the forward quote symbols enclosing the expression. When Maple sees these symbols it evaluates them as it evaluates just about everything else, but the result of evaluation is simply to remove them, with the result that you see. Instead of preventing full evaluation, it could be said that this technique protects `diff(x^2,x)` from full evaluation. What will result if we now type u? Here is the answer:

```
>u;
```

$$2\,x$$

This is just another example of full evaluation at work.

Using forward quotes is the main way to remove whatever assigned value a name has. For example, continuing from the last result, suppose you wanted to return u to being just a name. You would do the following:

```
>u:='u';
```

$$u := u$$

When the expression is evaluated, the quotes are removed, leaving the name. The previous value $2x$ is now lost. This is a technique that you will often have to use. It is the main way to "reset" or unassign a name so that you can use it for something else.

The technique of using forward quotes to protect expressions from evaluation can be nested as deeply as necessary for any particular case.

Automatic simplification

You would expect Maple to automatically simplify the fraction 2/4 to 1/2, and so it does. There are several other "automatic simplifications" that Maple performs, and you should be aware of them, especially because they can sometimes cause unexpected problems. In addition to the kind of simplification just mentioned, Maple automatically performs arithmetic simplifications such as replacing `(2+7+1.22)/2` by `5.11` and removes identical factors in rational expressions. Maple condenses sums and products as the following shows:

```
> (a*a+a*b-b*b-b*a)/3;
```

$$1/3 \ a^2 \ - \ 1/3 \ b^2$$

In the example above, products of like quantities have been simplified to exponent form, subtraction of equal quantities has resulted in their disappearance, and a numerical multiplier has been distributed over a sum. In contrast, no automatic simplification occurs in the next expression:

```
> (a^2-b^2)/(a+b);
```

$$\frac{a^2 \ - \ b^2}{a \ + \ b}$$

Automatic simplification will only cancel explicitly identical factors in the numerator and denominator.

Maple performs automatic simplifications on function values such as `sin(Pi/2)` (giving 1) and `log(1)` (giving 0).

Maple will automatically simplify expressions such as

```
>exp(ln(x));
```

$$x$$

Maple does not automatically simplify expressions if there is any ambiguity about the result. For example:

```
>sqrt(x^2);
```

$$(x^2)^{1/2}$$

To force Maple to take the positive branch, you can use the following option:

```
>sqrt(x^2,symbolic);
```

$$x$$

Another way to have Maple perform such simplifications to tell it about the arguments. For instance, we can do the following:

```
>assume(x>=0);
>sqrt(x^2);
```

$$x\sim$$

The ~ after x tells us that assumptions have been made about it (for instance, that it is nonnegative). The `assume()` function was introduced in Maple 5, Release 2. Although it is not yet completely integrated into Maple, it is nevertheless a powerful facility.

There is no central list of automatic simplifications available at the user level. In part because of this, automatic simplification is not something that you have much control over. (One promising idea might be to use forward quotes around the expression of interest; unfortunately, it doesn't work!) The fastest way to find out how and whether a particular expression is being automatically simplified is to try out a simple example that contains the essentials of the problem of interest.

More on types and type conversions

The general idea of a type was introduced earlier in connection with expressions. In this section we pursue the subject a little farther. The general subject of types in Maple is quite extensive, but the discussion here is short, consistent with the goals of the chapter.

In Expressions and Types we met the function `whattype()`. In this section we introduce another function called `type()`, which can be used to test whether an expression is of a given type. A function that does this is necessary because expressions can have more than one type. To illustrate this point look at the following example:

```
>e:=x+y;
```

$$e := x + y$$

```
> whattype(e);
```

$$+$$

This can be checked using the `type()` function as follows:

```
>type(e,`+`);
```

$$\text{true}$$

The plus sign is enclosed in back quotes to inform Maple that it is dealing with a string and not the arithmetic operator. To continue, e has another type:

```
>type(e,polynom);
```

$$\text{true}$$

Maple distinguishes between these two types by the way it has to check for them. Some types are recorded in the top level of the expression tree. Checking for these types (also using `type()`) is merely a question of verifying their presence or absence. Types found at the top level are called surface types; the type + is a surface type. Other types have to be checked by the more complex process of examining each part of the tree to make sure that the conditions for that type are met. They are called nested types, and the type polynom is one of these. Every expression has a surface type (a list of surface types can be found under `?type[surface]`), and that is what `whattype()` returns; `whattype()` cannot be used to find any other types. You must test for nested types with `type()`. Similarly, the `op()` function will also return surface types but not nested types.

Here are a few examples illustrating nested types:

```
>u:=exp(x);
```

$$u := \exp(x)$$

```
>type(u,mathfunc);
```

$$\text{false}$$

```
>u:=exp;
```

$$u := \exp$$

```
>type(u,mathfunc);
```

$$\text{true}$$

```
>type((x+1)^2,polynom);
```

$$true$$

```
>type((x+1)^2,expanded);
```

$$false$$

```
>type(x^2+2*x+1,expanded);
```

$$true$$

```
>s:=series(exp(x),x,4);
```

$$s := 1 + x + 1/2\ x^2 + 1/6\ x^3 + O(x^4)$$

```
>type(s,taylor);
```

$$true$$

There are a large number of possible nested types. A list can be obtained from online help by inputting ?type.

In addition to the built-in types, there is a mechanism for defining and testing for your own types. This is a more advanced topic and mainly used in programming. Chapter 11 contains additional information on this aspect.

There are times when you will need to change an expression from one type to another. Maple's primary way of making type changes (as well as numerous other conversions) is through a function called convert(). Here is a simple example of a case where a type change is necessary and how convert() is used to achieve it. The first step is to define a one-dimensional array a with four entries (arrays, sets, and lists are discussed in the following section, Working with Structured Data):

```
>a:=array(1..4,[2,5,1,8]);
```

$$a := [\ 2,\ 5,\ 1,\ 8\ ]$$

To find out if 1 is one of the array elements you could try:

```
>member(1,a);
```

```
Error, wrong number (or type) of parameters in
    function member;
```

The problem here is that member() only works for sets and lists, not for arrays. The convert() function can be used to solve this problem:

```
>member(1,convert(a,list));
```

$$true$$

Note that the type of a has not changed:

```
>type(a,array);
```

$$true$$

```
>type(a,list);
```

$$false$$

Many other type conversions are possible, but they all follow the above pattern in which the "target" type is the second argument. Online help contains a lengthy list of the capabilities of convert(), and Chapter 8 contains further discussion.

1.3 Some working tools

Most interaction with Maple consists of using its functions and possibly writing your own functions to accomplish specific tasks. Before getting to this, there is a relatively small body of notations and conventions to be digested that covers things such as on-screen operations, naming conventions, and Maple's notations for data objects such as lists and arrays. In addition, we will look at ways to define ranges for variables, at the difference between an equation and an assignment, and at a special class of functions for evaluating expressions. The subsections are

- Names and Naming
- Working with Structured Data

- Using Evaluators
- Assignments and Equations
- The `map()` Function
- Attributes and Assumptions for Variables
- Miscellany

Names and naming

Here we will discuss some basic facts about names in Maple. Most of the names we have used so far have contained just one or two letters. However, it is permissible for names to contain up to 512,000 characters consisting of letters, numbers, or underscores. Although these characters can be used in any combination that starts with a letter or underscore, you should avoid using an underscore for the first character in a name because Maple uses such names itself. Here is an example:

```
>solve(x^7+x-1);
```

$$
\mathrm{RootOf}(\ \_Z^7 + \_Z - 1)
$$

This example asks Maple to find the zeros of the polynomial shown. Because there is no explicit formula for these zeros, Maple records them implicitly in a `RootOf()` expression. The name `_Z` is used by Maple to specify the variable in the `RootOf()` expression. There is an extensive discussion on `RootOf()` in Chapter 7.

If you need to include spaces or other characters different from letters, numbers, and underscores in a name you can use a "quoted string." This is just a sequence of characters enclosed in back (or string) quotes. We have already used these a number of times. There is no restriction on the characters that are permitted between the quotes. Placing back quotes around characters tells Maple to ignore any predefined meaning the characters may have. Back quotes within a pair of back quotes are interpreted as a literal back quote. Quoted strings often occur when dealing with file names because these often contain slashes or periods. Names containing such characters must be enclosed in quotes. Note that the back quotes are not part of the name they enclose. They are simply there as markers to indicate the start and finish of the name.

You will sometimes see the expression

```
>``;
```

This is called the null string and returns no value but can be useful is some circumstances.

Maple is not very consistent about the use of case in its naming of things such as functions and variables, though this situation may change with a future release. Whereas most function names are written in lowercase, there are some that start with an uppercase letter; these are often, but not always, what are called inert functions (`Int()` is a good example). A few functions are written in all uppercase letters, the `GAMMA()` function being one of them.

There are thirty or so reserved names including, for example, the words used to set up loops and to test logical expressions. For the complete list, type `?keywords`. To use a reserved word as a name (the next subsection shows a case where this is necessary) you must enclose it in back quotes. Maple also has a name-protection scheme that will warn you if you attempt to assign to a system name such as `Pi` or `sin`. The name-protection scheme allows you to protect (and unprotect) your own variables also. Here is an illustration of the technique:

```
>a:=b;
```

$$a := b$$

```
>protect('a');
>a:=c;
Error, attempting to assign to `a` that is protected
>unprotect('a');
>a:=c;
```

$$a := c$$

Forward quotes are necessary in both cases. Otherwise, the argument is evaluated and the result of the evaluation is protected as the next illustration reveals (continuing from above):

```
>protect(a);
>a:=d;
```

$$a := d$$

```
>c:=e;
Error, attempting to assign to `c` that is protected
```

It is possible to unprotect system names, but that is not a good idea because you may be unable to reset the name to its original meaning without restarting Maple.

In the Full Evaluation subsection, we mentioned the use of forward quotes to delay or prevent evaluation of expressions. In connection with names, forward quotes are used to return a name to an unassigned status. To illustrate this, we assign x to the expression shown and then unassign it:

```
>x:=q*r/s;
```

```
                        q r
            x  :=  ---
                         s
```

```
>x:='x';
```

```
            x  :=  x
```

The result shows that x now has no assigned value. The expression that x initially referred to no longer has that name. The function unassign() allows several names to be unassigned simultaneously. Before it can be used, unassign() must be loaded from the library, as in the next statement:

```
>readlib(unassign);
```

```
proc()  ...  end
```

Now we will assign some names and then unassign() them:

```
>x:=1:y:=2:z:=3:
>unassign('x','y','z');
```

In unassign(), the forward quotes are essential. The unassign() function is one of the few that returns no value or NULL (see the following subsection), but it is easy enough to check that the names in the previous example are indeed unassigned. For example:

```
>x;
```

```
            x
```

There is an "evaluator" evaln() that evaluates expressions to a name, which will be discussed in the Assignments and Equations subsection.

Working with structured data

This subsection introduces some of the facilities that Maple offers for dealing with data, data structured into sets, lists, and arrays. We will look at Maple's notation for these items, how they can be created, and how their elements can be referenced. This will allow us to introduce a basic Maple construct called a range and to illustrate some of its uses.

Nearly as fundamental as the expression is the expression sequence. This is simply a list of expressions separated by commas. The expressions can be any Maple expressions. Expression sequences occur in many different settings. They can be created by functions or by explicit keyboard input. The following is a simple example:

```
>e:=p,q,r,s;
```

$$e := p, \ q, \ r, \ s$$

and its type can be easily checked:

```
>whattype(e);
```

```
exprseq
```

The expressions are p, q, r, and s and they could be just names standing for themselves or they could be previously assigned names of other expressions. An expression sequence can be empty. The empty expression sequence is denoted by the Maple variable called NULL mentioned above. The NULL variable prints as a blank line. There may be occasions when Maple is not responding to your input and seems to be ignoring you. Assuming you haven't forgotten the all important semicolon, there is a good chance that Maple is not really ignoring you but is "printing" NULL as a response.

A set in Maple is an expression sequence enclosed in braces. Although the expressions in the set are necessarily recorded in some particular order, for the purposes of calculation they are regarded as unordered. Here is an example of a set containing three expressions:

```
>s:={p,q,r,r};
```

$$s := \{r, \ q, \ p\}$$

The expressions are p, q, and r and, as usual, they could be just names standing for themselves or they could be the names of other expressions, including other sets. Note that following the mathematical definition of a set, duplicates are removed and order is not significant. Among other things, you can form unions and intersections and make membership tests on sets. For example:

```
> a := {sin,cos,tan};
```

$$a := \{cos, \ sin, \ tan\}$$

```
> b := {exp,ln,cosh,sin};
```

$$b := \{ln, \ exp, \ cosh, \ sin\}$$

```
> a union b;
```

$$\{ln, \ cos, \ exp, \ cosh, \ sin, \ tan\}$$

```
> a intersect b;
```

$$\{sin\}$$

You can also subtract sets with minus() and test an expression for membership with member(). The example above uses union and intersect as infix operators. To use them as prefix operators, you use, for example, `union`(a,b). The string quotes are needed because union is a reserved word.

A list is somewhat similar to a set in that it is built from an expression sequence. However, unlike a set, the expressions in a list are considered to be ordered. The two are distinguished by their enclosing symbols. For a list, the enclosing symbols are square brackets. The following is an example of a list:

```
>l:=[p,q,r,r];
```

$$l := [p, \ q, \ r, \ r]$$

In this case, the order of the expressions in the input is preserved in the output.

In both sets and lists, any Maple expressions can appear. The functions op() and nops() are useful in connection with sets and lists. The nops() function gives the length of a list or size of a set. Using op(), you can access the expression sequence inside the delimiters and also its individual expressions. For example, here is a way to augment a list:

```
>L1:=[sqrt(2),sqrt(3)];
```

$$L1 := [2^{1/2}, 3^{1/2}]$$

```
>L2:=[op(L1),sqrt(5)];
```

$$L2 := [2^{1/2}, 3^{1/2}, 5^{1/2}]$$

Notice how `op()` is used without a second argument to obtain the expression sequence of `L1`. Similar methods work for sets. The `nops()` and `op()` functions cannot be used with expression sequences as the following example shows:

```
>a:=v,n,g;
```

$$a := v, n, g$$

```
>nops(a);
Error,
wrong number (or type) of parameters in function nops;
>op(a);
Error,
wrong number (or type) of parameters in function op;
```

The problem here is that the argument a to `nops()` and `op()` is evaluated, thereby becoming three arguments, which are too many for these functions. The remedy is to enclose a in list brackets in the argument to the functions.

The `op()` function is not the only way to select from a multipart data structure such as a set or expression sequence. You can also use a selection operation or selector for short. In practice, this means that you place the description of the part you want in square brackets after the name of the structure. For example (after restarting Maple):

```
>l:=[a,b,{a,c,2},[2,b]]:

>l[2];
```

$$b$$

You can get at deeper parts by an extension of this procedure:

```
>l[3][2];
```

$$c$$

You can change the entries in an existing list by direct assignment. In addition, Maple will perform automatic arithmetic on lists of the same length. For example, you can form linear combinations of lists regardless of the nature of their entries. Deletions from a list can be made with subsop(). For instance, the following is an example in which the third entry in a list is first changed and then removed altogether:

```
>m:=[sin,cos,sec,tan];
```

$$m := [sin, cos, sec, tan]$$

```
>m[3]:=1/cos: m;
```

$$m := [sin, cos, \frac{1}{cos}, tan]$$

```
>subsop(3=NULL,m);
```

$$[sin, cos, tan]$$

The arguments to subsop() are equation(s) (see the Assignments and Equations subsection) and the expression that is to be evaluated. In each equation, the left side is the number of the operand that is to be substituted for. The value of m after the last evaluation is still given by its previous value because no assignment was made on the last step.

Two more data structures that we will discuss here are arrays and concatenated (joined) names. Before discussing these data structures, we need to introduce the idea of a range.

A range is an expression used to specify various kinds of intervals, which include continuous, discrete, and complex. The range below specifies integers from −5 through 11:

```
>rg:=-5..11;
```

$$rg := -5 .. 11$$

Because a range is an expression, it can be assigned to a name, in this case rg.

Ranges can be used to extract sublists (and subsets), as the following shows:

```
> l:=[you, me, eunuchs, DOS];

            l := [you, me, eunuchs, DOS]

> l[2..4][2..3];

                [eunuchs, DOS]
```

Ranges can also be used to define arrays. An array is a Maple type that is a special case of a more general type called a table. (Maple tables are discussed in Chapter 10.) To define an array, you call a function of the same name with one or more integer ranges, which specify the dimensions and indexing. For instance, the following defines a 3 × 2 array a indexed from 1 to 3 in the first dimension and from 1 to 2 in the second dimension:

```
>a:=array(1..3,1..2);

        a := array(1 .. 3, 1 .. 2, [])
```

The brackets will contain whatever Maple knows about the elements; right now that is nothing, and the brackets are empty. You can assign array entries using the method illustrated below, where the (3, 2) entry of a is defined:

```
>a[3,2]:=x;

            a[3, 2] := x
```

Notice that this is double indexing and not repeated single indexing.

To construct an array with specified entries, you can use a list of lists like the following:

```
>array(1..2,1..2,[[x,y],[z,w]]);

                [ x   y ]
                [       ]
                [ z   w ]
```

A one-dimensional array would use a single list and a three-dimensional array would use a list of lists of lists. One- and two-dimensional arrays with indexes starting from 1 are used as vectors and matrices. Chapter 4 discusses matrix computations and linear algebra.

The ranges in an array definition can cover any span of integers. However, you cannot refer to elements outside the ranges without getting a message:

```
>c:=array(-5..1);
```

$$c := array(-5 .. 1, [])$$

```
>c[2];
Error, 1st index, 2, larger than upper array bound 1
```

In other words, arrays are subject to index checking. The main difference between a table and an array is that a table can have more general indexing than integer ranges.

A different application of ranges is that of constructing a sequence of names using the dot or concatenation operator. The following illustrates the technique:

```
>day.(2..5);
```

$$day2, \quad day3, \quad day4, \quad day5$$

The expression to the left of the dot must be a name. The expression on the right of the dot (in this case the range) is evaluated and concatenated with the name to the left of the dot, resulting in the sequence of names shown. The names can be assigned like all names. At this stage, we merely have a method to create a sequence of names ending in a number. The novelty is that you can refer to particular names using the dot notation, allowing another form of representation for structured data. For example, if PayDay is assigned the value 4, then you can use it as a kind of index, as the following illustrates:

```
>PayDay:=4;
```

$$PayDay := 4$$

```
>day.PayDay;
```

$$day4$$

Sequences of concatenated names can sometimes replace other kinds of indexed data with a gain in simplicity.

Another (and ubiquitous) function using a range is seq(). Suppose you wanted to form the sequence of terms j^3, $j = 2, 3, 4$. Here is the way to do it with seq():

```
>seq(j^3,j=2..4);
```

$$8, \quad 27, \quad 64$$

The evaluation rules for seq() are that the expression on the left-hand side of the range equation is evaluated as far as the last name encountered in the evaluation ("evaluated to a name"), and the name is assigned to a range value before each evaluation of the first expression.

Sometimes it is possible to avoid the use of a range in seq(). This occurs when you are forming a sequence in the following general style:

$$seq(f(op(i,expr)), \quad i = 1..nops(expr))$$

where f denotes some Maple function of the operands. Often the expression expr will be a list. For example, the above example could be rephrased as "cube the elements in the list [2, 3, 4]." The Maple commands for this could be

```
>l:=[2,3,4];
```

$$l := [2, 3, 4]$$

```
>seq(op(k,l)^3,k=1..nops(l));
```

$$8, \quad 27, \quad 64$$

and f here is the cubing function. The shorthand that avoids the range and the explicit use of the op() function is

```
>seq(k^3,k=l);
```

$$8, \quad 27, \quad 64$$

The same technique works for general expressions and functions f; f(k) is used as the first argument to seq().

Ranges are also used for specifying the limits in definite integrals and sums as well as for plot intervals. There are many such examples scattered throughout the book.

The general definition of a range is two expressions separated by two or more periods (dots in Maple parlance). With numerical ranges, the lower range limit should not be greater than the upper limit, otherwise the range will be empty. You can evaluate the range limits using the functions lhs() and rhs() with the range as the argument. When using an upper range limit of the form, say, 0.1, be careful to include the zero. Otherwise, the three consecutive periods will be interpreted as the separator between the range limits. If you want to see an example, try the following plots (using semicolons in place of the colons):

```
>plot(sin(x),x=0..0.1):
>plot(sin(x),x=0...1):
```

Using evaluators

Sometimes you might want to fully evaluate an expression without necessarily using it for anything in particular. These and some related situations are handled with a class of functions called evaluators. To illustrate the use of evaluators, we will first look at a case where full evaluation is not performed. The following example defines a 2×2 matrix and sets its $(1, 1)$ element to u:

```
>a:=array(1..2,1..2); a[1,1]:=u;
```

$$a := \mathrm{array}(1 .. 2, 1 .. 2, [])$$

$$a[1, 1] := u$$

Asking for a to be printed (and presumably evaluated) gives the following:

```
>a;
```

$$a$$

This strongly suggests that full evaluation has not occurred because if it had occurred, we would expect to see the array printed in detail. It appears as if the array has somehow been evaluated up to the point of producing its name but no further. In fact, that is what has happened. Briefly, when the value of an expression is an array, the result of evaluating that expression is defined to be the last name evaluated, which will normally be the name of the array. To force Maple to fully evaluate an array or other item, you can use an evaluator called eval(). Here is the result for a:

```
>eval(a);
```

```
[    u       ?[1, 2] ]
[                    ]
[ ?[2, 1]   ?[2, 2] ]
```

Incidentally, to obtain a line-printed version of this (or any other expression) lprint() can be used:

```
>lprint(eval(a));
array(1 .. 2, 1 .. 2,[(1, 1)=u])
```

Use the `eval()` function when you want to evaluate expressions of the type called algebraic.

Another evaluator is `evaln()`. This function can be used to control the evaluation of parts of expressions by evaluating them, for instance, only as far as their name. The `evaln()` function can also be used to unassign a name. Here is an illustration of how this is done:

```
>x:=1:
>x:=evaln(x);
```

$$x := x$$

`x` is evaluated to a name and then assigned to itself.

There are several other evaluators. One of the most frequently used is called `evalf()`, which evaluates expressions using floating-point arithmetic in place of the exact (rational) arithmetic that is Maple's standard mode of operation. This is covered in Chapter 2. Another evaluator is `evalb()` for evaluations of Boolean expressions, and another is `evalm()`, which evaluates matrix expressions (covered in Chapter 4). To perform operations using Maple's algebra functions, there is an evaluator called `evala()` that is covered in Chapter 7.

Assignments and equations

This subsection explains the differences between Maple assignments and the Maple type called equation. Here, we will also introduce several new functions that have a direct bearing on the differences between equations and assignments or that depend on equations in a particularly significant way. Although the official name for the equation type is the equals sign "=," we will use the full word instead.

We have already seen numerous examples of assignments. They are the Maple input lines containing the assignment symbol ":=." We also mentioned earlier that these are not Maple types. Actually, they are members of a class of Maple entities called statements. There are just eight different kinds of statements. In addition to the assignment statement, there are the read, save, quit, and expression statements (yes, every expression is a statement), the selection and repetition statements (these are programming constructs unrelated to the similarly named ideas discussed in earlier parts of Section 1.3), and the empty statement (zero or more spaces followed by a ";").

In contrast to the assignment statement, an equation is merely a Maple type, although an important one. The equation type by definition consists of two expressions separated by an "=." As far as the definition goes, that is more or less the whole story, though it is not too informative. What is missing, and what really gives a meaning to Maple equations (and to all Maple types), is what you can do with them – in other words, what functions can be applied to them. Functions that can be applied to equations include `solve()` for finding zeros and the evaluator called `evalb()` for testing whether a given equation is true or false. There are many other situations where equations play a role, and we will see some examples further on in this subsection.

From the last two paragraphs, it follows that you can assign a name to an equation using an assignment statement. For example:

```
>eqn:=x=2;
```

$$eqn := x = 2$$

The name `eqn` now stands for the equation x=2 and could be used as a function argument in place of the equation itself. Now look at the following:

```
>x:=4;
```

$$x := 4$$

```
>eqn;
```

$$4 = 2$$

The first assignment sets x to 4, and there is in no reason to think that this contradicts the equation x=2. In the second step, full evaluation causes both sides of the equation to be evaluated with the result that you see. The result is a perfectly correct Maple equation even though it is not correct mathematically.

You should not be too concerned about this discrepancy. Properly written functions will check to make sure that their input arguments make sense, and `eqn` would be examined before it was accepted by a function. Having said that, observe that the form of `eqn` certainly makes sense for some functions, notably for `evalb()` (evaluate as Boolean). Here is what `evalb()` gives:

```
>evalb(eqn);
```

$$false$$

The left and right sides of an equation can be extracted using the functions `lhs()` and `rhs()`. The argument to these functions is just the equation at hand. The `lhs()` and `rhs()` functions also work for inequalities and other relations.

We will give three more examples relating to assignments and equations. These will also serve to introduce the Maple functions called `assign()`, `subs()`, and `alias()`. The `assign()` function lets you change equations to assignments. The `subs()` function lets you make substitutions for subexpressions of expressions using equations, and the `alias()` function lets you refer to Maple entities by alternative names.

The use of `assign()` is straightforward. For example, the following sets up an equation called z and immediately converts it to an assignment. It is m that gets assigned:

```
>z:=m=w1+w2;
```

$$z := m = w1 + w2$$

```
>assign(z);
>m;
```

$$w1 + w2$$

Note that the value of `assign()` (like `unassign()`) is NULL. (Full evaluation trivia question: what will result from typing z at the prompt?)

One of the main uses of the `assign()` function is in connection with solving equations. The solutions of systems of equations are usually returned as equations. If you wish to do additional computations with the solutions, they need to be assigned to names. The `assign()` function can be used for that purpose. The technique is illustrated in Systems of Equations in Section 2.4.

Now we will look at `subs()`, which is another function where equations are important. There are frequent uses of `subs()` scattered throughout this book. The idea here is to introduce the function and mention a connection with assignments.

Suppose that in the expression

```
>u:=p^2+q^2+r^2;
```

$$u := p^2 + q^2 + r^2$$

you wanted to substitute the particular value p=2. Here are two ways to do this. The first way is to make the assignment:

```
>p:=2;
```

$$p := 2$$

and then to evaluate u. The result is

```
>u;
```

$$4 + q^2 + r^2$$

Now suppose you wanted to see what happens with p=3. You can repeat the above steps using p=3, but first you have to unassign p as follows:

```
>p:='p':
```

```
>u;
```

$$p^2 + q^2 + r^2$$

The second and simpler approach uses subs(). Here is the technique:

```
>u:=p^2+q^2+r^2;
```

$$u := p^2 + q^2 + r^2$$

```
>subs(p=2,u);
```

$$4 + q^2 + r^2$$

Note that p is assigned through an equation. The expression u still evaluates to its original form:

```
>u;
```

$$p^2 + q^2 + r^2$$

Clearly, the approach using subs() is neater and more efficient. The subs() function is frequently used in Maple.

The subs() function performs syntactic substitutions; that is, the left-hand side of the substitution equation must be present in the expression tree of subs() second argument in order to be replaced by the expression on the right-hand side of the equation. More intricate substitutions can be done with algsubs(). The algsubs()

function will substitute for "compound" expressions, which subs() will not, as shown by the following examples:

```
> subs(x^2=a^2*(1-y^2/b^2),x^3/a^2+y^3/b^2);
```

$$\frac{x^3}{a^2} + \frac{y^3}{b^2}$$

```
> algsubs(x^2=a^2*(1-y^2/b^2),x^3/a^2+y^3/b^2);
```

$$\frac{(b^2 - y^2)\, x}{b^2} + \frac{y^3}{b^2}$$

Another function that uses equation arguments is alias(). The alias() function is used to give shorter or otherwise more convenient names to Maple functions or other entities. The arguments (or argument) to alias() are a sequence of equations specifying the new names for the old. For example, you may prefer to call the Riemann function Z() instead of the Maple name Zeta(). To do so, do the following:

```
>alias(Z=Zeta);
```

$$I, Z$$

Maple returns a list of all the aliases that it knows about. In this case, there is the Maple symbol for sqrt(-1), I, and the alias that we just defined. Now you can use Z() in place of Zeta() as the following demonstrates:

```
>Z(2);
```

$$1/6\ Pi^2$$

You can still use `Zeta()` as the name, and ignore the alias.
To remove the alias, you do the following:

```
>alias(Z=Z);
```

I

It is not a good idea to try to remove the alias by using forward quotes because
the alias is not an assignment. An additional restriction is that it is not possible to
`alias()` an `alias()`.

The `map()` function

It is often necessary to apply a function to the individual operands of a list or other data
structure. For a simple example, you might need a table of $\cos(k\pi)$, $k = 0, 1, 2, 3$.
The `map()` function is designed for this:

```
>s:=[seq(k*Pi,k=0..3)];
```

$$s := [0, \ Pi, \ 2 \ Pi, \ 3 \ Pi]$$

```
>CList:=map(cos,s);
```

$$CList := [1, \ -1, \ 1, \ -1]$$

Observe how the list `s` is created by using brackets around an expression sequence.
The operands of the list are its entries, and `map()` is then applied to each entry.

In general, `map()` takes two arguments. The second argument may be a general
expression but not an expression sequence because then there will be more than two
arguments, and an error message will result. You should transform an expression
sequence into a list, as in the example above. If necessary, the transformed expression
sequence can be recovered using `op()`.

If the function takes arguments, they are included as arguments to `map()` following the expression argument. For example, there is a function `irem()` that finds the
remainder of integer division:

```
>irem(19,13);
```

This function would be mapped as follows:

```
>map(irem,[19,21,26],13);
```

$$[6, \ 8, \ 0]$$

This only works because the divisor is the second argument of `irem()`. If it had been the first argument, `map()` would have produced an undesired result. To handle such cases, `map2()` is used. Suppose for instance that we needed the remainders when 29 was divided by multiples of 4. You could do the following to determine the remainders:

```
> map2(irem,29,[seq(4*j,j=1..7)]);
```

$$[1, \ 5, \ 5, \ 13, \ 9, \ 5, \ 1]$$

Generally, the specified function will be applied to all the operands of whatever expression is given.

Attributes and assumptions for variables

You can attach properties or attributes to Maple items such as names, and you can tell Maple that symbolic variables have specific properties such as positivity. Although these two ideas sound similar, they are implemented in different ways in Maple. In the first case, you attach to an item arbitrary properties that are unused by Maple until you, the user, tell Maple what use is to be made of the properties. The functions for this are called `setattribute()` and `attributes()`. In the second case, you use the functions `assume()`, `additionally()`, `addproperty()`, `is()`, and `about()`. These functions are quite different from the first two because properties set with them will (in theory) be used in all later calculations. This `assume` facility, as it is called, was introduced first in Maple V, Release 2. It is gradually being incorporated into the entire system, but we are not yet at the end of the road.

Here are some very basic illustrations of the functions mentioned above. First, we will set and query an attribute:

```
> setattribute(x,positive,IndependentVariable);
```

$$x$$

```
> attributes(x);
```

$$positive, \ IndependentVariable$$

You can set any Maple expression as an attribute. The most important point right now is that ownership of the attributes has no effect on any operations with x. For instance, you could assign x to a matrix or other object thereby contradicting its attributes. The presumption by Maple is that the attributes will be employed explicitly by a user rather than implicitly by Maple. A real-life application of attributes may be found in the discussion of the geometry[] package in Chapter 9.

The assume facility is used at a number of places in this book. Here we will give only a very simple (but significant) illustration:

```
> assume(m,integer);
> cos(m*Pi);
```
$$m\sim$$
$$(-1)$$
```
> sin(m*Pi);
```
$$0$$

Without the assume function, there is no reasonable way to get Maple to produce these results. Maple adds a tilde ~ after the names of variables that have assumptions.

To ask what assumptions have been made about a variable, you use about():

```
> about(m);
Originally m, renamed m~:
   is assumed to be: integer
```

You can remove assumptions by unassigning a name:

```
> m:='m';
```
$$m := m$$
```
> about(m);
m:
   nothing known about this object
```

Here is another illustration for assume(). This illustration also shows a way to assume more than one property:

```
> assume(x>0);
> additionally(x<1);
> abs(x+1)+abs(x-1);
```
$$2$$

It will become clear that the `assume` facility is a very powerful feature of Maple. However, it is not yet fully implemented as you may discover for yourself at some point. For now, here is a small quiz. Is `assume()` working correctly in the example that follows?

```
> assume(x>0);
```

```
> solve(x^2-1=0,x);
```
$$1, \ -1$$

```
> about(x);
Originally x, renamed x~:
    is assumed to be: RealRange(Open(0),infinity)
```

Miscellany

Here are some additional topics that you will need to know about.

1. To restart a session from scratch, you can use the `restart` function. This function takes no arguments and effectively starts a fresh Maple session. All assignments are lost and any specially loaded functions will need to be reloaded before they can be used again. Your initialization file will be reread. For more details on this see Section 8.2.

2. A frequently occurring concept in Maple is that of "returning unevaluated." Usually, this means that Maple is unable to perform an evaluation for some reason. The reason may be mathematical, for example, when an integral cannot be evaluated, or syntactic, for example, when you type an incorrect name for an input argument. We will see numerous examples of this as we proceed.

3. Maple has a class of functions called "inert" functions. These are functions that serve as placeholders for operations without performing the operations themselves. A simple example is the inert differentiation function called `Diff()`, which is the inert version of the regular differentiation function `diff()`. This function simply returns its input, possibly printed in a nice form. Another inert function is the integration function `Int()` whose active version is `int()`. This function is recognized by other Maple functions but does nothing by itself. For example `Int()` is recognized by `evalf()`, which interprets it as a request for a numerical integration on its argument. As these examples suggest, when an inert version of a function exists it is usually called by the same name as its active version except for a capitalized first letter.

4. You will frequently need to refer to previous results from your Maple session. The simplest way to do this is through "ditto" (double quote) notation. Using

ditto notation you can access the three most recent results, which covers most of the back referencing you will need. Here is a rather unnatural example that forms a cubic polynomial:

```
>x;
```

$$x$$

```
>a*"^0;
```

$$a$$

```
>"+b*""^2;
```

$$a + b\ x^2$$

```
>"+c*"""^3;
```

$$a + b\ x^2 + c\ x^3$$

A single ditto refers to the most recent result. Two consecutive dittos refer to the second most recent result and three dittos refer to the third most recent result.

Think of the ditto as equivalent to what would appear if you typed the corresponding result in full. Results within dittos are subjected to evaluation. More than three dittos generate an error message. There is a `history()` facility that is not restricted to just the three previous results and that lets you refer to any previous result by number. This facility is covered in Section 8.2.

5. You may want to add comments in your Maple session, for example, textual material inserted for informational rather than computational purposes. Comments can be inserted following a sharp symbol "#." The sharp may be inserted anywhere following a semicolon or colon on a line or at the start of a line. Maple simply ignores whatever text follows the sharp. Use comments to remind yourself what is going on, to give information about what to do in a given case, or to provide similar assistance. More structured text material can be supplied through a function called `TEXT()`. `TEXT()` provides a way to make help files for your own programs. The `TEXT()` function is discussed in Section 11.5.

1.4 Beginning graphics

Making graphs and other pictures with Maple is something you might want to do quite often. This section contains a brief introduction to the subject. The main goal is to demonstrate some graphics commands that will enable you to create simple two- and three-dimensional plots. In Chapter 6 we will cover Maple's graphics facilities in detail. The subsections here are

- Two-Dimensional Plotting
- Three-Dimensional Plotting
- The `plots[]` Package

Two-dimensional plotting

For plotting functions of a single variable, the principal command is `plot()`. There are several optional arguments to `plot()`, but we will discuss only the basic ones here. The two arguments that are usually present are the function(s) to be plotted and a range for the dependent variable. For example, here is a plot of the function xe^{-x} in the interval [0, 10] (see Figure 1.2):

```
>plot(x*exp(-x),x=0..10);
```

To plot several graphs on the same picture you can use a set like the following (see Figure 1.3):

```
>plot({x*exp(-x),x*exp(-2*x),x*exp(-4*x)},x=0..10);
```

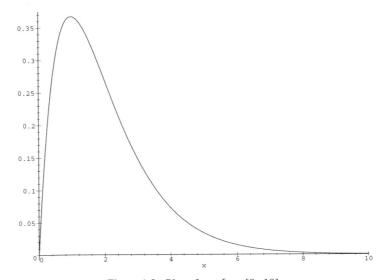

Figure 1.2: Plot of xe^{-x} on [0, 10].

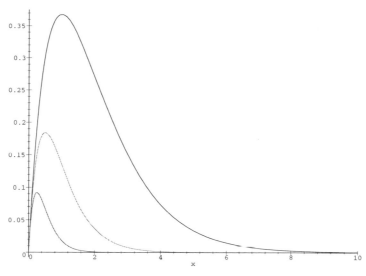

Figure 1.3: Multiple plots.

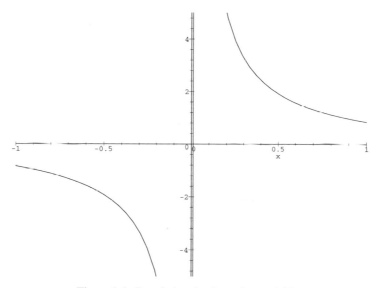

Figure 1.4: Restricting the dependent variable.

If a function can be large or unbounded in its range, it is a good idea to specify a range for the dependent variable as well as the independent variable. The details of the function can then be represented on a graph instead of being scaled out of existence. The next example illustrates the use of this plot option (see Figure 1.4):

```
>plot(sin(x)/x^2,x=-1..1,-5..5);
```

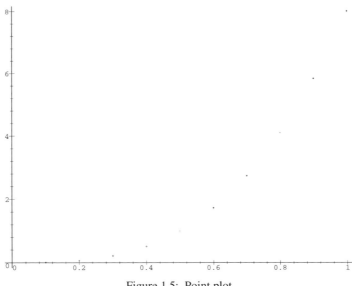

Figure 1.5: Point plot.

Try plotting this without the range restriction on the independent variable!

Sometimes you may want to plot a set of points without joining them. This can be done with an option called `POINT`. Here is an example to illustrate the use of this option (see Figure 1.5):

```
>plot({seq([i*0.1,(i*0.2)^3],i=0..10)},style=POINT);
```

This plots the points where the independent variable is equally spaced by 0.1 in the interval [0, 1]. The plot is defined as a set of lists of length 2. The sequence operator is used to avoid writing out the lists explicitly.

It is equally simple to make plots of parametrically defined functions. There is a special syntax for doing this that is illustrated in the following example and Figure 1.6:

```
>plot([2*sin(t/4),t,t=0..8*Pi]);
```

The arguments are entered in a list containing the two functions `x(t)`, `y(t)` and a range for the parameter `t`.

For polar plots, the technique is to define the polar curve parametrically, following the same method as in the last example, while incorporating a further argument specifying a polar plot. Defining the curve parametrically is usually a trivial matter for explicitly given polar expressions. To illustrate the method, the following example plots the polar curve $r = 2\sin(t/4)$ for t in the range $[0, 8\pi]$. Note that this differs from

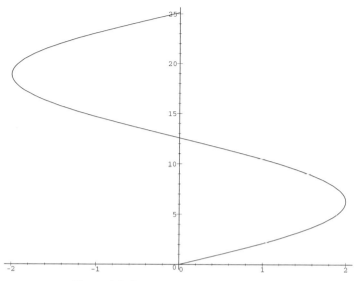

Figure 1.6: Parametric plot of $(2 \sin t/4, t)$.

the last example only in the presence of the polar and axes options. The default for the axes option is `normal` and that is what appeared in the previous plots. The scaling option produces a graph with similar length scales for the two axes (see Figure 1.7).

```
>plot([2*sin(t/4),t,t=0..8*Pi],coords=polar,
>axes=boxed,scaling-constrained);
```

A number of options for `plot()` concern things like axis labels and tick marks. There are also options for setting the resolution and sampling frequency of graphs, colors, and other things. These are discussed in Chapter 6.

Three-dimensional plotting

As with two-dimensional plotting, several kinds of three-dimensional plots are available. The principal function for three dimensional plotting is called `plot3d()`. This function is used much like `plot()`. Here is a plot of the two-variable trigonometric polynomial (see Figure 1.8).

$$z = \sum_{k,l=1}^{4} (k+l) \sin(kx) \sin(ly)$$

```
>plot3d(sum(sum(sin(k*x)*sin(l*y)*(k+1),k=1..4),l=1..4),
        x =- Pi..Pi,y=-Pi..Pi,grid=[50,50]);
```

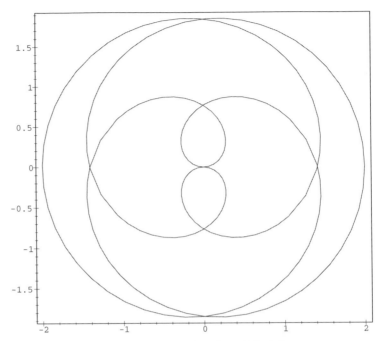

Figure 1.7: Polar plot of $r = 2 \sin \theta / 4$.

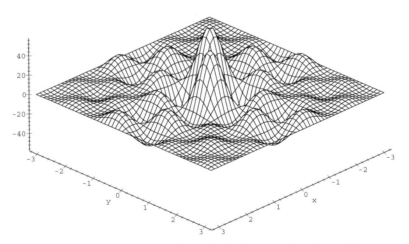

Figure 1.8: Plot of a two-dimensional trigonometric polynomial.

The function `sum()` that is used in this command is explained in Section 2.5. The argument `grid` appearing in the `plot3d()` command tells Maple to sample the function using a grid with fifty equally spaced points in each coordinate direction. The grid size can be deduced from its "image" on the surface.

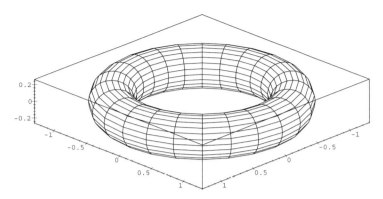

Figure 1.9: Plot of a torus.

Plots of parametrically defined surfaces are obtained similarly to parametric curves. As an example, we will plot a torus. The parametric equations of a simple torus are these:

$$x(\theta, \phi) = (R + r\cos(\phi))\cos(\theta),$$

$$y(\theta, \phi) = (R + r\cos(\phi))\sin(\theta),$$

$$z(\theta, \phi) = r\sin(\phi).$$

Here is a way to draw the torus that has $R = 1$ and $r = 1/4$ (see Figure 1.9):

```
>plot3d([(1+0.25*cos(u))*cos(v),(1+0.25*cos(u))*sin(v),
         0.25*sin(u)],u=0..2*Pi,v=0..2*Pi,
       scaling=constrained);
```

The parametric equations are supplied in a list, and ranges are used to define the domains of the independent variables, mirroring the two-dimensional parametric plot except that the ranges are outside the functions list. The default 25×25 grid option was used to make this plot.

There are many options available for three-dimensional plotting. The exact way you use the options is interface dependent. Using a graphics interface, you can rotate the plot, set different type of perspectives, choose from several possibilities for rendering surfaces, and choose from different lighting options. These options can usually be selected from menus. Chapter 6 discusses this in much more depth.

The `plots[]` package

The functions `plot()` and `plot3d()` are the foundation for a host of other plotting routines that are found in the package called `plots[]`. Some of the functions in

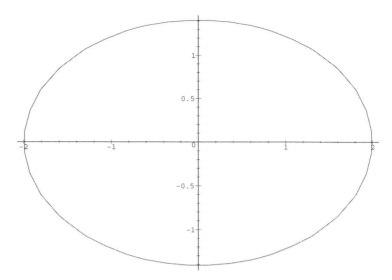

Figure 1.10: An implicitly defined function.

`plots[]` provide different ways to make some of the previous plots (the parametric plots for example) but most add new graph types. The `plots[]` package is described in Chapter 6. Here we will give one example to illustrate how it is used. We will plot an implicitly defined function (see Figure 1.10). As with all packages, you can either load the entire package or selectively access its functions. For the sake of illustration we will use the second technique. The function we need is called `implicitplot()`, and the following is how it is accessed and used:

```
>plots[implicitplot](x^2/4+y^2/2-1,x=-3..3,y=-3..3,
>labels=[` `,` `]);
```

Note how the arguments appear in parentheses after the brackets. The last option (which can also be used with `plot()` and `plot3d()`) has been included to suppress the printing of the axis labels because they collide with the axis numbering. Chapter 6 shows other means for controlling axis and other labeling.

1.5 Reference section

The tables that follow organize the functions and other items mentioned in the text by category. Permissible arguments to functions are immediately available from the online help system by typing ?, followed by the name of the function, followed by *return* or *enter*. Alternatively, use the functions `info()`, `usage()`, `example()`, or `related()`.

USING QUOTE SYMBOLS

`"`, `""`, `"""`	Ditto symbols are used to refer to the three most recent results.
`'`	Forward quote or apostrophe prevents evaluation of enclosed expression.
`` ` ``	Back quote is used to enclose strings.

USING DELIMITERS

`{ }`	Enclose the elements of a set
`[ ]`	Enclose the elements of a list or array selector
`( )`	Enclose function arguments

ARITHMETIC OPERATORS

`+`	Addition operator
`-`	Subtraction and negation (unary minus) operator
`*`	Multiplication operator
`^or **`	Exponentiation operator

FUNCTIONS FOR ANALYZING EXPRESSION TREES

`nops`	Find the number of operands in an expression
`op`	Find an operand of an expression
`type`	Test whether an expression has a given type
`whattype`	Find the topmost type of an expression
`has`	Tell if an expression has a specific subexpression
`hastype`	Tell if an expression has a specific type

TYPES MENTIONED IN THIS CHAPTER

`algebraic, array, equation(=), expanded, expression, exprseq, integer, list, mathfunc, polynom, range, series, set, string, taylor.`

EVALUATOR FUNCTIONS

`eval`	Force evaluation of general expressions
`evala`	Evaluate for algebra functions
`evalb`	Evaluate Boolean expression
`evalc`	Evaluate using complex numbers
`evalf`	Evaluate using floating-point (approximate) arithmetic

`evalm`	Evaluate matrix expression
`evaln`	Evaluate to a name

GRAPHICS FUNCTIONS

`plot`	Two-dimensional plotting function
`plot3d`	Three-dimensional plotting function
`plots[]`	Package containing numerous plotting functions

OTHER FUNCTIONS

`alias`	Set new name(s) for Maple objects
`array`	Form tables indexed by ranges
`assign`	Make assignments, especially of equations
`assume`	Make assumptions for Maple to check
`convert`	Change from one type (or representation) to another
`diff`	Differentiation function
`interface`	Set interface variables (unavailable for some interfaces)
`factor`	Factor algebraic expressions
`int`	Integration function
`intersect`	Form intersection of sets
`member`	Test for set menbership
`protect`	Prevent assignment to argument name
`unprotect`	Permit assignment to argument name
`restart`	Lose all assignments and start new session
`setattributes`	Set properties for explicit checking
`subs`	Replace subexpressions with different ones
`seq`	Form a sequence of expressions
`union`	Form union of sets

MISCELLANEOUS

`;` `:`	Execute the statement preceding ; or :
`#`	Comments follow this symbol
`.`	Concatenate a name with an expression

EXERCISES

1. Use the `op()`, `nops()`, and `whattype()` functions to determine the structure of the expression tree for
   (a) the actual expression `solve(a*x^2+b*x+c=0,x)`; and
   (b) the value of the expression `solve(a*x^2+b*x+c=0,x)`.

2. Show by examples how to perform the following operations on lists:
   (a) concatenation;
   (b) rotation (left or right);
   (c) reversal; and
   (d) flattening (removal of the inner list brackets from a list of lists).
3. Show by examples how to
   (a) sum the elements of a numerical list; and
   (b) make a list of lists of adjacent pairs of entries from a list containing an even number of entries, preserving the order of the entries of the original list.
4. Given a list `1`, find a way to check that all its entries are identical.
5. Explain the difference between the outputs from
   (a) `u1:= x<=1, x<=2, x<=3`; and
   (b) `u1:=seq(`x<=`.i,i=1..3)`.
6. Verify de Morgan's laws of set theory using Maple's functions for operations on sets (de Morgan's laws state $(A \cup B)' = A' \cap B'$ and $(A \cap B)' = A' \cup B'$, where the primes indicate complementation.).
7. Find Maple functions to effect the following transformations: `x*y*z` $\rightarrow$ `x+y+z` $\rightarrow$ `[x,y,z]`.
8. Obtain a plot of $y = \tan(x)$ for x in $[-\pi/2, \pi/2]$.
9. Identify five distinct types of automatic simplification performed by Maple and give an example of each type.
10. The following is a legal use of `subs()`: `subs(2=3,2*x)`. That being the case, explain the outputs from:
    (a) `subs(1=-1,1/x)`.
    (b) `subs(-1=1,1/x)`.
11. By using Maple's plot command, find the largest root of the equation

$$xe^{-x} - 0.25 = 0$$

correct to 2 decimal places.
Show your final plot with enough tickmarks on the x axis so that the accuracy of the root is clear. Color the graph green and give it a title. Make sure the axes are labeled.
12. The curve given parametrically by

$$x = \cos^3 t \qquad y = \sin^3 t$$

is traced out by a point on a circle of radius $1/4$ rolling on the inside of another circle of radius 1. For a suitable range of t, plot the curve and the larger circle on the same picture. Also on this picture, plot the smaller circle touching the larger one at $x = y = 1/\sqrt{2}$.

2 Numbers, functions, and basic algebra

This chapter and Chapter 3 parallel the usual sequence of precalculus, calculus, and differential equations courses. After finishing these chapters, you should be able to use Maple to solve many of the calculational problems (symbolic and numerical) that you met in those courses. The typical precalculus course discusses the number system, the elementary functions and their graphs, simple nonlinear equations, mappings, and one or two other topics. This is the kind of material that we cover in this chapter but at a higher level than in a precalculus course. For example, we will discuss solving algebraic equations and systems of algebraic equations of any degree, functions of several variables, floating-point numbers, and other relatively advanced topics. Topics that require the ideas of differentiation and integration are reserved for Chapter 3.

2.1 Numbers in Maple

Earlier, we mentioned that Maple does not automatically approximate numerical quantities such as rational numbers. Because the integers appearing in the numerators and denominators of rational numbers can grow quickly as a calculation proceeds, extended numerical calculations may consume excessive system resources. To avoid this difficulty we use floating-point numbers that use a fixed number of significant digits and a variable scale factor. Floating-point arithmetic suffers from the accumulation of roundoff errors in extended calculations. The only general protection against such accumulation is to use plenty of significant digits in the calculation. In standard procedural languages such as C or Fortran, you have only a few options for choosing the number of significant digits. In contrast, Maple has the powerful feature of letting you specify the number of digits to use. You can choose essentially any number of digits large or small. In part because of this feature, Maple is a highly useful environment for approximate computing. We will see many examples as we proceed through this book. In this section, we introduce the main features of exact and approximate numerical work with Maple. This section covers the following:

- Types of Numbers and Numerical Functions
- Numerical Approximations
- Numerical Types
- Constants
- Complex Numbers

Types of numbers and numerical functions

The three primary number types in Maple are integer, fraction, and float. An integer can have an explicit sign + or −. It can contain hundreds of thousands of digits, the precise maximum being a hardware-dependent quantity. You can see the exact number by inputting `kernelopts(maxdigits)`. (The `kernelopts()` function is covered in Chapter 8.)

A fraction is a pair of integers representing the numerator and denominator of the fraction. Maple automatically removes common factors from any fraction.

Any number containing a decimal point (a floating-point number) is called a float. A float is a pair of integers representing a mantissa, m, and a nonzero exponent, e, of the number. This means that the number has the value $m \times 10^e$. Normally, the maximum number of digits in m is given by a global variable called `Digits`, which is discussed in the Numerical Approximations subsection. The maximum number of digits in the exponent is hardware dependent and is usually around ten.

Fractions and floats are expressions, and both can be analyzed into their subexpressions using `nops()` and `op()`. The `op()` function gives the numerator and denominator of a fraction and the mantissa and exponent of a float. The following example finds the mantissa and exponent of a float:

```
>f:=123.456;
```
$$f := 123.456$$

```
>op(123.456);
```
$$123456, \ -3$$

There is a `convert()` function for converting between fractions and floats. Here is an example:

```
>convert(3.14,fraction);
```
$$\frac{157}{50}$$

There is also a similar way to use `convert()` to convert a fraction to a float.

Numbers may be combined using the standard symbols for addition and subtraction, $*$ for multiplication, and a / for division. Raising to a power is done with ^ or optionally with $**$. The order of precedence of these numerical operations is the usual one of negation followed by raising to a power, followed by multiplication and division, followed by addition and subtraction. Of course, you can also control the order of evaluation by using parentheses.

Some basic mathematical functions that work with numbers are the square root function `sqrt()`, the absolute value function `abs()`, and the `signum()` function (note that in Maple, `signum(0)` is undefined although it can be defined either by assigning a variable called `_Envsignum0` or through an additional argument). Other functions for working with numbers are `numer()` and `denom()`, which provide alternative ways for finding numerators and denominators (and not only of numbers); `trunc()`, `round()`, and `frac()`, which truncate and round to an integer and return the fractional part of a number, respectively: and `ceil()` and `floor()`, which produce the least integer not below the argument and the greatest integer not above the argument, respectively. The functions `max()` and `min()` return the largest and smallest of their arguments of which there can be any number.

Modular arithmetic can be performed using the `mod` function as follows:

```
>251 mod 9;
```

$$8$$

This function produces a result in the interval $[0, |m| - 1]$, where m is the modulus. Maple has two more functions for modular arithmetic; `modp()` represents `mod` as a standard function:

```
>modp(251,9);
```

$$8$$

and `mods()` produces a result in the symmetric range $[-int((|m| - 1)/2),$ $int(|m|/2)]$, where int denotes the integer part:

```
>mods(251,9);
```

$$-1$$

In these functions, the first argument can be any expression. If the expression is a list, for example, the function is applied to each entry. For a polynomial, the function is applied to the coefficients.

There are special techniques for computing powers of integers relative to a modulus that avoid work with large integers. To use this approach, you represent the power operation using an inert powering function as shown:

```
>839 &^ 416 mod 19;
```

$$9$$

The ampersand modifies the effect of the exponentiation symbol, and the power is not explicitly computed. Instead, the exponentiation is performed in mod, which calls on special algorithms for the computation.

Numerical approximations

Because Maple performs its calculations exactly, you need a way to obtain approximations from the exact results. For example, the quantity $\sqrt{2}$ is returned as follows:

```
>sqrt(2);
```

$$2^{1/2}$$

which is merely an automatic simplification. A more explicit result will require an approximation. How do you get an approximate result? In this case, the simplest way is to input a float:

```
>sqrt(2.0);
```

$$1.4142136$$

The number of digits, in this case eight, is the current setting of a global variable called Digits. Digits can be changed and the result recomputed as follows:

```
>Digits:=40: sqrt(2.0);
```

$$1.414213562373095048801688724209698078570$$

This value of Digits remains in effect until it is reassigned. The default value of Digits is 10.

As a rule, a numerical expression containing one or more floats is evaluated using approximate (floating-point) arithmetic. To approximately evaluate an expression not containing a float, you can use an important function called `evalf()`. The `evalf()` function will compute either with the number of significant digits given by the current value of `Digits` or with the number specified as a second argument. Using the last example, the following shows how to obtain the first fifty digits of the square root of 3:

```
>evalf(sqrt(3),50);
```

```
1.7320508075688772935274463415058723669428052538104
```

It is important to realize that giving a value to `Digits` or giving a second argument in `evalf()` are just ways to specify a length for the mantissa in the floats that occur in a calculation. The accuracy of the final result of an extended calculation can easily have far fewer correct digits than the value of `Digits` used in the calculation. This loss of significance is often unavoidable in floating-point computations. Its consequences are illustrated in Chapter 5.

Numerical types

There are several type tests that you can make for numerical quantities. In addition to integer, fraction, and float there are numeric (the previous three types also test positive for this), odd, even, positive, negative, posint, negint, nonnegint, and nonposint types. These are mostly used when programming.

Constants

An expression sequence named `constants` contains the names of the standard constants used by Maple. The sequence is as follows:

```
> constants;
     false, gamma, infinity, true, Catalan, FAIL, Pi
```

The standard constants have a type called `constant`, which can be tested with `type()`. You can add one or more new constants to this list, but you have to supply procedures for evaluating them. The `evalf()` function uses these procedures when you refer to the constants. In the sequence of standard constants, `true` and `false` are possible values of Boolean expressions, `gamma` is Euler's number, `Pi` is one-half the ratio of the circumference to the radius of a circle, and `Catalan` denotes the sum of the alternating series

$$1 - \frac{1}{9} + \frac{1}{25} - \cdots \frac{(-1)^n}{(2n+1)^2} \cdots$$

The constant called `infinity` is recognized as an argument in some functions, for example, as the upper limit of a definite integral.

Complex numbers

Complex numbers in Maple are defined using the symbol `I`, which is just an `alias` for `sqrt(-1)`. Complex arithmetic is performed automatically on complex arguments. For example:

```
> (I-1)*(I-2)*(I-3)/10;
```

$$I$$

You can input complex expressions to `evalf()` for floating-point evaluation:

```
> (1-I)*(1-I)/(2+I);
```

$$- 2/5 - 4/5 \ I$$

```
>evalf(");
```

$$- .4000000000 - .8000000000 \ I$$

There are functions for taking real and imaginary parts:

```
>v:=2*I+9;
```

$$v := 9 + 2 \ I$$

```
>Re(v);Im(v);
```

$$9$$

$$2$$

and for finding the modulus (absolute value) and argument:

```
>abs(v); argument(v);
```
$$85^{1/2}$$

$$\arctan(2/9)$$

Conjugation is performed with `conjugate()`.

There is a `convert()` for producing the polar form of a complex number:

```
>convert(v,polar);
```
$$\text{polar}(85^{1/2}, \arctan(2/9))$$

To convert to Cartesian form, you can use an evaluator `evalc()`, which evaluates its argument using complex arithmetic:

```
>evalc(");
```

$$2 I + 9$$

The evaluator `evalc()` can be used for other complex evaluations. It assumes that variables in its argument are real unless it explicitly knows that they are complex. There are times when this assumption is very helpful. However, it is advisable to beware of errors such as the following:

```
>evalc(conjugate(cos(I*z)));
```
$$\cosh(z)$$

This result is incorrect if z is not real. Automatic complex evaluation shows the problem:

```
>conjugate(cos(I*z));
```
$$\cosh(\text{conjugate}(z))$$

This is a user error; `evalc()` has merely made its standard assumption of real arguments.

Most of Maple's mathematical functions can be evaluated for complex arguments.

2.2 Basic mathematical functions

Maple comes equipped with a variety of mathematical functions. You can see a complete list in the online help system by typing ?inifcns. This section covers Maple's names and other properties of the functions that you meet in early mathematics courses. The subsections are

- Roots
- Trigonometric and Exponential Functions
- Factorial and Related Functions

Roots

Roots of numbers and functions are obtained by raising to the appropriate powers in the expected way. If it is really that simple, what is the reason for this subsection? Results such as the following are the reason:

```
> evalf((-1)^(1/3));
```

$$.5000000000 + .8660254038 \; I$$

This is not a problem with evalf(), which is there simply to force Maple to give us an explicit result; you could just as well have used simplify() (which is covered later in this chapter) to obtain a similar but exact complex result. The quantity returned here is the principal value of the cube root function evaluated at -1. Although we may have expected the answer -1, it is not the principal value even though it is one of the roots. For mathematical consistency, Maple must have a standard way of operating with multivalued functions and the complex result above is a consequence.

So how do you get the expected answer? You use a function called surd() which is programmed to produce real roots:

```
> surd(-1,3);
```

$$-1$$

Note the form of the second argument here (3, not 1/3).

The surd() function can be applied to other functions as well. To see that surd() really is useful, try plotting the function $f(x) = (x^2 - 1)^{1/3}$ from -2 to 2, first in the simple-minded way and then using surd(). (It may be an absurd name but it's a very useful function!)

Trigonometric and exponential functions

Maple uses the standard names `sin()`, `cos()`, and `tan()` for the trigonometric functions. The corresponding inverse functions are called `arcsin()`, `arccos()`, and `arctan()`. There is also a two-argument `arctan(,)` function that returns an angle in the interval $(-\pi, \pi]$. The other trigonometric functions are also called by the standard names `sec()`, `csc()`, and `cot()`, and their inverses are prefixed with `arc` as before. The exponential function (e^x) is denoted by `exp()`, and the logarithmic function is called `ln()` or `log()`:

```
>exp(ln(x));
```
$$x$$

For logarithms to base 10 and base b, you can use `log10()` and `log[b]()` as in

```
>evalf(log[2](1024));
```
$$10.00000000$$

The `simplify()` function (discussed in the next section) also produces a useful result in this case.

The hyperbolic functions are called by their standard mathematical names `sinh()`, `cosh()`, and `tanh()` together with their reciprocals `sech()`, `csch()`, and `coth()`. The inverse functions of all of these are obtained using the prefix `arc`. The elementary functions in this subsection can all be used with automatic complex arithmetic and can also be used in `evalc()`.

Factorial and related functions

Maple uses standard factorial notation:

```
>36!;
```
$$371993326789901217467999448150835200000000$$

The argument to the factorial must be a nonnegative integer. However, Maple knows about the gamma function, in effect extending the factorial function to all (complex) values of its argument except for nonpositive integers. (For positive-integer arguments the gamma function has the property $\Gamma(n + 1) = n!$). Maple uses the name GAMMA() for this function. (The name gamma is already used for Euler's constant.) You use GAMMA() in the same way as for other numerical functions:

```
>GAMMA(37);
```
$$371993326789901217467999448150835200000000$$

Some noninteger values of GAMMA() have automatic simplifications:

```
GAMMA(1/2);
```
$$Pi^{1/2}$$

but if Maple doesn't know an analytical form, the expression is returned unevaluated:

```
> GAMMA(2/3);
```
$$GAMMA(2/3)$$

To get a numerical approximation, you can use a floating-point argument or evalf():

```
> evalf(GAMMA(2/3));
```
$$1.354117939$$

For the binomial coefficients $\binom{n}{r}$ Maple uses the notation binomial(n,r):

```
>binomial(6,3);
```
$$20$$

Expressions can be converted with convert() to factorial and GAMMA formats. Here is an illustration:

```
> e:=binomial(m+n,m);
```
$$e := binomial(m + n, m)$$

```
> convert(e,factorial);
```
$$\frac{(m + n)!}{m!\ n!}$$

```
> convert(e,GAMMA);
```
$$\frac{GAMMA(m + n + 1)}{GAMMA(m + 1)\ GAMMA(n + 1)}$$

and this can be changed back to the `binomial` form as follows:

```
>convert(",binomial);
```

$$binomial(n + m, m)$$

`GAMMA()` can take complex arguments.

2.3 Simplifying and manipulating expressions

This section covers the principal Maple functions for changing mathematical expressions to different but equivalent forms. We will see that getting an expression into a specific form is not always easy and sometimes requires a fair amount of trial and error. The kind of operations we will look at include expanding and factoring polynomials and simplifying general expressions including trigonometric expressions. Maple has many different tools for this type of work and the main tools are introduced in this section. The subsections are

- Simplification
- Expanding Expressions
- Combining Expressions
- Polynomial Manipulations
- Transforming with `convert()`
- Converting to Partial Fractions

Simplification

There is no general definition of the "simplest" form of a computed result. Sometimes the shortest form of a result is the simplest one, and other times the most elementary form of a result is simplest. Nevertheless, Maple has a general command called `simplify()` that takes an expression and transforms it using a wide collection of rules. The rules perform operations such as putting things over a common denominator and applying multiple-angle formulas to trigonometric expressions. In addition, Maple will simplify exponents where it can be sure that there is no ambiguity. Here are some examples:

```
>simplify(a+b/x+c/x^2);
```

$$\frac{a x^2 + b x + c}{x^2}$$

```
>simplify(cos(2*x)+sin(x)^2);
                    2
                cos(x)
```

The previous example reveals Maple's preference for the use of $\cos^2(x)$ in place of $\sin^2(x)$. To make this explicit, examine these examples:

```
> simplify(sin(x)^2);
                         2
                1 - cos(x)
> simplify(cos(x)^2);
                      2
                  cos(x)
```

It can be difficult to persuade Maple to use the $\sin^2(x)$ form.

Algebraic expressions are simplified by removing common factors from quotients, which may not happen under automatic simplification:

```
>e:=(x^2+x)/(x+1)-1;
                   2
               x   + x
          e :=  ------ - 1
               x + 1
```

However, simplify() does cancel the common factor:

```
>simplify(");
                  x - 1
```

and simplify() can expand logarithms of products and combine exponents as follows:

```
> simplify(ln(x^p*y^q/z^r),symbolic);

           p ln(x) + q ln(y) - r ln(z)

> simplify((x^p*x^q/x^r));
                      p + q - r
                   x
```

If an expression contains combinations of trigonometric, logarithmic, or other expressions, `simplify()` applies its rules to the different parts. In the next example, `simplify()` has expanded the multiple-angle trigonometric function, evaluated the radical, and performed other trigonometric identities to produce the result shown:

```
>e:=ln((2*cos(3*x)+6*cos(x))^(2/3)/4+1/csc(x)^2);
```

$$e := \ln(1/4\ (2\ \cos(3\ x) + 6\ \cos(x))^{2/3} + \frac{1}{\csc(x)^2})$$

```
>simplify(e,symbolic);
```
$$0$$

Notice the use of the option `symbolic` in the last examples. If we omit it, the following is what we obtain:

```
> simplify(ln(x^p*y^q/z^r));
```
$$\ln(x^p\ y^q\ z^{-r})$$

```
> simplify(e);
```
$$\ln((\cos(x)^3)^{2/3} + 1 - \cos(x)^2)$$

In the previous example, Maple is unable to go any farther with the simplification because it does not have sufficient information to determine a value for the multivalued cube root function. The `symbolic` option tells Maple to proceed in the formal way that we first learn for such manipulations. The `symbolic` option must be specified explicitly if you wish to use this style of simplification. It may seem pedantic to have to be so explicit about simplification, but experience suggests that this is indeed the correct approach in a general-purpose program, where unwarranted assumptions can cause serious errors in extended calculations.

There is another way to ensure particular simplifications are made that uses the `assume` facility. For an illustration we will abstract from the previous example:

```
>simplify((u^3)^(2/3));
```
$$(u^3)^{2/3}$$

```
>assume(u>0);
>simplify((u^3)^(2/3));
```
$$u\sim^2$$

Knowing that u is positive enables Maple to select a specific cube root of u^3. The ~ means that properties have been assumed about u. Another way to use `assume` in association with `simplify()` is as an option of the form `assume=something`. Then all the variables in the expression to be simplified are assumed to be of the form `something`, for example, `real` or `> 0`.

It is possible to control the rules `simplify()` uses through other options. Initially, however, it is best to allow `simplify()` to use all of its rules to reduce an expression. If the results are unsatisfactory, you may need to get more involved with `simplify( ,radical)`, `simplify( ,trig)`, or one of the other options to be found in `related(simplify)`.

The `simplify()` function can be applied to numerical expressions as well. In the following example, note that e is not automatically simplified:

```
>e:=-1/4*(32)^(1/3)*(4)^(2/3);
```

$$e := -\,\frac{1}{4}\,32^{1/3}\,4^{2/3}$$

```
>simplify(e);
```

$$-2$$

As usual, Maple has used the principal values of the cube roots in order to obtain this result.

A case where `simplify()` does not do a good job of simplifying a numerical expression is the following:

```
>e:=(13*sqrt(15)+45)/(2*sqrt(15)+3);
```

$$e := \frac{13\,15^{1/2} + 45}{2\,15^{1/2} + 3}$$

```
>simplify(e);
```

$$\frac{13\,15^{1/2} + 45}{2\,15^{1/2} + 3}$$

The expression e can be further simplified to $5 + \sqrt{15}$ by rationalizing the denominator. One way to obtain this result is not through `simplify()` but through `rationalize()` and `expand()` as follows:

```
> readlib(rationalize);
```

```
proc(x::{relation,algebraic,list,set}) ... end
```

```
>rationalize(e);
```
$$1/51 \ (13 \ 15^{1/2} \ + \ 45) \ (- \ 3 \ + \ 2 \ 15^{1/2} \ )$$
```
>expand(");
```
$$15^{1/2} \ + \ 5$$

Note the use of `readlib()` to load the `rationalize()` function. (The `expand()` function is covered below.) In this instance, `factor()` can produce the final result more quickly; but that would not necessarily be the case for more general ratios (try replacing 15 with x in the above expression).

The `simplify()` function can take an argument that tells it to use "side relations" when simplifying an expression. Here is an illustration of the method:

```
>simplify(x^4-2*x^2-y^4+2,{x^2+y^2=1,x^2-y^2=1});
```
$$1$$

The side relations are polynomial equations are put in a set. The = may be omitted when the right-hand side is zero. Here is another example:

```
>simplify(x^2-y^2,{x+y=1});
```
$$- \ 2 \ y \ + \ 1$$

This result is correct, although perhaps not in the expected form. In the next case, Maple has not managed to simplify the expression to zero, its value under the side relations (divide the side relations to see the reason):

```
>simplify(a2*b3-a3*b2,{a1*b3-a3*b1,a1*b2-a2*b1});
```
$$a2 \ b3 \ - \ a3 \ b2$$

This situation can be remedied by using an additional argument – see Section 9.4 for this.

Expanding expressions

Maple has a function called `expand()` that expands expressions such as products of polynomials and trigonometric functions. It is often useful when `simplify()` doesn't do what you want, as in the next example:

```
>simplify(sin(x+y)+sin(x-y));
```

$$sin(x + y) + sin(x - y)$$

```
>expand(sin(x+y)+sin(x-y));
```

$$2 \, sin(x) \, cos(y)$$

Multiplying out polynomial expressions is one of the common applications of `expand()`:

```
>e:=(1+x)^3*(1+y)^2-(1-x)^3*(1-y)^2;
```

$$e := (1 + x)^3 \, (1 + y)^2 - (1 - x)^3 \, (1 - y)^2$$

```
>expand(e);
```

$$4 \, y + 6 \, x + 6 \, x \, y^2 + 12 \, x^2 \, y + 2 \, x^3 + 2 \, x^3 \, y^2$$

Maple has applied automatic simplification to the result of the expansion.

The `expand()` function will not attempt to do anything with the denominator of a rational function:

```
>e:=((x-1)*(x+1))/((x+4)*(x-4));
```

$$e := \frac{(x - 1) \, (1 + x)}{(x + 4) \, (x - 4)}$$

```
>expand(e);
```

$$\frac{x^2}{(x + 4)(x - 4)} - \frac{1}{(x + 4)(x - 4)}$$

However, `normal( ,expanded)` does expand both the numerator and denominator:

```
> normal(e,expanded);
```

$$\frac{x^2 - 1}{x^2 - 16}$$

Combining expressions

Neither `simplify()` nor `expand()` will replace the sum of two or more logarithms with the logarithm of their product:

```
>simplify(ln(a)+ln(b));
```

$$\ln(a) + \ln(b)$$

To do that, you can use another function called `combine()`:

```
> combine(ln(a)+ln(b),ln);
```

$$\ln(a) + \ln(b)$$

```
> combine(ln(a)+ln(b),ln,symbolic);
```

$$\ln(a\ b)$$

or alternatively:

```
> assume(a>0,b>0):
> combine(ln(a)+ln(b),ln);
```

$$\ln(a\sim\ b\sim)$$

The second argument can be used to restrict the rules that `combine()` uses. For example:

```
> assume(a>0,b>0):
> combine(ln(a)+ln(b),{trig,power});
```

$$ln(a\sim) + ln(b\sim)$$

The second argument must be present if the `symbolic` option is to be used.

You can specify a set of rules by using `exp`, `ln`, `power`, `trig`, `radical`, `abs`, `signum`, or one of several others (see `?combine` for the current list) as the second argument to `combine()`. If an expression needs more than one kind of rule applied, they can be applied separately or all together. To illustrate:

```
> e := ln(cos(x)^2-sin(x)^2)-ln(sin(2*x));
```

$$e := ln(cos(x)^2 - sin(x)^2) - ln(sin(2\ x))$$

```
> combine(e,trig);
```

$$ln(cos(2\ x)) - ln(sin(2\ x))$$

```
> combine(",ln,symbolic);
```

$$ln\left(\frac{cos(2\ x)}{sin(2\ x)}\right)$$

```
> combine(e,{trig,ln},symbolic);
```

$$ln\left(\frac{cos(2\ x)}{sin(2\ x)}\right)$$

The ability of `combine()` to "linearize" trigonometric polynomials is useful. The next example forms a sixth-degree trigonometric polynomial and `combine()`

removes the powers and replaces them with multiple angles:

```
> e:=x^6+y^4-2*x*y +1;
```

$$e := x^6 + y^4 - 2\,x\,y + 1$$

```
> f:=subs(x=cos(t),y=sin(t),e);
```

$$f := \cos(t)^6 + \sin(t)^4 - 2\,\cos(t)\,\sin(t) + 1$$

```
> combine(f,trig);
```

$$\frac{1}{32}\cos(6\,t) + \frac{5}{16}\cos(4\,t) - \frac{1}{32}\cos(2\,t)$$

$$+ \frac{27}{16} - \sin(2\,t)$$

You can sometimes undo the effects of combine() with expand():

```
>expand(");
```

$$\cos(t)^6 + \cos(t)^4 - 2\,\cos(t)^2 + 2 - 2\,\cos(t)\,\sin(t)$$

Polynomial manipulations

Polynomial manipulations, such as factoring and isolating coefficients, are handled with dedicated Maple functions. Some of the most often used functions are factor() for factoring, collect() for organizing sums of terms with respect to particular variables, and coeff() for picking off the coefficients of terms. Using factor() is straightforward:

```
>factor(x^5-1);
```

$$(x - 1)\,(x^4 + x^3 + x^2 + x + 1)$$

The `factor()` function also works on rational expressions:

```
>factor((x^2+5*x+6)/(x^4-x^2));
```

$$\frac{(x + 3) \ (x + 2)}{x^2 \ (x - 1) \ (x + 1)}$$

When you use `factor()` with a single argument, Maple will attempt to factor the expression over the field of rationals (using only factors with rational coefficients). You can change the field by using a second argument to `factor()`. A very simple example would be

```
>factor(x^2+1);
```

$$x^2 + 1$$

```
>factor(x^2+1,I);
```

$$(x + I) \ (x - I)$$

In the first case, there are no rational real factors and the expression is returned unevaluated. Extending the field by `I` allows factoring to occur. Chapter 7 contains further information on this topic.

For putting general expressions over a common denominator you can use either `simplify()` or `normal()`. The `normal()` function will automatically remove common factors from the numerator and denominator.

Another very useful manipulation tool is `collect()`. Here is an illustration of the basic operation of `collect()`:

```
>p:=(a*x^2+b*x+c)*(c*x^2+b*x+a);
```

$$p := (a \ x^2 + b \ x + c) \ (c \ x^2 + b \ x + a)$$

```
>collect(p,x);
```

$$c \ a \ x^4 + (c \ b + b \ a) \ x^3 + (c^2 + b^2 + a^2) \ x^2$$

$$+ \ (c \ b + b \ a) \ x + c \ a$$

The `collect()` function has arranged the terms as a polynomial in its second argument. Note that there is no need to apply `expand()` before collecting terms.

You can `collect()` with respect to any of the variables. Here the terms are collected with respect to a:

```
>collect(p,a);
```

$$x^2 a^2 + (b x + c + x^2 (c x^2 + b x)) a$$

$$+ (b x + c) (c x^2 + b x)$$

You can also specify a list of variables as the second argument to `collect()`. The effect of specifying two variables in a list is to cause the expression to be arranged as a polynomial in the first entry in the list, with coefficients arranged as a polynomial in the second variable. For example:

```
>collect(p,[a,x]);
```

$$x^2 a^2 + (c x^4 + b x^3 + b x + c) a + c b x^3$$

$$+ (c^2 + b^2) x^2 + c b x$$

If you want the collected form expanded out, you can specify a third option to `collect()` as follows:

```
>collect(p,[a,x],distributed);
```

$$x^2 a^2 + c a x^4 + b a x^3 + b a x + c a + c b x^3$$

$$+ (c^2 + b^2) x^2 + c b x$$

Now x and a appear on an equal footing; getting the variables organized in such a manner is often useful. The `distributed` option has no effect if there is only one variable in the second argument to `collect()`.

The function `coeff()` lets you access particular coefficients from an expression created by using `collect()`. For example, the coefficient of x^3 in the last result can be extracted in this way:

```
>coeff(",x^3);
```

$$c\ b\ +\ b\ a$$

If you want the coefficient of, say, ax^3 you have to be a bit more careful because `coeff()` can only find the coefficient of a power. It cannot find the coefficient of a product. Here is one way to extract the required coefficient:

```
>coeff(coeff("",a),x^3);
```

$$b$$

Whereas `coeff()` is the main function for getting at particular coefficients, there are also `lcoeff()` and `tcoeff()` for the leading and trailing coefficients of a polynomial, and `coeffs()`, which produces an expression sequence containing all the coefficients.

The functions `quo()` and `rem()` are used to obtain the quotient and remainder for polynomial division. Here is an example:

```
> quo(x^2+3*x+2,x-1,x,'r');
```

$$x\ +\ 4$$

```
> r;
```

$$6$$

```
> rem(x^2+3*x+2,x-1,x,'q');
```

$$6$$

```
> q;
```

$$x\ +\ 4$$

Transforming with `convert()`

There are times when none of the simplification and manipulation tools introduced above will do what you want. When that happens, you may be able to make progress using some facilities built into `convert()`. Among other things, these facilities allow you to convert trigonometric forms to exponentials and vice-versa and to convert combinatorial functions to factorials. Here are four examples of the conversion of an expression to another equivalent form:

```
>convert(sin(x),tan);
                     tan(1/2 x)
              2  ---------------
                               2
                 1 + tan(1/2 x)
```

```
>convert(binomial(n+m,m),factorial);

                      (n + m)!
                      --------
                       m! n!
```

```
>convert(cos(x),exp);
                                  1
              1/2 exp(I x)  +  ----------
                               2 exp(I x)
```

```
>convert(arccosh(x),ln);
                        1/2          1/2
          ln(x + (x - 1)      (x + 1)    )
```

Here is a simple example of how `convert()` can be helpful. Suppose that you wanted to rewrite the expression $\tan(\pi/4 + x/2)$ in terms of trigonometric functions of the angle x instead of the half angle $x/2$. It would be natural to first try the following:

```
> e:=tan(Pi/4+x/2);
              e := tan(1/4 Pi + 1/2 x)
```

```
> expand(");
                  tan(1/2 x) + 1
                  --------------
                  1 - tan(1/2 x)
```

This is still in half-angle form. It can be turned into the desired result using a further command (`simplify(")`), but to illustrate the use of `convert()`, we will solve the problem as follows:

```
> convert(e,exp);
```

$$-\ \frac{I\ (\exp(I\ (1/4\ Pi\ +\ 1/2\ x))^2\ -\ 1)}{\exp(I\ (1/4\ Pi\ +\ 1/2\ x))^2\ +\ 1}$$

```
> expand(");
```

$$\frac{\exp(1/2\ I\ x)^2}{I\ \exp(1/2\ I\ x)^2\ +\ 1}\ +\ \frac{I}{I\ \exp(1/2\ I\ x)^2\ +\ 1}$$

```
> combine(",{exp,power});
```

$$\frac{\exp(I\ x)}{I\ \exp(I\ x)\ +\ 1}\ +\ \frac{I}{I\ \exp(I\ x)\ +\ 1}$$

This expression involves the full angle, and the desired result can now be quickly obtained as follows:

```
> simplify(evalc("));
```

$$\frac{\sin(x)\ +\ 1}{\cos(x)}$$

Converting to partial fractions

There is a convert() function for changing a rational function to partial fraction form. Here is an example for this function:

```
>convert(1/(1+x^3)^2,parfrac,x);
```

$$\frac{1}{9\ (x\ +\ 1)^2}\ +\ \frac{2}{9\ (x\ +\ 1)}\ -\ 1/9\ \frac{-\ 3\ +\ 2\ x}{x^2\ -\ x\ +\ 1}$$

$$-\ 1/3\ \frac{x\ -\ 1}{(x^2\ -\ x\ +\ 1)^2}$$

The third argument is always needed, most obviously when the rational function contains parameters. In this example, the original function can be partially recovered as follows:

```
>simplify(");
```

$$
\frac{1}{(x + 1)^2 \; (x^2 - x + 1)^2}
$$

but it is more awkward to retrieve the initial form of the expression (try it!). An example for which `convert( ,parfrac, )` gives no result is the function $1/(1 + x^4)$. In this and other cases, a decomposition can be obtained from the function `genfunc[rgf_pfrac]()` using the additional argument `no_RootOf`.

2.4 Solving equations and inequalities

Symbolic mathematics programs are often used to solve polynomial equations, and Maple has extensive facilities for handling single equations and systems of equations. We will cover these facilities in this section. (Linear equations will be covered in Chapter 4.) The topics covered here are

- Using `solve()`
- Systems of Equations
- General Nonlinear Equations
- Equations with Radicals
- Inequalities
- Finding Numerical Roots

Using `solve()`

Maple's main facilities for finding closed-form solutions to polynomial equations and inequalities are in a function called `solve()`. The `solve()` function can also handle systems of polynomial equations including linear systems. In addition, `solve()` can sometimes obtain solutions to more general nonlinear equations and inequalities.

For polynomials of degree 4 or less, Maple can always produce the exact roots, although for the quartic case you have to tell Maple that you do indeed wish the roots to be explicitly printed. (If you feel that it would be better to have to tell Maple when you did *not* want the roots printed you are not alone.) For higher-degree polynomials, Maple can sometimes find a closed expression but not always, as we will see.

The first argument to `solve()` is the equation (or system) or inequality to be solved, and the second argument contains the variables to solve for. The simplest case has one equation and one variable as follows:

```
>solve(x^2-x+1=0,x);
```

$$1/2 + 1/2 \ I \ 3^{1/2} \ , \ 1/2 - 1/2 \ I \ 3^{1/2}$$

A short form lets you drop either or both of the $= 0$ parts and the variable x name if there is no ambiguity:

```
>solve(x^2-x+1);
```

$$1/2 + 1/2 \ I \ 3^{1/2} \ , \ 1/2 - 1/2 \ I \ 3^{1/2}$$

The roots are returned in an expression sequence. This next example selects just the first of four roots; even so it is an awkward expression containing relatively deeply nested radicals (setting _EnvExplicit to true is the way you tell Maple to print the results):

```
>_EnvExplicit := true:
>solve(x^4-x+1)[1];
```

```
                  /   2/3      \1/2
        1/2 |%1      + 48|                   1/2
  1/12 6    |----------|       + 1/12 6
            |     1/3   |
            \    %1     /


    /   / 2/3     \1/2          / 2/3      \1/2                    \ 1/2
    |   |%1  + 48|      2/3     |%1  + 48|          1/2  1/3|
    |-  |--------|      %1  -  48 |--------| + 12  6   %1   |
    |   |   1/3  |               |    1/3  |                    |
    |   \ %1     /               \ %1      /                    |
    |-----------------------------------------------------------|
    |                        /   2/3       \1/2                  |
    |                1/3 |%1       + 48|                         |
    |                %1      |----------|                        |
    |                        |     1/3   |                       |
    \                        \    %1     /                      /


                                 1/2
    %1 :=            108 + 12 I 687
```

The percent (`%`) assignments are genuine Maple names for the expressions they label, and consequently can be used in other Maple expressions later if necessary.

One way to cut down the formula for the zero is through `evalf()`:

```
>evalf(");
```

$$.7271360845 + .4300142883 \text{ I}$$

You might as well compute all of the roots:

```
>evalf(solve(x^4-x+1));
```

$$.7271360851 - .4300142884 \text{ I},$$

$$.7271360851 + .4300142884 \text{ I},$$

$$- .7271360853 - .9340992900 \text{ I},$$

$$- .7271360849 + .9340992900 \text{ I}$$

Because `evalf()` is a purely numerical facility, this approach does not work if the roots depend on parameters or the coefficients are nonnumeric.

There is no algebraic formula for the zeros of polynomials of degree 5 or higher. This result was proved in 1821 by Niels Abel for quintic polynomials and by Evariste Galois in 1829 for the general case. Still, higher-degree polynomials can sometimes be solved with special tricks. For example, `solve()` can find all six zeros of the next example, although only one of them is displayed:

```
>solve(x^6-3*x^5+3*x^4-x^3-1)[1];
```

$$\begin{array}{c} 1/2 \\ 1/2 + 1/2 \ 5 \end{array}$$

(oddly, `_EnvExplicit` does not have to be `true` for this). You can always check roots by substitution into the original equation:

```
>simplify(subs(x=",x^6-3*x^5+3*x^4-x^3-1));
```

$$0$$

If `solve()` cannot find the roots of a polynomial it returns as follows:

```
>solve(x^5-x+1);
```

$$5$$
$$RootOf(\_Z \quad - \_Z + 1)$$

This expression is a placeholder for the roots of the polynomial. `RootOf()` expressions have a number of applications in Maple, for instance, with algebraic numbers and finite fields (see Chapter 7). Here is how to use `RootOf()` to sum the fourth powers of the roots of the quintic given above (`sum()` is covered more fully in Sums and Products of Terms). Here, `r` is just a name and has no value after the calculation:

```
> sum(r^4,r=RootOf(x^5-x+1));
```

$$4$$

```
>eval(r);
```

$$r$$

The sum above can be checked by a floating-point calculation. To help with checking, we will use a function called `allvalues()` which will obtain explicit (floating-point if necessary) values from `RootOf()`. It returns an expression sequence:

```
>allvalues(RootOf(x^5-x+1));
```

$$-1.167303978, \quad - .1812324445 + 1.083954101 \; I,$$

$$- .1812324445 - 1.083954101 \; I,$$

$$.7648844336 + .3524715460 \; I,$$

$$.7648844336 - .3524715460 \; I$$

Summing gives the desired value, apart from a small roundoff error:

```
>sum(("[i])^4,i=1..5);
```

$$3.999999994$$

The `allvalues()` function will try to use `solve()` to find explicit values but if that does not work it will resort to numerical computations as shown in the previous example. The `allvalues()` function uses a function called `fsolve()` to compute

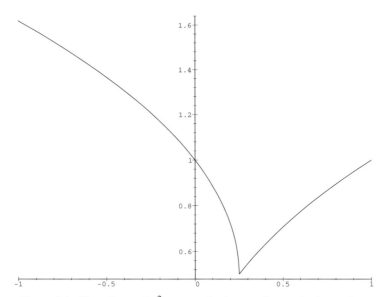

Figure 2.1: Plot of root of $x^2 + x + a$ having maximum absolute value.

these floating-point approximations. The `fsolve()` function is discussed in Finding Numerical Roots below and in Section 5.2.

Of course, polynomials may have literal coefficients as well as numerical co-efficients. For example, if you input a general quartic to `solve()`, Maple will produce the (very long) general solution formula for a quartic (remember to set `_EnvExplicit:=true`). The ideas already introduced remain valid with few exceptions.

As already mentioned, you cannot use `evalf()` on expressions containing non-numerical parameters. An obvious alternative is to use `plot()` or `plot3d()` to get pictures for a range of parameter values. For example, suppose we were interested in the variation of the roots of the quadratic equation $x^2 + x + a = 0$ as a function of a, where a denotes a parameter. The next example plots the root of maximum absolute value as a function of a (see Figure 2.1):

```
>r:=solve(x^2+x+a,x);
```

$$
r := -1/2 + 1/2 (1 - 4 a)^{1/2} , -1/2 - 1/2 (1 - 4 a)^{1/2}
$$

```
>plot(max(abs(r[1]),abs(r[2])),a=-1..1,labels
    =['','']);
```

Systems of equations

You can solve systems of polynomial equations analytically using `solve()`. This subsection briefly illustrates some difficulties with this relatively complicated subject. When you want to give sets of equations or unknowns to Maple, you can use Maple's set notation and enclose the set's elements in braces. Here is a set of two equations in two unknowns solved by Maple:

```
>solve({x+y=a,x-y=b},{x,y});
```

$$\{y = 1/2\ a\ -\ 1/2\ b,\ x\ =\ 1/2\ a\ +\ 1/2\ b\}$$

The solutions are also returned as a set of equations. Note that the roots do not have the names x and y here because we have equations, not assignments. To turn the equations into assignments, you can use `assign()`:

```
>assign(");
>x;y;
```

$$1/2\ a\ +\ 1/2\ b$$

$$1/2\ a\ -\ 1/2\ b$$

Here is a nonlinear example asking for the intersection of the circle centered on the origin and of radius a with two perpendicular lines through the origin:

```
>solve({x^2+y^2=a^2,y^2-x^2=0},{x,y});
```

$$\{y\ =\ \%1,\ x\ =\ \%1\},\ \{y\ =\ \%1,\ x\ =\ -\ \%1\}$$

$$\%1\ :=\qquad RootOf(2\ \_Z^2\ -\ a^2\ )$$

The sets in this result are the complete set of solutions to the equations (In this example, the variable _EnvExplicit was `false`.).

Often you will get more than one `RootOf` expression returned from this type of calculation. For example, the equations in the next example ask for the intersections of the unit circle with a parabola:

```
> solve({x^2+y^2=1,y-x^2=0},{x,y});
```

$$\{x = RootOf(-\ RootOf(\_Z + \_Z^{2} - 1) + \_Z^{2}),$$

$$y = RootOf(\_Z + \_Z^{2} - 1)\}$$

Figuring out which roots really solve the original equations is not always easy. A reasonable approach is to use `allvalues()` to list the roots explicitly, although this requires that the coefficients be numerical. In this instance, there are sixteen such possibilities and `allvalues()` does indeed list them all. They cannot all be the roots that we are looking for. For example, some are complex although only the real ones are of interest. Also, some of the combinations in the collection above are real but have negative y values, which is impossible from the second equation. Generally speaking, you have to be prepared to test which of the results represent honest roots, for example, by using `subs()`.

General nonlinear equations

The `solve()` function can sometimes find solutions to more general equations. A very simple example would be

```
> solve(sin(x)=x);
```

$$0$$

Closed-form solutions to general equations rarely exist. When `solve()` cannot find a solution to an equation or system it returns NULL as follows:

```
> solve(tan(x)=x^sin(x));
>
```

Frequently, `solve()` will return a `RootOf()` expression:

```
> solve(tanh(x)=x+1);
```

$$RootOf(tanh(\_Z) - \_Z - 1)$$

However, in contrast to the polynomial case (see Chapter 7), Maple has few facilities for manipulating roots of arbitrary equations. For example, if x is a root of the above equation then it follows that $\tanh^{-1}(x+1) = x$, but Maple doesn't detect it:

```
> rr := solve(tanh(x)=x+1):
> simplify(arctanh(rr+1));
```

$$\text{arctanh}(\text{RootOf}(\sinh(\_Z) - \_Z \cosh(\_Z) - \cosh(\_Z)) + 1)$$

Maple can determine all the solutions of certain simple transcendental equations and will do so when the environment variable _EnvAllSolutions is set to true. As a simple illustration, we solve $\tan(x) = \sin(x)$:

```
> solve(tan(x)=sin(x));
```

$$0$$

```
> _EnvAllSolutions := true;
```

$$\_EnvAllSolutions := true$$

```
> solve(tan(x)=sin(x));
```

$$\text{Pi } \_Z\sim$$

As explained in the help file for solve(), the variable _Z~ represents an arbitrary integer, _NN~ represents a nonnegative integer, and _B~ is a binary value, 0 or 1.

Equations with radicals

The solve() function can be applied to some types of equations involving radicals. A simple example of solving an equation with radicals is

```
> solve(x*sqrt(x)+x=2,x);
```

$$1$$

The solve() function handles these equations by converting them to systems of equations with the radicals as new variables. This is a process that might generate spurious solutions of the initial equation, so independent checking is advisable.

Inequalities

You can also use solve() to find solutions to a single inequality. This works well for polynomials with real roots that solve() can find. In the next example, solve()

has found the three disjoint sets where the "double-well potential" $(x^2 - 1)^2$ exceeds 1/2:

```
> _EnvExplicit:=true:
> solve((x^2-1)^2-1/2>0);
                                        1/2 1/2
    RealRange(- infinity, Open(- 1/2 (4 + 2 2    )    )),

                                1/2 1/2
    RealRange(Open(- 1/2 (4 - 2    2    )),
                            1/2 1/2
                Open(1/2 (4 - 2 2    )    )),

                            1/2 1/2
    RealRange(Open(1/2 (4 + 2 2    )    ), infinity)
```

When an inequality has no solutions `solve()` returns NULL:

```
>solve(x^2-x+1<0);
>
```

You can sometimes get solutions for nonpolynomial inequalities such as the following:

```
> solve(abs(x-1)>abs(x+1));

                    RealRange(- infinity, Open(0))

> solve(abs(x)>abs(x+1));

                    RealRange(- infinity, Open(-1/2))
```

Finding numerical roots

Most nonlinear equations cannot be solved in closed form, and it is necessary to use numerical approximations. In Maple, this is done by `fsolve()`. The `fsolve()` function treats univariate polynomial equations differently from other equations. For a polynomial (of any degree), it returns all the real roots; it returns all the roots if the option `complex` is given. To illustrate, we will find the real roots and then all the roots of a fifth-degree polynomial:

```
>p:=x^5-x^2+6;
```

$$p := x^5 - x^2 + 6$$

```
>fsolve(p);
```

$$-1.333778701$$

There is only one real root:

```
>fsolve(p,x,complex);
```

$$-1.333778701, \quad -.5208528939 - 1.418577334 \ I,$$

$$-.5208528939 + 1.418577334 \ I,$$

$$1.187742244 - .7477570027 \ I,$$

$$1.187742244 + .7477570027 \ I$$

Note that you have to specify which variable to solve for when using the `complex` option.

The next example uses `fsolve()` on a more general nonlinear equation:

```
>fsolve(x-tan(x)=0);
```

$$4.493409458$$

Only one root is returned, a wise policy in this instance because the equation $x - \tan(x) = 0$ has an infinite number of solutions. Which root is found depends on the initial approximation used in the iterative solver. You can control this to some extent by specifying an interval for the root. For instance, in an attempt to find the zero root of the equation, we might specify the interval $(-1, 1)$ as follows:

```
>fsolve(x-tan(x),x=-1..1);
```

$$0$$

By choosing other ranges, you can find other roots. We will return to this example in Section 5.2.

Systems of equations are handled in a similar way except that only one root will be returned, even for polynomial systems. The next example computes the solution to the earlier problem on the intersections of a parabola with the unit circle. First we will let Maple choose a root:

```
>fsolve({x^2+y^2=1,y-x^2=0});
```

$$\{x = -.7861513778, \ y = .6180339887\}$$

To find the remaining real root, we can specify a range for x:

```
>fsolve({x^2+y^2=1,y-x^2=0},{x,y},x=0..1);
```

$$\{y = .6180339887, \ x = .7861513778\}$$

You can also use `infinity` in the variable ranges. For example, here we specify a range for y:

```
>fsolve({x^2+y^2=1,y-x^2=0},{x,y},y=-infinity..0);
>
```

Because there is no solution in this case, `fsolve()` returns NULL. There is more on `fsolve()` in Chapter 5.

2.5   Sums and products of terms

It is often necessary to form sums and products of terms. This section discusses the functions `add()`, `sum()`, `mul()`, and `product()`. In addition, we will discuss how the ideas of indefinite summation and indefinite products relate to these functions and cover the use of a function called `eulermac()`, which makes Euler–MacLaurin expansions. The subsections are

- The `add()` and `sum()` Functions
- Indefinite Summation
- Euler–MacLaurin Summation
- Forming Products

The add() and sum() functions

You use the `add()` function to add up a specific number of terms as follows:

```
> add(i^3,i=3..6);
```
$$432$$

or:

```
> add(d[j]*x^j,j=0..3);
```

$$d[0] + d[1] \ x + d[2] \ x^2 + d[3] \ x^3$$

Do you remember the short form of the `seq()` function? The example we used earlier for this was

```
> l:=[2,3,4]: seq(k^3,k=1);
```

$$8, \ 27, \ 64$$

`add()` has a similar form:

```
> add(k^3,k=1);
```

$$99$$

For computing symbolic sums, the function is `sum()`. The most common form of `sum()` uses a range to specify the terms to be added. The following forms the sum of the first *n* positive integers:

```
>sum(j,j=1..n);
```

$$1/2 \ (n + 1)^2 \ - 1/2 \ n - 1/2$$

To get this example into the usual form, it needs to be rearranged:

```
>factor(");
```

$$1/2 \ n \ (n + 1)$$

Infinite ranges can be used also. Here is the sum of a simple geometric progression:

```
>sum(1/3^j,j=0..infinity);
```

$$3/2$$

Of course, Maple can do more interesting sums than this; for example:

```
>sum((-1)^j*(1/j),j=1..infinity);
```

$$- \ln(2)$$

You can nest `sum()` to perform multidimensional summations. Here is an example of how to do this for the sum $\sum_{i,j=1}^{\infty} 1/(i^2 j^2)$:

```
>sum(sum(1/(i^2*j^2),i=1..infinity),j=1..infinity);
```

$$\frac{1}{36} \text{ Pi}^4$$

As with `add()`, `sum()` can be used to define polynomial expressions:

```
>p:=sum(a[j]*x^j,j=0..4);
```

$$p := a[0] + a[1] \ x + a[2] \ x^2 + a[3] \ x^3 + a[4] \ x^4$$

Maple does recognize the last expression as a polynomial:

```
>type(p,polynom);
```
```
                               true
```

Numerical or other values can be given to the coefficients through straightforward assignments.

To sum over nonconsecutive integers, you can usually modify the summation index in the summand (not in the range). For example, to sum the squares of the odd integers the following can be done:

```
>sum((2*j-1)^2,j=1..n);
```

$$11/3 \ n + 8/3 - 4 \ (n + 1)^2 + 4/3 \ (n + 1)^3$$

```
>factor(");
```
$$1/3 \ n \ (2 \ n - 1) \ (2 \ n + 1)$$

Use a similar approach whenever a range step different from unity is needed.

Before a sum is computed, its arguments are evaluated, including the range arguments. The first range argument must evaluate to a name, otherwise an error message can result. If there is any problem with the range evaluation, you can enclose the arguments involved in forward quotes.

The second argument to `sum()` can be a `RootOf()` expression. In that case, Maple will try to sum the expression in the first argument over the roots. As a simple example, here is a way to find the sum of the squares of the roots of a cubic polynomial:

```
>sum(j^2,j=RootOf(x^3+x-1));
```
$$-2$$

This is useful because certain sums of this kind can be computed even when the individual roots cannot be found exactly. Chapter 7 has more on this topic.

Indefinite summation

Maple computes analytical sums by a process analogous to computing an indefinite integral and substituting in the limits. Just as in integration the indefinite integral yields a primitive, so does the summation. Although this primitive is needed less often than the definite result, it is very simple to inspect it when available. For an illustration, we will find a primitive for summing positive integers:

```
>sum(j,j);
```
$$1/2\ j^2\ -\ 1/2\ j$$

The result is the primitive. To find, say, the sum of the integers in the interval [Nmin,Nmax+1] you can do the following:

```
>subs(j=Nmax+1,")-subs(j=Nmin,");
```
$$1/2\ (Nmax\ +\ 1)^2\ -\ 1/2\ Nmax\ -\ 1/2\ -\ 1/2\ Nmin^2\ +\ 1/2\ Nmin$$

```
>factor(");
```
$$-\ 1/2\ (Nmin\ +\ Nmax)\ (Nmin\ -\ 1\ -\ Nmax)$$

This result gives the usual one if `Nmin` is zero. Of course, the same result could more easily be obtained by using `sum()` with a range, but the point here is to illustrate the idea of the summation primitive.

The package `sumtools[]` contains a number of functions for advanced work with indefinite sums.

Euler–MacLaurin summation

Maple knows a form of the Euler–MacLaurin summation formula. The standard formula can be obtained from Maple's formula by treating it as a primitive in the sense described in the Indefinite Summation subsection. To obtain an explicit sum, you have to evaluate the primitive at two different endpoints. The formula built into Maple can be found as follows:

```
>readlib(eulermac):
> eulermac(f(x),x);
```

```
    /
    |                                           /  d      \
    |   f(x)  dx  -  1/2 f(x)  +  1/12 |---- f(x)|
    |                                           \ dx      /
    /


                  /     3      \                  /     5      \
                  |    d       |                  |    d       |
        - 1/720 |----- f(x)|  +  1/30240 |----- f(x)|
                  |     3      |                  |     5      |
                  \    dx      /                  \    dx      /


                7
               d
        + O(----- f(x))
                7
              dx
```

This formula gives a value for the indefinite sum that Maple denotes by `sum(f(x),x)`. As a simple test, we can use the Euler–MacLaurin formula to approximate the sum of the reciprocals of the squares of the integers starting from 4.

The first step is to obtain the expansion:

```
>eulermac(1/x^2,x);
```

$$
- 1/x - \frac{1}{2x^2} - \frac{1}{6x^3} + \frac{1}{30x^5} - \frac{1}{42x^7} + O\left(\frac{1}{x^9}\right)
$$

Now we have to evaluate this result at the upper and lower limits and subtract the results. The result for the upper limit is zero, so we find the result:

```
>-evalf(subs(x=4,"));
```

$$
.2838230678 - O(1/262144)
$$

For comparison, the exact result is

```
>evalf(Pi^2/6-49/36);
```

$$
.283822957
$$

Ignoring the error term in the first result, we see that the approximation has almost six correct digits. To obtain more terms in this and other series expansions, you can reset a global variable called `Order`. Currently, `Order` is set to its default value, 6.

The `eulermac()` function can fail when the series terminates. The following shows what happens:

```
>eulermac(x^4,x);
Error, (in eulermac) division by zero
```

Mathematically, the Euler–MacLaurin formula gives the exact result in such a case, but `eulermac()` does not do so.

Forming products

To form a product of a specific number of terms there is `mul()`. This function is an analog of `add()`, and we will not discuss it further here.

Formation of symbolic products uses a function called `product()`:

```
>product((1-1/j^2),j=2..n);
```

$$1/2 \ \frac{\text{GAMMA}(n) \ \text{GAMMA}(n + 2)}{\text{GAMMA}(n + 1)^2}$$

```
>simplify(");
```

$$1/2 \ \frac{n + 1}{n}$$

The idea of finding a primitive works for products in a similar way as for sums except that instead of subtracting the primitive's endpoint values they have to be divided. Here is the primitive for the previous example:

```
>product((1-1/j^2),j);
```

$$\frac{\text{GAMMA}(j - 1) \ \text{GAMMA}(j + 1)}{\text{GAMMA}(j)^2}$$

Just as with summation, this result can be evaluated using `subs()`, but it is usually more convenient to give the limits directly in `product()`. The `product()` function returns unevaluated for infinite ranges.

Both `mul()` and `product()` can form polynomials from their roots. For example, the following shows one way to form the polynomial with roots 1, 2, 3, 4, 5:

```
>rts:=seq(i,i=1..5);
```

$$rts := 1, \ 2, \ 3, \ 4, \ 5$$

```
>product(x-rts[j],j=1..5);
```

$$(x - 1) \ (x - 2) \ (x - 3) \ (x - 4) \ (x - 5)$$

```
>expand(");
```

$$x^5 - 15 \ x^4 + 85 \ x^3 - 225 \ x^2 + 274 \ x - 120$$

If you wanted to use `i` in place of `j` in the second step, you would need to unassign it first because `seq()` has assigned `i` to 6.

2.6   Defining functions

So far, our dealings with mathematical functions such as polynomials have been at the expression level. We have simply set up expressions that represent these mathematical functions and applied Maple functions to them. However, there are many occasions when this approach is insufficient and we need to view mathematical functions more as "mappings." Maple offers some nice tools for defining mappings, and they are the subject of this section. The contents of this section are

- Arrow Notation
- Conditional Statements
- Using `unapply()`
- Piecewise-Defined Functions

Arrow notation

Arrow notation mimics the mapping notation of mathematics in that it represents the mapping of the input to the output by an arrow (formed using a minus and greater than symbol). Here is an example:

```
>s:=x->x^2;
```

$$s := x \rightarrow x^2$$

To square a number (or other expression) you do the natural thing:

```
>s(2);
```

$$4$$

The same method can be used for functions of more than one variable:

```
>f:=(x,y)->x^2+y;
```

$$f := (x,y) \rightarrow x^2 + y$$

(the parentheses around the x and y are necessary), and to compute the function you use standard notation:

```
>f(3,2);
```

$$11$$

You can compose and embed arrow functions too. Here, for example, the function f, defined above, is used as part of the definition of another function:

```
>g:=(a,b,c)->a*f(b,c);
```

$$g := (a,b,c) \rightarrow a\ f(b,\ c)$$

```
>g(2,3,1);
```

$$20$$

Arrow notation can be used to define vector-valued functions. The technique is a straightforward extension of the earlier cases, except that you must use parentheses on the right-hand side of the arrow:

```
>h:=(x,y)->(sin(x)*y,sin(y)*x,x*y);
```

$$h := (x,y) \rightarrow sin(x)\ y,\ sin(y)\ x,\ x\ y$$

```
>h(Pi,1);
```

$$0,\ sin(1)\ Pi,\ Pi$$

In all these cases, you can omit the function name. In the next case, the squaring function has no explicit name:

```
>(x->x^2)(2.1);
```

$$4.41$$

Such "anonymous" functions are often used with map().

Functions defined using the arrow notation can be recursive, meaning that they can call themselves during evaluation. Here is a function to compute $n!$ (a standard example for recursion) using arrow notation:

```
>g1:= n->n*g1(n-1);
```

$$g1 := n \rightarrow n\ g1(n-1)$$

The next condition puts an entry into the remember table of g1 (discussed in Section 11.3) and is essential for ending the recursion!

```
>g1(0):=1;
```

$$g1(0) := 1$$

To compute 20! and compare it with Maple's factorial function, you do the following:

```
>g1(20)-20!;
```

$$0$$

Be careful with recursions like these. They can cause a stack overflow error if they are applied to incorrect data or if there is no proper termination criterion.

Conditional statements

Arrow functions can incorporate "selection" statements; that is, those involving `if`, `then`, `else`, and so on. We will cover these in more detail in Chapter 10. Here we will show how to write an arrow function for computing a piecewise-defined mathematical function. Actually, Maple has a built-in function called `piecewise()` for defining and using piecewise-defined functions, which is covered in Piecewise-Defined Functions below.

In Maple the logical operators are `and`, `or`, and `not`. The relational operators are `<`, `<=`, `>`, `>=`, `=`, and `<>`. The `<>` relational operator stands for "not equal." Logical and relational operators are used to form expressions that can be evaluated and assigned a truth value of either `true` or `false`. (A third value, `FAIL` can be returned from a procedure when it is unable to perform its task.) The evaluator `evalb()` performs Boolean evaluations, for example:

```
>evalb(1<>1 or (1<>2 and 2<>2));
```

$$false$$

Selection statements in Maple have the general form:

```
if <expr> then <stmts> elif <expr> then <stmts>
    else <stmts> fi
```

where `<expr>` stands for an expression that has a truth value and `<stmts>` stands for a statement sequence. One or more of the keywords may be absent but `fi` must always be present to end the statement.

Now we will write an arrow function for:

$$g(x) = \begin{cases} x^2 & -1 \le x \le 0 \\ 2x & 0 < x \le 1/2 \\ (x-3/2)^2 & 1/2 < x \le 3/2 \end{cases}$$

Using the relational operators and selection statements to define the arrow function results in the following:

```
>g:= x-> if x<-1 or x>3/2 then print('Invalid argument')
>elif x>=-1 and x<=0 then x^2
>elif x>0 and x<=1/2 then 2*x
>else (x-3/2)^2 fi;


g := proc(x)
      options operator,arrow;
          if x < -1 or 3/2 < x then
              print('Invalid argument')
          elif -1 <= x and x <= 0 then x^2
          elif x > 0 and x <= 1/2 then 2*x
          else (x-3/2)^2
          fi
    end
```

After Maple has digested the input, it returns the procedure it has written for the function (procedures are discussed in detail in Chapter 11). Now we can evaluate g at any point:

```
>g(1/4);
                          1
                         ----
                          2
>g(-2);
```
Invalid argument

As an exercise, why not plot the graph of this procedure? (Do not give an argument to g in plot().)

Using `unapply()`

How can you obtain the arrow function corresponding to an expression? The answer lies in a function called `unapply()`. First we will illustrate the need for such a function. Here is an expression:

```
>p1:=2*x^4-x+1;
```

$$p1 := 2 x^4 - x + 1$$

This is not a function in the sense that you can get its value at, say, x=2, as the following shows:

```
>p1(2);
```

$$2 x(2)^4 - x(2) + 1$$

You could do the following:

```
>x:=2;
```

$$x := 2$$

and then ask for the value of the expression:

```
>p1;
```

$$31$$

To recover the original expression you have to unassign x, which may be inconvenient. The `unapply()` function provides an alternative. First, redefine the expression:

```
>x:='x';
```

$$x := x$$

```
>p1;
```

$$p1 := 2 x^4 - x + 1$$

and now do the following:

```
>f:=unapply(p1,x);
```

$$f := x \rightarrow 2 x^4 - x + 1$$

You can then compute with the arrow function as before:

```
>f(2);
```

$$31$$

The term "unapply" comes from viewing the operand expression as being obtained by applying an operator or mapping, say the squaring function, to x. The result of the application is the value at x of the squaring function. If you `unapply()` the expression x^2, you recover the original mapping, in this case the squaring function.

The `unapply()` function works in the same way if there are several dependent and/or independent variables. For illustration, we use a list-valued function of two variables:

```
>f:=[x^2+y^2,x^2-y^2];
```

$$f := [x^2 + y^2,\ x^2 - y^2]$$

```
>g:=unapply(f,x,y);
```

$$g := (x,y) \to [x^2 + y^2,\ x^2 - y^2]$$

In this example, the initial function is defined by a list. This technique does not work if f is defined by an array. You can then use a slightly different approach as is shown next. The first step is to set up the array of expressions:

```
>f:=array(1..2):
```

```
>f[1]:=x^2+y^2;f[2]:=x^2-y^2;
```

$$f[1] := x^2 + y^2$$

$$f[2] := x^2 - y^2$$

The `unapply()` function is now mapped onto the components of `f`:

```
>g:=map(unapply,f,x,y);
```

$$g := [\ (x,y) \ -> \ x^2 + y^2 , \ (x,y) \ -> \ x^2 - y^2 \ ]$$

Here is a test of this mapping:

```
>g(1,2);
```

$$[\ 5, \ -3 \ ]$$

Not suprisingly, `g` is itself an array and not a list:

```
>type(g,array);
```

$$true$$

The distinction between a Maple mapping and a Maple expression is essentially the same as the distinction between a mathematical function or mapping and its value at a point. This same distinction will be important in Section 3.1.

Piecewise-defined functions

Piecewise-defined functions are set up using the function `piecewise()`. To introduce `piecewise()`, we will use it to represent the same function that we used above to introduce selection statements; that is

$$g(x) = \begin{cases} x^2 & -1 \le x \le 0 \\ 2x & 0 < x \le 1/2 \\ (x-3/2)^2 & 1/2 < x \le 3/2 \end{cases}$$

and the corresponding Maple command is the following:

```
> g:=x->piecewise(x<-1,'undefined',x<=0,x^2,x<=1/2,2*x,

     x<=3/2,(x-3/2)^2);
  g := x -> piecewise(x < -1, undefined,
                2
       x <= 0, x , x <= 1/2,
                          2
       2 x, x <= 3/2, (x - 3/2) )
```

There are several things to notice here. First, g is defined as an arrow function. This is not required but is necessary if you wish to use the piecewise-defined function for specific arguments. For instance, we may now compute:

```
> g(1/4);
```
$$1/2$$

```
> g(-2);
```
$$\text{undefined}$$

```
> g(x);
```

```
PIECEWISE(
                                    2
     [undefined, x < -1], [x , x <= 0], [2 x, x <= 1/2],
                 2
     [(x - 3/2) , x <= 3/2])
```

Note that PIECEWISE is capitalized in the last case; we will discuss the reason for this below. Note also that the conditions are in lists.

The second point is to understand the structure of the definition itself. It is essentially what is called in other programming languages a "case" statement. It is read from left to right until a Boolean evaluates to true, at that point the expression following the Boolean is evaluated. If no Boolean evaluates to true, Maple assumes a default value of zero. As our first evaluation in g, we chose to use a string. The subsequent evaluations are the function values and, yes, we did slightly change the definition of the original function at the right-hand end to enable us to demonstrate the default case:

```
> g(2);
```
$$0$$

You can use more complicated expressions in the Boolean parts of the piecewise() statement. To show what can be done, here is an arrow function that we will use to define a piecewise function:

```
> fn:=x->x^2-3/2*abs(x)+1/2;
                          2
             fn := x -> x  - 3/2 abs(x) + 1/2
```

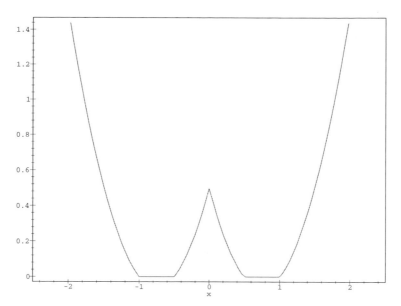

Figure 2.2: A plot of the piecewise-defined function r().

Here is the piecewise() function:

```
> r:=x->piecewise(abs(x)<=2 and fn(x)>=0,fn(x),
    fn(x)<0,0,`undefined`);
  r := x -> piecewise(

    abs(x) <= 2 and 0 <= fn(x), fn(x),
          fn(x) < 0, 0, undefined)
```

This example shows that the Booleans appearing in the definition of a piece-wise() function may contain absolute values and polynomial inequalities. To plot this function you can do the following (see Figure 2.2):

```
> plot(r,-2.5..2.5,axes=boxed);
```

Maple offers excellent support for piecewise() functions. In addition to being plotable, these functions can be combined algebraically, differentiated, integrated, and simplified. They can contain parameters and other complicated expressions. These are highly useful capabilities. You may find it instructive to apply some of these operations to the function r() defined above and to other fuctions of your own making.

Above, we encountered the capitalized form PIECEWISE(). This is actually the "applied" form of piecewise() and the unapply() function can be used to obtain the arrow form we have been working with above. For an example, we will use Maple's spline() function, which produces piecewise polynomial interpolants to data:

```
> readlib(spline):
```

```
> s:=spline([0,1,2],[1,0,1],x,linear);
```

$$s := \text{PIECEWISE}([1 - x, x < 1],$$
$$[x - 1, \text{otherwise}])$$

It is not possible to evaluate the spline in this form, so we unapply() as follows:

```
> ss:=unapply(s,x);
```

$$ss := x \rightarrow \text{piecewise}(x < 1,$$
$$1 - x, x - 1)$$

which allows computations such as

```
> ss(.25);
```

$$.75$$

The applied form may be more convenient in some situations, for example, when simplifying. There are two convert() functions that are useful with piecewise-defined functions. They are convert(,piecewise), used for converting various standard step functions and convert(,pwlist), that converts to a list.

2.7 Reference section

The tables that follow organize the functions and other material covered in this chapter by category. The arguments for these functions can be obtained from Maple's online help system by typing ?, followed by the name of the function, followed by *return* or *enter*.

FUNCTIONS FOR NUMERICAL WORK

abs	Absolute value function
ceil	Smallest integer not less than argument
denom	Denominator of expression
evalf	Floating-point evaluator
floor	Greatest integer not exceeding argument
frac	Fractional part of argument
max	Maximum of arguments
min	Minimum of arguments
mod	Evaluate relative to a modulus
modp	Function form of mod
mods	Symmetric form of modp
numer	Numerator of expression
round	Round to nearest integer
signum	Signum function
sqrt	Square root function
surd	Real roots function
trunc	Remove fractional part of argument

FUNCTIONS FOR COMPLEX NUMBERS

abs	Modulus of complex number
conjugate	Conjugate complex number
convert(,polar)	Convert to polar form
cvalc	Evaluate in complex field: real coefficients
evalf	Floating-point evaluation
Im	Imaginary part function
Re	Real part function

ELEMENTARY FUNCTIONS

{arc}sin{h}	{inverse} sine {hyberbolic}
{arc}cos{h}	{inverse} cosine {hyberbolic}
{arc}tan{h}	{inverse} tangent{hyberbolic}
{arc}csc{h}	{inverse} cosecant {hyberbolic}
{arc}sec{h}	{inverse} secant {hyberbolic}
{arc}cot{h}	{inverse} cotangent {hyberbolic}
arctan(,)	Produces an angle in $(-\pi, \pi]$
exp	Exponential function
ln, log	Natural logarithm function

`log10`	Base 10 logarithm function
`log[b]`	Base b logarithm function

TYPES MENTIONED IN THE TEXT

`constant, even, float, fraction, integer,`
`negative, negint, nonnegint, nonposint,`
`odd, posint, positive`

FACTORIALS AND RELATIVES

`!`	Factorial function
`binomial`	Binomial coefficients.
`convert( , factorial)`	GAMMAs → binomials
`convert( , GAMMA)`	binomials → GAMMAs
`GAMMA`	Gamma function

SIMPLIFICATION AND MANIPULATION FUNCTIONS

`coeff`	Pick off a coefficient in an expression; `collect()` first
`collect`	Collect terms in an expression
`combine`	Combine terms of a specified type in an expression
`convert( , parfrac, )`	Convert to partial fractions
`expand`	Expand an expression
`factor`	Factor an expression
`Factor`	Inert `factor()`
`normal`	Express as a ratio of polynomials
`simplify`	General simplifier
`coeffs`	Produce expression sequence of coefficients
`lcoeff`	Pick out leading coefficient in an expression
`radsimp`	Simplify the radicals in an expression
`tcoeff`	Pick out trailing coefficient in an expression

CONVERTING EXPRESSIONS

`convert( ,exp)`	Trigonometric terms → exponentials
`convert( ,expln)`	Terms → exponentials and logarithmics.
`convert( ,factorial)`	GAMMAs → binomials
`convert( ,GAMMA)`	binomials → GAMMAs
`convert( ,ln)`	Inverse trigonometrics → logarithmics
`convert( ,parfrac, )`	Rational function → partial fractions
`convert( ,radical)`	RootOfs → Radicals
`convert( ,RootOf)`	Radicals → RootOfs

```
convert( ,tan)          Trigonometrics → tangents (of half-angles usually)
convert( ,trig)         Exponentials → trigonometrics and hyperbolics
```

DEFINING FUNCTIONS: ARROWS, PIECEWISE, AND UNAPPLY

```
(x,y)->expr(p,q,x,y)
unapply                 Make function from an expression.
piecewise               Make a piecewise-defined mathematical function.
```

EQUATIONS AND INEQUALITIES

```
allvalues               Compute a RootOf expression; use fsolve() if
                          necessary.
assign                  Assigns the names to equations produced by
                          solve()
fsolve                  Numerical root finder
RootOf                  Placeholder for roots of an equation
solve                   Solves equation(s) or inequality
```

SUMMATION AND PRODUCTS

```
eulermac                Euler–MacLaurin summation primitive
product                 Form product of terms
Product                 Inert form of product()
sum                     Form sum of terms
Sum                     Inert form of sum()
```

EXERCISES

1. Simplify

$$\ln(\cos(y)\sin(x) - \cos(x)\sin(y)) - \ln(\cos(x)\cos(y) - \sin(x)\sin(y))$$

2. Express

$$\frac{x + 5\sqrt{x} + 6}{\sqrt{x} + 3}$$

as the sum of an integer and a radical.

3. Show that

$$\frac{\cos^2(x+y) - \cos^2(x-y)}{\cos^2(x+y) + \cos^2(x-y)} = -2\frac{\cos(x)\cos(y)\sin(x)\sin(y)}{\cos^2(x)\cos^2(y) + \sin^2(x)\sin^2(y)}$$

4. Transform $\tan(\pi/4 + x/2)$ to a form involving the full angle x (rather than $x/2$). Use a method different from that used in the text. (Hint: `simplify()` and `combine()` may be useful.)

5. The x derivative of

$$e := \frac{\sqrt{2}}{4} \arcsin\left(\frac{3\sin^2(x) - 1}{\sin^2(x) + 1}\right)$$

is $-1/(1 + \sin^2(x))$. Using simplification commands, get as close to this result as you can. (Use `diff(e,x)` to obtain the derivative.)

6. **(a)** Find the partial fraction expansion of

$$\frac{x^2 + 2x - 1}{2x^3 + 3x^2 - 2x}$$

   (b) Find the partial fraction expansion of $f(x) = 1/(4 + x^4)^2$. Can you simplify the result back to the given form of f?

7. Solve the equation $2x^3 - x + 7 = 0$ and find the sum and product of the resulting roots. Compare your answers with the appropriate coefficients of the equation.

8. Find all the roots in $[-5, 5]$ of the equation $x = \tan(x)$ correct to twenty significant figures.

9. Use Maple to solve for (x, y)

$$x + ay = 2 \qquad ax + y = 1$$

   When do the equations have exactly one solution?

10. **(a)** Make an expression sequence containing the first 100 digits of π.

   (b) Make a list of length 10 whose mth entry ($m = 1, 2, \ldots, 10$) is the number of times $m - 1$ occurs in this expression sequence. (Hint: there is a `convert()` that may be useful.)

11. Given a function $f(x)$ for $x \in [0, 10]$, obtain the `piecewise()` representation of the function

$$g(x) = f(i), \quad i \le x < i + 1, \ i = 0, \ldots, 9.$$

   Plot f and g on the same graph for $f(x) = x\sin(x/2)$.

12. Write an arrow function that can determine whether or not a given set contains the symbol V.

13. Verify the identities

$$\sum_{j=0}^{n} \binom{n}{j}^2 = \binom{2n}{n} \qquad \text{and} \qquad \sum_{j=0}^{n} \binom{a+j}{j} = \binom{a+n+1}{n}.$$

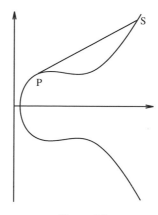

Figure 2.3

14. Make an arrow function and plot for

$$f(x) = \begin{cases} 1 & 2j < x \le 2j+1 \\ 0 & 2j-1 < x \le 2j \end{cases} \quad j = \cdots -2, -1, 0, 1, \ldots$$

Use only functions mentioned in this chapter and do not use any conditionals (if, etc.).

15. A vector field with Cartesian components $v_x(x, y, z)$ etc., can always be represented using spherical components $v_r(r, \theta, \phi)$ etc., as follows:

$$v_r = v_x \sin(\theta) \cos(\phi) + v_y \sin(\theta) \sin(\phi) + v_z \cos(\theta)$$
$$v_\theta = v_x \cos(\theta) \cos(\phi) + v_y \cos(\theta) \sin(\phi) + v_z \sin(\theta)$$
$$v_\phi = -v_x \sin(\phi) + v_y \cos(\phi)$$

Solve this system to obtain the Cartesian components in terms of the spherical components. The final result should closely resemble the formulas above.

16. Elliptic Curves of Genus One: Given a point $P = (p_x, p_y)$ on the curve $y^2 = x^3 - 2$ with $p_y \ne 0$, its tangent line intersects the curve at a second point $S = (s_x, s_y)$, as shown in Figure 2.3.

(a) Use Maple to explicitly compute the coordinates $s_x = s_x(p_x, p_y)$ and $s_y = s_y(p_x, p_y)$ in terms of the coordinates of the points P. Observe that if P has rational coordinates, so does S.

(b) Beginning with $P = (3, 5)$, compute the point $Q = (x, y)$ given by the above formula, and repeat the process beginning with Q to construct a third rational point R. Verify that these points lie on the curve $y^2 = x^3 - 2$.

17. Elliptic Curves of Genus One: Given two points $P = (p_x, p_y)$ and $Q = (q_x, q_y)$ on the curve $y^2 = x^3 - 2$ (with $p_y \ne -q_y$), the secant line through these points

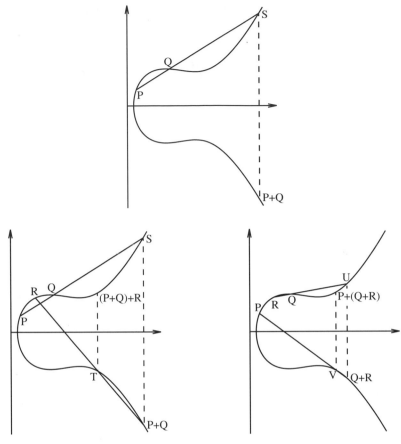

Figure 2.4

will intersect the curve at a third point $S = (s_x, s_y)$, as shown in Figure 2.4. Use Maple to explicitly construct the coordinates $s_x = s_x(p_x, q_x, p_y, q_y)$ and $s_y = s_y(p_x, q_x, p_y, q_y)$ as (arrow) functions of the coordinates of the points P and Q.

3 Calculus and differential equations

This chapter builds on the work of Chapter 2 and moves into differential and integral calculus and ordinary differential equations. It covers the important topics of differentiation, integration, and series. There is also a section on vector calculus covering divergence, gradient, and curl and the associated scalar and vector potentials. This section is followed by a section on differential equations and a section on transforms and solving finite-difference or recurrence equations. Finally, Maple's special functions are listed in a section of their own.

3.1 Limits and continuity

This section covers Maple's facilities for computing limits and testing the continuity of mathematical functions. The subsections are

- Using `limit()`
- Multidimensional Limits
- Testing Continuity

Using `limit()`

Computing limits is straightforward with Maple. The basic command is `limit()`. To illustrate the use of `limit()` we will evaluate

```
>limit((x^2+x)^(1/2)-(x^2+1)^(1/2),x=infinity);
```

$$1/2$$

Note that the second argument is written as an equation.

Maple can handle limits containing integrals:

```
>limit(int(sin(sin(t)),t=0..x)/x^2,x=0);
```

$$1/2$$

You can specify limits taken from the left and right by another option to `limit()`. For example:

```
>limit(abs(x)/x,x=0);
```

```
undefined
```

```
>limit(abs(x)/x,x=0,left);
```

$$-1$$

```
>limit(abs(x)/x,x=0,right);
```

$$1$$

When you use `x=±infinity` as the second argument, it is understood as a right/left limit. It is possible to override this by specifying `real` as the third argument to `limit()`, which is a synonym for bidirectional, or specifying `complex`, which denotes omnidirectional in the complex plane. For finite points, `real` is the default value.

Sometimes, `limit()` returns a range as in the next example:

```
>limit(sin(1/x),x=0);
```

```
-1 .. 1
```

No limit was found in this case (there isn't one), but the range gives bounds for the function values in some interval around the argument point 0.

Limits that Maple cannot find are returned unevaluated:

```
>limit(ln(sin(1/x)),x=0);
```

```
limit   ln(sin(1/x))
x -> 0
```

Here is a much harder limit than the previous ones:

$$\lim_{x \to 0} \frac{\sin(\tan x) - \tan(\sin x)}{\arcsin(\arctan x) - \arctan(\arcsin x)}$$

For Maple, this limit is a matter of just a few seconds work:

```
> limit((sin(tan(x))-tan(sin(x)))/(arcsin(arctan(x)) -
> arctan(arcsin(x))),x=0);
```

$$1$$

The assume() function can also be useful for computing limits. Here is a simple example:

```
>limit(exp(a*x),x=infinity);
```

```
limit              exp(a x)
x -> infinity
```

This limit is returned unevaluated because the result depends on the sign of a. Now we will tell Maple to assume that a is negative and recompute the limit:

```
>assume(a<0);
```

```
>limit(exp(a*x),x=infinity);
```

$$0$$

Multidimensional limits

The limit() function is also used for computing multidimensional limits. The main change is that the second argument becomes a set of equations defining the point. A simple example would be

```
>limit(a*x*y-b/(x*y),{x=1,y=1});
```

$$a - b$$

Unfortunately, because a multidimensional limit must be independent of the manner of approach to the point of interest, there will be many times when limit() will be unable to find a result. It will return unevaluated in such cases. For example, the value of the next limit is 2 but `limit()` returns unevaluated:

```
>limit(sin(x+y)/(sin(x)*sin(y)),{x=Pi/4,y=Pi/4});
```

$$\text{limit}\left(\frac{\sin(x + y)}{\sin(x)\ \sin(y)},\ \{x = 1/4\ Pi,\ y = 1/4\ Pi\}\right)$$

This does not mean that no limit exists, merely that `limit()` is unable to find one. If you are sure that a limit exists, you can usually compute it as an iterated limit. For example, the limit above can be computed as

```
>limit(limit(sin(x+y))/(((sin(x)*sin(y)),
                    x=Pi/4),y=Pi/4);
```

$$2$$

`limit()` can sometimes establish that a multidimensional limit does not exist. For instance, the well-known form

$$\lim_{x,y \to 0} \frac{x^2(1 + x) - y^2(1 - y)}{x^2 + y^2}$$

does not exist as a multidimensional limit as `limit()` discovers:

```
>e:=(x^2*(1+x)-y^2*(1-y))/(x^2+y^2);
```

$$e := \frac{x^2\ (1 + x) - y^2\ (1 - y)}{x^2 + y^2}$$

```
>limit(e,{x=0,y=0});
```

$$\text{undefined}$$

Testing continuity

Maple has a pair of `readlib()` defined functions called `iscont()` and `singular()` for checking the continuity of mathematical functions and finding their singularities. The `iscont()` function attempts to find whether a function in the form of an algebraic expression is continuous in a given interval (which may be of infinite extent). The interval you specify is assumed to be open, although there is an option to make it closed as in the following example:

```
>readlib(iscont):readlib(singular):
>iscont(tan(x),x=0..Pi/2);
```

$$true$$

```
>iscont(tan(x),x=0..Pi/2,closed);
```

$$false$$

Note also the following:

```
>iscont(exp(-1/(x^2)),x=-1..1);
```

$$false$$

The singularity at $x = 0$ is removable, but `iscont()` still regards the function as discontinuous. The `singular()` function is used similarly to find the points where functions are undefined or unbounded, but where no range can be specified. For the previous example `singular()` gives

```
>singular(exp(-1/(x^2)));
```

$$\{x = 0\}$$

If a function contains several variables, an option to `singular()` is used to define the argument for testing.

3.2 Differentiation

Maple has not just one but two differentiation functions called `diff()` and `D()`. These reflect the two principal ways in which a mathematical function can be given in Maple. The first is the one we use most often to demonstrate various commands;

you simply write a Maple assignment with a "formula" appearing on the right-hand side. The second way to define a mathematical function is to use an arrow function. When you are dealing with differentiation, it is necessary to make the distinction between formulas and arrow functions.

The Maple function `diff()` is used for differentiating formulas. The `diff()` function returns another formula representing the derivative of the input formula. The using `diff()` subsection gives examples of this and illustrates the capabilities of `diff()`.

The second differentiation function `D()` is analogous to the mathematical differentiation operator of the same name. This is the differentiation operator for mappings, and, as with the mapping itself, it does not depend on the particular name(s) of the independent variable(s). It is no surprise then that the `D()` operator produces another mapping from its input mapping. The `D()` function is also used to represent quantities such as $f'(0)$. Expressions like this are used to specify initial conditions for differential equations, among other things. The `diff()` function cannot be used to represent these quantities.

The `diff()` and `D()` functions are not unrelated. For example, sometimes `diff()` will return a result involving `D()`, whereas `D()` might call on the same differentiation rules as `diff()` in specific cases. There are several illustrations of these links in this section.

The topics in this section are

- Using `diff()`
- The `D` Operator
- Defining Derivatives at Points
- Implicit and Total Differentiation

Using `diff()`

The `diff()` function is very simple to use. Its first argument is always the function to be differentiated. This argument must be an expression that is of a type called algebraic. The remaining arguments specify the variable(s) to be used. The `diff()` function performs partial differentiation, so there may be any number of these differentiation variables. Here is a function of two variables:

```
>u:=x*tan(x*y);
```

$$u := x \tan(x\,y)$$

and here is how to use `diff()` to calculate some of its derivatives:

>`diff(u,x);`

$$\tan(x\ y)\ +\ x\ (1\ +\ \tan(x\ y)\ ^2)\ y$$

>`diff(u,y);`

$$x\ ^2\ (1\ +\ \tan(x\ y)\ ^2)$$

>`diff(u,x,y);`

$$2\ (1\ +\ \tan(x\ y)\ ^2)\ x\ +\ 2\ x\ ^2\ \tan(x\ y)\ (1\ +\ \tan(x\ y)\ ^2)\ y$$

A convenient way to express a higher derivative uses Maple's $ notation. The $ notation produces expression sequences somewhat like `seq()` does, but it is more concise. The following example uses $ to produce a third derivative with respect to y:

>`diff(x^2*y^3,y$3);`

$$6\ x\ ^2$$

Here, `y$3` represents the expression sequence `y,y,y`. (See `?$` for more information on the use of this notation.)

The `diff()` function can also be used to differentiate arrow functions provided they are evaluated (in the mathematical sense). Here is an illustration:

>`diff((x->x^2)(y),y);`

$$2\ y$$

The presence of the variable y in the first argument effectively turns the mapping into a formula. Observe also that the result is not a mapping but a formula. You could turn the formula into a mapping with `unapply()` as we will see below.

There is an inert version of `diff()` called `Diff()`. It acts as a place holder for the derivative expressed in its arguments that does not undergo derivative evaluation. The `Diff()` function's arguments are similar to those of `diff()`.

The D operator

The most basic use for `D()` is differentiating mappings. Here is an example that defines a mapping $f : \mathbf{R}^2 \to \mathbf{R}$, corresponding to the expression used above with `diff()`, then computes some partial derivatives:

```
>f:=(x,y)->x*tan(x*y);
```

$$f \; := \; (x,y) \; \to \; x \; \tan(x \; y)$$

```
>D[1](f);
```

$$(x,y) \; \to \; \tan(x \; y) \; + \; x \; (1 \; + \; \tan(x \; y)^2) \; y$$

```
>D[1,2](f);
```

$$(x,y) \; \to \; 2 \; (1 \; + \; \tan(x \; y)^2) \; x \; + \; 2 \; x^2 \; \tan(x \; y)$$
$$(1 \; + \; \tan(x \; y)^2) \; y$$

The results of the differentiations are also mappings. Observe the syntax for `D()`. The argument is the mapping to be differentiated. A list of differentiation variables comes before the argument. In this list, the number j refers to the jth variable in the list of arguments of the arrow function. The `$` operator can be used within this list to specify higher derivatives in the same way as for `diff()`.

D() can be applied to compositions of mappings. As an illustrative example, suppose you wanted to compute

$$\frac{d}{dt} \sin(x(t)), \quad x(t) = t^2$$

without directly substituting and differentiating. We will set up the composition and then use `D()` for the differentiation. Here are the steps, where the @ symbol stands for composition:

```
>f:=x->sin(x);
```

$$f \; := \; \sin$$

```
>x:=t->t^2;
```

$$x \; := \; t \; \to \; t^2$$

```
>D(f@x);
```

$$\cos@x \; (t \; \to \; 2 \; t)$$

This product of mappings is the correct result, although not in a particularly readable form. The mapping becomes more readable when it is applied: The result is

```
>"(t);
```

$$2 \cos(t^2) \ t$$

Now we will do the same calculation using `diff()`. Incidentally, note that in this example, `diff()` produces a result involving `D()`:

```
>f:='f':x:='x':
>q:=diff(f(x(t)),t);
```

$$q := \left[\frac{d}{dt} \ x(t)\right] \ D(f)(x(t))$$

This result implies that `f` must be defined as a mapping while `x(t)` must be defined as a formula. Now we will calculate the derivative:

```
>x(t):=t^2;
```

$$x(t) := t^2$$

This is an unusual assignment and is one we have not met before. It does not define a Maple function that squares its argument. For now, it is enough to think of `x(t)` as a name. An explanation of the assignment will be provided in Section 11.3. Continuing with the example:

```
>f:=x->sin(x);
```

$$f := \sin$$

```
>q;
```

$$2 \ t \ \cos(t^2)$$

As usual, `diff()` produces a formula, not a mapping.

`D()` always assumes that `D[1,2]=D[2,1]` as this shows (`g` is any name):

```
>D[1,2](g)-D[2,1](g);
```

$$0$$

The mathematical analog of this is certainly true if both sides are continuous functions but may be false otherwise. In the usual examples where it fails to be true, the discontinuity occurs at a single point. A classic case is the function

$$f(x, y) = \begin{cases} \frac{xy(x^2-y^2)}{x^2+y^2} & x^2 + y^2 \neq 0, \\ 0 & x^2 + y^2 = 0. \end{cases}$$

Away from the origin, the partial derivatives of this function can be computed by the usual algebraic rules and are equal. At the origin, the algebraic rules do not apply and the derivatives must be computed from first principles. However, `diff()` performs only the algebraic calculation.

You might find it interesting to check (using `diff()` or `D()` and `limit()`) that

$$\frac{\partial^2 f}{\partial x \partial y}(0, 0) \neq \frac{\partial^2 f}{\partial y \partial x}(0, 0).$$

Maple's assumption of equal partials is wrong for this function. Be alert to this situation!

Defining derivatives at points

In some instances, you may need to work with the values of derivatives defined at points. A simple example of this occurs in specifying the initial conditions for differential equations. For instance, you might want to prescribe $y'(0) = y_0$. This is one of the things the `D()` operator is designed to do. Another application occurs in writing the Taylor expansion of a general function, where the derivatives need to be evaluated at the center of the expansion. By way of illustration, here is a way to represent the third derivative of an unknown function g at a point x:

```
> (D@@3)(g)(x);
```

$$(3)$$
$$D \quad (g)(x)$$

The `D()` operator is composed with itself three times and all the parentheses are significant. The repeated composition operator `@@` is used to create multiple compositions.

Implicit and total differentiation

Implicit and total differentiation can be done with `diff()`. For example, the following shows a method for implicit differentiation:

```
>diff(x^2*y(x)+y(x)^2*x,x);
```

```
             2 [  d      ]              [  d      ]        2
2 x y(x)  + x  [---- y(x)] + 2 y(x) x [---- y(x)] + y(x)
               [ dx      ]              [ dx      ]
```

To find the derivative, assuming that the implicit derivative is zero, you can do the following:

```
>solve(",diff(y(x),x));
```

$$- \frac{2 x y(x) + y(x)^2}{x^2 + 2 x y(x)}$$

Total derivatives can be found in a similar way. Here is an example:

```
>diff(sin(x(t)*y(t)),t);
```

```
               [[  d      ]             [  d      ]]
cos(x(t) y(t)) [[---- x(t)] y(t) + x(t) [---- y(t)]]
               [[ dt      ]             [ dt      ]]
```

A similar approach works for more independent variables and higher-order derivatives.

3.3 Integration

Integration is more straightforward than differentiation because there is only one Maple function involved, but, as we will see, it is less foolproof. This section covers both definite and indefinite integration. In addition, it briefly mentions how to use numerical integration for checking definite integrals. Chapter 5 contains a more thorough account of numerical integration. The topics in this section are

- Indefinite and Definite Integration
- Numerical Integration
- Multiple Integrals
- Infinite Ranges
- Errant Integrals

Indefinite and definite integration

The basic integration command is `int()` and it is used this way:

```
>int(sin(ln(x)),x);
```

$$1/2 \; x \; (sin(ln(x)) - cos(ln(x)))$$

The second argument is the integration variable. To check:

```
>diff(",x);
```

```
1/2 sin(ln(x)) - 1/2 cos(ln(x))
                  [ cos(ln(x))    sin(ln(x))   ]
        + 1/2 x [ ---------  +  ----------   ]
                  [      x              x        ]
```

```
>simplify(");
```

$$sin(ln(x))$$

In this case, it was easy to simplify the derivative into the desired form. Sometimes you have to experiment with different simplification commands to get what you want.

To compute a definite integral, you include a range expression with the integration variable:

```
>int(sqrt(1-x^2),x=0..1);
```

$$1/4 \; Pi$$

Definite integrals take more work to check. The obvious way is to compute the indefinite integral and substitute the limits:

```
>int(sqrt(1-x^2),x);
```

$$1/2 \; x \; (1 - x^2)^{1/2} + 1/2 \; arcsin(x)$$

```
>subs(x=1,")-subs(x=0,");
```

$$1/2 \; arcsin(1) - 1/2 \; arcsin(0)$$

```
>simplify(");
```

$$1/4 \; Pi$$

Unfortunately, this only works when Maple has an explicit primitive, which is not always the case. For example:

```
>int(x*ln(sin(x)),x=0..Pi);
```

$$- 1/2 \; Pi^2 \; ln(2)$$

but the indefinite integral is returned unevaluated:

```
>int(x*ln(sin(x)),x);
```

$$\int x \; ln(sin(x)) \; dx$$

which means that Maple can do nothing more with it in the present form.

Numerical integration

Numerical integration is discussed in detail in Section 5.3. Here, we will briefly introduce this subject as a means of checking analytical results.

Numerical integration uses an inert integration function analogous to the inert differentiation function. The following example illustrates a syntax for numerical integration by checking the earlier definite integral:

```
>evalf(Int(x*ln(sin(x)),x=0..Pi));
```

$$-3.420544232$$

`Int()` is the inert integration function and is used as an argument to `evalf()`. The exact result for the integral, from above, is

```
>evalf(-Pi^2*ln(2)/2);
```

$$-3.420544233$$

The slight discrepancy is due to roundoff. It is important to use the inert function `Int()`. If you use `int()` instead, you may end up with the result of `evalf()`

applied to the result of the definite integral; no check will have been done, as the following shows:

```
>evalf(int(x*ln(sin(x)),x=0..Pi));
```

$$-3.420544233$$

This result agrees with the analytical result, not the numerical result. This distinction is moot for an unevaluated integral, which will be automatically treated as a numerical calculation by `evalf()`.

Multiple integrals

You can nest calls to `int()` to evaluate multiple integrals, although usually it is easier to evaluate the integrals separately. The next statement nests `int()` to compute the volume of the tetrahedron bounded by the coordinate planes and the plane $x/a + y/b + z/c = 1$:

```
>int(int(int(1,z=0..c*(1-x/a-y/b)),
    y=0..b*(1-x/a)),x=0..a);
```

$$1/6 \; c \; a \; b$$

Maple does not add constants of integration, so for indefinite integrals you should add constants into nested evaluations.

Infinite ranges

You can use the constant `infinity` in the range of integrals, as the following shows:

```
>int(exp(-x),x=0..infinity);
```

$$1$$

Doubly infinite integrals follow a similar pattern; for example, here is a Fourier transform:

```
>int(exp(-x^2)*exp(-I*w*x),x=-infinity..infinity);
```

$$Pi^{1/2} \quad exp(-1/4 \; w^2)$$

Divergent integrals can return `infinity` also:

```
>int(-x^2,x=0..infinity);
```

$$- \; infinity$$

Errant integrals

Integration does not always go as smoothly as the earlier examples suggest. One such situation arises when a positive integrand over a positive interval produces a negative result. We will illustrate this with a simple example. We will define an expression to be integrated and then find its indefinite integral:

```
>e:=sqrt(1+cos(2*x));
                                               1/2
                      e := (1 + cos(2 x))
>int(e,x);
                          1/2
                         2    sin(x)
```

There is a problem with this result, which becomes clear when we manipulate e:

```
>expand(1+cos(2*x));
                                    2
                             2 cos(x)
>sqrt(");
                     1/2          2 1/2
                    2      (cos(x) )
```

As you see, Maple has been cautious and retained the explicit square root because it does not know enough about $\cos(x)$ to make a choice of sign. It seems that int() is not so cautious; it has picked the positively signed root and then performed the integration with the result we see above. You may be thinking that this is a reasonable thing to do, but notice what happens if we now evaluate the integral using the above result over the interval $(\pi, 3\pi/2)$. The result is $-\sqrt{2}$, a negative result for a positive integrand! However, if we evaluate over $(0, \pi/2)$ we obtain the correct result. Although we have performed the above substitutions mentally, Maple does indeed give the same results:

```
>int(e,x=Pi..3*Pi/2);
                              1/2
                          - 2
>int(e,x=0..Pi/2);

                           1/2
                          2
```

This example shows that the correct choice of branch depends on the interval of integration. The rational way to handle this situation is to `assume()` the integration variable into the given interval so that Maple can make the necessary choices. However, that does not work at present. You should be aware that the type of behavior illustrated above is becoming rare in symbolic mathematics programs (although they all exhibit it to some extent). Eventually it should disappear altogether, but we are some way from that today. In the meantime, be on the lookout for weird results and be prepared for some independent checking of integrals.

3.4 Working with series

Maple has a general series command that produces whatever series expansion is considered appropriate for a function. Maple will produce Taylor expansions as well as inverse and fractional power expansions. In addition, series can be inverted.

In this section we discuss

- Series Expansions
- Unevaluated Integrals
- Multidimensional Expansions
- Laurent-Type Expansions
- Fractional Power Expansions
- Other Expansions
- Inverting Expansions

Series expansions

Maple has a command for producing Taylor and related expansions. Here is a basic example:

```
>series(arctan(x),x=0,10);
```

$$x - 1/3\ x^3 + 1/5\ x^5 - 1/7\ x^7 + 1/9\ x^9 + O(x^{10})$$

The first argument is the function you want to expand. The second is the expansion point. If this point is 0, as it is here, it is sufficient to merely write the name of the expansion variable. The third argument is the order of accuracy, the final term in the output, which is optional. The default value is set by a global variable called `Order`, just as `Digits` is a global variable for `evalf()`. `Order` is initially set to 6.

In the next illustration, `Order` is reset to 4 and a general Taylor expansion is displayed:

```
>Order:=4;
                    Order := 4
```

```
>series(u(x),x);
                                    (2)        2
        u(0) + D(u)(0) x + 1/2 D    (u)(0) x

                  (3)        3        4
        + 1/6 D    (u)(0) x   + O(x )
```

This is an example of the use of `D()` to represent pointwise values of derivatives.

The expressions produced by `series()` are a surface type called series. There is also a nested type called taylor (not all of Maple's `series()`, are Taylor series, as we will see below). The surface type is found using `whattype()`:

```
>whattype(");
                       series
```

The nested taylor type has to be checked explicitly:

```
>type("",taylor);
                        true
```

How do you get a Taylor expansion for $u(x + h)$ about the point x? Here is the quickest way; note how x becomes the expansion point with this use of the second argument:

```
>series(u(x+h),h=0);
                                    (2)        2
        u(x) + D(u)(x) h + 1/2 D    (u)(x) h

                  (3)        3        4
        + 1/6 D    (u)(x) h   + O(h )
```

You should be aware of some unexpected features of series types. First, you cannot add series types together and have the terms combined. For example, look at the following:

```
>series(exp(x),x)+series(exp(-x),x);
```

$$(1 + x + 1/2\ x^2 + 1/6\ x^3 + O(x^4))$$

$$+ (1 - x + 1/2\ x^2 - 1/6\ x^3 + O(x^4))$$

The most obvious things, such as using simplification commands, will have no effect on this expression and will not cancel the positive and negative terms.

There are several ways around this difficulty. The most general way is to use a `convert()` from series to polynom. The disadvantage is that you lose the order terms. Here is the calculation for the example given above:

```
>u:=series(exp(x),x);
```

$$u := 1 + x + 1/2\ x^2 + 1/6\ x^3 + O(x^4)$$

```
>v:=series(exp(-x),x);
```

$$v := 1 - x + 1/2\ x^2 - 1/6\ x^3 + O(x^4)$$

```
>convert(u,polynom)+convert(v,polynom);
```

$$2 + x^2$$

An alternative is to let `series()` do the work:

```
>series(u+v,x);
```

$$2 + x^2 + O(x^4)$$

Sometimes it is possible to put all the terms you want to expand in the argument to `series()`. In that case, you preserve an accurate order term. To illustrate this approach, the next example shows that the difference quotient in the `series()`

argument below is a second-order-accurate finite-difference approximation in h:

```
>series((u(x+h)-2*u(x)+u(x-h))/h^2,h=0);
```

$$D^{(2)}(u)(x) + 1/12\ D^{(4)}(u)(x)\ h^2 + O(h^4)$$

As mentioned above, there is an assignable Maple variable called `Order` (default value 6) that controls the maximum number of terms returned by `series()`. `Order` can be assigned or included as a third argument to `series()` as in the examples that follow. These examples show that `series()` can produce different order terms depending what has gone on before:

```
>series(sin(x),x=0,4);
```

$$x - 1/6\ x^3 + O(x^4)$$

```
>series(sin(x),x=0,6);
```

$$x - 1/6\ x^3 + 1/120\ x^5 + O(x^6)$$

```
>series(sin(x),x=0,4);
```

$$x - 1/6\ x^3 + O(x^5)$$

The first and third results are both correct mathematically. The discrepancy comes from the fact that `series()` is one of a number of functions that "remember" their previous results. Here, the third result has been computed from the remembered second result. To confirm this, perform the following calculation:

```
>readlib(forget):
>forget(series);
>series(sin(x),x=0,4);
```

$$x - 1/6\ x^3 + O(x^4)$$

Remembering and forgetting results is discussed in more detail in Section 11.3.

An inconvenience of series types is that `subs()` cannot be used with them. An example is given below. As before, the simplest solution is to `convert()` to a polynom type; then `subs()` will work as usual. Additionally, if for some reason you wish to keep an order term, you can convert to $+$ and then make the substitution.

Here is an example:

```
>s:=series(sin(x),x=0);
```

$$s := x - 1/6\ x^3 + 1/120\ x^5 + O(x^6)$$

```
>subs(x=1,s);
Error, invalid substitution in series
```

```
>convert(s,'+');
```

$$x - 1/6\ x^3 + 1/120\ x^5 + O(x^6)$$

```
>subs(x=1,");
```

$$\frac{101}{120} + O(1)$$

You can add and perform other operations on series in a similar way.

You cannot easily apply convergence tests to Maple's series because a general formula for the coefficients is not provided.

Unevaluated integrals

You can apply `series()` to an integral that has been returned unevaluated. The integral appearing below is returned unevaluated, although this is not shown explicitly. The first few terms of the series around $x = 0$ are shown:

```
>Order:=8;
```

$$Order := 8$$

```
>series(Int(sin(x)/(x^2+1),x),x);
```

$$1/2\ x^2 - 7/24\ x^4 + \frac{47}{240}\ x^6 + O(x^8)$$

Multidimensional expansions

Maple has a `readlib()` defined function called `mtaylor()` for multidimensional Taylor polynomials. This function returns a polynomial type without an order term. Before using `mtaylor()`, you have to load it:

```
>readlib(mtaylor);
```

```
proc() ... end
```

Here is a simple example for `mtaylor()`:

```
>mtaylor(arcsin(x+y),[x,y],4);
```

$$x + y + 1/6\ x^3 + 1/2\ y\ x^2 + 1/2\ y^2\ x + 1/6\ y^3$$

You can check that this has type polynom; it is not a series type.

The first argument to `mtaylor()` is the function to be expanded. The second is a list of the expansion variables, and the optional third argument is one greater than the maximum degree in the expansion. There is an optional fourth argument that gives more control over the degrees of the variables.

Laurent type expansions

Sometimes `series()` will produce results containing inverse powers of the variable like the following:

```
>series(1/(z*(z^2+1)),z,6);
```

$$z^{-1} - z + z^3 - z^5 + O(z^7)$$

Maple assigns a type laurent to these and some other `series()`:

```
>type(",laurent);
```

$$true$$

It is important to realize that `series()` may not produce a desired Laurent expansion. For instance, the Laurent expansion of $1/z$ in $1 < |z - 1| < \infty$, is

$$\frac{1}{z} = \frac{1}{z-1} - \frac{1}{(z-1)^2} + \frac{1}{(z-1)^3} - \cdots$$

but `series()` gives:

```
>series(1/z,z=1);
```

$$1 - (z - 1) + (z - 1)^2 - (z - 1)^3 + O((z - 1)^4)$$

which is the Taylor expansion of the function. The result given is the Laurent expansion for the annulus $0 < |z - 1| < 1$.

Fractional power expansions

Maple can also produce expansions involving fractional powers of the variable. When this occurs, the type is no longer series, but merely $+$. This means that `subs()` will produce numerical results without further ado:

```
>series(sqrt(sin(x)),x);
```

$$x^{1/2} - 1/12\ x^{5/2} + O(x^{7/2})$$

```
>whattype(");
```

$$+$$

```
>subs(x=1,"");
```

$$\frac{11}{12} + O(1)$$

Other expansions

Maple has a command called `asympt()`, which automatically substitutes $1/x$ for x in a series. This is occasionally useful in cases where a direct use of `series()` fails:

```
>series(sin(1/z),z);
Error, (in series/trig) unable to compute series
>asympt(sin(1/z),z);
```

$$1/z - \frac{1}{6\ z^3} + O(\frac{1}{z^4})$$

Similar results are produced when the expansion point is given as `z=infinity`.

Inverting expansions

You can invert expansions using `series()` and `solve()`. As an illustration of this, suppose that you wanted to have a formula for the roots of (Kepler's equation) $x - 0.1 \sin(x) = y$. In this equation, y is a variable and there is a different solution for each y. How can you obtain a function of y whose value is the corresponding root x? The answer is to expand the left side of the equation as a series in x and then to use `solve()` to invert the expansion. Here are the steps:

```
>u:=series(x-(1/10)*sin(x),x);
```

$$u := 9/10 \ x + 1/60 \ x^3 - 1/1200 \ x^5 + O(x^6)$$

Now use `solve()` as follows:

```
>solve(u=y,x);
```

$$10/9 \ y - \frac{500}{19683} \ y^3 + \frac{47500}{14348907} \ y^5 + O(y^6)$$

This the expansion for y. It certainly appears that it should be convergent for some interval of y values. If you recompute the expansion with `Order` set to higher values, say 20 or more, you will get further evidence of this.

Before evaluating the series, convert it to a polynomial:

```
>v:=convert(",polynom);
```

$$v := 10/9 \ y - \frac{500}{19683} \ y^3 + \frac{47500}{14348907} \ y^5$$

Evaluating at $y = 0.5$, for example, gives

```
>subs(y=0.5,v);
```

$$.5524836752$$

To check this, you can use the numerical equation solver:

```
>fsolve(x-(1/10)*sin(x)-1/2,x);
```

$$.5524799869$$

The series approach has produced around five good digits. This is not at all bad for such a small number of terms. Inverting a series is one of the few ways to produce analytical expressions for the roots of general equations.

3.5 Vector calculus

This section covers div, grad, and curl and related operators of multivariable calculus. In Maple, these operators are part of the important package called `linalg[]`, which contains most of Maple's linear algebra and matrix facilities. The next chapter is devoted to the algebraic aspects of `linalg[]`. This section is restricted to discussing the calculus operators in `linalg[]`. In this section, we will make our first use of the evaluator `evalm()`. Remember that `evalm()` uses matrix algebra to evaluate expressions. The subsections here are

- Vector Algebra
- Vector Calculus

The illustrations in this section assume that the `linalg[]` package has been loaded by the command `with(linalg):`.

Vector algebra

This subsection covers the `linalg[]` functions for forming products of two- and three-dimensional vectors. These are dot and cross products, and the associated functions are `dotprod()` and `crossprod()`. There is also a related function (`angle()`) for computing the angle between two vectors. With complex data, `dotprod()` computes the Hermitian inner product in which $(u, v) \equiv \bar{u}^t v$, where the bar denotes complex conjugation. The `dotprod()` function can multiply any pair of compatible vectors, but `crossprod()` is limited to three-dimensional vectors.

To illustrate these functions, we will now check a well-known vector identity. Some obvious outputs are supressed to save space, and `alias()` is used to make the main statement easier to read:

```
> with(linalg):
Warning, new definition for norm
Warning, new definition for trace
Warning, new definition for transpose

> a:=vector([a1,a2,a3]): b:=vector([b1,b2,b3]):
  c:=vector([c1,c2,c3]):
```

(The function `vector()` is covered in Chapter 4.)

```
> alias(XX=crossprod): alias(DD=dotprod):
```

```
> XX(a,XX(b,c))-DD(a,c)*b+DD(a,b)*c;
```

```
[ a2 (b1 c2 - b2 c1) - a3 (b3 c1 - b1 c3),

      a3 (b2 c3 - b3 c2) - a1 (b1 c2 - b2 c1),

      a1 (b3 c1 - b1 c3) - a2 (b2 c3 - b3 c2) ]

       - (a1 c1 + a2 c2 + a3 c3) b

      + (a1 b1 + a2 b2 + a3 b3) c
```

This result must be simplified, but `simplify()` will not work yet. The expression must be evaluated using the matrix evaluator `evalm()`. This will insert the coordinates of b and c and arrange the result as a vector onto which we will map `simplify()`. The result is

```
>evalm("):
```

```
>map(simplify,");
```

$$[0, 0, 0]$$

The `evalm()` function merely expands the vector terms in its input and does not simplify the result. That is the reason for using `simplify()`.

Vector calculus

The functions in `linalg[]` for vector calculus are the first-order derivative operators `diverge()`, `grad()`, `jacobian()`, and `curl()` for the divergence, gradient, Jacobian (vector gradient), and curl. The second-order derivatives are `laplacian()` for the Laplacian of a scalar field and `hessian()` for the matrix of second partial derivatives of a scalar field. There are two further functions for computing scalar and vector potentials, when they exist, called `potential()` and `vecpotent()`.

Here are some applications of these functions:

```
>u:=C*sin(x)*sin(y);
```

$$u := C \sin(x) \sin(y)$$

```
>diverge(grad(u,[x,y]),[x,y]);
```

$$- 2 C \sin(x) \sin(y)$$

```
>laplacian(u,[x,y]);
```

$$- 2 C \sin(x) \sin(y)$$

The variables must be given in a list (or set) in the manner illustrated. They may not be omitted.

The following shows one way to compute the vector Laplacian:

```
>u:=vector([x^2+y^2,x^2-y^2,0]):
>vars:=[x,y,z]:
>grad(diverge(u,vars),vars)-curl(curl(u,vars),vars);
```

$$[2, -2, 0] - [-2, -2, 0]$$

```
>evalm(");
```

$$[4, 0, 0]$$

In Cartesian coordinates, there is an easier way:

```
>map(laplacian,u,vars);
```

$$[4, 0, 0]$$

but this approach is incorrect in other coordinate systems.

The Jacobian of u is computed as follows:

```
>jacobian(u,vars);
```

$$
\begin{bmatrix}
2\,x & 2\,y & 0 \\
2\,x & -\,2\,y & 0 \\
0 & 0 & 0
\end{bmatrix}
$$

and the Hessian is computed similarly.

To find whether or not a potential for a three-dimensional vector field exists, you can use `potential()`. For a demonstration, begin by computing a gradient field:

```
>v:=grad(x*sin(2*x*y),[x,y]);
```

$$v := [\sin(2\ x\ y) + 2\ x\ \cos(2\ x\ y)\ y,\ 2\ x^2\ \cos(2\ x\ y)]$$

The `potential()` function returns `true` or `false`, depending whether a scalar potential was found or not. If it returns `true`, the last argument to `potential()` will contain the scalar field. The third argument must evaluate to a name, and that is the reason for enclosing it in forward quotes:

```
>potential(v,[x,y],'potl');
```

$$true$$

```
> potl;
```

$$2\ x\ \sin(x\ y)\ \cos(x\ y)$$

A minor simplification is needed to produce the original form:

```
> combine(",trig);
```

$$x\ \sin(2\ x\ y)$$

A vector potential is computed in a similar way when it exists (which is when div $v = 0$).

For an example, first make a vector field with divergence equal to zero by taking the curl of some arbitrary field:

```
>v:=curl([x*y,0,-z*x],[x,y,z]);
```

$$v := [0,\ z,\ -\ x]$$

The `vecpotent()` function should produce something that differs from this by (at most) a gradient:

```
>vecpotent(v,[x,y,z],'vptl');
```

$$true$$

```
>eval(vptl);
```

$$[1/2\ z^2 + x\ y,\ 0,\ 0]$$

This is not the original potential. However, the result is a correct one and it can be checked directly by taking its curl:

```
> curl(vptl,[x,y,z]);
```

$$[\ 0,\ z,\ -\ x\ ]$$

```
> evalm("-v);
```

$$[\ 0,\ 0,\ 0\ ]$$

The functions `diverge()`, `curl()`, `grad()`, and `laplacian()` can take an additional option specifying the coordinate system. This option may be either `coords=spherical`, `coords=cylindrical`, or a list of three scale factors defining an orthogonal curvilinear coordinate system. For instance, here is a divergence computation for spherical coordinates using the scale factors approach:

```
>diverge([sin(t)/r^2,cot(f),r],[r,t,f],[1,r,r*sin(t)]);
```

$$\frac{\cot(f)\ \cos(t)}{r\ \sin(t)}$$

You can check this using the `coords=spherical` option in place of the last list.

3.6 Differential equations

This section covers the Maple function called `dsolve()`, which is a collection of routines for solving ordinary differential equations. The `dsolve()` function can be used for constant coefficient equations with both smooth and impulsive right-hand sides, for systems of equations, for general first-order nonlinear equations, and for series solutions to equations around ordinary and regular singular points. The `dsolve()` function can also obtain numerical solutions.

The topics in this section are

- Entering Equations and Checking Solutions
- First-Order Equations and Systems
- Second-Order Equations and Higher-Order Equations
- The `DESol()` Structure
- The `laplace` Option
- Numerical Methods
- Partial Differential Equations

Entering equations and checking solutions

This subsection discusses ways to define equations and initial conditions for dsolve() and also explains how to check solutions by substituting them into their equations.

The principal way to define differential equations uses diff(). The example that follows defines a second-order equation (an Euler-type equation) using the diff() notation and then solves it:

```
>e:=t^2*diff(x(t),t$2)-2*t*diff(x(t),t)+2*x(t)=0;
```

```
                 [    2      ]
            2 [   d      ]           [  d     ]
     e := t   [----- x(t)] - 2 t [---- x(t)] + 2 x(t) = 0
            [    2      ]           [  dt    ]
          [ dt      ]
```

```
>s:=dsolve(e,x(t));
```

```
                                                 2
                    s := x(t) = _C1 t + _C2 t
```

In defining the equation, dsolve() assumes the right-hand side to be zero if it is omitted. This is the same convention that is used with solve(). The dsolve() function always precedes its integration constants with underscores as shown here.

Solutions can be checked using the following method:

```
>simplify(subs(s,lhs(e)));
```

```
                          0
```

Initial conditions are included in the input data to dsolve() by including them in a Maple set with the equation(s) as follows:

```
>dsolve({diff(x(t),t)+t*x(t),x(0)=1},x(t));
```

```
                              2
                 x(t) = exp(- 1/2 t )
```

As expected, there is no integration constant.

The `D()` operator is used to define initial conditions on derivatives. The syntax follows the same lines as in the previous examples. For example, the following solves a second-order initial value problem:

```
>dsolve({diff(x(t),t,t)-x(t),x(0)=1,D(x)(0)=0},x(t));

                                 2
                      1/2 exp(t)    + 1/2
            x(t)  =  ------------------
                          exp(t)
```

Higher-order initial conditions are handled similarly. You cannot use `diff()` to specify initial conditions on derivatives.

First-order equations and systems

The `dsolve()` function is good at solving many kinds of equations, including first-order linear and nonlinear equations. Here is an easy example of solving a first-order homogeneous equation:

```
>e:=diff(x(t),t)+t/x(t)=0:
>dsolve(e,x(t));
                         2      2
              x(t)   = - t    + _C1
```

The solution just obtained defines `x(t)` implicitly in terms of `t`. This is a common situation with homogeneous equations. The `dsolve()` function does have an option that will produce explicit formulas for the solution. Here is what it does with the previous example:

```
>dsolve(diff(x(t),t)+t/x(t),x(t),explicit);

                  2       1/2                2       1/2
   x(t) = - (- t   + _C1)    ,  x(t) = (- t   + _C1)
```

Imposing the condition $x(0) = 1$ in the example above gives

```
>dsolve({e,x(0)=1},x(t));
                         2      1/2
              x(t)  = (- t   + 1)
```

so that Maple has selected the correct solution satisfying the differential equation.

Here is a first-order separable equation and its solution:

```
>e:=diff(x(t),t)-x(t)*cos(t)/(1+2*x(t)^2)=0:
>dsolve(e,x(t));
```

$$\ln(x(t)) + x(t)^2 - \sin(t) = \_C1$$

Imposing an initial condition produces

```
>dsolve({e,x(0)=1},x(t));
```

$$x(t) = \exp(-1/2\ W(2\ \exp(2\ \sin(t) + 2)) + \sin(t) + 1$$

In other cases, it may be desirable to obtain the integration constant manually. For the equation above, the steps are

```
>s:=dsolve(e,x(t));
```

$$s := \ln(x(t)) + x(t)^2 - \sin(t) = \_C1$$

```
>eval(subs(t=0,x(0)=1,s));
```

$$1 = \_C1$$

Observe the differing forms of the solutions.

The last calculation illustrates a point about subs(). The substitutions were done sequentially, from left to right. If they had been defined as a set or list they would have been applied simultaneously, which is not required in this setting. The following equation shows what happens when a set is used:

```
>eval(subs({t=0,x(0)=1},s));
```

$$\ln(x(0)) + x(0)^2 = \_C1$$

A further substitution would be necessary at this stage.

To use dsolve() for systems of equations, the procedure is similar. For example, here we solve a 2×2 linear initial value problem:

```
>e1:=diff(x(t),t)-2*x(t)+5*y(t)=0:
>e2:=diff(y(t),t)-x(t)+2*y(t)=0:
>i1:=x(0)=0: i2:=y(0)=1:
>dsolve({e1,e2,i1,i2},{x(t),y(t)});
```

$$\{y(t) = -2\ \sin(t) + \cos(t),\ x(t) = -5\ \sin(t)\}$$

The solution can be substituted using a similar approach to the earlier one:

```
>eval(subs(",lhs(e1)));
```

$$0$$

The `dsolve()` function will not usually be able to find explicit solutions for systems of nonlinear equations even when they exist. However, both series solutions and numerical methods are available for this case. Numerical solutions are covered below and in Section 5.4. Series solutions are illustrated in Section 3.7.

Second- and higher-order equations

The `dsolve()` function can handle second- and higher-order equations with constant coefficients in a straightforward way, provided the forcing terms are combinations of simple functions such as exponentials, trigonometrics, or polynomials. If the forcing terms are impulse functions, you can use a Laplace transform option to `dsolve()`, which is covered in the Section 3.7. An additional option to `dsolve()` can be used to obtain a solution basis for linear equations. Here is an illustration of the syntax:

```
>e:=diff(x(t),t$2)-2*diff(x(t),t)+x(t)=0;

          [   2      ]
          [  d       ]        [  d       ]
    e  := [----- x(t)]  -  2 [---- x(t)]  +  x(t)  =  0
          [   2      ]        [ dt       ]
          [ dt       ]

>dsolve(e,x(t),output=basis);

                    [exp(t),  exp(t) t]
```

An important class of linear second-order equations has a well-developed solution approach that uses series. The `dsolve()` function's series option implements this approach. Here is a series solution for Airy's equation (`Order` is currently set to 8):

```
>dsolve(diff(x(t),t,t)-t*x(t),x(t),series);

                                           3                4
    x(t)  =  x(0)  +  D(x)(0) t  +  1/6 x(0) t   +  1/12 D(x)(0) t

                      6                7            8
        +  1/180 x(0) t   +  1/504 D(x)(0) t   +  O(t )
```

Because no initial conditions were given, the solution contains the arbitrary parameters x(0) and D(x)(0). It is usually more convenient to have the solution expressed as the sum of two separate expressions multiplied by these parameters. Here is a way to do it:

```
>collect(convert(rhs("),polynom),{x(0),D(x)(0)},
        distributed);
```

$$(1 + 1/6\ t^3 + 1/180\ t^6)\ x(0)$$

$$+ (t + 1/12\ t^4 + 1/504\ t^7)\ D(x)(0)$$

The type `polynom` is recognized by `collect()`, but the order term is lost with this approach. The order term could be explicitly added back to the result if necessary.

The `dsolve()` function can solve other second-order linear equations. For example, here is an equation that can be transformed to a Bessel equation and for which `dsolve()` finds the general solution:

```
>e:=t^3*diff(x(t),t$2)+t^2*diff(x(t),t)+x(t)=0:
```

```
>dsolve(e,x(t));
```

$$x(t) = \_C1\ BesselJ(0,\ \frac{2}{t^{1/2}}) + \_C2\ BesselY(0,\ -\frac{2}{t^{1/2}})$$

For this example, `dsolve()` returns NULL if you request a series solution.

The `DESol()` structure

Just as we can manipulate polynomial roots without knowing them explicitly (using `RootOf()`), we can sometimes manipulate the solutions of differential equations. Solutions of differential equations are represented by `DESol()`. These are placeholders for the solutions. At present, Maple can do four things with a `DESol()`: integrate, differentiate, series expand, and numerically evaluate. To illustrate, here is a differential equation set up in a DESol():

```
>e:=diff(x(t),t$2)+sin(x(t))*x(t)=0;
```

```
          [   2       ]
          [  d        ]
    e  :=  [----- x(t)] + sin(x(t)) x(t) = 0
          [   2       ]
          [ dt        ]
```

```
>d:=DESol(e,x(t));
```

```
              [   2       ]
              [  d        ]
    d  :=  DESol({[----- x(t)] + sin(x(t)) x(t)}, {x(t)})
              [   2       ]
              [ dt        ]
```

Now we can obtain an equation satisfied by the integral of the solution:

```
>int(d,t);
```

```
DESol(

     /  3     \
     | d      |              d       / d     \
    {|----- w(t)| + sin(---- w(t)) |---- w(t)|}, {w(t)} )
     | 3      |             dt       \ dt    /
     \ dt     /
```

To obtain a series expansion around 0, you do the following (after setting Order to
4 to shorten the output):

```
>series(d,t=0);
```

```
                                           2
x(0) + D(x)(0) t - 1/2 sin(x(0)) x(0) t   +

(- 1/6 sin(x(0)) D(x)(0) - 1/6 cos(x(0)) D(x)(0) x(0))

    3       4
   t  + O(t )
```

The other choices are accessed in a similar way using `diff()` for differentiation and `evalf()` for numerical results.

The `laplace` option

Equations with impulsive forcing terms can be solved using Laplace transforms. The `dsolve()` function has an option that lets you specify that Laplace transforms are to be used. To define the basic impulsive functions, Maple uses the procedures `Heaviside()` and the `Dirac()`. `Heaviside()` produces the usual step function and `Dirac()` produces the Dirac delta function or its derivatives. Here is a typical example of using the `laplace` option to solve an equation with impulsive data:

```
>e:=diff(x(t),t$2)+4*x(t)-Dirac(t-1)=0:
>ic1:=x(0)=1: ic2:= D(x)(0)=0:
>dsolve({e,ic1,ic2},x(t),laplace);
```

$$x(t) = \cos(2\ t) + 1/2\ \text{Heaviside}(t - 1)\ \sin(2\ t - 2)$$

You do have to specify the initial conditions at $t = 0$ to use the `laplace` option. A transformation will be necessary to handle other cases.

You can solve higher-order equations and use more singular data as in this next example, which has the second derivative of the delta function as a forcing function:

```
>e:=diff(x(t),t$4)+diff(x(t),t$2)-Dirac(2,t-1)=0:
>ic1:=x(0)=1: ic2:=D(x)(0)=0: ic3:=(D@@2)(x)(0)=0:
>ic4:=(D@@3)(x)(0)=0:
```

The previous initial condition, for example, means the `D` operator composed with itself three times (that is, a third derivative) applied to `x` and evaluated at 0. The solution to the differential equation and initial conditions is now obtained from:

```
>dsolve({e,ic1,ic2,ic3,ic4},x(t),laplace);
```

$$x(t) = 1 + \text{Heaviside}(t - 1)\ \sin(t - 1)$$

The `laplace` option can be used to solve equations with other kinds of data such as polynomials and exponentials and their combinations. Success in this approach depends on whether there is enough information in Maple's transform table to compute and then invert the transforms that occur in the solution. Maple does not currently have the ability to evaluate the contour integral inversion formula for the Laplace transform.

The package `DEtools[]` contains a number of utilities for processing differential equations. We will mention some graphics functions in the next subsection. In addition, there are functions for changing variables (dependent and independent), for reducing the order using a known solution, and for other common differential equation operations.

Numerical methods

In addition to analytical solutions, `dsolve()` can also produce numerical solutions that can be easily plotted. The option to `dsolve()` that produces a numerical result is `numeric`. The algorithm used is the standard Runge–Kutta–Fehlberg technique with automatic step size control. This is a fourth-order finite difference method in which the time step is continuously adjusted to achieve a solution accuracy (relative or absolute) within prescribed limits. When you invoke `dsolve( ,numeric)`, a function is returned. This function can be evaluated for particular values of t to obtain approximate solutions to the equations. In addition, it can be used as an argument to a function in `plots[]` called `odeplot()` that automatically produces graphical output.

We will illustrate the process of numerically solving differential equations by plotting the space trajectory of a solution to the famous Lorentz equations. These equations are a now-classical example of a system having a strange attractor. The equations are

$$\dot{x} = \sigma(y - x)$$
$$\dot{y} = rx - y - xz$$
$$\dot{z} = xy - bz$$

where σ, r, and b are positive parameters. We will choose $\sigma = 3$, $r = 30$, and $b = 1$, and take the initial position to be $(0, 1, 0)$:

```
>e1:=diff(x(t),t)-3*(y(t)-x(t)):
>e2:=diff(y(t),t)-30*x(t)+y(t)+x(t)*z(t):
>e3:=diff(z(t),t)-x(t)*y(t)+z(t):
>i1:=x(0)=0: i2:=y(0)=1: i3:=z(0)=0:

>q:=dsolve({e1,e2,e3,i1,i2,i3},{x(t),y(t),z(t)},
        numeric):
```

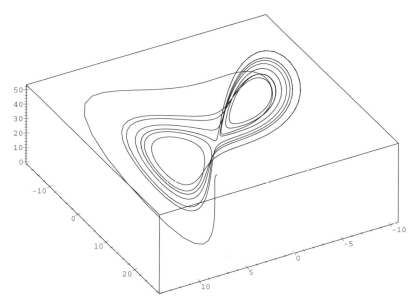

Figure 3.1: Orbit for Lorentz equations.

To evaluate the solution at, say, $t = 2$ you would simply enter q(2):

```
>q(2);
```

```
[t = 2, x(t) = -1.488454045650566,
```

```
  y(t) = -2.671726416776653,  z(t) = 19.03067385782937]
```

The result is a list containing the time value and the corresponding solution components. Maple automatically used the available math coprocessor to compute this
example. How this occurs is discussed further in Section 5.7.

Usually, a plot of one or more components of the solution of the differential equation will be needed. Such plots can be obtained by using dsolve(,numeric) as
an argument to plots[odeplot](). For example, to plot the the space trajectory
of the Lorentz equations, you can use odeplot() as follows:

```
>with(plots):
>odeplot(q,[x(t),y(t),z(t)],0..25,numpoints=1000);
```

In odeplot(), the range argument is the time interval for the plot, and the
numpoints option ensures that enough points are used to give a reasonably smooth

trajectory. Section 5.4 contains more details on numerical methods for ordinary differential equations.

Partial differential equations

Maple can obtain analytical solutions (usually, the general solution) to a limited class of partial differential equations. You will have most success with linear – especially first-order linear – equations in two independent variables. Here is one equation of this type that can be solved with pdesolve():

```
> pdesolve((1+x^2)*diff(u(x,y),x)-y^2*diff(u(x,y),y),
           u(x,y));
```

$$u(x, y) = \_F1\left(- \frac{y \ arctan(x) - 1}{y}\right)$$

In this output, _F1 denotes an "arbitrary" function, which is usually fixed by specified initial conditions. To keep the output readable, we avoided using a right-hand side in this example. However, pdesolve() will usually be able to handle polynomial and trigonometric right-hand sides, although the output can soon grow unmanageably long.

Higher-order equations, particularly those with constant coefficients can be solved in some cases. Again, two independent variables is the most favorable case. For instance, here is d'Alembert's solution for the wave equation:

```
> pdesolve(diff(u(x,t),t,t)-diff(u(x,t),x,x),u(x,t));
```

$$u(x, t) = \_F1(t + x) + \_F2(t - x)$$

where again _F1 and _F2 can be fixed by using initial conditions.

It hardly needs to be said that it is extremely simple to produce equations that pdesolve() cannot handle. Often when this happens, the response will be simply returned unevaluated. For instance, that is the case with the wave equation in two space dimensions. In other cases, you may encounter weird error messages. Try the following equations for a sample of these messages:

$$uu_x + u_y = 0$$
$$u_{xx} + u_{yy} = 0$$

The first of these equations has at least one solution, $x/(1 + y)$, and the second is Laplace's equation.

There is a function in `DEtools[]` that is designed to plot the solution surfaces of first-order quasilinear partial differential equations. See `?DEtools[PDEplot]` for information on this function.

3.7 Other calculus functions

There are some other calculus-related functions that belong in this chapter. These include functions for computing several kinds of transforms and for solving difference equations (recurrence relations).
The contents of this section are

- Transforms
- Solving Difference Equations with `rsolve()` and `LREtools[]`

Transforms

Maple has tables (to which you can add entries using `inttrans[addtable]()` with arguments consisting of the transform name, the function, its transform, the transform variable, and the independent variable) for Fourier (including separate sine and cosine transforms), Hankel, Hilbert, Laplace, Mellin, and z transforms. Except for the last, these functions are in a package called `inttrans[]`. The use of Laplace transforms for ordinary differential equations has been mentioned earlier. For other kinds of equations, it is necessary to have Maple explicitly make the necessary transform(s) and invert the result. As an example, here are the steps to form and solve a Volterra integral equation. First, we define the equation and then take its Laplace transform:

```
>with(inttrans):
>e:=u(t)+int((t-x)*u(x),x=0..t)-cos(t);
```

$$
e := u(t) + \int_0^t (t - x)\, u(x)\, dx - \cos(t)
$$

```
>laplace(e,t,s);
```

$$
\mathrm{laplace}(u(t),\, t,\, s) + \frac{\mathrm{laplace}(u(t),\, t,\, s)}{s^2} - \frac{s}{s^2 + 1}
$$

Second, we solve for the transform:

```
>solve(",laplace(u(t),t,s));
```

```
                  s
        -------------------
         2     [      1 ]
        (s  + 1) [1 + ----]
                 [      2 ]
                 [      s ]
```

and finally, we invert the transform:

```
>invlaplace(",s,t);
```

```
           - 1/2 t sin(t) + cos(t)
```

In a similar way, the Fourier (`fourier()`), Hankel (`hankel()`), Hilbert (`hilbert()`), Mellin (`mellin()`), and *z* transforms (`ztrans()`) can be used to solve different kinds of equations. Among many other things, the Fourier transform is appropriate for equations in **R** (or **R**^{n}), and the *z* transform is used to solve initial value problems for linear finite-difference equations. The Mellin transform essentially records information about the moments of a function.

Solving difference equations with `rsolve()` and `LREtools[]`

The difference equation solver `rsolve()` is analogous to `dsolve()` in its capabilities. This function can solve linear first-order equations, single equations, systems of equations with constant coefficients, and some additional miscellaneous equations. As with `solve()`, sets are used to input multiple equations and initial conditions and to specify unknowns. Zero is assumed for the right-hand side of an equation if it is omitted. Here are two first-order equation examples to illustrate the basic methods for using `rsolve()`:

```
>rsolve({u(n+1)-u(n)/(n+1)=1/(n+1)!,u(0)=1},u);
```

```
                  n + 1
               -----------
               GAMMA(n + 1)
```

The next example is a nonlinear Ricatti-type equation:

```
>rsolve(u(n+1)*u(n)-2*u(n)+1,u);
```

$$\frac{-n + u(0)\ n + u(0)}{-n + 1 + u(0)\ n}$$

Note that (and this is typical) the initial condition is specified to be at zero. If you want to use some other starting point, you could substitute the appropriate value for n in the above result and solve the resulting equation for u(0). More directly, you can also specify initial conditions in the argument list, as in the next example:

```
>rsolve({a(k+1)-b(k)=1,-a(k)+b(k+1)=0,a(2)=1,
      b(2)=-1},{a,b});
```

$$\{a(k) = 1/2\ k - 3/4 + 3/4\ (-1)^k,$$

$$b(k) = 1/2\ k - 5/4 - 3/4\ (-1)^k\}$$

With rsolve(), you can obtain a generating function for the solution to a linear equation or system with constant coefficients. This is often useful when the explicit solution is not in the form you want. To illustrate this, we will look at the three-term recurrence formula for the Chebychev polynomials:

$$T_{n+1}(x) - 2xT_n(x) + T_{n-1}(x) = 0, \quad T_0(x) = 1,\ T_1(x) = x.$$

The solution to this second-order constant coefficient difference equation is surely a polynomial, but rsolve() returns it in a more complicated form:

```
> q:=rsolve({T(n+1)-2*x*T(n)+T(n-1),T(0)=1,T(1)=x},T):
> simplify(q);
```

$$1/2\ \left(\frac{1}{x + (x^2 - 1)^{1/2}}\right)^n + 1/2\ \left(\frac{1}{-x + (x^2 - 1)^{1/2}}\right)^n$$

Instead of trying to simplify the last result, we will use the generating-function approach, which calls for the additional argument shown below:

```
>rsolve({T(n+1)-2*x*T(n)+T(n-1),T(0)=1,T(1)=x},
        T,'genfunc'(z));
```

$$\frac{-1 + x\ z}{-1 + 2\ x\ z - z^2}$$

In the third argument, `genfunc` (mandatory) and `z` (any name) must be unassigned. Now we shall expand the generating function in a series in its variable `z`. The next command produces the series up to fourth-order terms:

```
>simplify(series(",z,4));
```

$$1 + x\ z + (-1 + 2\ x^2)\ z^2 + (-3\ x + 4\ x^3)\ z^3 + O(z^4)$$

The coefficients of the series in `z` are the Chebychev polynomials. Higher-order polynomials in the sequence can be produced by increasing the order of the series and perhaps using `coeff()`. This example shows how the generating function can produce more explicit solutions than the straightforward approach.

The `asympt()` function is often useful in connection with difference equations. For example, the following gives an asymptotic approximation for the Fibonacci number F_n:

```
>simplify(asympt(rsolve({y(n+2)-y(n+1)-y(n),
        y(1)=1,y(2)=1},y),n));
```

$$-\frac{4}{5}\frac{5^{1/2}\ 2^n\ ((1 + 5^{1/2})^{-n}\ \exp(n\ \mathrm{Pi}) - (-1 + 5^{1/2})^{-n})}{(-1 + 5^{1/2})\ (1 + 5^{1/2})}$$

The same technique sometimes works even when `rsolve()` returns unevaluated.

The `rsolve()` function has a `makeproc` option that returns a procedure to evaluate the solution of a linear difference equation or system.

More functions for working with linear difference or recurrence equations are provided in the package `LREtools[]`. The main functions in this package perform various useful simplifications and manipulations of these equations. For instance, there are functions for creating procedures to perform direct numerical computation of the solutions `REtoproc()`, to plot the solutions `REplot()`, and to create `RESol()` structures analogous to `DESol()` structures.

3.8   Special functions of mathematics and mathematical physics

This section contains two lists of special mathematical functions that are supplied in Maple. The lists are of special functions occurring in mathematics and in mathematical physics. These categories are not very well defined or mutually exclusive, so consult both lists if you are seeking a particular function. A minor difficulty is the relatively large number of variations that can occur within a single class of special functions. We have not attempted to list the variations individually; instead we have chosen to use a more generic approach. The help file `?inifcns` describes the detailed variations.

SPECIAL FUNCTIONS OF MATHEMATICS

`bernoulli`	Bernoulli numbers and polynomials
`Beta`	The beta function
`Ci, Si, Ei`	Cosine, sine, exponential integrals
`Chi, Shi`	Hyperbolic cosine, hyperbolic sine integrals
`dilog`	Dilogarithm function
`erf, erfc`	Error and complementary error functions
`euler`	Euler numbers and polynomials
`Fresnel`	Fresnel sine and cosine integrals
`GAMMA, lnGAMMA`	The gamma function and its logarithm
`GaussAGM`	The arithmetic–geometric mean iteration
`harmonic`	Partial sums of the harmonic series
`Li`	Logarithmic integral
`MeijerG`	The Meijer G-function
`polylog`	Polylogarithm function
`Psi`	Derivatives of the logarithm of the gamma function
`W`	Solution of the algebraic equation $We^W = x$
`Weierstrass`	Weierstrass P and other functions
`Zeta`	Riemann zeta function

SPECIAL FUNCTIONS OF MATHEMATICAL PHYSICS

Airy	Airy functions
Anger	Anger J function
Bessel	Bessel functions and modified Bessel functions
Elliptic	Complementary elliptic integrals
Hankel	Hankel functions
hypergeom	The generalized hypergeometric function $_jF_k$
Jacobi	Jacobi elliptic functions
JacobiTheta	Jacobi theta functions
JacobiZeta	Jacobi zeta functions
Kelvin	Kelvin's combination of Bessel functions
Legendre	Complete elliptic integrals
Struve	Struve functions
Weber	Weber functions

3.9 Reference section

LIMITS, DERIVATIVES AND INTEGRALS

diff	Differentiation function
Diff	Inert differentiation function
D	Differentiation operator
int	Integration function
Int	Inert integration function
limit	Compute a limit

FUNCTIONS AND TYPES FOR SERIES EXPANSIONS

asympt	Make a series valid for large arguments
convert(,polynom)	Deletes the order term from the series and changes the type of the result to polynom
laurent	A Maple type
Order	Order of the error term in series()
polynom	A Maple type
series	A Maple type
series	General series expansion function
solve(series=y,x)	Invert the series in x around the point y
taylor	A Maple type

VECTOR ALGEBRA AND ANALYSIS FUNCTIONS

angle	Angle between two vectors
crossprod	Cross product of vectors

curl	Curl of a vector field
diverge	Divergence of a vector field
dotprod	Dot product of vectors
grad	Gradient of a scalar field
hessian	Matrix of second derivatives of a scalar
jacobian	Jacobian matrix of a vector
laplacian	Laplacian of a scalar field
potential	Find a scalar potential for a field
vecpotent	Find a vector potential for a field

EQUATION SOLVERS

DESol	Place holder for solutions of ordinary differential equations
dsolve	Initial value solver for ordinary differential equations
dsolve(,explicit)	Represent solution as an explicit function
dsolve(,laplace)	Solve using Laplace transforms
dsolve(,series)	Find a series solution
dsolve(,numeric)	Numerical solution for initial value problem
dsolve(,output=basis)	Solution basis for ordinary differential equations
LREtools	Package for manipulating and processing linear recurrence (difference) equations
pdesolve	Partial differential equation solver
rsolve	Initial value solver for difference equations
rsolve(,genfunc(z))	Represent solution as a generating function in z
rsolve(, makeproc)	Return a procedure to evaluate the solution

INTEGRAL TRANSFORMS

The last three entries below must be defined with readlib(). The rest are in the inttrans[] package.

addtable	Add entry to transform table
(inv)fourier	Fourier transform and its inverse
fouriercos	Fourier cosine transform
fouriersin	Fourier sine transform
hankel	Hankel transform
(inv)hilbert	Hilbert transform and its inverse
(inv)laplace	Laplace transform and its inverse
mellin	Mellin transform
mellintable	Add to the table of Mellin transforms
(inv)ztrans	z transform and its inverse

EXERCISES

1. Explain why the following command produced zero instead of $2x+2y+2z$

```
> F := [x^2,y^2,z^2]:
> X := [x,y,z]:
> sum(diff(F[i],X[i]),i=1..3);
```

$$0$$

How would you modify the last line to give the "correct" answer ?

2. Define $f(x) = x^3 + \sin(\arctan(x)) - \tan(\arcsin(x))$. Find the lowest-order derivative of f that is nonzero at $x = 0$ and its corresponding value. Plot $f(x)$ over the interval $-0.001 \le x \le 0.001$.

3. Numerically evaluate

$$\int_{-\pi/2}^{\pi/2} \ln(|\sin(x)|)\,dx$$

and check the result analytically. Briefly explain any discrepancies.

4. Problem Integrals: Use Maple to (help you) compute the following integrals:

   (a) $\displaystyle\int \frac{1}{x^{1/5} - x^{1/3}}\,dx$

   (b) $\displaystyle\int x \ln(2x + \sqrt{1 + x^2})\,dx$

   (c) $\displaystyle\int_{-1}^{0} \sqrt{x^2 - x^4}\,dx$

5. Use Maple to decide the probable convergence or divergence of the series

   (a) $\displaystyle\sum_{n=2}^{\infty} \frac{1}{\ln(n)}$

   (b) $\displaystyle\sum_{n=1}^{\infty} \frac{n!}{(2n)!}$

   (c) $\displaystyle\sum_{n=1}^{\infty} \sin(1/n)$

6. Raleigh–Ritz approximations: Consider the problem of finding $\alpha > 0$ that minimizes the area of revolution of the curve

$$y(x) = \frac{1}{2} + 2x^\alpha$$

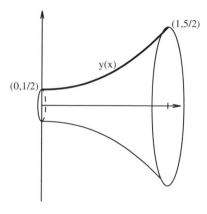

Figure 3.2

The area of revolution, shown in Figure 3.2, is given by

$$J = 2\pi \int_0^1 y(x)\sqrt{1 + y'(x)^2}\,dx$$

(a) Plot $J = J(\alpha)$ for $\alpha \in [1, 3]$, and estimate the minimizing value of α. (Note: Numerical calculation of the integral takes a long time, so do not plot too many points.)

(b) Calculate and plot $dJ/d\alpha$ over a small range containing the minimizing value of α, and get a better estimate of the minimizer by estimating where the derivative vanishes (crosses the x-axis). What is the value of the area for your best estimate of α ?

(c) The curve passing through $(0, 1/2)$ and $(1, 5/2)$ having minimal area of revolution is approximately

$$Y(x) \simeq 0.4837\cosh(2.0674x + 0.25885).$$

Calculate the area for this curve, and plot the curves $y(x) = 1/2 + 2x$, $y(x)$ with α computed from part (b), and $Y(x)$ using the same set of axes, with $Y(x)$ as a dotted curve.

7. Plot successive partial sums (that is, sums of the first N terms for various values of N) of the Fourier series

$$\frac{1}{\pi}\sum_{n=1}^{\infty}\frac{4}{2n - 1}\sin(\pi x)$$

and use them to decide what function the series is derived from. Plot this function and some partial sums on the same graph.

8. Least Squares Approximation: Given data points $\{(x_i, y_i)\}_{i=1}^{N}$ that are supposed to lie on a line $f(x) = a_0 + a_1 x$, the method of least squares estimates the intercept a_0 and slope a_1 by minimizing the error

$$e(a_0, a_1) = \sum_{i=1}^{N} e_i^2 = \sum_{i=1}^{N} (f(x_i) - y_i)^2.$$

This error will be a minimum when

$$\frac{\partial e}{\partial a_0} = 0 \quad \text{and} \quad \frac{\partial e}{\partial a_1} = 0.$$

(a) Given the data

```
> xx := [0.0 ,0.2 ,0.4 ,0.6 ,0.8 ,1.0 ];
> yy := [0.46,0.62,0.83,1.09,1.43,1.87];
```

corresponding to points $(x_i, y_i) = (xx[i], yy[i])$, use Maple to compute the coefficients a_0 and a_1 of the least squares approximation.

(b) Plot the given points and the line using the same axes, and compute the error e.

9. Let $f : \mathbf{R}^2 \to \mathbf{R}$ be defined by

$$f = \begin{cases} \frac{xy(x^2 - y^2)}{x^2 + y^2} & (x, y) \neq (0, 0) \\ 0 & (x, y) = (0, 0) \end{cases}$$

Show that $\partial f/\partial x$, $\partial f/\partial y$, $\partial^2 f/\partial x \partial y$, and $\partial^2 f/\partial y \partial x$ exist at $(0, 0)$ but the two mixed derivatives are not equal.

10. Let $h > 0$ be given and consider the function

$$F(x) = a_{-2} f(x - 2h) + a_{-1} f(x - h) + a_0 f(x)$$
$$+ a_1 f(x + h) + a_2 f(x + 2h)$$

where the constants a_i $i = -2, -1, \ldots, 2$ are to be determined by the fact that we want $F(x)$ to approximate $f''(x)$.

(a) To do this, choose the five constants so that as many as possible of the terms in the series for F about $h = 0$ vanish, except for the term involving the second derivative of f whose coefficient should be unity.

(b) For $f(x) = x \sin(x)$ plot both $f''(x)$ and $F(x)$ for $h = 4, 2,$ and 1.

11. If you draw n nonparallel lines in the plane such that no three of them intersect in the same point, the plane will be divided into R_n regions, where R_n satisfies the equation $R_{n+1} = R_n + n + 1$. Verify this recurrence and use Maple to solve it.

12. A pendulum made from a weightless string of length l and unit mass is oscillating in a vertical plane under gravity. The angle θ denotes the deflection of the string from the vertical and satisfies the differential equation

$$\theta'' + \frac{g}{l}\sin(\theta) = 0.$$

Take $l = 1$, $g = 9.81$, and chose initial conditions $\theta(0)$ and $\theta'(0)$ to illustrate the two kinds of solution that may arise. Use Maple to plot these solutions in the phase plane.

13. Solve the equation

$$2x(1-x)y''(x) + (6x+1)y'(x) + 2y(x) = 0$$

using the `series` option to `dsolve()`. Set `_C1=1, _C2=0` in the solution and obtain an explicit series for the resulting function.

14. Find a general solution of $y''(x) = \lambda y(x)$, $\lambda < 0$. Let e1 and e2 denote the equations resulting from substituting $x = 0$ and $x = \pi$ into the general solution. Solve these equations. If $y(0) = 0$ and $y(\pi) = 0$ use the solution to decide for what values of λ the differential equation has nonzero solutions.

15. Picard iteration is a technique for obtaining solutions of differential equations. Given a first-order differential equation and initial condition

$$y'(x) = f(x, y(x)), \quad y(0) = a,$$

the idea is to convert it into an integral equation of the form

$$y(x) = a + \int_0^x y'(s)\,ds = a + \int_0^x f(s, y(s))\,ds.$$

Given an initial guess for the solution, for example, $y_0(x) = a$, this process is iterated according to

$$y_{n+1}(x) = a + \int_0^x f(s, y_n(s))\,dx.$$

Use Maple to solve the differential equation $y' = f(x, y) = \cos(x)y$ with initial condition $y(0) = 1$. Beginning with $y_0(x) = 1$, use Maple to compute the first four Picard iterates and plot them along with the exact solution (use the range $0 \le x \le 6$ and make the exact solution dotted).

4 Matrices, linear algebra, and the `linalg[]` package

In Chapters 2 and 3, we covered Maple's precalculus and calculus features. Now it is time to look at matrices and linear algebra. Most of Maple's matrix and linear algebra capabilities are in a package called `linalg[]`. The `linalg[]` package is a relatively large package, containing over 100 different functions. These functions cover things you expect such as linear equations and eigenvalues, but there are also extensive facilities for creating and modifying matrices, for finding bases for various spaces, and for reducing matrices to normal forms.

This chapter starts with a section on defining and changing matrices in `linalg[]`. From there, we continue with a section on matrix algebra. The following two sections cover the solution of linear systems of equations and functions to generate bases for subspaces. We then look at the important topic of eigenvalues and eigenvectors. The remaining sections cover normal forms, checking for matrix properties such as positive definiteness, and methods for making submatrices and supermatrices from existing matrices.

Where appropriate, the examples in this chapter assume that the linear algebra package has been loaded through the command `with(linalg);`.

4.1 Creating and changing matrices

This section deals with matrix creation and modification in Maple. The subsections contents are

- Defining Matrices with `array()`
- Defining Matrices with `linalg[]`
- Indexing Functions
- Programmed Matrices

- Matrix Exponential: Wronskian
- Parameterized Matrices
- Using `map()` and `subs()` with Matrices

Defining matrices with `array()`

In Section 1.3, we very briefly introduced the main library function called `array()`. We saw that `array()` can be used to define numerically indexed data arrays. The dimensions of the array are defined by range expressions, and the entries are contained in lists. In general, the ranges in an `array()` definition can be any integer ranges. However, for using `evalm()` (the linear algebra evaluator, see below) or `linalg[]` functions with an `array()`, it is essential that each lower range expression is 1. In other words, if an array represents a vector or matrix in `evalm()` or `linalg[]` the range expression(s) in it must have the form `1..n` for some numerical valued expression n. Such arrays are a specific Maple type called vector or matrix as appropriate. For example, the following defines a general four dimensional vector v:

```
>v:=array(1..4);
```

$$v := array(1 .. 4, [])$$

The empty list in the output indicates that no explicit values have been given for the components of v. Similarly, the following defines a 3×4 matrix with unassigned entries:

```
>A:=array(1..3,1..4);
```

$$A := array(1 .. 3, 1 .. 4, [])$$

The entries of an `array()` can be assigned in several ways. To assign some entries when the array is created, include them in a set or list. The following examples illustrate the procedure for both a vector and a matrix:

```
>v:=array(1..4,{(1)=q,(3)=s});
```

$$v := [q, v[2], s, v[4]]$$

```
>d:=array(1..3,1..2,{(1,1)=4,(3,2)=0});
```

$$
d := \begin{bmatrix} 4 & d[1, 2] \\ d[2, 1] & d[2, 2] \\ d[3, 1] & 0 \end{bmatrix}
$$

If all the entries of an array are to be assigned when it is created, it is not necessary to include the range argument. The argument is inferred from the data and automatically started at 1:

```
>v:=array([2,w,1,z]);
```

$$
v := [\ 2,\ w,\ 1,\ z\ ]
$$

```
>type(v,vector);
```

$$
true
$$

In a similar way, a list of (row) lists is treated as a matrix type. The actual entries in a matrix can be any Maple expressions. However, many of the `linalg[]` package's functions are set up to work with particular classes of matrices. For instance, many functions work with rational symbolic matrix entries, whereas others work for smaller classes such as complex numerical matrices.

Assignments such as

```
>v[3]:=4;
```

$$
v[3] := 4
$$

```
>A[1,2]:=x;
```

$$
A[1, 2] := x
$$

can be used to set values for particular entries of arrays. The same notation is used to print or perform other operations on selected entries.

Note that `array()` provides no way to describe the typography of v, that is, whether it is to be a row or column. That is to be expected because there are many applications of arrays where such typography is meaningless. Still, `linalg[]` does have to know what is intended, and the convention adopted is that v denotes a column vector. Even though a one-dimensional array is interpreted by Maple as a column vector, it is printed as a row vector. This is inconsistent with Maple's notation for matrices, which does print an $n \times 1$ matrix type as a column: In Maple, a vector type is not quite the same as an $n \times 1$ matrix type!

Recall from Section 1.3 that `array()` follows different evaluation rules from most other expressions. This is apparent when you want to display an `array()`. For example, trying to display the `array()` d, created above, by typing its name merely gets the name printed back:

```
>d;
```

$$d$$

One way to force Maple to display or evaluate a matrix or vector is to use `eval()`:

```
>eval(d);
```

```
[    4        ?[1, 2] ]
[                     ]
[ ?[2, 1]   ?[2, 2] ]
[                     ]
[ ?[3, 1]      0     ]
```

The entries with question marks have not been assigned.

Defining matrices with `linalg[]`

In addition to the main library function `array()`, some functions in `linalg[]` provide useful alternatives for defining matrices and vectors. Two of these functions (not to be confused with the Maple types of the same names) are called `matrix()` and `vector()` and they can be used in several different ways. The `matrix()` function takes the dimensions of the matrix as its first two arguments. There are several alternatives for the third argument. You can give a list of explicit entries as follows:

```
>matrix(2,3,[1,-1,2,-1,4,1]);
```

```
[  1   -1   2 ]
[             ]
[ -1    4   1 ]
```

and more generally, you can build matrices whose elements are prescribed functions
of position:

```
>f:=(r,s)->r^2+s^2;
```

$$f := (r,s) \rightarrow r^2 + s^2$$

```
>matrix(2,3,f);
```

$$\begin{bmatrix} 2 & 5 & 10 \\ 5 & 8 & 13 \end{bmatrix}$$

General procedures can be used here, not just arrow functions. Also, similar constructions can be used with `vector()`. For example:

```
>vector(4,i->2*i);
```

$$[\ 2,\ 4,\ 6,\ 8\ ]$$

Useful special cases of this approach are

```
>Z:=matrix(2,3,0);
```

$$Z := \begin{bmatrix} 0 & 0 & 0 \\ 0 & 0 & 0 \end{bmatrix}$$

```
>C:=matrix(2,3,a);
```

$$C := \begin{bmatrix} a(1,\ 1) & a(1,\ 2) & a(1,\ 3) \\ a(2,\ 1) & a(2,\ 2) & a(2,\ 3) \end{bmatrix}$$

The Programmed Matrices subsection gives a more complex example of this technique.

It is sometimes necessary to enter the matrix elements one by one and have Maple read each element before the next element is entered. The function for this is `entermatrix()`. Here is a simple example:

```
> m:=matrix(2,2);
```

$$m := array(1 .. 2, 1 .. 2, [])$$

```
> entermatrix(m);
enter element 1,1 > x^2-1;
enter element 1,2 > x^2+1;
enter element 2,1 > 2*x;
enter element 2,2 > -2*x;
```

```
            [   2           2        ]
            [  x  -  1    x   +  1    ]
            [                        ]
            [     2 x        -  2 x  ]
```

The `linalg[]` package contains several facilities for simplifying the creation of particular matrices. There is a function called `diag()` (or equivalently `BlockDiagonal()`), which sets up block diagonal matrices, and one called `band()`, which sets up band matrices with constant diagonals. Both of these matrices use the `sparse` indexing function, an idea that is explained in the Indexing Functions subsection. For building a matrix from prescribed submatrices, there is `blockmatrix()`. There is also a function called `JordanBlock()`, which creates a bidiagonal matrix with a constant diagonal and unit upper diagonal.

Another facility built into `linalg[]` can extract the coefficient matrix and data from a system of linear equations. Here is an illustration:

```
> genmatrix([a*x+b*y=f1,c*x+d*y=f2],{x,y},'flag');
```

```
            [ a   b   f1 ]
            [            ]
            [ c   d   f2 ]
```

The final argument is optional and can be any name, or `flag`. If this argument is a name, the data vector is assigned to that name, and as shown above, `flag` causes the augmented matrix to be formed. You can enter the equations and variables as sets or lists. Use lists to avoid the kind of situation that follows:

```
>genmatrix({a*x+b*y=f1,c*x+d*y=f2},{x,y});
```

$$\begin{array}{ccc} [& c & d &] \\ [& & &] \\ [& a & b &] \end{array}$$

To copy a submatrix of an existing matrix into another, possibly larger, matrix, `linalg[]` provides the function `copyinto()`. Related to `copyinto()` is extend(), which lets you enlarge an existing matrix by appending additional rows and columns, optionally initialized. Another pair of functions that (just) belong in this section are `swaprow()` and `swapcol()`, which are used to exchange a pair of rows or columns in an already created matrix.

The `linalg[]` package contains three functions, `companion()`, `bezout()`, and `sylvester()`, which construct the companion matrix of a polynomial and the Bezout and Sylvester matrices of a pair of polynomials.

The matrix and vector-building functions in `linalg[]` do not generate new types. Their outputs are of the standard types `matrix` and `vector`.

Indexing functions

While `array()`, `matrix()`, and `vector()` are Maple's tools for general matrix building, there are also some preprogrammed matrix structures that can save time and effort. These structures are called indexing functions and appear as optional first arguments to `array()`. There are five standard indexing functions, which are called `antisymmetric`, `diagonal`, `identity`, `sparse`, and `symmetric`. As its name suggests, `identity` automatically makes a matrix with 1s on its main diagonal. It is not necessary that the matrix be square:

```
>eval(array(identity,1..2,1..3));
```

$$\begin{array}{ccc} [& 1 & 0 & 0 &] \\ [& & & &] \\ [& 0 & 1 & 0 &] \end{array}$$

One reason for indexing functions is to define a structure for a matrix. For example, you cannot use the option `identity` to make a general matrix with 1s on its diagonal and nonzeros in some other positions. It is part of the definition of the indexing function `identity` that its off-diagonal elements are zero, and trying to assign them will result in an error message.

The symmetric option can be used to automatically build a symmetric matrix from the input data:

```
>elems:={(1,1)=a,(2,2)=b,(1,2)=c};

        elems := {(2, 2) = b, (1, 1) = a, (1, 2) = c}

>eval(array(symmetric,1..2,1..2,elems));
```

$$
\begin{bmatrix} a & c \\ & \\ c & b \end{bmatrix}
$$

The antisymmetric option builds a skew-symmetric array.

As you have already guessed, diagonal builds a diagonal array, but what about sparse? The sparse function is simply a "zero default" option for a matrix: An element is assumed to be zero unless explicitly defined otherwise. This conforms with standard terminology, which designates as "sparse" a matrix with relatively few nonzero entries. Sparse matrices are common across a range of disciplines, and, consequently, the sparse option is a very useful one. An array with a sparse indexing function can be used more efficiently (for example, in algebraic operations) than a similar matrix without the indexing function. Here is an example that uses sparse to make a small permutation matrix:

```
>data:={(1,2)=1,(2,3)=1,(3,1)=1};

        data := {(2, 3) = 1, (1, 2) = 1, (3, 1) = 1}

>eval(array(1..3,1..3,sparse,data));
```

$$
\begin{bmatrix} 0 & 1 & 0 \\ & & \\ 0 & 0 & 1 \\ & & \\ 1 & 0 & 0 \end{bmatrix}
$$

The linalg[] package contains a function called indexfunc() that returns the indexing function of its argument matrix if there is one, and returns NULL otherwise. You cannot use the predefined indexing functions to define an array that is both `sparse` and `symmetric` because `array()` takes just a single indexing function as an (optional) argument. For cases like this, and in more general situations, you can supply your own indexing function in the form of a Maple procedure. Indexing functions are not available with `matrix()` and `vector()`.

Programmed matrices

Maple has some preprogrammed matrices that can be produced with a single command: They are the Hilbert matrices `hilbert()`, the Toeplitz matrices `toeplitz()`, the Vandermonde matrices `vandermonde()`, and what Maple calls `fibonnaci()` matrices, which are generated from the standard recursion formula for Fibonacci numbers with matrix-starting conditions. There is also a function `randmatrix()` for generating random matrices, satisfying a variety of conditions. The first three of these functions are used in the expected way. For example, here is a 4 × 4 Toeplitz matrix with a generic row listed as `[a,b, c,d]`:

```
>toeplitz([a,b,c,d]);
```

$$
\begin{bmatrix} a & b & c & d \\ b & a & b & c \\ c & b & a & b \\ d & c & b & a \end{bmatrix}
$$

The `randmatrix()` function is more varied in what it can produce. Its first two arguments always give the dimensions of the desired random matrix:

```
>randmatrix(2,3);
```

$$
\begin{bmatrix} -85 & -55 & -37 \\ -35 & 97 & 50 \end{bmatrix}
$$

The matrix entries default to uniform (pseudo) random integers in the range [−99, 99]. To obtain integer entries in a different range, include another argument like the following:

```
>randmatrix(2,3,entries=rand(-1..1));
```

```
[ 1   1    0 ]
[            ]
[ 0   0   -1 ]
```

The entries are uniform random integers in $[-1, 1]$. You are not limited here to the use of rand(integer..integer). You can use any of Maple's random-number generators and more complex creations based on them such as random polynomials.

The remaining option to randmatrix() permits you to define a structure for the matrix. The options are antisymmetric, dense, sparse, symmetric, and unimodular (having unit determinant). The dense option is the default. Here is a random 3×3 skew-symmetric matrix:

```
>randmatrix(3,3,antisymmetric);
```

```
[  0   -50   -12 ]
[                ]
[ 50    0    -18 ]
[                ]
[ 12    18    0  ]
```

One way to obtain floats in the matrix above is to divide it by 100. More generally, you can use options in the random-number generators. (See Section 8.4 for more on random-number generators.)

To create a random vector there is a function called randvector() that is used similarly to randmatrix().

Matrix exponential: Wronskian

To compute the exponential of a matrix, $\exp(tA)$, linalg[] has a function called exponential(). This takes the matrix A as its first argument and the scalar parameter t as its second optional argument. The exponential() function works by finding the eigenvalues and (generalized) eigenvectors of A. Ignoring some difficulties associated with computing eigensystems, exponential() does what you expect. For example:

```
> a := matrix(3,3,[p,1,0,0,p,1,0,0,p]);
```

$$
a := \begin{bmatrix} p & 1 & 0 \\ 0 & p & 1 \\ 0 & 0 & p \end{bmatrix}
$$

```
> exponential(a);
```

$$
\begin{bmatrix} \exp(p) & \exp(p) & 1/2\ \exp(p) \\ 0 & \exp(p) & \exp(p) \\ 0 & 0 & \exp(p) \end{bmatrix}
$$

There is also a function to create the square Wronskian matrix whose (i, j) element is defined as $d^i f_j / dx^i$, where the functions f_j are given. For example:

```
>Wronskian([sin(x),cos(x)],x);
```

$$
\begin{bmatrix} \sin(x) & \cos(x) \\ \cos(x) & -\sin(x) \end{bmatrix}
$$

The functions must be in a list or a vector.

Parameterized matrices

Large structured matrices that are parameterized in some way by their order often occur in practice. Using the tools defined above, it is possible to set up such matrices in some interesting cases. For example, the famous partial difference operator and boundary conditions

$$
(Lu)_{ij} = u_{i,j-1} + u_{i-1,j} - 4u_{i,j} + u_{i+1,j} + u_{i,j+1} \qquad i, j = 1, 2, \ldots, n
$$
$$
u_{i,j} = 0, \quad i \text{ or } j = 0 \text{ or } n + 1
$$

correspond to a discretization of the Laplace operator and homogeneous boundary conditions relative to a unit mesh in a square domain. To set this up as a matrix expression, we first order the mesh interior points lexicographically and number them sequentially from 1 to n^2. Using this labeling of the mesh points, the next step is to define an arrow function for the matrix entries. Only the result of the arrow function definition is shown below: This function was created as an arrow function in a similar way to the example in Section 2.6:

```
>print(L);
proc(r,s)
options operator,arrow;
    if r = s then -4
    elif s = r-1 and r mod n <> 1 then 1
    elif s = r+1 and r mod n <> 0 then 1
    elif s = r+n then 1
    elif s = r-n then 1
    else 0
    fi
end
```

Now we set a value for n, in this case 3, which yields a 9×9 matrix for the difference operator corresponding to the nine interior mesh points of the square:

```
>n:=3:
>matrix(9,9,L);
```

$$
\begin{bmatrix}
-4 & 1 & 0 & 1 & 0 & 0 & 0 & 0 & 0 \\
1 & -4 & 1 & 0 & 1 & 0 & 0 & 0 & 0 \\
0 & 1 & -4 & 0 & 0 & 1 & 0 & 0 & 0 \\
1 & 0 & 0 & -4 & 1 & 0 & 1 & 0 & 0 \\
0 & 1 & 0 & 1 & -4 & 1 & 0 & 1 & 0 \\
0 & 0 & 1 & 0 & 1 & -4 & 0 & 0 & 1 \\
0 & 0 & 0 & 1 & 0 & 0 & -4 & 1 & 0 \\
0 & 0 & 0 & 0 & 1 & 0 & 1 & -4 & 1 \\
0 & 0 & 0 & 0 & 0 & 1 & 0 & 1 & -4
\end{bmatrix}
$$

With the help of the simplest programming tools, you could use L as part of an autonomous procedure to return the Laplace matrix of any order.

Using `map()` and `subs()` with matrices

This subsection covers two general techniques for changing the elements of existing matrices. In the first technique, a function is applied to each element of a matrix. In the second technique, one or more parameters in a matrix have substitutions made for them.

The `map()` function is used to apply a function to every element of a vector or matrix. The argument list of `map()` contains the function to be used, followed by the expression, followed by any auxiliary arguments that may be needed by the function. As an example (without auxiliary arguments), we will add (modulo 2) 1 to a matrix of random quadratic polynomials with binary coefficients. The first step is to define the addition function:

```
>f:=u->u+1 mod 2;
```

$$f := u \rightarrow (u + 1) \mod 2$$

The matrix is defined using a function called `Randpoly()`, which can produce random polynomials in several different formats:

```
>A:=matrix(2,2,[seq(Randpoly(2,x) mod 2,i=1..4)]);
```

$$A := \begin{bmatrix} x^2 + 1 & x^2 + x \\ x^2 + x + 1 & x^2 + x + 1 \end{bmatrix}$$

The final step is to apply the `map()` function:

```
>map(f,A);
```

$$\begin{bmatrix} x^2 & x^2 + x + 1 \\ x^2 + x & x^2 + x \end{bmatrix}$$

You cannot directly apply f to A for this result; `map()` is the easiest way to obtain it.

Another common situation calls for a substitution to be made for a variable in a matrix. For example, you may want to substitute x=2 in the matrix:

```
>a:=matrix(2,2,[1,1,x,x^2]);
```

$$
a := \begin{bmatrix} 1 & 1 \\ & 2 \\ x & x \end{bmatrix}
$$

The most obvious thing to do is the following:

```
>subs(x=2,a);
```

$$
a
$$

but it does not work, as the next example shows:

```
>eval(subs(x=2,a));
```

$$
\begin{bmatrix} 1 & 1 \\ & 2 \\ x & x \end{bmatrix}
$$

Here is a method that works:

```
>subs(x=2,eval(a));
```

$$
\begin{bmatrix} 1 & 1 \\ 2 & 4 \end{bmatrix}
$$

Remember that arrays are subject to last-name evaluation rules. You have to force the evaluation of a so that substitution has the desired effect.

4.2 Matrix algebra

This section covers Maple's facilities for basic matrix operations. The topics covered are

- Main Library Facilities
- Addition and Multiplication with `linalg[]`
- Transposition
- Inverting Matrices
- Scalars from Matrices

Main library facilities

The main library contains some facilities for linear algebra, which we will discuss here. These algebraic facilities are always available in a Maple session and it is not necessary to preload `linalg[]` to use them. The main library functions allow you to use most of the usual algebraic symbols to combine matrices and vectors, the main exception being the symbol for matrix multiplication, which is not * but rather `&*`. The distinction here is between commutative and noncommutative multiplication. Once an expression is set up with matrices and the algebraic operators, it can be evaluated with `evalm()`, the main library function for evaluating matrix expressions.

Here are some examples to illustrate basic matrix algebra: First, we will define two matrices and a vector (note the syntax of the next assignments, where no ranges are used):

```
>A:=array([[a,b],[c,d]]);
```

$$
A := \begin{bmatrix} a & b \\ c & d \end{bmatrix}
$$

```
>B:=array([[1,-1],[2,0]]);
```

$$
B := \begin{bmatrix} 1 & -1 \\ 2 & 0 \end{bmatrix}
$$

```
>v:=array([x,y]);
```

$$
v := \begin{bmatrix} x, & y \end{bmatrix}
$$

Addition, subtraction, and exponentiation are performed with the usual symbols.

The scalar multiplication symbol can be used to multiply a matrix by a scalar. For example:

```
>C:=A^(-1)&*B +2*A;
```

$$C \; := \; (1/A \; \&* \; B) \; + \; 2 \; A$$

In this result, there is no indication that matrices are involved. The presence of a matrix is only recognized by `evalm()`, which is the evaluator for matrix expressions. This is what it gives here:

```
>evalm(C);
```

```
[   - d + 2 b                 d              ]
[ - ---------- + 2 a  - ---------- + 2 b ]
[   a d - b c              a d - b c       ]
[                                          ]
[   - c + 2 a                 c              ]
[   --------- + 2 c   --------- + 2 d ]
[   a d - b c              a d - b c       ]
```

Let's (indirectly) verify that vectors are column vectors in `linalg[]`:

```
>evalm(B&*v);
```

$$[\; x \; - \; y, \; 2 \; x \;]$$

```
>evalm(v&*B);
Error, (in linalg[multiply])
matrix dimensions incompatible
```

The function `linalg[multiply]` for matrix multiplication is discussed in the following subsection.

The previous subsection mentioned the use of the identity-indexing function for making a unit matrix. In addition, Maple provides the symbol `&*()` for a unit matrix. This symbol can appear in algebraic expressions and will be appropriately interpreted as a unit matrix. For instance (using an `alias` to enhance readability):

```
>alias(U=&*()):
>evalm(A-lambda*U);
```

```
             [ a - lambda          b       ]
             [                              ]
             [       c         d - lambda   ]
```

```
>evalm(v-3*U);
```

```
             [ x - 3, y - 3 ]
```

Note that in the last example, a rectangular unit matrix has been created. This is similar to the way the identity-indexing function operates.

Addition and multiplication with `linalg[]`

In this subsection, we will discuss the `linalg[]` package's facilities for matrix algebra.

Addition and multiplication of matrices is performed using two functions called `matadd()` and `multiply()`. The `matadd()` function can handle just two matrices or vectors at a time, although it can also form linear combinations of the matrices. The first two arguments to `matadd()` are the compatible matrices that are to be added. The next two arguments, which are optional, are the coefficients of the linear combination. There is no explicit need for `evalm()` with these functions: The result is automatically computed.

The multiplication routine `multiply()` can produce the product of any number of compatible matrices and vectors. For forming the inner product of two vectors, there is a function called `dotprod()`. A multiplication function called `innerprod()` is used for computing bilinear and quadratic forms. Here is a simple example of its use:

```
>u:=vector([1,0]): v:=vector([0,1]):
>innerprod(u,matrix([[p,q],[r,s]]),v);
```

```
             q
```

There are three more multiplication functions that allow you to multiply selected rows or columns or an entire matrix by a scalar expression. These functions are called `mulrow()`, `mulcol()`, and `scalarmul()`.

Related to the functions already mentioned are addrow() and addcol(), which add a multiple of a row or column to another row or column. Another related function called pivot() can perform the basic step of Gaussian elimination, consisting of "elimination" of a column of the matrix.

Transposition

Transposition is performed by transpose(), and simultaneous conjugation and transposition of complex matrices is done by htranspose(). For example:

```
>a:=vector([p,q]);
```

$$a := [\ p,\ q\ ]$$

```
>b:=vector([r,s]);
```

$$b := [\ r,\ s\ ]$$

```
>multiply(transpose(a),b);
```

$$p\ r\ +\ q\ s$$

The next example computes the Hermitian inner product of a matrix with itself:

```
>f:=(r,s)->r+I*s;
```

$$f\ :=\ (r,s)\ ->\ r\ +\ I\ s$$

```
>a:=matrix(2,2,f);
```

$$a := \begin{bmatrix} 1+I & 1+2\ I \\ 2+I & 2+2\ I \end{bmatrix}$$

```
>multiply(htranspose(a),a);
```

$$\begin{bmatrix} 7 & 9+3\ I \\ 9-3\ I & 13 \end{bmatrix}$$

Inverting matrices

Matrix inversion is done through the `inverse()` function. For arrays defined using the `sparse` indexing function and for all matrices of order 4×4 or less, `linalg[]` uses Cramer's rule to do the inversion. In the remaining cases, `linalg[]` uses Gauss–Jordan elimination. The argument to `inverse()` must be an invertible square matrix. Maple does not have explicit facilities for generalized inversion. However, `linalg[]` has enough tools to make most generalized inverses easy to compute with just a few steps.

To have Maple compute an inverse using fixed length floating-point numbers (possibly for reasons of efficiency), you can include a decimal point in some entry of the matrix. Another possibility is to multiply the matrix by 1.0 using `scalarmul()` and a third possibility is to `convert()` the matrix to floats in conjunction with `map()`. You should not use `inverse()` as an argument to `evalf()` for a floating-point inversion, as that might merely compute the exact inverse and then evaluate it in floating-point arithmetic.

For larger matrices, it is worth knowing something about the computational complexity of inversion. For example, floating-point numerical inversion takes an amount of time proportional to the cube of the size of the coefficient matrix; doubling the size of the matrix will increase the inversion time by a factor of 8 for sufficiently large matrices. Exact numerical computing (with rational numerical matrices) could take longer, depending on the length of the integers that are generated during the inversion. Symbolic inversion of relatively large, dense matrices can generate many long expressions, and it is quite easy to use up a lot of computer memory in the process of generating and storing them. For purely symbolic matrices, the amount of time will depend on the complexity of the formulas defining the matrix entries, but it is likely to be larger than for rational matrices of comparable size.

To illustrate some of these points, the next example generates a random matrix of order 15, multiplies it by 0.1 to convert the entries to floating-point numbers in the interval $[-10, 10]$ and applies `invert()` to the result. The computations are carried out using floating-point numbers of length given by `Digits` $(=10)$:

```
>a:=scalarmul(randmatrix(15,15),0.1):
>tzero:=time():
>inverse(a): time()-tzero;
```

$$7.700$$

The `time()` function's value (covered in Section 8.2) is the amount of CPU time so far used, measured in seconds. Here is a similar calculation with a matrix of order 30:

```
>a:=scalarmul(randmatrix(30,30),0.1):
>tzero:=time():
>inverse(a): time()-tzero;
```
$$56.571$$

The time ratio is reasonably close to the limiting theoretical value of 8. Repeating the first calculation, this time with exact matrix entries gives

```
>a:=randmatrix(15,15):
>tzero:=time():
>inverse(a): time()-tzero;
```
$$11.600$$

This calculation takes roughly fifty percent longer than the first one because of the long integers that have to be handled. For example, the "first" element of the inverse is the following:

```
>""[1,1];
```

$$- \ \frac{29327645834822733055774864367}{2577556339827400239097662001 0481}$$

Repeating the calculation with a 30×30 matrix gives

```
>a:=randmatrix(30,30):
>tzero:=time():
>inverse(a): time()-tzero;
```
$$117.929$$

The time used is about twice the corresponding floating-point time. The deterioration in the relative performance has occurred because the integers in the solution have more than doubled in length:

```
>""[1,1];
```

```
-
81229757374272506975666337065346294767854891390449622 2\
5708827324
-----------------------------------------------------
56508979797028683553741770648725493777893986 9766046645\
5797378470495
```

Related to the inverse of a matrix is the transposed matrix of cofactors. This is formed by the function adjoint() that also has the abbreviation adj(). The resulting matrix is the inverse of the original, multiplied by its determinant (mentioned in the next section) as the following illustrates:

```
>multiply(a,adjoint(a)/det(a));
```

$$\begin{bmatrix} 1 & 0 & 0 \\ 0 & 1 & 0 \\ 0 & 0 & 1 \end{bmatrix}$$

For floating-point matrix calculations, bear in mind that almost no calculation can be performed exactly. You might as well assume that Maple generates a roundoff error each time it does a floating-point operation. This means being alert to the possibility of considerable inaccuracy caused by accumulation of roundoff errors. Although there are some theoretical results about this, a simpler approach is to compute twice, using different values of `Digits`. A sure sign of roundoff problems is if the two sets of results differ greatly. Section 5.5 contains an illustration of how this works in practice.

Scalars from matrices

Several algebraic operations on matrices yield scalar results. An easy-to-compute example is the trace operation, called `trace()`, that returns the sum of the diagonal entries of a matrix. Other scalar-valued functions are the determinant function, called `det()` in `linalg[]` and the permanent function called `permanent()`.

The algorithms for computing determinants and computing inverses are closely related, and the comments above about efficiency and floating-point accuracy apply to determinants also.

Two more scalar functions are used for computing norms and condition numbers. The function `norm()` can evaluate the standard ℓ^1, ℓ^2, and ℓ^∞ norms, the last being the default. Remember that the second of these norms uses the eigenvalues of the matrix, in contrast to the other two, which use relatively trivial algebraic computations. The condition number, which is defined for a square matrix A as $\|A\|\|A^{-1}\|$, is returned by the function `cond()`. This could also be an expensive calculation, since the inverse of the matrix is needed.

4.3   Matrix decompositions

This section covers three matrix decomposition functions in `linalg[]`. These functions are

- LU Decomposition
- Cholesky Decomposition
- QR Decomposition

LU decomposition

The function for LU decomposition is `LUdecomp()`. This function can handle symbolic and numerical rectangular matrices, including matrices with complex floating-point entries. It can produce the determinant and rank of the input matrix as well as pivot information generated for floating-point decompositions. In addition, an option is available for producing the row-reduced echelon form of the input matrix. For an illustration of this function, we will use a 3×3 Vandermonde matrix:

```
> A:=vandermonde([x1,x2,x3]);
```

$$
A := \begin{bmatrix} 1 & x1 & x1^2 \\ 1 & x2 & x2^2 \\ 1 & x3 & x3^2 \end{bmatrix}
$$

`LUdecomp()` returns the upper triangular factor. Other information is obtained by supplying names for assignment. For instance, the unit lower triangular factor and the determinant are set in the following call to `LUdecomp()`:

```
> LUdecomp(A,L='L',det='d');
```

$$
\begin{bmatrix} 1 & x1 & x1^2 \\ 0 & x2 - x1 & x2^2 - x1^2 \\ 0 & 0 & x1\,x2 - x1\,x3 + x3^2 - x2\,x3 \end{bmatrix}
$$

Any names can be used on the right sides of the equations in the argument sequence.

The lower triangular factor is then:

```
> eval(L);
```

$$
\begin{bmatrix}
1 & 0 & 0 \\
1 & 1 & 0 \\
1 & \dfrac{-x3 + x1}{-x2 + x1} & 1
\end{bmatrix}
$$

and the determinant is

```
> d;
```

$$(x2 - x1)\ (x1\ x2 - x1\ x3 + x3^2 - x2\ x3)$$

Putting this result into the usual form is easy:

```
> factor(");
```

$$- (- x2 + x1)\ (x2 - x3)\ (- x3 + x1)$$

`LUdecomp()` cannot explicitly make use of the sparsity structure of a matrix.

Cholesky decomposition

The real Cholesky decomposition is a more symmetric form of the LU decomposition, and it can be obtained for real positive definite matrices (symmetric $n \times n$ matrices such that $z^t A z > 0$ for every nonzero n-dimensional vector z). The real Cholesky decomposition produces a decomposition in the form $A = LL^t$, where L is lower triangular and t denotes transposition. Maple's function for this is `cholesky()`. To illustrate this function, we first build a positive definite matrix using a technique introduced in the earlier Parameterized Matrices subsection:

```
> l:=(r,s)-> if r=s then 2 elif abs(r-s)=1 then
    -1 else 0 fi;
    l := proc(r,s)
        options operator,arrow;
            if r = s then 2 elif abs(r-s) = 1
                    then -1 else 0 fi
        end
```

The matrix is then defined as follows:

```
> A:=matrix(4,4,1);
```

$$
A := \begin{bmatrix} 2 & -1 & 0 & 0 \\ -1 & 2 & -1 & 0 \\ 0 & -1 & 2 & -1 \\ 0 & 0 & -1 & 2 \end{bmatrix}
$$

and `cholesky()` gives:

```
> cholesky(A);
```

```
[      1/2                                                    ]
[     2                   0             0            0        ]
[                                                             ]
[          1/2         1/2                                    ]
[ - 1/2 2          1/2 6             0            0           ]
[                                                             ]
[                      1/2          1/2                       ]
[         0        - 1/3 6       2/3 3           0            ]
[                                                             ]
[                                   1/2          1/2         ]
[         0            0        - 1/2 3       1/2 5           ]
```

The lower triangle is returned.

If the input matrix had contained a decimal point, the calculations would have been done using floating-point arithmetic, and a floating-point matrix would have been returned.

The `cholesky()` function can handle complex symmetric matrices. However, it cannot factor the more frequently occurring Hermitian matrices, even though the Cholesky decomposition is well defined in the Hermitian positive definite situation.

Another point to note is that `cholesky()` really does demand a positive definite matrix and will not factor merely symmetric (even positive semidefinite) matrices. In addition, the `cholesky()` function cannot explicitly use sparsity in a matrix.

QR decomposition

In the QR decomposition, the matrix A is represented as the product QR where Q is orthogonal or unitary and R is upper triangular. This decomposition arises whenever you do a Gram–Schmidt orthogonalization of a set of linearly independent vectors. In that case, Q contains the orthogonalized vectors, and the columns of R record the linear combinations that produce the original set of vectors.

The QR function is called `QRdecomp()` and it returns the R term of the decomposition. The Q term and some additional information can be obtained by inserting names in the parameter list.

The input matrix A can be symbolic or numeric, and possibly complex. As usual, inclusion of a decimal point in a numerical matrix will ensure that the computations are done using floating-point arithmetic. Symbolic output from `QRdecomp()` can be very long, even for small matrices so we will not show too much of it below. Here is a small symbolic matrix, which we will decompose:

```
> A:=matrix([[x,1],[y,1],[0,1]]);
```

$$
A := \begin{bmatrix} x & 1 \\ y & 1 \\ 0 & 1 \end{bmatrix}
$$

We will decompose this fully to begin with, meaning that Q will contain a full basis for R^3. It is done as follows:

```
> QRdecomp(A,Q='Q');
```

```
[     2    2 1/2                x + y              ]
[ (x  + y )             -----------                ]
[                          2    2 1/2              ]
[                        (x  + y )                 ]
[                                                  ]
[                                   / 2          2\1/2 ]
[                             1/2 |x  - x y + y |     ]
[         0             2        |------------- |     ]
[                                |    2    2    |     ]
[                                \  x  + y    /       ]
[                                                  ]
[         0                         0              ]
```

In this case, Q is inordinately long so we will not print it here. To see it on your screen type

```
eval(Q):
```

using a semicolon in place of the colon. Note that it is a 3×3 matrix.

Thinking again about Gram–Schmidt, we realize that the last column of Q is somewhat irrelevant, and looking at the last row of R above merely strengthens this view. We would then like to compute the decomposition without the extraneous data, which is done using an additional option to QRdecomp():

```
> QRdecomp(A,Q='Q',fullspan=false);
```

```
        [    2       2 1/2                    x + y            ]
        [ (x    + y )                      ----------          ]
        [                                    2      2 1/2       ]
        [                                  (x    + y )          ]
        [                                                       ]
        [                                 / 2              2\1/2 ]
        [                          1/2  |x   - x y + y |         ]
        [           0        2          |-------------|          ]
        [                               |    2      2  |         ]
        [                               \   x    + y   /         ]
```

and this time Q has just two columns (orthogonal of course) as you can easily check.

4.4 Solving linear equations

This section covers the linalg[] package's facilities for solving linear systems of equations, including underdetermined and overdetermined systems. The topics are

* Using linsolve()
* Least Squares Solutions

Using linsolve()

The linalg[] package's function for solving linear systems of equations is called linsolve(). The linsolve() function takes for its arguments the coefficient matrix of the linear system and either a vector or matrix of data ("right-hand sides"). The coefficient matrix can be of any shape. For an inconsistent system, linsolve() returns NULL. In all other cases, linsolve() returns a vector or matrix type.

Nonunique solutions are parameterized using a sequence of global variables called
`_t1[1]`, `_t[2]`, etc., although the details of this scheme can be controlled through
an option. Using `linsolve()` is straightforward. Here is a basic example:

```
> a:=matrix(3,3,[1,1,1,1,3,1,1,1,3]);
```

$$a := \begin{bmatrix} 1 & 1 & 1 \\ 1 & 3 & 1 \\ 1 & 1 & 3 \end{bmatrix}$$

```
> b:=vector([2,4,0]);
```

$$b := [2, 4, 0]$$

```
>linsolve(a,b);
```

$$[2, 1, -1]$$

Underdetermined and overdetermined systems are handled similarly. For example,
here is a rectangular homogeneous underdetermined system and its solution:

```
> a:=matrix(4,3,[4,-2,5,1,-1,1,5,-1,7,-3,1,-4]);
```

$$a := \begin{bmatrix} 4 & -2 & 5 \\ 1 & -1 & 1 \\ 5 & -1 & 7 \\ -3 & 1 & -4 \end{bmatrix}$$

```
> b:=vector([0,0,0,0]);
```

$$b := [0, 0, 0, 0]$$

```
> linsolve(a,b);
```

$$[- 3/2 \ \_t[1], \ - 1/2 \ \_t[1], \ \_t[1]]$$

Here, _t[1] is Maple's name for the free parameter occurring in this underdetermined system.

A recurring difficulty concerns matrices with parameters. For some values of the parameters, you may have something unusual such as a singular matrix, although linsolve() can only give you a solution for the "generic" case. Here is an example:

```
>a:=matrix(3,3,[c,4,1,1,1,1,2,-2,1]);
```

$$
a := \begin{bmatrix} c & 4 & 1 \\ 1 & 1 & 1 \\ 2 & -2 & 1 \end{bmatrix}
$$

```
>b:=vector([1,1,1]);
```

$$
b := [\ 1,\ 1,\ 1\ ]
$$

```
>linsolve(a,b);
```

$$
[\ 0,\ 0,\ 1\ ]
$$

This solution does not even depend on c, yet for c=0 the matrix is not invertible. In fact, the determinant is

```
>det(a);
```

$$
3\ c
$$

Note that the solution that linsolve() found is still a solution even when c=0. However, there are more solutions for the particular case c=0. Of course, they can always be obtained by a separate calculation:

```
> a[1,1]:=0;
```

$$
a[1,\ 1]\ :=\ 0
$$

```
> linsolve(a,b);
```

$$
[\ 3\ \_t[1],\ \_t[1],\ -\ 4\ \_t[1]\ +\ 1\ ]
$$

so that the earlier solution corresponds to _t[1]=0.

Because `linsolve()` returns a vector or matrix type, simplification commands should be applied using `map()`.

The `linsolve()` function will use floating-point arithmetic with partial (row) pivoting if the system of equations contains any floats. You can check that the solution is not unduly contaminated by roundoff errors by repeating the calculation with the value of `Digits`, say, doubled. It is not sufficient to substitute the computed solution into the equations. The result can be close to zero, even though the solution is far from correct. The next chapter contains an example of this phenomenon (Section 5.5).

Least squares solutions

For overdetermined systems that have no ordinary solution, a least squares solution is often acceptable. The `linalg[]` function for this is called `leastsqrs()`. The next example computes the least squares straight line fit for the points $(0, 0)$, $(1, 1)$, and $(1, -1)$:

```
>a:=matrix(3,2,[0,1,1,1,1,1]);
```

$$a := \begin{bmatrix} 0 & 1 \\ 1 & 1 \\ 1 & 1 \end{bmatrix}$$

```
>b:=vector([0,1,-1]);
```

$$b := [\ 0,\ 1,\ -1\ ]$$

```
>leastsqrs(a,b);
```

$$[\ 0,\ 0\ ]$$

so that the equation of the straight line is $y=0$, which is clearly the correct result.

It is often more convenient to enter the equations themselves rather than use matrix notation. The syntax is the following:

```
>leastsqrs({m*0+c=0,m*1+c=1,m*1+c=-1},{m,c});
```

$$\{c\ =\ 0,\ m\ =\ 0\}$$

Both the equations and variables are entered as sets, and the equations come first.

The `leastsqrs()` function will use floating-point arithmetic if the equations contain floating-point coefficients. The earlier comments about the loss of precision and the need to check results with higher-precision arithmetic are particularly important – least squares systems are notorious for being poorly behaved with respect to roundoff errors. One way to perform a check is to factor the coefficient matrix using `QRdecomp()`, then multiply both sides of the least squares equations by Q, and follow this with back substitution using R.

4.5 Bases and spaces

This section covers the `linalg[]` package's functions for finding bases for vector spaces and related computations. The functions fall naturally into three sets. In the first set are functions for finding bases from a given set of vectors. The second set contains functions for performing Gaussian elimination, and functions for finding bases for the null space and range spaces of a matrix form the third set. The topics for this section are

- Computing and Orthogonalizing Bases
- Elimination Functions
- Matrix Spaces

Computing and orthogonalizing bases

Functions in this set can extract a basis from a set of vectors (`basis()`) and also find a basis for the direct sum of spaces (`sumbasis()`) as well as for the intersection of spaces (`intbasis()`). Also in this set is a function for orthogonalizing a basis (`GramSchmidt()`). To illustrate these commands, begin by defining four vectors in three dimensions:

```
>v1:=vector([1,0,0]):
>v2:=vector([0,1,0]):
>w1:=vector([1,1,0]):
>w2:=vector([1,1,1]):
```

The first three functions give the following results:

```
>basis({v1,v2,w1,w2});
```

$$\{v1, \ v2, \ w2\}$$

```
>sumbasis({v1,w1},{v2,w2});
```

$$\{v1, \ v2, \ w2\}$$

```
>intbasis({v1,w1},{v2,w2});
```

$$\{[\ 0,\ 1,\ 0\ ]\}$$

The arguments to these functions can also be presented as lists.

The function `GramSchmidt()` is used as follows:

```
>v1:=vector([1,1,1]):
>v2:=vector([1,1,0]):
>v3:=vector([1,0,0]):
>GramSchmidt({v1,v2,v3});
```

$$\{[\ 1,\ 1,\ 1\ ],\ [\ 1/3,\ 1/3,\ -2/3\ ],\ [\ 1/2,\ -1/2,\ 0\ ]\}$$

The result depends on the order in which the input vectors are presented:

```
>v1:=vector([1,0,0]):
>v3:=vector([1,1,1]):
>GramSchmidt({v1,v2,v3});
```

$$\{[\ 0,\ 1,\ 0\ ],\ [\ 1,\ 0,\ 0\ ],\ [\ 0,\ 0,\ 1\ ]\}$$

Again, you can use either a list or a set to input the vectors.

You can orthogonalize a basis using floating-point arithmetic by inputting one or more floating-point entries in (one or more of) the vectors. Be alert to the possibility of serious roundoff errors in that case – it is well known that the Gram–Schmidt process can be poorly behaved when the input vectors are nearly linearly dependent.

Elimination functions

The main elimination function is `gausselim()`, which applies Gaussian elimination to an input matrix. For a matrix with rational numerical or rational function entries, standard elimination is used. For floating-point (real or complex) matrices, partial pivoting is used, meaning that the pivot row is taken to be the one with the largest absolute leading coefficient. Options to this function let you retrieve the determinant of a leading (square) matrix, and the rank of the matrix as well as let you terminate elimination at a specified column. Here is an example that illustrates the option for returning the rank of the matrix:

```
>A:=matrix(3,2,[a,1,b,0,c,a]);
```

$$
A := \begin{bmatrix} a & 1 \\ b & 0 \\ c & a \end{bmatrix}
$$

```
>gausselim(A,rr);
```

$$
\begin{bmatrix} a & 1 \\ 0 & -\,b/a \\ 0 & 0 \end{bmatrix}
$$

```
>rr;
```

$$
2
$$

Corresponding to `gausselim()`, there is a similar function for Gauss–Jordan elimination called `gaussjord()`. The options to `gaussjord()` are similar to those of `gausselim()`. The `gaussjord()` function has the synonym `rref()`, which is shorthand for row-reduced echelon form.

Of the remaining elimination routines, `ffgausselim()` performs elimination on matrices without permitting fractions. This is a specialized function most useful for matrices with polynomial entries. The two routines `hermite()` and `ihermite()` produce row-reduced echelon forms using only polynomials and only integers, respectively. No fractions appear in the results of these functions.

The function `pivot()` will eliminate the column below a specified entry in the matrix. There is an option that controls the range of rows to which the elimination is applied. To do back substitution on an augmented matrix (augmented by the last column) to which `gausselim()`, `ffgausselim()`, or `gaussjord()` has been applied, use `backsub()`. The two functions `pivot()` and `backsub()` can be used to do a step-by-step solution of a linear system, as the next example illustrates. The first command sets up a random 3×3 matrix and augments it with a data vector.

The following is the system that will be solved:

```
>a:=augment(randmatrix(3,3),vector([1,1,1]));
```

$$a := \begin{bmatrix} -53 & -61 & -23 & 1 \\ -37 & 31 & -34 & 1 \\ -42 & 88 & -76 & 1 \end{bmatrix}$$

Next, choose the (1, 1) element as the pivot and eliminate its column:

```
>a1:=pivot(a,1,1);
```

$$a1 := \begin{bmatrix} -53 & -61 & -23 & 1 \\ 0 & \dfrac{3900}{53} & -\dfrac{951}{53} & \dfrac{16}{53} \\ 0 & \dfrac{7226}{53} & -\dfrac{3062}{53} & \dfrac{11}{53} \end{bmatrix}$$

Then choose the (2, 2) element as the pivot and back substitute to obtain the solution of the equations:

```
>a2:=pivot(a1,2,2);
```

$$a2 := \begin{bmatrix} -53 & 0 & -\dfrac{49237}{1300} & \dfrac{1219}{975} \\ 0 & \dfrac{3900}{53} & -\dfrac{951}{53} & \dfrac{16}{53} \\ 0 & 0 & -\dfrac{15943}{650} & -\dfrac{343}{975} \end{bmatrix}$$

```
>backsub(a2);
```

$$\left[- \frac{1079}{31886}, \frac{727}{95658}, \frac{686}{47829} \right]$$

Matrix spaces

The functions described here are for finding bases for the row and column spaces of matrices (`rowspace()`, `colspace()`, `rowspan()`, and `colspan()`) and their dimension (`rank()`, the rank of a matrix). These functions also find the null space or kernel of a matrix (`nullspace()`).

The functions `rowspace()`, `colspace()`, and `nullspace()` can be applied to matrices of rational functions or rational numbers and numerical matrices. Here is a simple example:

```
>a:=matrix(3,2,[1,1+z,1,0,0,z]);
```

$$a := \begin{bmatrix} 1 & 1+z \\ 1 & 0 \\ 0 & z \end{bmatrix}$$

Its column space is returned as

```
>colspace(a);
```

$$\left\{ \left[1, 0, \frac{z}{1+z} \right], \left[0, 1, -\frac{z}{1+z} \right] \right\}$$

These vectors are certainly independent, but there is a problem with their definition when z=-1. The function `colspan()`, which produces fraction-free results, offers a way around this. Here is what it produces in this instance:

```
>colspan(a);
```

$$\{ [1, 1, 0], [0, -1-z, z] \}$$

No fractions appear in the result and the value of z is immaterial.

Here is an example that shows that `colspan()` can generate difficulties of its own:

```
>a:=matrix(3,3,[u,1,0,0,0,1,1,v,1]);
```

$$
a := \begin{bmatrix} u & 1 & 0 \\ 0 & 0 & 1 \\ 1 & v & 1 \end{bmatrix}
$$

```
>colspace(a);
```

$$
\{[\ 1,\ 0,\ 0\ ],\ [\ 0,\ 0,\ 1\ ],\ [\ 0,\ 1,\ 0\ ]\}
$$

```
>colspan(a);
```

$$
\{[\ u,\ 0,\ 1\ ],\ [\ 0,\ u,\ u\ ],\ [\ 0,\ 0,\ v\,u - 1\ ]\}
$$

If u=0, the first result continues to give a correct basis for the column space (although not if uv=1). In that case, the second result degenerates rather badly, even though "generically" the basis is good. Consequently, by using `colspan()` in place of `colspace()` you might be trading one kind of generically correct result for another. Similar remarks hold for `rowspan()` and `rowspace()`.

The row and column space functions can all take a second argument to return the rank of the matrix. Alternately, the rank can be computed using `rank()`.

Unlike `colspace()` and `rowspace()`, `nullspace()` will accept a general symbolic matrix as its main argument. For instance:

```
>B:=matrix(2,2,[2.0*cos(t),sin(t),2.0*cos(t),sin(t)]);
```

$$
B := \begin{bmatrix} 2.0\ \cos(t) & \sin(t) \\ 2.0\ \cos(t) & \sin(t) \end{bmatrix}
$$

```
>nullspace(B,r);
```

$$\left\{\left[\begin{array}{ccc} 1, & -2. & \dfrac{\cos(t)}{\sin(t)} \end{array}\right]\right\}$$

```
>r;
```

$$1$$

The vector produced forms a basis for the null space. The optional second argument returns the dimension of the null space. You can use the synonym `kernel()` for this function.

4.6 Eigenvalues and eigenvectors

This section covers the `linalg[]` package's routines for computing eigenvalues and eigenvectors. There are options for both analytical and approximate numerical computations. Numerical computations can be especially important for eigenvalues because for matrices of order higher than four, the characteristic equation does not have closed-form solutions except in special cases. The topics are

- Using `eigenvals()` and `eigenvects()`
- Singular Values and Singular Vectors
- Characteristic and Minimum Polynomials

Using `eigenvals()` and `eigenvects()`

The main eigenvalue and eigenvector functions in `linalg[]` are called `eigenvals()` and `eigenvects()`. The `eigenvals()` function works by solving the characteristic equation $\det(A - \lambda C) = 0$. The matrix C is not necessarily the identity matrix, although that is the most common case. To illustrate, here is a computation of the eigenvalues of a 3×3 random skew-symmetric matrix:

```
>a:=randmatrix(3,3,antisymmetric);
```

$$a := \begin{bmatrix} 0 & 79 & 56 \\ -79 & 0 & 49 \\ -56 & -49 & 0 \end{bmatrix}$$

```
>eigenvals(a);
```

$$0, \text{ I } 11778^{1/2}, \text{ } - \text{ I } 11778^{1/2}$$

As they should be, the eigenvalues are purely imaginary complex conjugates, and
one of them is zero. There is, of course, no restriction to real matrix entries. For the
generalized eigenvalue problem, the matrix C is included as a second argument to
`eigenvals()`.

For a matrix of order five or greater, the eigenvalues may have no explicit form. In
that case, `eigenvals()` will return a `RootOf()` expression. Here is an example:

```
>a:=matrix(5,5,0):
>a[1,5]:=-1: a[2,1]:=1: a[2,5]:=1:
>a[3,2]:=1: a[4,3]:=1: a[5,4]:=1:
>eval(a);
```

$$\begin{bmatrix} 0 & 0 & 0 & 0 & -1 \\ 1 & 0 & 0 & 0 & 1 \\ 0 & 1 & 0 & 0 & 0 \\ 0 & 0 & 1 & 0 & 0 \\ 0 & 0 & 0 & 1 & 0 \end{bmatrix}$$

```
>eigenvals(a);
```

$$\text{RootOf}(\_Z^5 - \_Z + 1)$$

You can always obtain a `RootOf()` expression for the eigenvalues by including
the option `implicit` as follows:

```
>a:=matrix(2,2,[1,-1,2,0]);
```

$$a := \begin{bmatrix} 1 & -1 \\ 2 & 0 \end{bmatrix}$$

```
>eigenvals(a,'implicit');
```

$$\text{RootOf}(- \_Z + \_Z^2 + 2)$$

It is desirable to enclose the option in forward quotes because then any existing assignment to the name `implicit` will not affect the option. If the option is omitted in this example, the explicit roots will be returned. The option `radical` will produce explicit eigenvalues where possible. The `eigenvals()` function works for symbolic as well as numerical matrices. For example, the following finds the eigenvalues of an orthogonal matrix:

```
> b:=matrix(2,2,[cos(t),-sin(t),sin(t),cos(t)]);
```

$$b := \begin{bmatrix} \cos(t) & -\sin(t) \\ \sin(t) & \cos(t) \end{bmatrix}$$

```
> eigenvals(");
```

$$\cos(t) + (\cos(t)^2 - 1)^{1/2}, \quad \cos(t) - (\cos(t)^2 - 1)^{1/2}$$

```
> map(simplify,["],symbolic);
```

$$[\cos(t) + I \sin(t), \cos(t) - I \sin(t)]$$

The examples so far have contained exact numerical or symbolic entries. For matrices containing one or more floats (real or complex), the situation is different: `eigenvals()` handles such matrices by numerical methods, so they may not contain symbolic entries. In addition, bear in mind that numerical methods use floating-point arithmetic, so that roundoff errors, possibly accumulated, can affect the results. The easiest way to check for roundoff problems is to redo the calculation with an increased value of `Digits`.

Here is an illustration of the numerical aspects of `eigenvals()`:

```
>a:=matrix(3,3,[2.,-1,0,-1,2,-1,0,-1,2]);
```

$$a := \begin{bmatrix} 2. & -1 & 0 \\ -1 & 2 & -1 \\ 0 & -1 & 2 \end{bmatrix}$$

```
>eigenvals(a);
```

$$.5857864387, \; 2.000000001, \; 3.414213563$$

Checking with the exact eigenvalues shows that these results are in error in the last decimal place. Note that a single float in the matrix is all that is necessary to obtain a floating-point result.

Next, we will see how to use the `linalg[]` package's eigenvector routine `eigenvects()`. The `eigenvects()` function handles the eigenvalues calculation itself; you do not do a separate calculation. Here is an example:

```
>a:=matrix(2,2,[0,1,1,0]);
```

$$a := \begin{bmatrix} 0 & 1 \\ 1 & 0 \end{bmatrix}$$

```
>eigenvects(a);
```

$$[-1, \; 1, \; \{ [\; -1, \; 1 \;] \}], \; [1, \; 1, \; \{ [\; 1, \; 1 \;] \}]$$

The result is a sequence (an expression sequence) of lists. In each list, the first entry is an eigenvalue and the second entry is the algebraic multiplicity of the eigenvalue (its multiplicity in the characteristic equation). The third and last entry in a list is a set of eigenvectors corresponding to the eigenvalue. This is a maximal set of independent eigenvectors for the eigenvalue. Recall from linear algebra that there are usually as many eigenvectors as the algebraic multiplicity, but there can be less.

An eigenvector set can be extracted from its list by noting that it forms the third operand of the list. Any particular eigenvector can then be obtained as an element of the set. The only unusual point is that an expression sequence (in this case, the result of `eigenvects()`) cannot be an argument to `nops()` or to `op()`. Enclose it in set or list brackets before using these functions.

When the eigenvalues cannot be found explicitly, the output of `eigenvects()` will contain `RootOf()`. Even if there is an explicit form for the eigenvalues, the `RootOf()` notation can be clearer than the explicit result, especially when the eigenvalues contain nested radicals. You can force Maple to give the implicit form by using an option. For illustration, here is a small test matrix and its eigensystem:

```
>a:=matrix(2,2,[1,-1,2,0]);
```

$$m := \begin{bmatrix} 1 & -1 \\ 2 & 0 \end{bmatrix}$$

```
>eigenvects(a);
```

$$[1/2 + 1/2 \ I \ 7^{1/2}, 1, \{[\ 1/4 + 1/4 \ I \ 7^{1/2}, 1 \ ]\}],$$

$$[1/2 - 1/2 \ I \ 7^{1/2}, 1, \{[\ 1/4 - 1/4 \ I \ 7^{1/2}, 1 \ ]\}]$$

To obtain the implicit form you do the following:

```
>eigenvects(a,implicit);
```

$$[\text{RootOf}(\_Z^2 - \_Z + 2), 1,$$

$$\{[\ 1/2 \ \text{RootOf}(\_Z^2 - \_Z + 2), 1 \ ]\}]$$

You have to take each `RootOf()` in turn to generate the eigenvalues with their corresponding eigenvectors. Apart from that, the structure of the result follows the previous case.

It is true that a result expressed using `RootOf()` is of limited usefulness when the eigenvalues cannot be found. The problem is most serious with symbolic matrices, because in other cases, numerical methods are available.

For a matrix containing one or more floats and all numerical entries, `eigen-vects()` uses a purely numerical algorithm (the QR algorithm). We will illustrate with the matrix used above to show numerical facilities of `eigen-vals()`:

```
>a:=matrix(3,3,[2.,-1,0,-1,2,-1,0,-1,2]);
```

$$a := \begin{bmatrix} 2. & -1 & 0 \\ -1 & 2 & -1 \\ 0 & -1 & 2 \end{bmatrix}$$

```
>eigenvects(a);

[1.999999999, 1,

                                -9
        {[ .7071067808, .14*10   , -.7071067812 ]}],


        [3.414213562, 1, {[ .5000000000, -.7071067813,
            .5000000001 ]}],


        [.585786435, 1, {[ -.4999999998, -.7071067814,
            -.5000000002 ]}]
```

Note that the eigenvalues are slightly different from before. This is due to the different effects of roundoff in the two algorithms (`fsolve()` and QR). In this example, the coefficient matrix is symmetric, but this is not exploited by `eigenvects()`. However, if a symmetric matrix is created with the symmetric indexing function (in `array()`), the symmetry can be used by `eigenvects()` to improve efficiency.

`eigenvects()` can work on numerical matrices and matrices with rational or algebraic function entries. It does not work with more general matrices, such as the 2×2 orthogonal matrix used above to illustrate `eigenvals()`. Chapter 5 contains more on numerical methods for eigenvalues and eigenvalues.

Singular values and vectors

The `linalg[]` package has a procedure called `singularvals()` for computing the singular values of a matrix. The singular values of a matrix A are the nonzero eigenvalues of A^*A (or of AA^*). This procedure involves nothing new in that it uses `transpose()`, `multiply()`, and `eigenvects()` to do its work. The main library contains a more powerful numerical facility called `Svd()` for computing the singular value decomposition. Chapter 5 illustrates this function.

Characteristic and minimum polynomials

The `linalg[]` package has straightforward facilities for computing the characteristic matrix (`charmat()`) and its determinant, the characteristic polynomial (`charpoly()`), as well as the minimum polynomial (`minpoly()`). The `charpoly()` and `charmat()` functions can be used with `nullspace()` to compute eigensystems in a step-by-step way, as we will illustrate next.

In one-dimensional gas dynamics, the eigenvalues of the matrix

$$\begin{bmatrix} u & \rho & 0 \\ a^2/\rho & u & p_s/\rho \\ 0 & 0 & u \end{bmatrix}$$

are of interest, where u, ρ, and p denote velocity, density, and pressure, respectively, and s denotes entropy. Here, a is the local sound speed. In the following example, we will find the eigenvalues and eigenvectors of this matrix:

```
>A:=matrix(3,3,[u,r,0,a^2/r,u,ps/r,0,0,u]);
```

```
                         [    u     r    0   ]
                         [                   ]
                         [    2              ]
                         [    a          ps  ]
              A  :=  [   ----   u    ----  ]
                         [    r          r   ]
                         [                   ]
                         [    0     0    u   ]
```

The characteristic polynomial is

```
>p:=charpoly(A,x);
```

```
          3       2            2     3     2       2
p := x   - 3 x  u + 3 x u   - u   - a  x + a  u
```

and its roots, the eigenvalues, are given by:

```
>q:=solve(p,x);
```

```
q  :=  u,  - a + u,  a + u
```

The corresponding eigenvectors can now be found as the nullspaces of the characteristic matrices:

```
>seq(nullspace(charmat(A,q[i])),i=1..3);
```

$$
\{[\ 1,\ 0,\ -\ \dfrac{a^2}{ps}\ ]\},\ \{[\ -\ r/a,\ 1,\ 0\ ]\},\ \{[\ r/a,\ 1,\ 0\ ]\}
$$

This technique provides a more explicit approach to eigenvalue and eigenvector calculation.

4.7   Checking matrix properties

Several functions are available for finding sizes and other properties of matrices. To find the dimensions of vectors and matrices, there is `vectordim()` for vectors and `rowdim()` and `coldim()` for matrices. To find out if a matrix is identically zero, you can input it to the function `iszero()`, and you can test for exact equality of matrices using the related function `equal()`. The last two functions will be most useful when you are doing exact computations. Floating-point results are usually contaminated by roundoff errors, which prevent things from being exact. The `fnormal()` function can be very helpful in avoiding this problem.

To find the indexing function of a matrix, you use `indexfunc()`. This function returns NULL if no indexing function has been defined for the matrix.

Two additional tests are possible with `definite()` and `orthogonal()`. The `definite()` function can test positive and negative definiteness and semidefiniteness for both numerical and symbolic matrices. Floating-point matrices can be tested only within the limitations imposed by roundoff errors caused by the testing algorithm. The input matrix must be symmetric for an affirmative result to be possible. The next example shows what happens with a general symbolic matrix:

```
>m:=matrix(3,3,[a,h,g,h,b,f,g,f,c]);
```

$$
m := \begin{bmatrix} a & h & g \\ h & b & f \\ g & f & c \end{bmatrix}
$$

```
>definite(m,positive_def);
```

$$(-a < 0) \text{ and } (-ab + h^2 < 0) \text{ and}$$

$$(-abc + af^2 + h^2c - 2hgf + g^2b < 0)$$

The left sides of the inequalities are the determinants of the principal minors, reflecting the `linalg[]` package's algorithm for testing definiteness. The `definite()` function appears to check for symmetry rather than Hermitian conjugacy and so it is most useful for real matrices.

To test whether a matrix is orthogonal, you can use the function `orthog()`. This function works with numerical and symbolic matrices, with the usual caveat about roundoff. Here is a symbolic example:

```
>a:=matrix(2,2,[cos(x),-sin(x),sin(x),cos(x)]);
```

```
            [ cos(x)   - sin(x) ]
    a  :=  [                    ]
            [ sin(x)     cos(x) ]
```

```
>orthog(a);
```

```
                true
```

This function does not test for unitary matrices.

4.8 Submatrices and supermatrices

This section deals with methods for producing submatrices of a given matrix and with methods for building larger matrices from smaller ones through bordering. The topics are

- Making Submatrices
- Making Supermatrices

Making submatrices

A number of commands enable you to extract submatrices of various species. Two functions, `row()` and `col()`, return any contiguous set of rows or columns from a matrix. The rows or columns are in the form of a matrix. The desired rows or columns are expressed as a range or as a single number if there is only one.

More general submatrices can be extracted using `submatrix()`. In `submatrix()` you can specify a range of rows and columns that define what you want, or you can specify separate lists of rows and columns if they are not contiguous. The following example uses both techniques simultaneously:

```
>a:=matrix(3,3,[1,2,3,4,5,6,7,8,9]);
```

$$
a := \begin{bmatrix} 1 & 2 & 3 \\ 4 & 5 & 6 \\ 7 & 8 & 9 \end{bmatrix}
$$

```
>submatrix(a,2..3,[1,3]);
```

$$
\begin{bmatrix} 4 & 6 \\ 7 & 9 \end{bmatrix}
$$

It is not necessary for the list to be in natural order as the following shows:

```
>submatrix(a,2..3,[3,2]);
```

$$
\begin{bmatrix} 6 & 5 \\ 9 & 8 \end{bmatrix}
$$

To extract a part of a row or column as a vector rather than a matrix, use the function `subvector()`. The arguments are similar to the arguments for `submatrix()`.

Any $(n - 1)$ order minor of an $n \times n$ matrix can be extracted directly using `minor()`. Related to `minor()` are `delrows()` and `delcols()`, that let you delete a specified range (but not list) of rows or columns from a matrix.

Making supermatrices

There are two commands that "paste" matrices together, one for horizontal pasting called `augment()` or `concat()` and one for vertical pasting called `stack()`. The matrices to be pasted must fit together properly: For `augment()` they must have the same number of rows, and for `stack()` they must have the same number of columns. In both cases, a vector can be used to extend the matrix. With `stack()` the vector is interpreted as a row vector and with `augment()` as a column vector. Both functions return a single matrix.

The commands `extend()` and `copyinto()`, already mentioned in Defining Matrices with `linalg[]`, are often used in conjunction with the functions discussed in this section.

4.9 Normal forms

The `linalg[]` package can compute the Frobenius, Smith, and Jordan forms of a matrix. Here is an example of computing a Jordan form:

```
> a:=matrix(3,3,[1,1,0,1,1,0,0,0,0]);
```

$$
a := \begin{bmatrix} 1 & 1 & 1 \\ 1 & 1 & 0 \\ 0 & 0 & 0 \end{bmatrix}
$$

```
> jordan(a,t);
```

$$
\begin{bmatrix} 2 & 0 & 0 \\ 0 & 0 & 1 \\ 0 & 0 & 0 \end{bmatrix}
$$

```
> eval(t);
```

$$
\begin{bmatrix} 2/3 & 2/3 & 1/3 \\ 1 & -1 & -1 \\ 0 & 0 & 1 \end{bmatrix}
$$

The second argument returns the transformation matrix.

The `jordan()` function will automatically switch to floating-point arithmetic to approximate the eigenvalues of the matrix if this is necessary. If that happens, the transformation matrix as well as the Jordan matrix are only approximate.

The Frobenius and Smith forms are computed with `frobenius()` and `smith()`. There is a version `ismith()` for integers. Both of these forms are computed by row operations on the original matrix.

4.10   Reference section

FUNCTIONS FOR DEFINING MATRICES

array	Basic matrix/vector definition
band	Create an n × n band matrix
blockmatrix	Create a matrix from given matrices
diag	Create a block diagonal matrix
entermatrix	Element by element matrix entry
genmatrix	Take the coefficient matrix from equations
indexfunc	Select an indexing function
JordanBlock	Create a Jordan bidiagonal matrix
matrix	`linalg[]` function for defining a matrix
vector	`linalg[]` function for defining a vector
Wronskian	Make the Wronskian of given functions

BUILT-IN MATRICES

fibonacci	Matrix satisfying Fibonacci recurrence
hilbert	Hilbert matrix
randmatrix	Random matrix: selectable distribution
randvector	Random vector: selectable distribution
toeplitz	Toeplitz matrix
vandermonde	Vandermonde matrix

ENLARGING AND REORDERING MATRICES

augment	Join matrices horizontally
copyinto	Copy submatrices to another matrix
extend	Add more rows and columns to a matrix
stack	Join matrices vertically
swapcol	Swap columns of a matrix
swaprow	Swap rows of a matrix

PARTS OF MATRICES AND VECTORS

col	Form a vector from a matrix column
delcols	Delete columns of a matrix
delrows	Delete rows from a matrix
minor	Form a minor
row	Form a vector from a matrix row
submatrix	Take a submatrix
subvector	Take a subvector

FINDING MATRIX PROPERTIES

coldim	Find the number of columns in a matrix
definite	Test positive/negative definiteness
equal	Test equality of matrices
indexfcn	Find the indexing function of a matrix
iszero	Test for a zero matrix
orthogonal	Test for an orthogonal matrix
rowdim	Find the number of rows in a matrix
vectdim	Find the dimension of a vector

MATRIX ALGEBRA AND FUNCTIONS OF MATRICES

matadd	Add matrices
addcol	Add a multiple of one row to another row
addrow	Add a multiple of a column to another column
adjoint	Transposed matrix of cofactors
det	Determinant of a matrix
dotprod	Inner product of vectors
exponential	Exponential of matrix
hadamard	Upper bound on a determinant
htranspose	Hermitian transpose of a matrix
innerprod	Extended inner products of vectors and matrices
inverse	Inverse of nonsingular matrix
mulcol	Multiply a column by a scalar expression
mulrow	Multiply a row by a scalar expression
multiply	Multiply matrices
norm	The norm of a matrix
scalarmul	Multiply a matrix by a scalar expression
trace	Form the trace of a matrix
transpose	Transpose a matrix

DECOMPOSITION FUNCTIONS

cholesky	Cholesky factorization of matrix
LUdecomp	LU decomposition of matrix
QRdecomp	QR decomposition of matrix

SOLVING LINEAR EQUATIONS

leastsqrs	Solve by the least squares technique
solve	Solve general linear systems

EIGENVALUES AND EIGENVECTORS

charmat	Form the characteristic matrix
charpoly	Form the characteristic polynomial
eigenvals	Find the eigenvalues of a matrix
Eigenvals	Inert eigenvalue function
eigenvects	Find the eigenvalues of a matrix
minpoly	Form the minimum polynomial
singularvals	Find singular values and vectors of a matrix

FUNCTIONS FOR COMPUTING BASES

basis	Form a basis for the span of vectors
GramSchmidt	Orthogonalize a set of vectors
intbasis	Form a basis for the intersection of spaces
sumbasis	Form a basis for the sum of spaces

FUNCTIONS FOR SPACES ASSOCIATED WITH MATRICES

colspace	Find the column space of a matrix
colspan	Find the column space in fraction free form
kernel	Find the null space of a matrix
rank	Find the rank of a matrix
rowspace	Find the row space of a matrix
rowspan	Find the row space in fraction-free form

FUNCTIONS ASSOCIATED WITH ELIMINATION

backsub	Do back substitution for triangular equations
ffgausselim	Fraction-free Gaussian elimination
gausselim	Gaussian elimination function
gaussjord	Gauss–Jordan elimination function
hermite	Find the row-reduced echelon form
ihermite	Integer version of hermite
pivot	Choose a pivot row and eliminate

FUNCTIONS FOR PRODUCING NORMAL FORMS

frobenius	Make the Frobenius normal form of a matrix
ismith	Integer version of Smith
jordan	Make the Jordan normal form of a matrix
smith	Make the Smith normal form of a matrix

MAKING MATRICES FROM POLYNOMIALS

bezout	Make the Bezout matrix of polynomials
companion	Make the companion matrix of a polynomial
sylvester	Make the Sylvester matrix of polynomials

MAIN LIBRARY FUNCTIONS FOR MATRICES

&*	Noncommutative multiplication
&*()	Identity matrix, size inferred from context
evalm	Evaluate matrix expressions
Svd	Numerical singular value decomposition
Det	Inert determinant function
Eigenvals	Inert eigenvalue/eigenvector function
Nullspace	Inert nullspace function used with mod
Hermite	Inert hermite function used with mod
Smith	Inert Smith function used with mod

EXERCISES

1. (a) The matrix $A = \begin{bmatrix} -2 & 1 \\ 1 & -1 \end{bmatrix}$ transforms the vector $\begin{bmatrix} 1 \\ (1+\sqrt{5})/2 \end{bmatrix}$ into a multiple of itself. Find this multiple.

   (b) There is another vector of the form $v = \begin{bmatrix} 1 \\ u \end{bmatrix}$ that A transforms to a multiple of itself. Estimate the value of u such that Av is a multiple of v by plotting both v and Av for various values of u.

2. Use Maple to check that any matrix of the form $\begin{bmatrix} \cos(\theta) & -\sin(\theta) \\ \sin(\theta) & \cos(\theta) \end{bmatrix}$ transforms $\begin{bmatrix} a \\ b \end{bmatrix}$ to $\begin{bmatrix} a' \\ b' \end{bmatrix}$ where $a^2 + b^2 = a'^2 + b'^2$.

3. Let

$$A = \begin{bmatrix} 1 & 1 \\ -1 & 2 \end{bmatrix} \qquad B = \begin{bmatrix} 3 \\ -2 \end{bmatrix} \qquad C = \begin{bmatrix} 1 & -1 \\ 2 & 0 \\ 0 & 3 \end{bmatrix}$$

Using Maple, compute all products of the form PQ where P and Q are any of A, B, and C and their transposes, excluding products of a matrix with its transpose. If you give a product PQ as part of your solution, do not also give the product $Q^T P^T$.

4. Solve the equations

$$2x + y - z = 2$$
$$2x + 2y + z = 8$$
$$x - y + 2z = 3$$

using the inverse matrix and check the result with `solve()`.

5. Construct a matrix that is its own inverse and that is not an identity matrix.

6. Use Maple to obtain the generic 2×2 and 3×3 determinants, and verify the following formula: If A is a 3×3 matrix, then

$$\det(A) = a_{11} \det(A_{11}) - a_{12} \det(A_{12}) + a_{13} \det(A_{13})$$

where A_{ij} denotes the 2×2 submatrix of A obtained by omitting the ith row and jth column.

7. Find two solutions, that are not multiples of each other, of the system $Ax = b$, where

$$A = \begin{bmatrix} 0 & 2 & 4 \\ 1 & -1 & -3 \\ 0 & 1 & 2 \end{bmatrix} \qquad b = \begin{bmatrix} 2 \\ -1 \\ 1 \end{bmatrix}$$

(Perform the entire calculation with Maple using the `linalg[]` functions as much as possible.)

8. Let C be a 4×4 matrix. Use Maple to
(a) Compute $\det(C)$.
(b) Compute the sum

$$c_{11} \det(C_{11}) - c_{12} \det(C_{12}) + c_{13} \det(C_{13}) + c_{14} \det(C_{14})$$

where the notation is the same as in question 6.

9. Let $V_{i,j} = x_i^j$ where $x_i = 1/(1+i)$, $i = 0, \ldots, n$. Find the eigenvalues of V when $n = 9$.

10. A formula in linear algebra states that

$$\begin{bmatrix} A & u \\ v & a_{n,n} \end{bmatrix}^{-1} = \begin{bmatrix} A^{-1} + \frac{A^{-1}uvA^{-1}}{\alpha} & -\frac{A^{-1}u}{\alpha} \\ -\frac{vA^{-1}}{\alpha} & \frac{1}{\alpha} \end{bmatrix}$$

where A is a square invertible matrix and u and v are column and row vectors of appropriate orders, and $\alpha = a_{n,n} - vA^{-1}u$. Use Maple to verify this formula and then generalize it to the case where u, v, and α are matrices. Verify your generalization.

11. Using Maple as a computational assistant, for each pair u, v, characterize the solutions of the linear system $Ax = b$, where

$$A = \begin{bmatrix} 0 & u & 1 & 0 & v \\ 0 & 1 & 0 & u & 0 \\ u & 0 & 1 & 0 & 0 \\ 0 & 1 & o & v & 0 \end{bmatrix}$$

and b is arbitrary.

5 The last resort: Numerical methods

The previous chapters covered Maple's functions for a variety of problems in algebra and calculus. On several occasions, we found numerical methods useful either as an adjunct to symbolic techniques or as an independent approach. For example, we used numerical methods in finding roots for nonlinear equations, in numerical integration, and for problems in linear algebra such as solving linear systems and finding eigensystems. Because the main focus of earlier chapters was on symbolic techniques, our treatment of the numerical aspects was necessarily limited. This chapter takes the development of numerical methods a step farther. We will look more closely at the numerical functions discussed in earlier chapters and introduce more of Maple's numerical facilities.

The chapter begins by recalling the essential facts about floating-point arithmetic in Maple. Following this, we retrace our steps from the previous chapters, covering finding roots for nonlinear equations and systems, numerical integration, numerical methods for differential equations, and numerical linear algebra. After that, we move on to some new functions, starting with Maple's Fast Fourier transform (FFT) algorithm. The FFT is used to illustrate a very useful evaluator, `evalhf()`, which speeds up floating-point calculations by using floating-point hardware when it is available. In the remaining sections, we cover a number of approximation-theory topics, including best approximation, splines, and rational approximation.

5.1 Floating-point computing

This section recalls the basic definitions from Chapter 2 and summarizes some general issues of floating-point computing. The two subsections are

- Floating-Point Arithmetic
- Approximate Zeros

Floating-point arithmetic

A float is defined as a pair of integers representing the mantissa (or significand) and the exponent (in base ten) of a number. The number of digits in the mantissa is set by the global variable `Digits`. The number of digits in the exponent is not under user control but is usually around ten. The maximum value for `Digits` is of the order of hundreds of thousands. There is no lower limit (other than one) for `Digits`.

There are two ways to have a calculation performed in floating-point arithmetic. First, if an expression contains a float, Maple will normally perform the evaluation of that expression using floating-point arithmetic, obtaining a floating-point result or results. The second approach uses `evalf()`. Expressions are used as arguments to `evalf()` in the manner illustrated in earlier chapters and below.

An evaluator called `evalhf()` is able to dispatch a limited set of mathematical operations to specialized floating-point hardware, a math coprocessor being the usual example. Unlike `evalf()`, which can operate with any number of significant digits, `evalhf()` computes with the number of digits allowed by the hardware. This value can be obtained through the following command:

```
>evalhf(Digits);
```

$$14.$$

The `evalhf()` function is illustrated in the Using Floating-Point Hardware subsection below.

Because of accumulated roundoff errors, the results of floating-point calculations are, at best, approximations to exactly defined quantities. The accuracy of the approximations depends on several factors. The main determinants of accuracy are the number of significant digits used in the calculations and something called the "condition" of the problem being solved. The worse the condition of the problem, the more significant digits you have to use to achieve a fixed level of accuracy. In practice, it is usually difficult to measure the condition of a problem unless it falls into one of the standard categories. Even then, estimating the condition can cost as much as solving the original problem. The condition of a problem becomes less of an issue when arbitrary precision computing is available because you may be able to compute the same problem with varying amounts of precision and compare the results. Serious roundoff problems will usually show up as excessively different solutions to the same problem. For an illustration see Matrix Inversion in Section 5.5.

Approximate zeros

The quantity computed below would be zero if performed in exact arithmetic rather than in the approximate floating-point arithmetic `evalf()` of the following (the current value of `Digits` is 10, which is the default value):

```
>evalf(arcsin(sqrt(3)/2))-arcsin(evalf(sqrt(3)/2));
```

$$-.1*10^{-8}$$

The discrepancy is caused by roundoff errors and has no mathematical significance. It makes sense to eradicate it. A function called `fnormal()` can be used to zero out this and other roundoff effects:

```
>fnormal(");
```

$$0$$

The `fnormal()` function sets sufficiently small quantities to zero. Sufficiently small means within a tolerance that can be given as an option in `fnormal()`. The default value is $10^{2-\text{Digits}}$. The `fnormal()` function can be applied to lists, sets, series, equations, and other expressions. To apply it to a matrix, `map()` can be used as in the next example (using `linalg[]` functions):

```
>a:=scalarmul(randmatrix(2,2),1.0);
```

$$a := \begin{bmatrix} 41.0 & -58.0 \\ -90.0 & 53.0 \end{bmatrix}$$

```
>a:=multiply(a,inverse(a));
```

$$a := \begin{bmatrix} 1.0000000 & -.4*10^{-7} \\ -.1*10^{-6} & 1.0000000 \end{bmatrix}$$

The off-diagonals are roundoff errors so we will zero them:

```
>map(fnormal,a);
```

$$\begin{bmatrix} 1.0000000 & 0 \\ 0 & 1.0000000 \end{bmatrix}$$

We will use `fnormal()` again in the final example of the next section.

5.2 Nonlinear equations and systems of equations

This section covers the numerical solution of algebraic and transcendental equations and systems. Maple's main function for this is called `fsolve()` and it can be thought of as an extension to `solve()`. The `fsolve()` function behaves differently for ordinary polynomials and more general equations and systems. For a polynomial with real coefficients, it will automatically produce numerical approximations (as accurate as you like) to all the real roots. The complex roots are optional. Here is an example:

```
>fsolve(x^3-1,x);
```

$$1.000000000$$

```
>fsolve(x^3-1,x,complex);
```

$$- .5000000000 + .8660254038 \text{ I},$$
$$- .5000000000 - .8660254038 \text{ I}, \ 1.000000000$$

If the polynomial has one or more complex coefficients, then all of the roots will be computed. To illustrate

```
>fsolve(x^3-I,x);
```

$$.8660254038 + .5000000000 \text{ I},$$
$$- .8660254038 + .5000000000 \text{ I}, \quad - 1.000000000 \text{ I}$$

In contrast to polynomials, `fsolve()` will compute at most one root of a more general equation. To some extent, you can control which root is computed by specifying a range (which can be infinite) where you want to find a solution. The `fsolve()` function will return unevaluated if it cannot find a zero in the specified range. A point to note is that too large a range can cause `fsolve()` to return unevaluated even when a root exists. For example, an equation with many roots is $x = \tan(x)$. Here is a sequence of results that illustrates what happens as the range increases from smaller to larger:

```
>fsolve(x=tan(x),x=0..1);
```

$$0$$

```
>fsolve(x=tan(x),x=0..2);
```

$$0$$

```
>fsolve(x=tan(x),x=0..3);
```

$$fsolve(x = tan(x), \ x, \ 0 \ .. \ 3)$$

```
>fsolve(x=tan(x),x=0..4);
```

$$fsolve(x = tan(x), \ x, \ 0 \ .. \ 4)$$

```
>fsolve(x=tan(x),x=0..5);
```

$$4.493409458$$

In the first two cases, the range is small enough that the zero root was found. In the next two cases, `fsolve()` returned unevaluated. In the last case, it is the second root that `fsolve()` has found. There are no roots between these two. This suggests is that you should constrain `fsolve()` as much as possible (through the range argument) to reduce the chances of missing a root.

The `fsolve()` function can be used to solve nonlinear systems of equations. At most, one solution will be found. For example, here is the numerical solution of the system we solved previously with `solve()`:

```
>sys:={x^2+y^2=1,y-x^2=0};
```

$$sys := \{x^2 + y^2 = 1, \ y - x^2 = 0\}$$

```
>fsolve(sys);
```

$$\{x = -.7861513778, \ y = .6180339887\}$$

To find the other real root, we can constrain x:

```
>fsolve(sys,{x,y},{x=0..1});
```

$$\{y = .6180339887, \ x = .7861513778\}$$

It is necessary to include the set of variable names as the second argument, otherwise the range restrictions are not recognized as such, even though this is not the case with a single equation.

In some cases, `fsolve()` can handle complex solutions to systems of equations. Here is an example:

```
>sys1:={x^2+y^2=1,(x-3)^2+y^2=1};
```

$$sys1 := \{x^2 + y^2 = 1, (x - 3)^2 + y^2 = 1\}$$

```
>fnormal(fsolve(sys1,{x,y},complex));
```

$$\{x = 1.500000000, \ y = 1.118033989 \ I\}$$

The `fnormal()` function is used here to zero out an imaginary roundoff error in x. The results can be easily checked as follows:

```
>assign(");
>lhs(sys1[1]);
```

$$.999999999$$

```
>lhs(sys1[2]);
```

$$.999999999$$

In this sense, the results are correct up to roundoff.

The `fsolve()` function has two additional optional arguments for specifying the number of solutions that will be computed for a scalar polynomial and for controlling the precision of the intermediate calculations.

5.3   Numerical integration

This section examines the accuracy, and some limitations, of Maple's numerical integration functions.

Numerical integration is done using `evalf(Int())`. The inert integration function `Int()` takes any arguments that its active version `int()` takes. Note that if `int()` can compute a result for a definite integral, `evalf(int())` merely provides a floating-point evaluation of the result of `int()`. Otherwise, `evalf(int())` has the same effect as `evalf(Int())`. Maple's approximate integration procedures combine both analytical and numerical techniques. In a finite interval, the basic approach is to compute an expansion of the integrand and use its convergence behavior to detect singularities. Special series and other techniques are used to approximate near the singularities wherever possible. For the rest of the interval, the procedures are Curtis–Clenshaw quadrature, based on integration of Chebyshev series, or a combination of Curtis–Clenshaw quadrature and adaptive techniques. Integrals on infinite ranges are transformed to a finite range, provided the integrand is smooth.

You can control some finer points of the integration by the use of additional arguments to `Int()`. The details can be found by typing `?int[numerical]`.

Here are several examples of numerical integration that illustrate the accuracy of Maple's approach. The first integration is on a finite interval and the function has no singularities (unlike its derivatives):

```
>int(sin(x)^(1/3),x=0..Pi/2);
```

$$\int_{0}^{1/2\,Pi} \sin(x)^{1/3}\, dx$$

```
>evalf(");
```

$$1.293554780$$

The exact value (from a table of integrals) is

```
>evalf(GAMMA(2/3)*GAMMA(1/2)/(GAMMA(7/6)*2));
```

$$1.293554779$$

showing that the numerical result is accurate up to roundoff.

The next example is slightly singular at the endpoints of the domain:

```
>evalf(Int(log(abs(log(x))),x=0..1));
```

$$-.5772156649$$

The exact value of this integral is the negative of Euler's constant, γ, which is

```
>evalf(-gamma);
```

$$-.5772156649$$

Again, the result is accurate to within roundoff.

The next example combines a singularity with an infinite interval:

```
>evalf(Int(cos(x)/x^(1/2),x=0..infinity));
```

$$1.253314137$$

The exact result is

```
>evalf(sqrt(Pi/2));
```

$$1.253314137$$

Generally, the numerical integration routines are good at handling algebraic singularities whether they are inside the domain or on its boundary.

Because of the way `evalf(Int())` handles infinite ranges, it can sometimes produce good results for an infinite interval while being unable to compute the same integrand over a finite interval. This occurs, for instance, with the (highly oscillatory) Fresnel integral in the following example:

```
>evalf(Int(sin(x^2),x=-infinity..infinity));
```

$$1.253314137$$

Maple can also do this analytically:

```
>int(sin(x^2),x=-infinity..infinity);
```

$$\frac{1}{2} \, 2^{1/2} \, Pi^{1/2}$$

```
>evalf(");
```

$$1.253314137$$

so that once again, the numerical solution is about as good as possible. However, a result for a sufficiently large finite interval cannot be obtained:

```
> evalf(Int(sin(x^2),x=-22..22));
Error, (in evalf/int) unable to handle singularity
```

Presumably, the rapid oscillations of the integrand cause the expansion to have convergence difficulties, even though there are no singularities in the finite plane. A result can be obtained if the interval is restricted sufficiently:

```
>evalf(Int(sin(x^2),x=-21..21));
```

$$1.234994322$$

The exact result is

```
>evalf(int(sin(x^2),x=-21..21));
```

$$1.234994306$$

and the numerical result is still good, although not as good as the earlier results. You can always split a finite interval into smaller pieces to get around the problem found in this example, but this is not a very good solution for highly oscillatory integrands.

Finally, here is a piecewise constant integrand, which should be susceptible to numerical integration:

```
>u:=x-> if x<=0 then 0 else 1 fi;

u := proc(x)
        options operator,arrow;
            if x <= 0 then 0 else 1 fi
        end
```

Attempted integration gives the following:

```
>evalf(Int(u(x),x=-1..1));
Error, (in u) cannot evaluate boolean
```

This error results from specifying the argument to the procedure u. The correct syntax and result is

```
>evalf(Int(u,-1..1));
```

$$1.000000000$$

5.4   Ordinary differential equations

In Numerical Methods in Section 3.1, we illustrated the numerical aspects of
`dsolve()`, Maple's ordinary differential solver. We will look at `dsolve( , numeric)` again in this subsection and cover some more details of its operation.

In Section 3.1, we also showed how to use `plots[odeplot]` to obtain graphical
output for differential equations. We will extend these plotting techniques in this
section. The subsections are

- About `dsolve( ,numeric)`
- Plotting Solutions with `plots[odeplot]`

About `dsolve( ,numeric)`

Recall that for numerical computation, `dsolve()` takes three main arguments:
the differential equations and initial conditions in a set, the (set of) variable(s) to
solve for, and the `numeric` option. The equations can be a system of equations of
mixed orders, and enough initial conditions must be provided to fix the solution. The
`dsolve( ,numeric)` function returns a procedure that takes a value of the independent variable as input and returns the corresponding (approximate) value of the
solution. This procedure is actually a fourth-order adaptive Runge–Kutta–Fehlberg
program tailored for your specific system of equations. It can be used to produce a
table of solution values, or it can be used in conjunction with `plots[odeplot]`
to produce graphical output.

Sometimes, the procedure returned by `dsolve( ,numeric)` can return with an
error condition flag. Such error conditions are often related to the adaptivity aspects
of the procedure and arise, for instance, because the requested accuracy could not be
achieved. The remedy is to change either or both of two options that set the accuracy.
These options can be changed from their default values through additional arguments
to `dsolve()`. The help file `?dsolve[numeric]` explains how to do this. You can
also get an error message when you first try to run the solution procedure. This is
usually caused by errors in the input to `dsolve()` such as having the wrong number
or type of initial conditions.

Where possible, `dsolve( ,numeric)` uses `evalhf()` rather than Maple's
floating-point software. However, `evalhf()` can only be used if the current value of
`Digits` is not greater than the number of digits used by the floating-point hardware,
which is found as follows:

```
>evalhf(Digits);
```

14.

In addition to the default Runge–Kutta–Fehlberg algorithm, Maple has a good collection of other ODE solvers. These are accessed by a further option to `dsolve()`. The available algorithms include classical Runge–Kutta methods of orders one through four, and Adams–Bashforth and Adams–Moulton predictor–corrector methods as well as the Taylor series method. There are stiff equation solvers also – Gear's method and the Livermore stiff ODE solver. In addition there is a 7/8th-order adaptive Runge–Kutta solver for use when high efficiency is necessary. These solvers and the numerous options available are covered in the online help system; start by looking in `?dsolve[numeric]`.

Plotting solutions with `plots[odeplot]`

Once you have obtained the procedure for solving the differential equations, it can be used as an argument to `plots[odeplot]` for graphical output. This function can make two- or three-dimensional plots of the solution. The plots can be of any pair or triplet of variables. The main arguments to `plots[odeplot]` are the name of the procedure, the list of variables for plotting, and, possibly, one or more ranges for the variables.

To illustrate solution plotting, here is a method for making phase plane plots. Although `plots[odeplot]` can be used directly for this approach, we will use it to plot the solution in (`t`, `x`, `y`,) space. It can then be projected onto the (`x`, `y`) plane using graphics options. This approach has the advantage of showing the phase plot and the three-dimensional trajectory in the same plot. All you have to change is the orientation.

For illustration, we will use the Van der Pol equation (see Figure 5.1):

$$\frac{d^2x}{dt^2} - (1 - x^2)\frac{dx}{dt} + x = 0$$

written as a system of first-order equations:

$$\frac{dx}{dt} = y, \qquad \frac{dy}{dt} = (1 - x^2)y - x,$$

with initial conditions $x(0) = 0.1$, $y(0) = 0$. First, we will set up the equations and the initial conditions:

```
>eqns:={D(x)(t)=y(t),D(y)(t)=(1-x(t)^2)*y(t)-x(t)};
```

$$eqns := \{D(x)(t)=y(t), \ D(y)(t)=(1-x(t))y(t)-x(t)\}$$

```
>ics1:={x(0)=0.1,y(0)=0};
```

$$ics1 := \{x(0) = .1, \ y(0) = 0\}$$

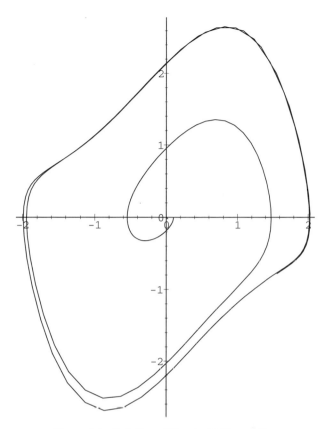

Figure 5.1: Solution of Van der Pol's equation

Here, p1 is the name of the procedure for solving the system:

```
>p1:=dsolve(eqns union ics1,{x(t),y(t)},numeric);
p1 := proc(rkf45_x) ... end
```

The command that follows makes the phase plot and shows the limit cycle of the Van der Pol equation:

```
>plots[odeplot](p1,[t,x(t),y(t)],0..20,numpoints=200
>,orientation=[0,90],color=black,scaling=constrained,
>axes=normal);
```

The graphics options are almost self-explanatory. The numpoints function specifies the number of samples used to make the plot over the time interval $t=0$ to $t=20$;

the orientation is chosen so we are looking along the time axis onto the phase plane; we have chosen axes with equal scales through the `constrained` option, and for printing purposes, the graph `color` is chosen as `black`. (Graphics options are covered in detail in Chapter 6.)

The package `DEtools[]` contains several additional functions for differential equation plots.

5.5 Numerical methods for matrices

In this section, we will amplify our previous discussion of matrix inversion, linear equations, and eigenvalue/eigenvector calculations. Mainly, we want to illustrate the effects of roundoff for linear systems and matrix inversion and look more closely at numerical methods for eigensystems. The subsections are

- Matrix Inversion
- Linear Equations
- Numerical Methods for Eigenproblems
- Singular Values and Vectors

Matrix inversion

The pitfalls of numerical matrix inversion can be easily illustrated using a Hilbert matrix, one of a notoriously roundoff sensitive ("ill-conditioned") family of matrices. In this example, with `Digits` set to 10, the Hilbert matrix of order 10 is converted to floating-point form, inverted, and the result multiplied by the original matrix. The fifth row of the product matrix is then printed out:

```
>a:=map(convert,hilbert(10),float):
>b:=multiply(a,inverse(a)):
>row(b,5);

  [.00001, -.0017, 0, -.06, 1.9, 1.0, -.21, -.6, .3, .1]
```

If you do this experiment without the floating-point conversion, you will get the expected identity matrix for the result. The floating-point calculation, however, has gone badly wrong. Here is the same calculation done with more digits:

```
>Digits:=20:
>a:=map(convert,hilbert(10),float):
```

```
>b:=multiply(a,inverse(a)):
>row(b,5);
```

$$\begin{array}{cccc} -13 & -12 & -10 & -9 \\ [\ .12*10 & ,\ -.4*10 & ,\ -.3*10 & ,\ .2*10 & , \end{array}$$

$$\begin{array}{cccc} & -8 & -8 & -8 \\ 1.0000000006,\ .2*10 & ,\ -.1*10 & ,\ -.4*10 & , \end{array}$$

$$\begin{array}{cc} -8 & -9 \\ .2*10 & ,\ .4*10 &] \end{array}$$

These results are completely different from the previous ones, and roundoff is the culprit. You can see that approximately thirteen digits of accuracy out of the initial twenty have been lost. Because the first calculation was performed with just ten digits, it is not too surprising that the results were essentially meaningless.

This example illustrates what we have said many times: repeating a calculation with a greater setting for Digits is one of the best ways to check the effects of roundoff.

Linear equations

Now we will use the Hilbert matrix of order five to illustrate how a "solution" with a small residual, say $Ax - b$, may not be as accurate as you might guess. Here, we will solve a linear system using both exact and floating-point arithmetic and compare the solutions as well as the residuals:

```
>A:=scalarmul(hilbert(5),1.0):
>b:=randvector(5):
>s1:=linsolve(A,b):
>s2:=multiply(inverse(hilbert(5)),b):
```

The data vector b has random entries between 0 and 99. The names s1 and s2 are the floating-point and exact solutions. Now we will print both residuals, the second one as a check on the approach we are using:

```
>r1:=matadd(multiply(A,s1),b,1,-1);
```

$$r1\ :=\ [\ 0,\ 0,\ -.00006,\ -.00012,\ -.00010\ ]$$

```
>r2:=matadd(multiply(hilbert(5),s2),b,1,-1);
```

$$r2 := [0, 0, 0, 0, 0]$$

The difference between the floating-point and exact solutions is

```
>matadd(s1,s2,1,-1);
```

$$[-.050300, .9799, -4.3319, 6.654, -3.2962]$$

a result that shows errors in the floating-point result. Although the relative errors here are quite small, the lesson is clear: Don't rely on the residuals if you suspect that your problem is not well conditioned relative to the value of Digits.

The only general way to avoid such floating-point difficulties is to compute with more precision, which means using a larger value for Digits. Unfortunately, knowing what value of Digits to use is a matter of trial and error.

Numerical methods for eigenproblems

The main library has an inert eigenvalue function Eigenvals(), which is used with evalf() to compute eigenvalues and eigenvectors numerically (by the QR algorithm). As an illustration of its use, here are some commands to generate a random 3×3 matrix and find its eigenvalues and eigenvectors numerically:

```
>a:=randmatrix(3,3);
```

$$a := \begin{bmatrix} 31 & -26 & -62 \\ 1 & -47 & -91 \\ -47 & -61 & 41 \end{bmatrix}$$

```
>evalf(Eigenvals(a));
```

$$[18.86184938, 106.3995940, -100.2614433]$$

Eigenvals() can take two optional arguments. The first optional argument is used to define the matrix that multiplies the eigenvalue when you want to solve a generalized eigenvalue problem of the form $\det(A - \lambda C) = 0$. It defaults to the identity matrix. The second optional argument is the name of an $n \times n$ matrix, which will return the eigenvectors of the matrix. Confusion can result if the first optional argument is omitted but the second is present. Using an unassigned name for the eigenvector matrix avoids problems. For example:

```
>b:='b':
>evalf(Eigenvals(a,b));
```

$$[\ 18.86184938,\ 106.3995940,\ -100.2614433\ ]$$

```
>eval(b);
```

```
[  -.800696605    .4739300034   .3849771869 ]
[                                            ]
[   .4860642735    .4592432326   .8070632518 ]
[                                            ]
[  -.3605910824   -.7689428068   .4765970428 ]
```

For well-conditioned problems, it is easy to check the result of this eigenvalue–eigenvector computation as follows:

```
>multiply(inverse(b),a,b);
```

```
[                              -6            -7   ]
[ 18.86184932     -.119*10        -.26*10         ]
[                                                 ]
[            -7                              -7   ]
[  -.7*10          106.3995940    -.1*10          ]
[                                                 ]
[            -7               -7                  ]
[  -.2*10          .5*10          -100.2614434    ]
```

This suggests that roundoff has not been entirely insignificant, given that the results were computed using ten-digit arithmetic.

You can run into a difficulty with what is called the remember table of `evalf()` if you reuse the names for new matrices. For example, carrying on from the example above, suppose a is redefined as follows:

```
>a:=matrix(2,2,[0,1,1,0]);
```

$$a := \begin{bmatrix} 0 & 1 \\ 1 & 0 \end{bmatrix}$$

Computing as before gives the following:

```
>evalf(Eigenvals(a,'b'));
```

```
[ 18.86184938, 106.3995940, -100.2614433 ]
```

This somewhat disconcerting effect results from Maple "remembering" the result it previously obtained for a. There are good reasons for wanting to remember some kinds of results, but not here! The `remember` option is one that you can include when you write Maple procedures. Right now, we need to use a procedure called `forget()`, which you have to load first as it is not part of the main library:

```
>readlib(forget);
```

```
proc(f) ... end
```

```
>forget(evalf);
>b := 'b':
>evalf(Eigenvals(a,'b'));
```

```
[ 1.000000000, -1.000000000 ]
```

```
>eval(b);
```

$$\begin{bmatrix} .7071067812 & -.7071067812 \\ .7071067812 & .7071067812 \end{bmatrix}$$

This time the answers are correct.

You will find that enclosing a in forward quotes is not sufficient to remove it from the remember table. However, b is not in the remember table and can be cleared by forward quoting it. There is more on remember tables and related topics in Section 11.3.

When a real matrix has complex eigenvectors, Eigenvals() returns the eigenvectors in the form of a matrix of the same order as the input matrix, with the real and imaginary parts of an eigenvector occupying adjacent columns. To interpret this, recall that the complex eigenvalues of a real matrix occur in conjugate complex pairs and the corresponding eigenvectors are also complex conjugates. The eigenvectors appear in the same order as their corresponding eigenvalues. Here is a simple illustration:

```
>z:=matrix(2,2,[0,1,-1,0]);


                              [  0   1 ]
                      z  :=  [          ]
                              [ -1   0 ]
>evalf(Eigenvals(z,'zvec'));


          [ 1.000000000 I,  - 1.000000000 I ]
```

and the eigenvector matrix becomes

```
>eval(zvec);
                    [ 1.000000000   0 ]
                    [                 ]
                    [      0        1 ]
```

The correct eigenvectors are complex. Corresponding to the first eigenvalue, I is the complex eigenvector (1,I) obtained from the columns of the matrix. The second eigenvalue is the complex conjugate of the first as we expected, and reading from the matrix, we find the conjugate complex eigenvector (1,-I). The eigenvectors are orthogonal with respect to the standard Hermitian inner product, as they must be because the initial matrix is skew-symmetric (skew Hermitian).

If a matrix has one or more complex entries, the eigenvectors are printed in full, avoiding shorthand. For example, the following forms a small complex matrix and finds its eigensystem:

```
>forget(evalf):
>a:=matadd(randmatrix(3,3),scalarmul(randmatrix(3,3),I));
```

```
            [ 63 + 77 I    57 + 66 I   - 59 + 54 I ]
            [                                       ]
    a  :=  [  45 - 5 I   - 8 + 99 I   - 93 - 61 I ]
            [                                       ]
            [ 92 - 50 I    43 - 12 I   - 62 - 18 I ]
```

```
>b:='b':
>evalf(Eigenvals(a,b));
```

$$[\ - 77.88670608 - 53.5955488 \ I,$$

$$69.37863342 + 144.0612493 \ I,$$

$$1.508072650 + 67.53429966 \ I \ ]$$

Here are the eigenvectors in all their gory detail:

```
>eval(b);
```

$$[\ - .2434383129 \ - \ .1641436092 \ I,$$
$$- \ .3403303554 \ + \ .7768577166 \ I,$$
$$.2145680161 \ + \ 1.106265273 \ I]$$

$$[.4382475902 \ - \ .3825315313 \ I,$$
$$- \ .2961732127 \ + \ .02486705756 \ I,$$
$$- \ .6188404297 \ - \ 1.053305541 \ I]$$

$$[.7481141321 \ - \ .1254136572 \ I,$$
$$.3318912201 \ + \ .2993187174 \ I,$$
$$.6011516877 \ + \ .0277580906 \ I]$$

The eigenvectors are normalized to be unit vectors (excluding roundoff effects):

```
>q:=col(b,1):
>multiply(htranspose(q),q);
```

$$.9999999995$$

Singular values and vectors

Maple has a main library function for numerically computing singular-value decompositions called `Svd()`. This function, which is inert and used as an argument to `evalf()`, can compute the singular values and the left- and right-singular vectors of rectangular matrices. `Svd()` works only for numerical matrices and finds the singular values and vectors using floating-point operations. In the example that follows, the singular values are returned together with the left- and right-singular vectors, which are saved in the arrays U and V.

```
>a:=array([[1,0,-1],[0,1,1]]);
```

$$
a := \begin{bmatrix} 1 & 0 & -1 \\ 0 & 1 & 1 \end{bmatrix}
$$

```
>s:=evalf(Svd(a,U,V));
```

$$
s := [\ 1.732050808,\ 1.000000000\ ]
$$

```
>eval(U);
```

$$
\begin{bmatrix} -.7071067814 & .7071067808 \\ .7071067808 & .7071067814 \end{bmatrix}
$$

```
>eval(V);
```

$$
\begin{bmatrix} -.4082482907 & .7071067805 & .5773502691 \\ .4082482901 & .7071067816 & -.5773502691 \\ .8164965811 & .6*10^{-9} & .5773502691 \end{bmatrix}
$$

Note that the singular values are returned in a list.

If you want to check the decomposition, you must first put the singular values into a rectangular diagonal matrix of the same order as the original matrix. Here is one way to do this:

```
>DD:=array(diagonal,1..2,1..3,{seq((i,i)=s[i],i=1..2)});
```

$$
D := \begin{bmatrix} 1.732050808 & 0 & 0 \\ & & \\ 0 & 1. & 0 \end{bmatrix}
$$

Now the check proceeds as follows:

```
>multiply(U,DD,transpose(V));
```

$$
\begin{bmatrix} 1.000000000 & -.3*10^{-9} & -1.000000000 \\ & & \\ -.3*10^{-9} & 1.000000000 & 1.000000000 \end{bmatrix}
$$

Apart from the inevitable roundoff effects, this agrees with the initial matrix.

You can choose to save the left- or right-singular vectors alone by giving the name of the matrix for the result and the option `left` or `right` as appropriate. You can also discard both sets of singular vectors by not giving any destination in the argument list of `Svd()`.

5.6   Fast Fourier transform

Maple has a pair of functions for computing discrete Fourier transforms for data sets of length $n := 2m$ where m is a positive integer. The formula for the transform is

$$
F_k = \sum_{j=0}^{n-1} f_j e^{2\pi ijk/n}
$$

The Maple function `FFT()` efficiently computes these sums. The inverse transform is performed by `iFFT()`. To illustrate these fast transforms, we will compute the convolution of two vectors. The first two lines set up the real and imaginary parts of the vectors. In both cases, the imaginary parts are zero. The output reproduces the input and is suppressed.

```
>sr:=array([1,2,1,2]): si:=array([0,0,0,0]):
>tr:=array([0,1,0,1]): ti:=array([0,0,0,0]):
```

FFT() takes as arguments the exponent m of the number of coefficients and the arrays containing the real and imaginary parts of the data to be transformed. These arrays are overwritten by the real and imaginary parts of the coefficients that FFT() computes. The printed output from FFT() is just the exponent m and is suppressed in the next step:

```
> readlib(FFT):
> FFT(2,sr,si): FFT(2,tr,ti):
```

The computed coefficients arc found by combining the real and imaginary parts of the output. In this case, the imaginary parts are zero (due to an evenness property of the input data):

```
>linalg[matadd](sr,si,1,I);
```

$$[\ 6,\ 0,\ -2,\ 0\ ]$$

```
>linalg[matadd](tr,ti,1,I);
```

$$[\ 2,\ 0,\ -2,\ 0\ ]$$

According to the convolution theorem, the pointwise product of these vectors is the transform of their convolution. Manually forming this product and forming the inverse transform writes the results into the two arrays.

```
>ur:=array([12,0,4,0]): ui:=array([0,0,0,0]):
>iFFT(2,ur,ui):
```

The final result is then

```
>linalg[matadd](ur,ui,1,I);
```

$$[\ 4,\ 2,\ 4,\ 2\ ]$$

which is correct. (Note that readlib(FFT); also loads iFFT()). This calculation used only integer arithmetic. Most of the time, FFT() and iFFT() are used as floating-point functions. Inputting the data as floats will ensure that a floating calculation is performed. These functions can be used with evalhf(), as we illustrate next.

5.7   Using floating-point hardware

Maple does floating-point computations using software in association with the computer's integer facilities. This accounts for the ease with which you can specify the number of digits in a computation. It also gives numerical results that are machine independent. The drawback of this approach is the loss of speed compared with using the computer's floating-point hardware, typically a math coprocessor. In making this comparison, bear in mind that the number of digits carried by the floating-point hardware is fixed so that the hardware approach has little flexibility. Still, it would be nice to be able to use the floating-point hardware as there are likely to be good-sized speed increases to be had. Maple provides a function called evalhf() for just that purpose.

The argument to evalhf() is a single expression. The input expression is severely circumscribed in terms of what it can contain, being limited essentially to purely numerical operations. This is to be expected when you remember that the various subexpressions are going to be fed to (for example) a math coprocessor. It does mean that structural operations and the like are ruled out, although Boolean operations are permitted. Typical uses for evalhf() would be numerical linear algebra and function evaluation. An example using function evaluation occurs within Maple itself – the graphics routines use evalhf() to compute function values for plotting.

Most of Maple's functions cannot be used with evalhf() precisely because they are likely to contain structural and other operations that have no simple numerical interpretation. The main use for evalhf() is most likely with your own specially written procedures. However, one function that can work with evalhf() is FFT(), which was described above. FFT() provides a useful function for testing the speed increases available from evalhf(). To show what can be expected, the example that follows compares the times to compute a 256-point FFT, first using evalf() and then using evalhf(). The timings are done using the Maple function time() (see Section 8.2), which gives the elapsed time from the start of the session.

First the data is generated as a vector, using the shorthand procedures supplied in linalg[], then FFT() is read from the library.

```
>f:=x->evalf(ln(x));
```

$$f := x -> evalf(ln(x))$$

```
>a:=linalg[vector](256,f):
>b:=linalg[vector](256,0):
>readlib(FFT);
```

```
proc(m,x,y) ... end
```

The data generated in this way has zero imaginary part and has real parts given by the logarithm indicated.

Next, the CPU time since the start of the session is read, and the first calculation is performed and timed. Then the second calculation is done in a similar way.

```
>start:=time(): FFT(8,a,b): time()-start;
```

$$5.000$$

The names a and b must be reset because they are overwritten in `FFT()`.

```
>a:=linalg[vector](256,f):
>b:=linalg[vector](256,0):
>start:=time(): evalhf(FFT(8,a,b)): time()-start;
```

$$1.000.$$

These times are given to the nearest second and show that the `evalhf()` calculation is around five times faster than the regular calculation. How many digits did `evalhf()` carry during this calculation? The answer is

```
>evalhf(Digits);
```

$$14.$$

5.8 Interpolation and approximation

The functions in this section allow you to easily form several kinds of polynomial and rational approximations to mathematical functions and data. The subsections are

- The Interpolation Polynomial
- Cubic and Other Spline Approximations
- Bernstein Polynomial Approximations
- Rational Function Approximations
- Min-Max Approximations

The interpolation polynomial

The function `interp()` forms the unique polynomial of degree n or less that interpolates the data set (x_i, y_i), $i = 1, 2, \ldots, (n + 1)$. As an example of the use of `interp()`, here is a method for determining the weights in Gaussian quadrature formulas when the nodes are given. For example, with weight function $w(x) = 1$, the nodes are given by the zeros in $(-1, 1)$ of the Legendre polynomial of appropriate order. If you want a formula exact for all seventh-degree polynomials, say, then you need the zeros of the fourth-degree Legendre polynomial. These zeros can be found using `fsolve()`. The required polynomial is contained in Maple's orthogonal polynomial package `orthopoly[]` under the name P.

The first step, then, is to form the polynomial and to find its zeros:

```
>p:=orthopoly[P](4,x);
```

$$p := 35/8 \ x^4 \ - \ 15/4 \ x^2 \ + \ 3/8$$

```
>nodes:=[fsolve(p)];
```

```
nodes :=

    [-.8611363116, -.3399810436, .3399810436, .8611363116]
```

The zeros have been placed in a list. The `interp()` function can accept data in the form of a list or of a vector.

To find the Gaussian quadrature weights, the Lagrangian basis polynomials that take the value 1 at one node and zero at the others must be integrated over the interval $(-1, 1)$. The basis polynomials are formed with `interp()`. To find the first basis polynomial, the call is the following:

```
>q:=interp(nodes,[1,0,0,0],x);
```

$$q := \ - \ .9275675067 \ x^3 \ + \ .7987620635 \ x^2 \ + \ .107214847 \ x \ - \ .092326598$$

The data lists are the first and second arguments, and the name of the variable in the polynomial is the third argument. The `interp()` function has no optional arguments.

To obtain the weight for the leftmost node, this polynomial must be integrated. The result is

```
>int(q,x=-1..1);
```

$$.3478548463$$

For the second node, the corresponding calculations are

```
>q:=interp(nodes,[0,1,0,0],x);
```

$$q := 2.349431172 \ x^3 \ - \ .798762065 \ x^2 \ - \ 1.742234190 \ x$$
$$+ \ .5923265986$$

```
>int(q,x=-1..1);
```
$$.6521451539$$

By symmetry considerations, the weights on the two positive nodes are the same as on the corresponding negative nodes. As a simple check on the results, the weights do indeed sum to 2, as they must.

It would be desirable to automate the computation of the weights. This can be done with the help of a few basic programming tools.

Cubic and other spline approximations

Maple has a function for efficiently computing natural cubic splines and spline functions of other degrees (in one dimension). Here, we will look at the cubic case. The other splines are obtained through an option to `spline()`.

Recall that a cubic spline is a twice continuously differentiable piecewise cubic that interpolates a table of data. Natural cubic splines are distinguished by the following property: of all twice continuously differentiable functions f interpolating the same data in an interval $[a, b]$, they have the least "curvature" or "oscillation" in the sense that they minimize

$$I(f) = \int_a^b f''(x)^2 \, dx$$

This property is the main reason for the ubiquity of cubic splines in graphics and engineering applications.

The `spline()` function is called much like `interp()` with two lists and a name for the independent variable. Its output is more complicated because of the piecewise definition of the spline. Here is a straightforward illustration. We will interpolate the function x^3 at a uniformly spaced set of four nodes in [0,1].

```
>readlib(spline);
proc(X,Y,z,d) ... end

>X:=[seq(i/3,i=0..3)];
```

$$X := [0, 1/3, 2/3, 1]$$

```
>Y:=[seq(X[i]^3,i=1..4)];
```

$$Y := [0, 1/27, 8/27, 1]$$

```
> spline(X,Y,x);
```

$$\text{PIECEWISE}([1/45\ x + 4/5\ x^3,\ x < 1/3],$$

$$[-\ 2/45 + \frac{19}{45}\ x - 6/5\ x^2 + 2\ x^3,\ x < 2/3],$$

$$[\frac{62}{45} - \frac{269}{45}\ x + 42/5\ x^2 - 14/5\ x^3,\ \text{otherwise}])$$

The three cubics listed are the components of the spline in the natural left-to-right order. (Numerical methods trivia question: Why is the cubic spline not equal to x^3?) To evaluate the spline at a point, say $x = 1/3$, use `subs()`:

```
> simplify(subs(x=1/3,"));
```

$$1/27$$

A better approach is illustrated at the end of Section 2.6.

Bernstein polynomial approximations

Given a continuous function f defined in the interval [0,1], its Bernstein polynomial approximation of degree n is defined by

$$B_m(x) = \sum_{k=0}^{n} f\left(\frac{k}{m}\right) \binom{m}{k} x^k (1-x)^{n-k}.$$

These polynomials have many uses, for example, in computational geometry under the name of Bezier curves.

To use Maple to construct Bernstein polynomials, the function to be approximated must be defined as a procedure. Here we will use procedures defined by arrow functions. The `bernstein()` function returns unevaluated if you try to use a simple expression instead of a procedure for the function. For example, the following attempts direct use of the `sin` function

```
>readlib(bernstein);
proc(n,f,x) ... end
>bernstein(4,sin(x),x);
                bernstein(4, sin(x), x)
```

The correct way is as follows:

```
>bernstein(4,sin,x);
```

$$(4 \ x \ - \ 12 \ x^2 \ + \ 12 \ x^3 \ - \ 4 \ x^4) \ \sin(1/4)$$

$$+ \ (6 \ x^2 \ - \ 12 \ x^3 \ + \ 6 \ x^4) \ \sin(1/2)$$

$$+ \ (4 \ x^3 \ - \ 4 \ x^4) \ \sin(3/4) \ + \ x^4 \ \sin(1)$$

Usually, you need to form the Bernstein polynomial that interpolates a table rather than an explicit function. Here is an example that forms the quadratic Bernstein polynomial, which interpolates generic data at the independent variable values $x = 0, 1, 2$. First, we will make the procedure to return the data values:

```
>f:=x->if x=0 then f[0] elif x=1/2
             then f[1] else f[2] fi;

f := proc(x)
        options operator,arrow;
            if x = 0 then f[0]
            elif x = 1/2 then f[1]
            else f[2]
            fi
        end
```

The procedure merely returns one of three values depending on whether it is called with the leftmost, middle, or rightmost point of the interval. A call to bernstein() now gives

```
>bernstein(2,f,x);
```

$$(1 - 2x + x^2)\ f[0] + (2x - 2x^2)\ f[1] + x^2\ f[2]$$

To finish the job, it is nice to arrange this in powers of x:

```
>collect(",x);
```

$$(f[0] - 2\ f[1] + f[2])\ x^2 + (-2\ f[0] + 2\ f[1])\ x + f[0]$$

You may recognize the finite differences in the coefficients of this result. A similar approach can be used with purely numerical tables.

Rational function approximations

This subsection illustrates Maple's functions for making Padé approximations and rational collocation (point-matching) functions. Recall that a Padé approximation to a function f is a rational function with degrees m and n in the numerator and denominator that matches f through its $(m + n)$th derivative at some fixed point. The standard way to make a Padé approximation is to match an appropriate rational function to the Taylor approximation through $(m+n)$th derivatives of f. This means that the first step in the calculation is to find the Taylor approximation. In Maple, you can either perform the steps separately or use a function called numapprox[pade] that does the steps for you.

First, we will illustrate the use of numapprox[pade]. Here is a Padé approximation for the exponential:

```
>pade(exp(x),x=0,[2,2]);
```

$$\frac{1 + 1/2\ x + 1/12\ x^2}{1 - 1/2\ x + 1/12\ x^2}$$

The second argument is the matching point and the third contains the degrees m and n. In the second argument the "=0" is assumed if it is omitted; values other than 0 must appear explicitly.

Now we will make a related approximation the hard way. The first step is to make the expansion, and we do have to specify its order:

```
>series(exp(-x),x,5);
```

$$1 - x + 1/2\ x^2 - 1/6\ x^3 + 1/24\ x^4 + O(x^5)$$

The Padé approximation is formed by a `convert()`:

```
>convert(",ratpoly);
```

$$\frac{1 - 1/2\ x + 1/12\ x^2}{1 + 1/2\ x + 1/12\ x^2}$$

Note that we did not specify m and n explicitly. Maple follows a standard convention in that the degrees are chosen to differ by 0 or 1 with the numerator having the higher degree in the second case. If you want to use different degrees, they can be third and fourth arguments to the `convert( ,ratpoly)`.

Matching values of f at $(m + n + 1)$ distinct points is analogous to polynomial interpolation (and is polynomial interpolation when $n = 0$). There are several methods for forming such rational interpolation functions. One of the best known is Thiele's method, which takes $m = n$. Thiele's approach generalizes Newton's divided-difference technique, which builds a sequence of interpolating polynomials of increasing degree. In the rational-function setting, the difference table is replaced by what is called a reciprocal difference table, and the intermediate results appear as a sequence of continued fractions. These calculations are done in the function `thiele()`. To illustrate `thiele()`, let's approximate e^{-x} again, this time by equal-interval rational interpolation in [-1,1]. First, we will compute the interpolation table in two lists, X and Y:

```
>X:=[seq(-1+i*(2./4),i=0..4)];
   X := [-1., -.5000000000, 0, .500000000, 1.000000000]

>Y:=[seq(exp(X[i]),i=1..5)];
Y := [.3678794412, .6065306597, 1, 1.648721271,
      2.718281828]
```

Next, we call `thiele()` to form the interpolant. The `normal()` function is used here to clear the continued fraction representation:

```
>readlib(thiele):
>normal(thiele(X,Y,x));
```

$$\frac{7.627052840 + 3.812241098\ x + .6224593260\ x^2}{7.627052841 - 3.812241129\ x + .6224593412\ x^2}$$

The coefficients are slightly different in the numerator and denominator: this may be a roundoff effect.

To compare the numerator, say, with the numerator of the Padé approximation do the following:

```
>numer(")/coeff(numer("),x^2);
```

$$12.25309433 + 6.124482257\ x + .9999999999\ x^2$$

In this form, the numerator is directly comparable with the numerator of the Padé approximation.

Min-max approximations

Maple has a function `numapprox[minimax]` for computing the best rational (including polynomial) approximation of given degrees, to functions defined on finite intervals. Here, best means having the least possible pointwise error relative to all rational functions of the same degrees.

Here is an example that estimates the best linear approximation to the exponential in [0, 1]:

```
> with(numapprox):
> minimax(exp,0..1,1);
```

$$x \to .8941114810 + 1.718281828\ x$$

The first argument is the function to be approximated. It must be represented as a procedure or operator. The second argument is the range of the independent variable, and the third argument specifies the degree of the polynomial approximation. For a rational approximation, this is specified as a list. There are two optional arguments; the first specifies a weight function for measuring the error (default 1) and a name for returning the maximum error.

Here is another example that computes the best (2, 2) rational approximation to the exponential function in $[-1, 1]$.

```
> minimax(exp,-1..1,[2,2],1,'err');
```

$$
x \rightarrow \frac{.9626684195 + (.4896106850 + .08261833500\ x)\ x}{.9625985884 + (-.4727261450 + .07480282320\ x)\ x}
$$

```
> e := normal("(x));
```

$$
e := \frac{.9626684195 + .4896106850\ x + .08261833500\ x^2}{.9625985884 - .4727261450\ x + .07480282320\ x^2}
$$

To compare the numerator with the previous approximations' numerators, do the following:

```
> numer(")/coeff(numer("),x^2);
```

$$
11.65199492 + 5.926174681\ x + 1.000000000\ x^2
$$

The maximum error of the rational function is given as

```
> err;
```

$$
.000086927
$$

5.9   Reference section

FUNCTIONS FOR INTERPOLATION AND APPROXIMATION

`bernstein`	Make a Bernstein polynomial
`bspline`	Make a B-spline function
`chebyshev`	Make a Chebyshev expansion
`convert( ,ratpoly)`	Convert from a series to a rational polynomial
`interp`	Lagrangian interpolating polynomial
`minimax`	Find a best rational approximation (`numapprox[]`)
`pade`	Form a Padé approximation (`numapprox[]`)
`spline`	Make a spline interpolant
`thiele`	Make a rational-function interpolant

FUNCTIONS FOR NUMERICAL COMPUTING

`dsolve(, numeric)`	Numerical ODE solver
`evalf(Int)`	Numerical integration
`evalhf`	Evaluate using floating-point hardware
`FFT`	Fast Fourier transform function
`fsolve`	Nonlinear algebraic equation solver
`iFFT`	Inverse fast Fourier transform
`plots[odeplot]`	Graph solutions from `dsolve(, numeric)`

FUNCTIONS FOR NUMERICAL LINEAR ALGEBRA

`evalf(Eigenvals)`	QR algorithm for eigensystems
`evalf(Svd)`	Find singular values and vectors
`linsolve`	Linear equation solver: include float(s) for numerical computation

6 Graphs and graphics

We introduced Maple graphics in Section 4 of Chapter 1. In that section we discussed the basic strategies for plotting curves and surfaces and mentioned that most of Maple's graphics facilities are in the functions `plot()` and `plot3d()` and in the `plots[]` package. This chapter provides a more comprehensive look at Maple's graphics tools and ways to use them.

The chapter starts with a section containing general information about plotting with Maple. Following this are two sections on two-dimensional graphics and three-dimensional graphics. In both these sections, we begin with a short discussion of the options available in the basic plot commands (`plot()` and `plot3d()`, respectively) and continue with illustrations of the additional plots and facilities provided in `plots[]`. We then cover techniques for animating plots. Following that, there is a section on `PLOT` structures. A `PLOT` structure is a Maple data structure that results from a `plot()` or `plot3d()` command. It contains the mathematical data from which the screen image is created. It can be quite handy to know how to modify `PLOT` structures, and we will look into that.

Where appropriate, the examples in this chapter assume that the command `with(plots):` has been issued.

6.1 Graphics in general

In this section we will cover some aspects of plotting that apply to more or less all plots, whether two- or three-dimensional. The topics are

- Interfaces for Graphics
- How to Plot Procedures and Mappings
- Assigning Plots

Interfaces for graphics

The most powerful type of interface for graphics work is, not surprisingly, the GUI
or Graphical User Interface. Specific examples are the X interface, which runs under
the UNIX operating system, and Microsoft Windows. In these environments, Maple
assigns each plot to its own standard window. Normally, the plot windows are re-
sizable and a number of options are available through menu choices. Selection of
options and other features is usually done with a mouse.

GUIs are not the only interfaces supported by Maple. An example of a non-GUI
would be Maple's MS-DOS interface. For graphics, this interface imitates a GUI
by providing menus (activated from the keyboard). The menus control more or the
less the same options as the typical GUI. However, the graphic occupies the entire
screen and can neither be viewed simultaneously with the command that generated
it nor resized. The graphs are similar in quality to those of a GUI running on the
same hardware, and both interfaces can produce, say, Postscript output.

You may also encounter a "terminal" interface, especially when computing by
modem. Usually, you are limited to character plots in this setting. There is not much
to say about terminal graphics except, perhaps, that they truly are terminal!

One reason for this digression on interfaces is that a number of graphics options
are now available in menus and no longer have to be typed. For interactive work, this
menu/mouse approach is overwhelmingly more flexible, and some of the illustrations
in this chapter were changed interactively. In these cases, the picture on your screen
may be slightly different from the one in the text. Still, it should be easy to reproduce
the text picture. Most of the changes from the initial plot are changes of viewpoint
only.

How to plot mappings and procedures

In Section 1.4, we discussed how to plot functions defined by formulas. For plotting
mappings such as arrow functions as well as functions defined by more general
procedures, the syntax is slightly different. The essential point is that if no arguments
are given for the mapping(s), then for the independent variable(s) the range(s) should
be specified as range expressions and not as equations. For example, the following
forms and plots a pair of arrow functions (see Figure 6.1):

```
>f:=x->x*ln(x):
>g:=x->ln(x):
>plot({f,g},0..2,-1.5..1.5);
```

In this example, the dependent variable is also restricted by a range. It is permissible to
use an equation for this range. Below, we show how to label the graphs in Figure 6.1.

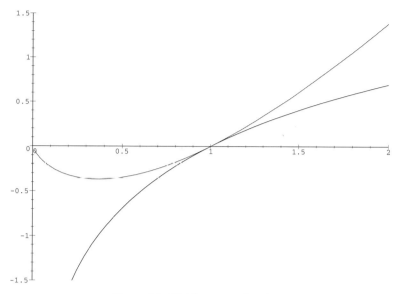

Figure 6.1: Plotting arrow functions

Functions defined by more general procedures are treated in a similar way. For example, the procedure called `sin`, which we normally deal with in its "formula" style `sin(x)`, would be plotted as

```
>plot(sin,0..2*Pi);
```

producing the plot shown in Figure 6.2. The point to remember is that it is an error to use a name for the independent variable range in a plot of a procedure that is not evaluated as a formula.

Assigning plots

Previously, we plotted graphs directly to the computer screen. To obtain the underlying data structure of a graphic, you simply assign it to a name. The effect is to assign the name to a Maple data structure and type called a `PLOT` structure. The `PLOT` structure contains all the information that is needed to render the graph(s). It is often possible to explicitly modify `PLOT` structures to achieve some special effect. This aspect is covered in Section 6.6. Another reason to assign plots is to display different kinds of graphs in a single picture. This is covered in the Section 6.2.

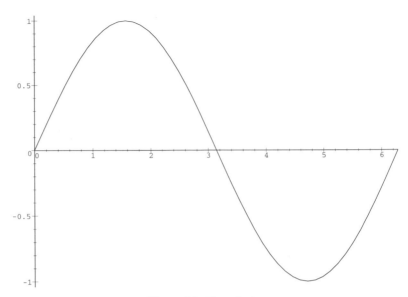

Figure 6.2: Plot of `sin`

As an illustration of plot assignments, the logarithmic plots from above could be assigned to a name as follows:

```
s:=plot({f,g},0..2,-1.5..1.5):
```

The output from this command is not a picture but rather its corresponding PLOT structure. This structure is too long to reproduce here, but you can view it by using a semicolon in place of the colon in the above command. To obtain the picture from the PLOT structure, you can type the name, in this case s, or use `print(s)`. Either method will reproduce the original picture on your screen.

Most things that you can plot on the screen can be assigned to a name in a similar way, and that name is then assigned to the underlying PLOT structure. To inspect the PLOT structure rather than the picture that it represents, you `lprint()` it. That way you get its line-printed version instead of the prettyprinted version produced by `print()`.

6.2 Two-dimensional graphics

This section covers plane graphs and other two-dimensional items. First, we discuss the options available with `plot()` and then we go on to cover the two-dimensional graphing functions in `plots[]`. The topics are

- Options to `plot()`

- Superimposing Graphs with `display()`
- Adding Text with `textplot()`
- Logarithmic and Scaled Axes
- Conformal Maps
- Vector Fields
- Contour and Density Plots
- Making a Histogram
- Drawing Polygons
- Plotting Real-Valued Functions of Complex Arguments
- Plotting Linear Inequalities
- Root Locus Plots

Options to `plot()`

An "`I`" following the name of an option in the next paragraph means that the option is commonly available as a menu choice in graphics windows in addition to being an option to `plot()`.

We have already used the `style(I)` and vertical range options of `plot()` in Section 1.4. The remaining options are `title` and `titlefont`, `xtick-marks`, `ytickmarks`, `linestyle(I)`, `thickness(I)`, `font`, `symbol(I)`, `discont`, `numpoints`, `resolution`, `adaptive`, `sample`, `coords`, `scaling(I)`, `axes(I)`, `labels`, `labelfont`, `axesfont`, and `color(I)`. The title option lets you define a title for the plot, and `titlefont` sets its font. The `x` and `y` `tickmarks` options let you specify the number of tickmarks to be placed on the axes of the plot. The `linestyle` and `linethickness` options refer to graphs. The `font` option sets the font for text items in the graph, and `symbol` sets one of a handful of characters for marking points on graphs. The `discont` option lets Maple handle plot discontinuities more carefully than would otherwise be the case; `numpoints` lets you specify the minimum number of samples of the function that are to be used to create the plot. Maple uses an adaptive sampling scheme and may sample more points than `numpoints`. Remember that you can use the `style=POINT` option to see the actual points used in the plot. Adaptive plotting can be switched off using `adaptive=false` and initiated at specific points using `sample`. The `resolution` option is a parameter that sets the ultimate fineness of adaptive sampling. The option for scaling can be either `constrained` or `unconstrained`. The effect of the `constrained` option is to make the `x` and `y` scales equal. Otherwise, Maple chooses a suitable scale ratio. The choice for `axes` can be `boxed`, `frame`, `normal`, or `none`. The `normal` option refers to a pair of Cartesian axes through the origin, and `none` means that no axes will be drawn. The `frame` and `boxed` axes do not necessarily pass through the origin; they are drawn as bounds to the graph. The `labels` option lets you label the axes of the

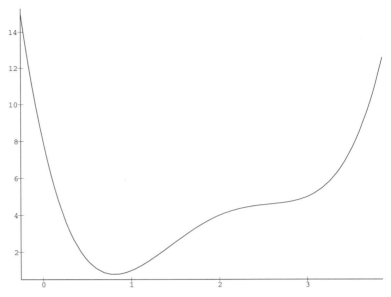

Figure 6.3: Double-well potential

plot. It takes a two-variable list as its argument. For a simple illustration, Figure 6.3 shows a framed graph with specified tickmarks, a title, and no axis labeling that was produced by:

```
>q:=x^4-8*x^3+22*x^2-22*x+8:
>plot(q,x=-.25..3.85,xtickmarks=5,ytickmarks=5,
>title='Double well potential',axes=frame,
>labels=[' ',' ']);
```

It is usually best to experiment with the choice of axes and type of scaling through menus. It is easy enough to impose the ultimate selections as explicit options if necessary.

There are two more options to plot(); view and tickmarks. These provide alternative ways to specify which part of a plot to display and the values of xtickmarks and ytickmarks. The form of these options is the option name followed by an equals (as for all plot() and plot3d() options) followed by a two-member list. For view, the list entries are ranges for the independent and dependent variables. The effect is the same as specifying the ranges as the second and third options to plot(). For tickmarks, the list entries are xtickmarks and ytickmarks. In either case, both list entries must be present.

The `view` and `tickmarks` options are essential for controlling the corresponding features in `plot3d`.

For changing Maple's default option settings for `plot()`, you can use a function in `plots[]` called `setoptions()` whose arguments select options in the standard way. The specified options will remain in force throughout the session or until you change them again. The corresponding function for three-dimensional plots is called `setoptions3d()`. The `setoption()` and `setoption3d()` commands can also be placed in your initialization file.

You can usually use `plot()` options with the functions in `plots[]` when they make sense. In addition, some functions in `plots[]` have their own options. We will mention these where appropriate.

Superimposing graphs with `display()`

We know how to plot a set of graphs that share the same options (plot them as a set or list), but how do you plot graphs with different options in the same picture? For example, how do you plot a LINE graph and a POINT graph in the same picture? The answer is to use `display()`, which is a function in `plots[]`. To illustrate how `display()` is used, we show the commands used to generate Figure 6.4 and then Figure 6.5, which shows the superposition of two plots. The first plot will consist of the points $(i/10, y_i)$, $i = 0, \ldots, 10$ where the y_i are defined by $y_i = 3x_i - 2 + r_i$ and where r_i denotes a random perturbation with magnitude less than 0.2. The second plot is a simple graph of the function $y - 3x - 2$. To begin, we will define the random-number generator for the perturbations (see Random-Number Generators in Chapter 8 for information on this) and form the point data. Here are the steps with the outputs suppressed:

```
>r:=rand(-99..99)/500:
>pts:=seq([i*.1,3*(i*.1)-2+r()],i=0..10):
```

Next, we will generate and assign the plots. Here, p1 and p2 are the names of PLOT structures:

```
>p1:=plot([pts],style=POINT):
>p2:=plot(3*x-2,x=0..1):
```

The last step is to use `display()` to make the plot shown in Figure 6.4:

```
>plots[display]({p1,p2});
```

As demonstrated, `display()` can also be used with `plot()` options.

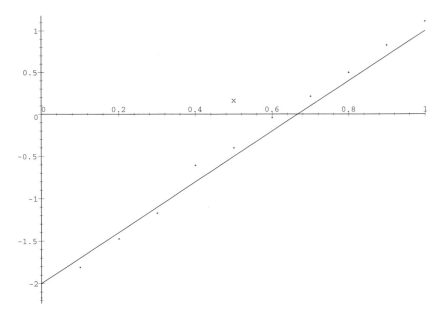

Figure 6.4: Using the `display()` function for `POINT` and `LINE` plots

On the subject of plotting lists of points, the method used in `p1` above is by no means the only possible approach, although it is the most basic. The plots package contains the functions `pointplot()` and `listplot()`, which can make point plots. The first of these plots sets or lists of two-element lists representing Cartesian coordinates. It can also plot simple lists containing an even number of entries. The second plots a list of numbers, automatically using an integer-valued independent variable.

Adding text with `textplot()`

Another function in `plots[]` called `textplot()` lets you to place text anywhere on a graph. The `textplot()` function's arguments consist of one or more lists containing the coordinates of the point where the text is to be placed, together with a string containing the text. We will illustrate this function by labeling the plot of the logarithm functions made above. The earlier definition of the `PLOT` structures is still in force. Here are the `textplot()` definitions:

```
>t1:=textplot([0.4,-1,'y = x ln x']):
>t2:=textplot([1.6,1.25,'y = ln x'],align=RIGHT):
```

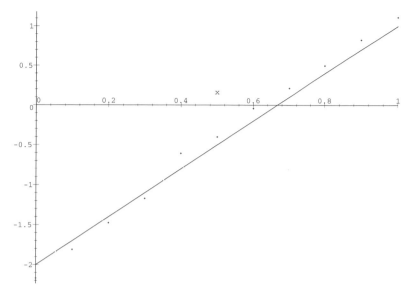

Figure 6.5: Logarithm plots

The align option allows you to specify that the text should be placed LEFT, RIGHT, ABOVE, or BELOW the point. The text will be centered over the point if no alternative is given. The textplot() command produces a PLOT structure, so we will use display() again to draw the multiple plot structures, this time including a plot() option in display:

```
>display({t1,t2,s},title='Logarithm plots');
```

Another use for textplot() is making character plots with text symbols.

Logarithmic and scaled axes

The plots[] package contains a function called logplot() for producing two-dimensional graphs with a logarithmically scaled dependent variable. This means that equal length intervals on the dependent variable axis correspond to equal multiples of the value of that variable. This is a natural way to plot data that tend to change in time by percentages of their current values. Economic statistics such as stock market averages or the national debt vary in this way. Generally, any data

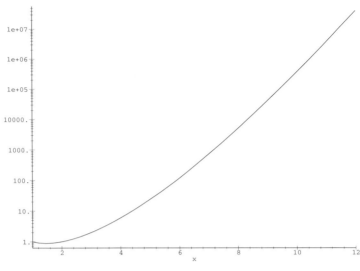

Figure 6.6: Log plot of $\Gamma(x)$

that tend to show approximate exponential behavior are candidates for a logarithmic scale. In the next example, Figure 6.6, we plot the GAMMA function; remember that for positive integers, $\Gamma(n) = (n-1)!$:

```
>logplot(GAMMA(x),x=1..12);
```

The `plots[]` package also has a function `semilogplot()` for producing plots with a logarithmic scale on the independent variable's axis and a function `loglogplot()` for producing graphs with logarithmic scales on both coordinate axes.

There is also an option for defining a function for scaling the axis of the independent variable.

Conformal maps

The `plots[]` package contains some functions for graphing higher-dimensional functions in a plane. For representing conformal maps, there is a function called `conformal()`, which displays the image of a uniform square grid under the conformal mapping. One of the prominent uses of conformal maps is for solving Laplace's equation. To illustrate this application of `conformal()`, we will display

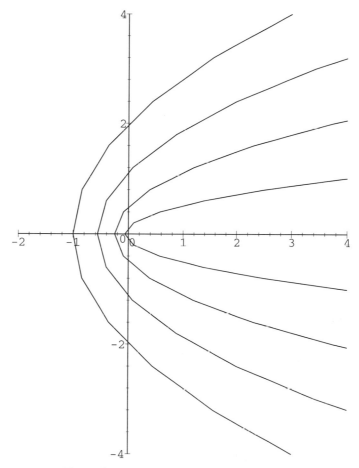

Figure 6.7: Conformal plot showing streamlines

the streamlines of the steady flow of an incompressible frictionless fluid around a flat plate:

```
>conformal(z^2,z=-4..4+I,-2-4*I..4+4*I,grid=[2,5],
>scaling=constrained);
```

The plate occupies the positive real axis (and is extended perpendicular to the plane of the paper in both directions). This is a two-dimensional flow, and Figure 6.7 shows the fluid flowing around the plate from one side to the other.

The arguments to `conformal()`, apart from the mapping itself, are (complex) ranges for the uniform square grid and its fineness as defined by the number of grid lines in each direction. The grid in this example covers the rectangle with lower left and upper right corners at $(-4, -2 - 4I)$ and $(4 + I, 4 + 4I)$, respectively. The choice of just two grid lines in the x direction ensures that only the flow lines will be plotted, not their orthogonal trajectories. There is also an option to `conformal()` that allows you to specify the number of sample points on the mesh lines.

Vector fields

The `plots[]` package contains some functions for plotting vector fields. The function `fieldplot()` draws appropriate vectors at a uniform set of mesh points. Here is an illustration of `fieldplot()` (see Figure 6.8):

```
>fieldplot([exp(x*y),2*x*y],x=-1..1,y=-1..1,
>arrows=THICK,axes=boxed);
```

The `fieldplot()` function can take two options in addition to the options for `plot()`. The `arrow` option allows you to specify a particular style for the arrows used to make the plot. In addition to `THICK`, the possibilities are `THIN`, `LINE`, and `SLIM`. The `grid` option allows you to specify the number of field samples in each coordinate direction.

Vector fields with critical points do not always graph nicely because the field vectors become too small to be represented. You have several alternative approaches in

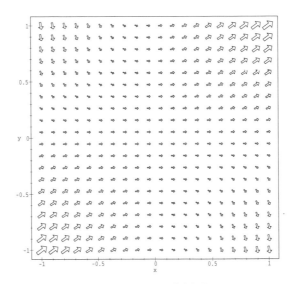

Figure 6.8: Vector field plot

this case. If the field is a gradient field, you can plot the contours of the potential function. Failing that, you can plot the direction field and simply ignore the magnitudes of the vectors. In the following subsection, we will illustrate the contour-plotting function. For plotting direction fields, there is the function `dfieldplot()`.

Contour and density plots

As a simple example for a contour plot, Figure 6.9 shows the contours of a cubic potential function produced by

```
>contourplot(y-x^2*y,x=-2..2,y=-2..2,grid=[70,70],
>axes=boxed,scaling=constrained,contours=15);
```

The `grid` option specifies the size of the grid where the function is evaluated to make the contours. This example uses fifteen contours representing equally spaced values of the potential function. The spaces between contours can be flooded with (appropriately scaled) color using the `fill` option. The `contourplot()` func-

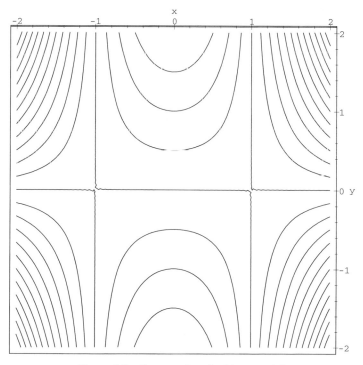

Figure 6.9: Contour plot of cubic potential

tion is really a specialization of a three-dimensional plot. In the next section, more available options are covered.

Another two-dimensional representation of a surface can be obtained from the function `densityplot()`. This produces a grayscale representation with darker areas corresponding to greater function values.

Making a histogram

Maple does not have a function specifically for making histograms. However, it is possible to obtain a histogram using a function called `matrixplot()`. We will give a simple example to illustrate the technique. First, we will generate some data, indexed by consecutive integers starting from 1. This data will be plotted in the histogram. It must be recorded in an $n \times 1$ matrix:

```
>c:=linalg[matrix](8,1,[seq(j! mod 11,j=1..8)]):
```

To generate the histogram shown in Figure 6.10, a function called `matrixplot()` is used:

```
>matrixplot(c,heights=HISTOGRAM,orientation
          =[-90,90],axes=frame);
```

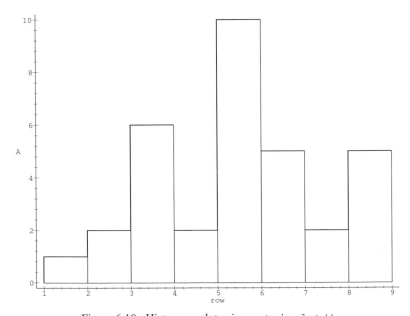

Figure 6.10: Histogram plot using `matrixplot()`

Specifying `orientation` as shown produces a two-dimensional histogram with the independent variable increasing from left to right. You can see a three-dimensional histogram by varying the `orientation` with menu options or varying the `plot3d()` orientation option. Similar to `contourplot()`, this is a projection of a three-dimensional plot, and additional options are available. The histogram above uses the grayscale option, which was obtained through the interface color menu.

Drawing polygons

For plotting polygonal figures, you can use the `polygonplot()` function. A polygon can be described by a list or set of vertices, each of which is a list of two points. To illustrate this function, we will generate three polygons and plot them as a set. The data is generated in the following three assignments:

```
>head:=[0,0],[-10,0],[-18,6],[-18,14],[-14,17],[-14,24],
>[-10,20],[0,20],[10,20],[14,24],[14,17],[18,14],[18,6],
>[10,0]:
>lcye:=[-10,14],[-7,12],[-10,10],[-13,12]:
>reye:=[10,14],[7,12],[10,10],[13,12]:
```

The plot, shown in Figure 6.11, is generated by the following:

```
>polygonplot({[head],[leye],[reye]},axes=none);
```

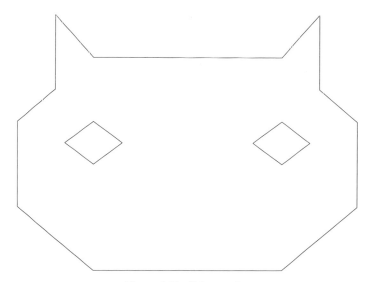

Figure 6.11: Polygon plot

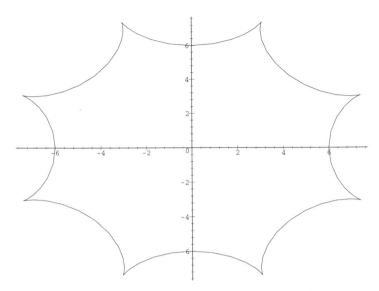

Figure 6.12: A complex-valued function of a real variable

Some experimentation may be needed for plotting nonconvex polygons because the vertices can determine more than one polygon. You can vary the order of the input list or try using sets of vertices to achieve a desired effect.

Plotting real-valued functions of complex arguments

In some situations, you may need to make a plot of a real-valued function of a complex argument (see Figure 6.12), for instance, a Fourier transform. Maple's function for this is complexplot(). The basic way to use this function is to specify the function and the range of the real independent variable. To illustrate, here is a way to make a plot of a seven-sided curvilinear polygon:

```
> complexplot(7*exp(I*t)-exp(-7*I*t),t=0..2*Pi);
```

The complexplot() function can plot the same kinds of functions as plot(), including lists of functions, procedures, and numerical lists.

Plotting linear inequalities

The plots[] package contains a function called inequalplot() for plotting the solution sets of systems of linear inequalities in two variables. Because these sets are defined by the intersections of half spaces, they are (planar) convex sets that may

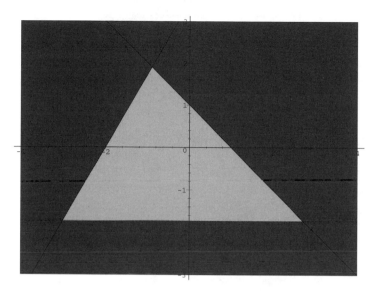

Figure 6.13: A plot of the solution set of three inequalities

be open, closed, or neither open nor closed depending on whether the inequalities are strict or not. In the example that follows, only the first inequality is strict:

```
> inequalplot({y>-sqrt(3),x+y<=1,x-1/sqrt(3)*y>=-2},
               x=-4..4,y=-3..3);
```

In Figure 6.13, the open boundary segments are extended as broken lines and the closed boundary segments are extended as regular lines. The solution set is distinguished from the remaining points by color (shade in Figure 6.13). The `inequalplot()` function has four options that allow you to specify the colors of the regions and boundaries and the line styles of the boundaries. The help file for `inequalplot()` contains information on these options.

Root-locus plots

If p and q denote two polynomials, their root-locus plot is a plot of the roots of the polynomial $1 + \lambda p/q$ in the complex plane as the real parameter λ varies in some interval. The `plots[]` package has a function `rootlocus()` for making these plots. As a simple example of the use of `rootlocus()`, we will make a plot of the roots of the quartic polynomial $x^4 + \lambda(2x^2 + 1)$ as λ varies from 0 to 1.05. Here is

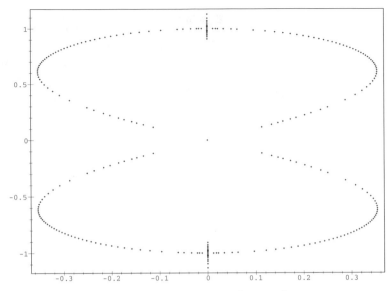

Figure 6.14: A plot of the zeros of $x^4 + \lambda(2x^2 + 1) = 0$

the required command:

```
> rootlocus((2*x^2+1)/x^4,x,0..1.05,style=point);
```

As you can see, for $\lambda = 0$ and $\lambda = 1$ the quartic is easily solved to give a quadruple zero at the origin and double roots at $\pm i$. Figure 6.14 shows that as λ increases between these values, the roots trace out paths in the complex plane. The four paths are shown in the output of the `rootlocus()` command. At the value $\lambda = 1$, the distinct roots coalesce into the two double roots. As λ increases a little more, these two double roots split into pairs of simple roots, two of which are moving toward the origin and two are moving away from it along the imaginary axis.

It is easy enough to track the behavior of the roots in this simple case, but it can be more difficult in other situations. In addition, because Maple uses numerical computation to compute the roots for each value of the parameter, the possibility of roundoff errors confusing the root paths at an intersection or bifurcation is real.

The `point` option was specified in the example in order to make the plot more visible on the printed page. Without this option, `rootlocus()` produces a continuous color-coded plot with a different color for each root. Do remember that these color-coded paths are really the result of a guess about where each root goes with what after the polynomial's roots have been found for consecutive values of the parameter.

Options to `rootlocus()` allow you to control the sampling rate for the parameter and control whether the sampling is done uniformly or at an adaptively chosen set of points.

6.3　Three-dimensional plots

We discussed some aspects of three-dimensional plotting in Section 1.4. Now we will look at `plot3d()` in more detail and discuss some interesting functions available in `plots[]`.

- Options for `plot3d()`
- Using `plot3d()`
- Using `plots[]` Functions for Three Dimensions
- Plotting Space Curves and Tubes
- Drawing Polyhedra
- Plotting Nodal Data
- Plotting Three-Dimensional Point Data
- Other Functions in `plots[]`

Options for `plot3d()`

There is a long list of options available for use with `plot3d()`. Many of the options are common to both `plot` and `plot3d`. In the following paragraph, we will mention the main options we did not mention earlier in connection with `plot`. An (`I`) following an option means that it can be adjusted through interface menu commands as well as through the appropriate plot command. We will not attempt to give detailed descriptions of the options because they are readily available through online help in `?plot3d[options]`. Instead, we will illustrate in the following subsections how the options can be used in practice.

Using options, you can specify the number of samples to be used to make the plot through `grid` or `numpoints`. The `gridstyle` option can be either `rectangular` or `triangular`. The `tickmarks` option is used slightly differently from the `plot()` version and an example follows. Axis types can be assigned through `axes(I)` and the method used to render the plot (`hidden line`, `wireframe`, `patch`, etc.) can be set using `style(I)`. There are options for `color(I)`, `shading(I)`, `ambientlight(I)`, and `light(I)` (which sets a position for an illumination source) and for a `lightmodel` and `shading` scheme. You can choose a coordinate system (`cartesian`, `polar`, or `cylindrical`) using `coords`, and a viewpoint by using `orientation(I)` and `projection(I)`. You can choose how much of a plot to display using `view` and how many contours to show with

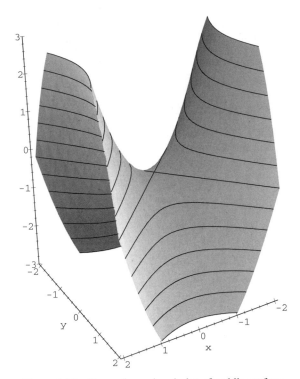

Figure 6.15: Three-dimensional plot of saddle surface

contours. Finally, there is a `scaling(I)` option for choosing the length scale (`constrained` or `unconstrained`) on the coordinate axes.

The `plot3d()` function does not take a third range option analogous to the second range option with `plot()`. In order to control the range of the dependent variable, the `view` option is used.

To override the `plot3d()` default options, use `plots[setoptions3d]()` either in the session or in your initialization file.

Using `plot3d()`

This subsection contains four plots to illustrate the main uses for `plot3d()` and its options. For the first example, we will plot the simple saddle surface shown in Figure 6.15. We will use a patch and contour method to render the plot in which the contours are not merely projected onto a plane but are drawn on the surface itself. The `view` option is used to restrict the independent variable. The axes are of the `frame` variety and an `orientation` is specified to display specific characteristics of the picture. In addition, a fairly wide-angle `projection` is used with `constrained`

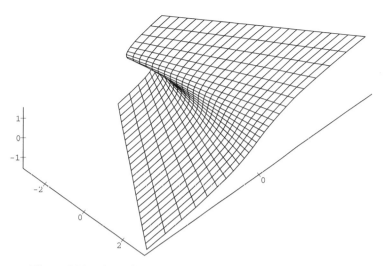

Figure 6.16: Three-dimensional parametric plot of roots of a cubic

axes. All of these options are explicitly imposed on the command line. Here is the plotting command and its output:

```
>plot3d((x^2-y^2),x=-2..2,y=-2..2,view=-3..3,
>style=patchcontour,scaling=constrained,axes=frame,
>projection=.25,orientation=[60,60]);
```

Next, we will illustrate the use of `plot3d()` for obtaining plots of parametrically defined surfaces. This is done by inputting a list of three expressions followed by two ranges for the parameters. To illustrate the use of this technique, we will plot a graph of the real roots of a cubic polynomial $p(x) = 4x^3 + 2ax + 4b$ that depends on two parameters. We will use the cubic equation $b = -(4x^3 + 2ax)/4$. The plot command for this and its result, shown in Figure 6.16, are given next:

```
>plot3d([(-2*a*x-4*x^3)/4,a,x],a=-3..3,x=-1.5..1.5,
>axes=frame,tickmarks=[2,2,3],scaling=constrained);
```

Because it is the variable x which is of interest, it is the last item to appear in the list. The first entry in the list is just b. A hidden-line rendering was chosen through the interface `style` menu. This plot also shows how to use the `tickmarks` option in `plot3d()`. Note that the usage is slightly different from the `plot()` usage. The graph shows the expected result, that is, that the cubic has either one or three real roots counting multiplicity.

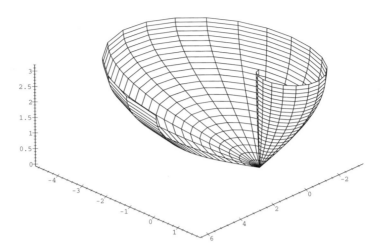

Figure 6.17: Three-dimensional plot using cylindrical coordinates

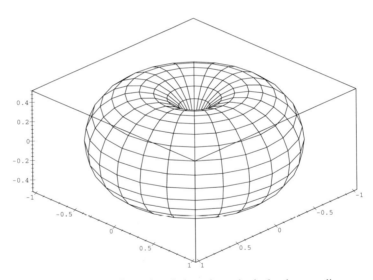

Figure 6.18: Three-dimensional plot using spherical polar coordinates

In the next two examples, Figures 6.17 and 6.18, we illustrate the use of the `coords` option for producing plots in `cylindrical` and `spherical` polar coordinates. First is an illustration for `cylindrical` coordinates:

```
>plot3d(sin(z/2)*theta,theta=0..2*Pi,z=0..Pi,
>coords=cylindrical,axes=frame);
```

The `orientation` and several other characteristics of this hidden-line plot were chosen using menu commands. The final orientation is $\theta = -30$, $\phi = 70$.

Second is a `spherical` polar plot produced from `plot3d()`:

```
>plot3d(sin(t),f=0..2*Pi,t=0..Pi,coords=spherical,
>axes=boxed,style=hidden,color=black);
```

In this plot, the `style` option is used to obtain hidden-line rendering and a color is chosen using the `color` option. In addition, the plot is `constrained`.

Cylindrical and spherical polar plots can also be obtained directly from the `plots[]` functions `cylinderplot()` and `sphereplot()`.

Using `plots[]` functions for three dimensions

The `plots[]` package contains numerous functions for different kinds of three-dimensional graphics. As we saw in the previous subsection, some of these functions are extensions of similar two-dimensional functions. For example, `fieldplot()` and `gradplot()` have three-dimensional versions called `fieldplot3d()` and `gradplot3d()`. Here is an example using `gradplot3d()` (Figure 6.19):

```
>gradplot3d((x^2+y^2+z^2),x=-1/4..1/4,y=-1/4..1/4,z=-
>1/4..1/4,arrows=THICK);
```

The option `shading=Z_GRAYSCALE` has been applied through the color menu on the interface.

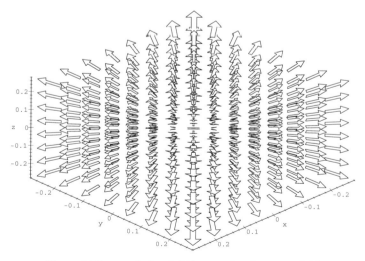

Figure 6.19: `gradplot3d()` example of a vector field

Other three-dimensional versions of two-dimensional `plots[]` functions are `implicitplot3d()`, `polygonplot3d()`, `display3d()`, and `textplot3d()`. These functions are used in a similar way to their two-dimensional counterparts. Type `?plots[]` to see the the full list of `plots[]` functions.

In the subsections that follow we will explain the use of the remaining three-dimensional functions in the `plots[]` package.

Plotting space curves and tubes

First, we will draw a space curve that is defined by a parameterized three-dimensional vector. The function for this is called `spacecurve()`, and it takes a list (or set of lists if there are several curves) as its first argument and a named range for its second argument. The standard options are available with `spacecurve()`. As an example of this function, we will give a representation of the Fresnel integrals by using them to parameterize a three-dimensional curve. The `numpoints` option specifies that 100 sample points are to be used to make the plot:

```
>spacecurve([u/2,FresnelS(u),FresnelC(u)],u=1..5,
>numpoints=100,axes=boxed,tickmarks=[5,2,4]);
```

The projections of the curve, shown in Figure 6.20, onto the coordinate planes give graphs of the two Fresnel integrals and a curve known as a Cornu spiral.

A close relative of `spacecurve()` is a function called `tubeplot()`, which constructs a tubular surface of circular cross section around one or more curves

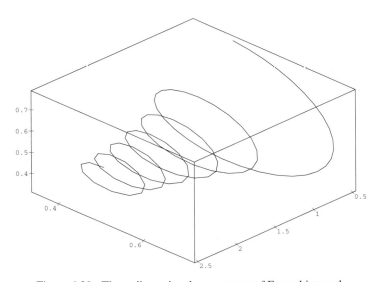

Figure 6.20: Three-dimensional space curve of Fresnel integrals

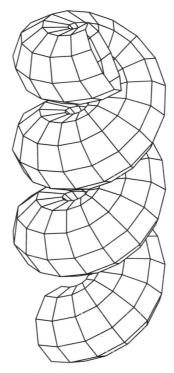

Figure 6.21: Three-dimensional tubeplot

drawn in three-dimensional space. The illustrative plot shown in Figure 6.21 is drawn without axes and has been reorientated from the default position. It is rendered with patches rather than by hidden-line rendering.

```
>tubeplot([cos(t),sin(t),t/2],t=0..20);
```

There are some options for `tubeplot()` that allow you to specify the radius of the tubes as well as the number of samples on the curve and around the tubes.

Drawing polyhedra

A function for drawing regular polyhedra is `polyhedraplot()`. This function takes a list of three numbers as its minimal argument expression. These numbers define the position around which a regular polyhedron will be drawn. Alternative arguments are a list of such points (for a polyhedron to be drawn around each of them), an argument that defines the type of polyhedron to be drawn (the default type is `tetrahedron`), and a scale variable that controls the size of the polyhedron. The

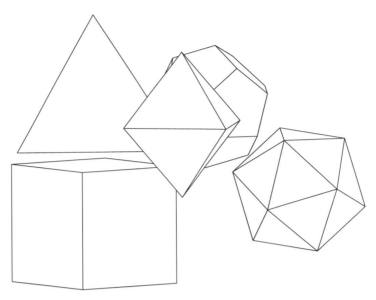

Figure 6.22: `polyhedraplot()` example

following example, shown in Figure 6.22, illustrates the use of `polyhedraplot()`:

```
>p1:=polyhedraplot([1,1,1],polyscale=.2):
>p2:=polyhedraplot([1/2,1,1],polytype=octahedron,
                polyscale=.25):
>p3:=polyhedraplot([1/2,1/2,3/4],polytype=icosahedron,
                polyscale=.2):
>p4:=polyhedraplot([1,1/2,1],polytype=dodecahedron,
                polyscale=.2):
>p5:=polyhedraplot([1,1,5/8],polytype=hexahedron,
                polyscale=.2):

>display3d({p1,p2,p3,p4,p5},orientation=[143,85]);
```

To draw custom polyhedra in three dimensions, use `polygonplot3d()`.

Plotting nodal data

For plotting data defined at the nodes of a rectangular mesh or grid, `plots[]` provides the functions `surfdata()`, `listplot3d()`, and the related function contourlistplot(). Here, we will cover the use of surfdata(). Use of surfdata() is straightforward and involves little more than correctly organizing the input data. This means supplying the data in a list of lists of points, where a point is itself a list of the form [x,y,z], with x and y denoting the independent variables and z denoting the dependent variable. Each list of points therefore contains one line of mesh data, either an $x =$ constant line or a $y =$ constant line, depending on how the inner lists are structured. As an example, we will use data generated from the function

$$\Phi(x, y) = 2y + \ln\left(\sqrt{x^2 + (y - 1/2)^2}\right) + \ln\left(\sqrt{x^2 + (y + 1/2)^2}\right)$$

This is another fluid-flow example. Φ denotes the stream function of a uniform flow past a pair of point vortices. The fluid is incompressible and inviscid, and the flow is two-dimensional. We will fit a surface to the mesh data and plot its contours. The contours, shown in Figure 6.23, give the paths of the fluid particles in this instance and are usually of more interest than the graph of the surface itself. Here are the steps:

```
>psi:=(x,y)->2*y+ln((x^2+(y-1/2)^2)/(x^2+(y+1/2)^2))/2:
```

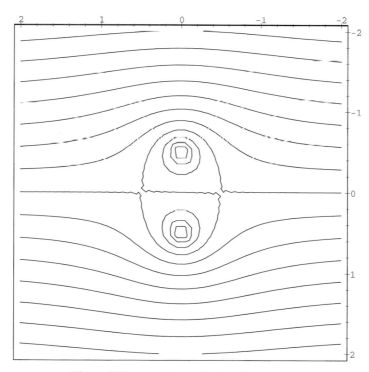

Figure 6.23: surfdata() plot of streamlines

```
>data:=[seq([seq([-2+4*i/41,-2+4*j/41,psi(-2+4*i/41,
>-2+4*j/41)],i=0..41)],j=0..41)]:
>surfdata(data,contours=15,orientation=[90,0],
>style=contour,color=black,scaling=constrained,
    axes=boxed);
```

This example serves as a model for contour plotting of numerical data, a frequently occurring problem in scientific computing. The help file for surfdata() contains some useful suggestions to simplify the preparation of input data.

As we mentioned above, plots[] contains alternative functions for plotting numerical data in three dimensions. The functions listplot3d() and contourlistplot() are functionally similar to the above use of surfdata(). The pointplot3d() function generalizes pointplot() to three dimensions and is discussed in the next subsection.

At present, Maple does not have a function for plotting data that do not lie on a regular mesh.

Plotting three-dimensional point data

Earlier, we saw how to plot numerical lists in two dimensions. For instance, to plot a list of points in two dimensions you can use plot() with a single argument giving the list of points or use pointplot(). For three dimensions, corresponding to pointplot() there is pointplot3d() (see Figure 6.24). The pointplot3d() function has a greater significance than its two-dimensional counterpart because plot3d() cannot be used to plot points in the same way as plot(). As with the two-dimensional case, the input to pointplot3d() can be a set or list of three element lists representing three-dimensional Cartesian coordinates or a simple list containing $3n$ elements. As an illustration, here is a way to plot forty random points in space:

```
>r:=stats[random,uniform[-1,1]]:
>p:=[seq([r(),r(),r()],i=1..40)]:
>pointplot3d(p,axes=boxed,tickmarks=[5,5,5],color=black,
>scaling=constrained,orientation=[-142,66]);
```

An interface command was used to set the point style.

The textplot3d() function can be used as in two dimensions to plot specific keyboard symbols and text strings at designated points on a plot.

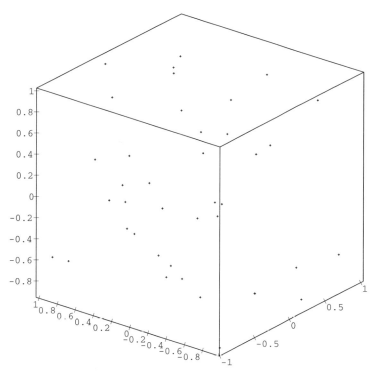

Figure 6.24: `pointplot3d()` example

Other functions in `plots[]`

It is often useful to be able to plot the curves or surfaces of coordinate systems. The `plots[]` package contains two functions for this purpose, one for two-dimensional coordinate systems (`coordplot()`) and one for three-dimensional coordinate systems (`coordplot3d()`). A complete list of the available coordinate systems may be found in `?plots[coordchange]`. The `plots[]` package contains one more function that must be mentioned here, `sparsematrixplot()`. This is a relatively specialized procedure that gives a picture of the positions of the nonzero elements of a matrix. It is particularly useful for understanding the extent of nonzero fill in sparse matrix operations such as Gaussian elimination.

6.4 The `plottools[]` package

This package contains a number of functions for producing graphics primitives and some tools for manipulating them. The primitives include basics such as ellipses, curves, arrows, and polygons and also a number of three-dimensional objects, includ-

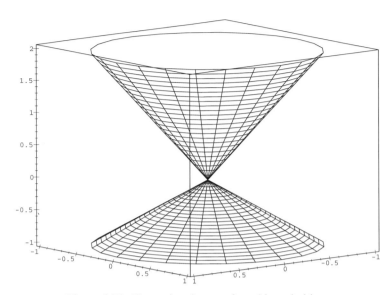

Figure 6.25: Illustrating the use of graphics primitives

ing torii and cones. Five functions are supplied for modifying the primitives. These are rotate(), scale(), stellate(), transform(), and translate(). The rotate() and translate() functions allow images to be rotated around the coordinate axes and translated. The transform() function lets you apply a specified mapping to all points of the primitive. The scale() function performs a scale change, and stellate() takes as an argument a polyhedron and produces a stellated form of it. To illustrate the use of these functions, we will make a picture of a pair of cones standing tip to tip. The standard cone produced by the cone() function has its tip pointing upward so we will use the rotate() command to reorient it. Here are the steps:

```
> cone1:=cone([0,0,0],1,2):
> cone2:=cone([0,0,0],1,1):
> rcone2:=rotate(cone2,Pi,0,0):
> display({cone1,rcone2});
```

The results are shown in Figure 6.25.

6.5 Animating plots

Maple contains some facilities for simple animations. Although we cannot demonstrate animation in a book, we will discuss it a little and suggest some examples to try.

The animation functions (which are in `plots[]`) are called `animate()` and `animate3d()`. To create an animation, you can incorporate an additional parameter in a function (think of it as time) and simply tell `animate()` or `animate3d()` how many times and in what time interval to evaluate the surface. The animation functions can then play the time sequence of plots in sufficiently rapid sequence to create the appearance of motion.

In the GUI setting, the animation appears in its own window, with various controls laid out in a way analogous to a video tape recorder (VTR). In addition to on and off controls, the VTR interface has speed controls, a playback direction control, and a loop control that causes the animation to cycle until the stop button is pressed. Here are two suggestions for you to try that will demonstrate more clearly than any amount of writing what you can do with animation. The first illustration is of the transverse motion of a string, such as a guitar or violin string, vibrating in its third overtone. The function that is animated is a solution of the classical linear wave equation subject to suitable boundary and initial conditions, which are immediately evident from the plot:

```
>animate(cos(3*t)*sin(3*x),x=0..Pi,t=0..2*Pi,frames=30,
>color=black,scaling=constrained);
```

A three-dimensional analog of this plot for the vibrations of a membrane (or drum) is

```
>animate3d(cos(3*t)*sin(3*x)*cos(3*y),x=0..Pi,y=0..Pi,
>t=0..2*Pi,frames=20,color=black,scaling=constrained);
```

This three-dimensional animation takes considerably longer to prepare than the one-dimensional plot. However, it can be viewed at basically the same rate.

Suppose you have a sequence of plots that you want to animate. How can you do it? The answer is to use `display()` with a new option. Here is an illustration of the technique. First, we will make a sequence of plots. Although this sequence is formed using a discrete time-like parameter, it is important to realize that the animation works for any sequence of plots. They merely have to be assembled into a suitable aggregate data object:

```
>p:=seq(plot([[0,0],[cos(2*Pi*t/100),sin(2*Pi*t/100)]]),
        t=0..100):
```

As a rule, sequences of `PLOT` structures can be very long and be very messy to print.

To display the successive plots, you use `display()` with the `insequence` option and whatever other options you need:

```
>display([p],insequence=true,scaling=constrained,
        axes=none);
```

(Note the use of the list brackets in the first argument.) You can use this animation to experiment with the VTR speed controls on your interface. You can also use `display()` to superimpose a static and an animated plot.

6.6 PLOT/PLOT3D structures

When you use `plot()` or `plot3d()`, Maple creates what it calls a PLOT or PLOT3D structure (we will refer to both as PLOT structures). These are data structures that can be rendered by the hardware to produce a picture. Typically, these structures contain lists of points, together with values for options. Usually, you do not have to worry about PLOT structures, but there are times when it is useful to know how to create or modify them. For example, you might have waited a long time for a complicated plot to appear, only to realize that you forgot the axis labeling or some other option not available from the menus. Do you now have to repeat the whole calculation? The answer is no, and this section discusses the appropriate techniques.

We will begin by generating a short PLOT structure:

```
> a:=plot({[[0,0],[1,1]],[[0,0],[1,2]]},
>scaling=constrained,tickmarks=[3,3],view=[0..1,0..1]);

a := INTERFACE_PLOT(

    CURVES([[0, 0], [1., 1.]], COLOUR(RGB, 1.0, 0, 0)),

    CURVES([[0, 0], [1., 2.]], COLOUR(RGB, 0, 1.0, 0)),

    SCALING(CONSTRAINED), AXESTICKS(3, 3),
        VIEW(0 .. 1., 0 .. 1.)

    )
> type(a,PLOT);
                              true
```

Examination of the `plot()` command shows that the picture is going to consist of two straight lines joining the points $(0, 0)$ and $(1, 1)$ and the points $(0, 0)$ and $(2, 2)$. The picture will use equal scales along the coordinate axes due to the use of the scaling option.

The PLOT structure that is returned is a Maple expression and can be analyzed into its constituent operands. Let's look at these operands:

```
> nops(a);
```

$$5$$

```
> seq([i,op(i,a)],i=1..5);
  [1,CURVES([[0, 0], [1., 1.]], COLOUR(RGB, 1.0, 0, 0))],

  [2,CURVES([[0, 0], [1., 2.]], COLOUR(RGB, 0, 1.0, 0))],

  [3,SCALING(CONSTRAINED)], [4, AXESTICKS(3, 3)],

  [5,VIEW(0 .. 1., 0 .. 1.)]
```

The first and second operands of the PLOT structure contain a list of points and a color, each presented as arguments to CURVES. The remaining operands are associated with options. Observe that they are expressed as functions, not as equations. Also, the names may differ slightly from the corresponding option name. Usually, the correspondence between options and the functions appearing in the PLOT structure will be evident. For instance, in the structure above it is reasonable to suppose that the tickmarks option corresponds to the AXESTICKS function. In case of doubt, you could change an option and observe the corresponding change in the operands.

How can you modify a PLOT structure other than by modifying options in the plot() command? The answer is that you use subsop() directly on the PLOT structure. To illustrate this, let's change the view option to view=[0..1/2,0..1/2]. The effect of this change will be that Maple will display only the indicated part of the plot. The substitution is straightforward:

```
> a:=subsop(5=VIEW(0..1/2,0..1/2),a);
  a := INTERFACE_PLOT(

      CURVES([[0, 0], [1., 1.]], COLOUR(RGB, 1.0, 0, 0)),

      CURVES([[0, 0], [1., 2.]], COLOUR(RGB, 0, 1.0, 0)),

      SCALING(CONSTRAINED), AXESTICKS(3, 3),

      VIEW(0 .. 1/2, 0 .. 1/2))
```

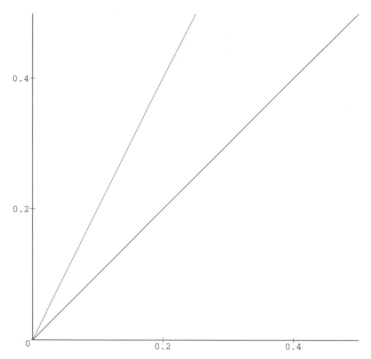

Figure 6.26: Plot obtained with modified PLOT structure

Figure 6.26 shows the plot resulting from the following change:

```
>a;
```

In some cases, it can be helpful to examine other PLOT and PLOT3D structures in order to get ideas for making nonstandard plots. An example of this is joining a succession of points in three dimensions with line segments. We have been working with a two-dimensional version of the same problem above. Taking a similar approach in three dimensions merely produces a message:

```
>plot3d([[0,0,0],[1,1,1]]);
```

```
Error, (in plot3d)
at least three arguments are required
```

and there is no other obvious function to use. Looking around for a remedy, we soon realize that spacecurve() must know how to join points in three dimensions and indeed, a glance at a PLOT3D structure produced by spacecurve() does tell us what to do. You simply have to give a list of points to CURVE in a PLOT3D structure. It is perfectly acceptable to write a PLOT structure from scratch, and that is what we

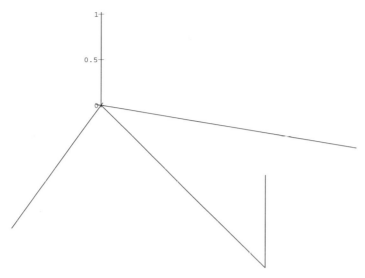

Figure 6.27: Three-dimensional line plot from a PLOT3D structure

will do here:

```
> b:=PLOT3D(CURVES([[0,0,0],[1,1,0],[1,1,1]]),
              AXESTICKS(0,0,3));
b := INTERFACE_PLOT3D(

    CURVES([[0, 0, 0], [1, 1, 0], [1, 1, 1]]),
          AXESTICKS(0, 0, 3)


    )
```

The resulting picture, shown in Figure 6.27, is produced by

```
>b;
```

These examples show the value of knowing how to build and modify PLOT structures.

6.7 Reference section

For a complete list of options to plot() and plot3d() see ?plot[options] and ?plot3d[options]. For information on the plottools[] package start at ?plottools.

The rest of this section contains a summary of the functions in `plots[]`. In the `plots[]` summary, a (3d) following the name of a function means that the three-dimensional version of the function has "3d" appended to the name of the corresponding two-dimensional version.

THE PLOTS PACKAGE

`animate(3d)`	Animation facility
`complexplot`	Real-valued function of complex variable
`complexplot3d`	Real part colored by imaginary part
`conformal`	Mesh images under conformal maps
`contourplot(3d)`	Plot contours of a function of two variables
`coordplot(3d)`	Lines and surfaces of coordinate systems
`cylinderplot`	Regular and parametric cylindrical polar plots
`densityplot`	Plane grayscale plots
`display(3d)`	Display `PLOT/3D` structure(s)
`fieldplot(3d)`	Arrow plots of vector fields
`gradplot(3d)`	Arrow plots of gradient fields
`inequalplot`	Linear inequalities
`listcontourplot(3d)`	Contours of numerical list data
`listplot(3d)`	Plot from lists of numerical data
`loglogplot`	Both variables on logarithmic scales
`logplot`	Dependent variable on logarithmic scale
`matrixplot`	Plot matrix entries as mesh data
`odeplot`	Trajectory plotter used with `dsolve( ,numeric)`
`parametricplot(3d)`	Graph curves or surfaces given parametrically
`pointplot`	Plot points in three dimensions
`polarplot`	Polar graphs in the plane
`polygonplot(3d)`	Draw polygon(s) in the plane or in space
`polyhedraplot`	Draw platonic solid(s)
`replot`	Superceded by `display()`
`rootlocus`	Plot roots as a function of a parameter
`semilogplot`	Independent variable on logarithmic scale
`setoptions(3d)`	Change default settings
`spacecurve`	Three-dimensional trajectory plotter
`sparsematrixplot`	Graph the sparsity structure of a matrix
`sphereplot`	Regular and parametric spherical polar plots
`surfdata`	Surface plots from numerical data
`textplot(3d)`	Position text at a specified location
`tubeplot`	Make a tube from a space curve

7 Computational algebra with Maple

This chapter covers Maple's main facilities for calculating in algebraic number fields over the rationals and calculating in finite fields. We will discuss computing in rings of polynomials defined over these fields and their associated quotient fields.

There are several reasons to become familiar with the techniques presented in this chapter. For instance, algebraic computing is finding a growing number of applications in digital technologies such as cryptography. A more mundane reason is to gain greater insight into Maple's ubiquitous `RootOf()` function. This chapter is a good place to discover some of the many applications of `RootOf()`.

To follow the chapter in detail, you will need a modest background in abstract algebra, mainly field theory. Even without this background you may find some of the material useful for the insight it gives into the way Maple is constructed. We suggest that you at least skim the chapter, looking for useful information.

7.1 Computing with algebraic numbers

This section covers Maple's tools for computing in algebraic extensions of the rational numbers. Included is a discussion of how Maple represents such numbers and the fundamentals of how to manipulate them. The subsections are

- Introducing `RootOf()`
- Simplification and `RootOf()`
- Factoring Over Algebraic Fields
- The Evaluator `evala()`
- Roots Dependent on Parameters

Introducing `RootOf()`

Recall that an algebraic number over the set of rational numbers $\mathbf{Q}$ is one that can be expressed as the root of a polynomial, $p(x)$, with coefficients in $\mathbf{Q}$. For each algebraic number ξ (called "xi" below), there is a unique monic polynomial (that is, a polynomial with a unit leading coefficient) of minimal degree, with coefficients in **Q** having ξ as a root (we will show below how to find this polynomial using `Primfield()`). Maple has two ways to represent algebraic numbers. The simplest is to use an expression containing radicals, such as the following:

```
>solve(x^2+x+5=0,x);
```

$$- 1/2 + 1/2 \; I \; 19^{1/2} \quad , \quad - 1/2 - 1/2 \; I \; 19^{1/2}$$

The alternative way uses a `RootOf()`:

```
>xi:=solve(x^4+x+5=0,x);
```

$$xi := RootOf(\_Z^4 + \_Z + 5)$$

Algebraic numbers can be defined directly with `RootOf()` and may involve symbolic quantities. When there is more than one name in the equation, the second argument specifies which variable is the indeterminate (or "unknown"). Here is an example:

```
>xi := RootOf(x^2+a*x+5,x);
```

$$xi := RootOf(\_Z^2 + a \_Z + 5)$$

The second argument to `RootOf()` may be omitted when _Z is used as the indeterminate. `RootOf()` always writes the indeterminate as _Z even when there is just one name in its argument. If you wish, you can include the "=0" part of the equation that defines the `RootOf()`.

Is a `RootOf()` an aggregate or a specific number? The answer is that both interpretations are useful. Usually, algebraic manipulations of a `RootOf()` expression will produce results that are valid for any of the particular algebraic numbers represented by the `RootOf()`. To illustrate, here is an example that obtains the inverse of an algebraic number defined by a `RootOf()`:

```
>xi := RootOf(x^4+x+5);
```

$$xi := RootOf(\_Z^4 + \_Z + 5)$$

```
>1/xi;
```

$$\cfrac{1}{\text{RootOf}(\_Z^4 + \_Z + 5)}$$

```
>simplify(");
```

$$- \frac{1}{5} \text{RootOf}(\_Z^4 + \_Z + 5)^3 - \frac{1}{5}$$

Even though you might have in mind a particular root, this result is correct for any of the algebraic numbers defined by the formula for xi.

A case where a RootOf() is better viewed as an aggregate occurred earlier in connection with the sum() function. We presented a example showing that sum() could be used to find the sum of the roots of a polynomial represented by a RootOf() (see "The sum() Function" in Section 2.5).

Note also that a RootOf() is a (nested) Maple type:

```
>type(xi,RootOf);
```

$$\text{true.}$$

Now we will discuss the numerical evaluation of RootOf() expressions. The main function for this is allvalues(), which will find numerical values for each of the components of a RootOf(). These values will be floating-point approximations if exact results are unobtainable. As an example, we will apply allvalues() to xi defined above. This gives

```
>evalf(allvalues(xi));
```

$$- 1.060298235 - .9425760606\ I,$$
$$- 1.060298235 + .9425760606\ I,$$
$$1.060298235 - 1.166196839\ I,$$
$$1.060298235 + 1.166196839\ I$$

The allvalues() function will attempt to find the exact roots (and will certainly succeed for polynomials of degree no greater than four provided _EnvExplicit is true) and otherwise uses `fsolve()` to approximate the roots. In the above example, we used `evalf()` to minimize the rather lengthy output. The `allvalues()` function does distinguish multiple roots.

You can also obtain floating-point approximations from `evalf()`. When a `RootOf()` appears as an argument to `evalf()`, a root is selected in an arbitrary fashion, as in the next example:

```
>evalf(xi);
```

$$- 1.060298235 - .9425760606 \text{ I}$$

(That this equals the first root produced by `allvalues()` is accidental.) You can gain control over what `evalf()` produces by using a third argument in the `RootOf()`. The `evalf()` function will approximate the root closest to the third argument:

```
>xi := RootOf(x^4+x+5,x,1-I);
```

$$xi := RootOf(\_Z^4 + \_Z + 5, 1 - I)$$

```
>evalf(xi);
```

$$1.060298235 - 1.166196839 \text{ I}$$

Because `RootOf()` expressions can be somewhat lengthy, it is common to use `alias()` to reduce them to more readable format. For instance, here is a more legible rendering of one of our earlier results (remember that the value of `alias()` is a sequence of all current `alias()` names):

```
>alias(xi=RootOf(x^4+a*x+5,x));
```

$$I, \text{ } xi$$

```
>simplify(1/xi);
```

$$- 1/5 \text{ } xi^3 - 1/5 \text{ } a$$

Simplification and `RootOf()`

There is a standard approach for simplifying expressions that are defined in extended fields. We will recall this approach here in order to point out that `simplify()` is capable of performing similar simplifications. The technique is based on the the standard representation of an algebraic number in the field $\mathbf{Q}(\xi)$ as a polynomial of degree $(n - 1)$, where n is the degree of the minimal polynomial $p(x)$ having root ξ. Then, using the division algorithm, any polynomial $P(x)$ over $\mathbf{Q}$ may be written as $P(x) = q(x)p(x) + r(x)$, where the degree of r is less than n. Evaluating at ξ gives $P(\xi) = r(\xi)$; in this way it is possible to simplify results to lower degree. Here is an example of such a simplification:

```
>alias(xi=RootOf(x^4+x+5));
```

$$I, \ xi$$

```
>simplify(xi^5);
```

$$\begin{array}{cc} & 2 \\ - \ xi & - \ 5 \ xi \end{array}$$

Similar manipulations can be used to simplify quotients of algebraic numbers in the field $\mathbf{Q}(\xi)$. For example, to simplify the quotient $1/Q(x)$, where $Q(x)$ is a polynomial relatively prime to $p(x)$ (otherwise $Q(x)$ is a zero divisor), the Euclidean algorithm can be used to find $P(x)$ and $q(x)$ such that $q(x)Q(x) + p(x)P(x) = 1$. Because $p(\xi) = 0$, it follows that $1/Q(\xi) = q(\xi)$. To illustrate this, with `xi alias()`'d as above, we define and simplify a quotient:

```
>f := (3*xi^3 - 2*xi + 2)/(5*xi^3-3);
```

$$f := \frac{3 \ xi^3 \ - \ 2 \ xi \ + \ 2}{5 \ xi^3 \ - \ 3}$$

```
>simplify(f);
```

$$- \frac{3216}{79661} xi^3 - \frac{11491}{79661} xi + \frac{10050}{79661} xi^2 + \frac{42651}{79661}$$

A number of other simplifications can yield lower degree results·for similar reasons. The subsection Linear Algebra in Section 7.3 contains a further illustration of this use of `simplify()`.

Factoring over algebraic fields

In Chapter 2, we discussed the basic use of Maple's factoring function `factor()`. Now we will see how the usefulness of `factor()` can be increased by using extensions of **Q**. Most of the time it is not possible to factor polynomials over **Q** by remaining in **Q**. Instead, we usually have to extend **Q** by one or more algebraic numbers to make factoring possible. In fact, `factor()` can handle both univariate and multivariate polynomials over algebraic fields. The field to factor over is specified in a second argument to `factor()`. If this argument is not present, Maple will decide the field from the coefficients of the argument polynomial. Here is a case with a single argument:

```
>factor(x^2+x+5);
```

$$x^2 + x + 5$$

The given polynomial is irreducible over **Q**. In the next example, the field is more complicated, but Maple is able to figure out what it is and factor the expression accordingly:

```
>alias(xi=RootOf(x^2+19));
```

$$I, xi$$

```
>five := (1+xi)*(1-xi)/4;
```

$$five := 1/4 \ (1 + xi) \ (1 - xi)$$

```
>factor(x^2+x+five);
```

$$1/4 \ (2 \ x + 1 - xi) \ (2 \ x + 1 + xi)$$

Explicit extensions are possible also. As an example, we will start by appending $\sqrt{2}$ to **Q** and factoring $x^4 - 2$:

```
>factor(x^4-2,2^(1/2));
```

$$(x^2 + 2^{1/2}) \ (x^2 - 2^{1/2})$$

Each of the factors is irreducible over the extended field. To obtain a more complete set of factors, a slightly different extension can be used:

```
>factor(x^4-2,2^(1/4));
```

$$(x^2 + 2^{1/2}) \ (x + 2^{1/4}) \ (x - 2^{1/4})$$

It is clear that a further extension to the field is necessary if we are to find additional factors, so now we append twice to **Q**. This causes no problem to `factor()`:

```
>factor(x^4-2,{2^(1/4),I});
```

$$(x + I \ 2^{1/4}) \ (x - I \ 2^{1/4}) \ (x + 2^{1/4}) \ (x - 2^{1/4})$$

The previous example specified the algebraic field to be $\mathbf{Q}(\sqrt{2}, i)$, the extension of **Q** containing both the fourth root of 2 and the square root of -1. Incidentally, this field is called the splitting field for the given polynomial: Essentially, it is the smallest field containing all the roots of the polynomial.

You can use `RootOf()` to specify extensions of **Q**. As an illustration, the next example shows the steps to factor a polynomial over an algebraic extension containing two of its roots:

```
>alias(xi=RootOf(x^5-x+1)):
>factor(x^5-x+1,xi);
```

$$(x - xi) \ (x^4 + xi \ x^3 + xi^2 \ x^2 + xi^3 \ x - 1 + xi^4)$$

Note that this extension is by a single element. To continue the factorization, we have to isolate the second factor:

```
>p:= op(2,");
```

$$p := x^4 + \xi x^3 + \xi^2 x^2 + \xi^3 x - 1 + \xi^4$$

```
>alias(eta=RootOf(p)):
>factor(x^5-x+1,{xi,eta});
```

$$(\xi^3 + \xi^2 x + \xi x^2 + x^3 + eta^3 + \xi eta^2 x + \xi^2 eta$$

$$+ \xi eta^2 + eta^2 x + eta^2 x)\ (x - eta)\ (x - \xi)$$

```
>map(collect,",x);
```

$$(\xi^3 + \xi^2 eta + \xi eta^2 + eta^3$$

$$+ (\xi^2 + \xi eta + eta^2)\ x + (\xi + eta)\ x^2 + x^3)$$

$$(x - eta)\ (x - \xi)$$

Note that in order to have a well-defined extension of **Q** (and to avoid an error message), roots appended must be of an irreducible polynomial. Also, for extensions involving more than one `RootOf()`, be sure that the polynomials are independent (for example, a `RootOf()` of a low-order polynomial doesn't exist in the extension given by the `RootOf()` of a higher-order polynomial).

The evaluator `evala()`

In addition to factoring, Maple can perform many other algebraic computations in extensions of **Q**. Typically, this is done through the use of inert functions. For example, the greatest common divisor function in the main library, gcd(), can only work with polynomials defined over the rationals. To find the greatest common divisor of a set of polynomials in $\mathbf{Q}(\xi)[x]$, the inert Gcd() function is used as an argument to evala() in the following way:

```
>alias(xi=RootOf(x^2-2*x+5)):
>p:=x^2+(xi-2)*x-(xi-1):
>q:=x^2+xi*x+(xi-1):
>evala(Gcd(p,q));
```

$$x - 1 + xi$$

Here is a list of inert functions recognized by evala():

Content	Divide	Expand	Factor	Factors
AFactor	AFactors	Normal	Prem	Primpart
Quo	Rem	Resultant	Sprem	Sqrfree
Norm	Trace	Indep	Primfield	Gcd
Gcdex	Frobenius	Issimilar		

This list was obtained from the help file for evala(). In addition to Factor() and Gcd(), there is an inert version of expand() as well as inert versions of the division, quotient, and remainder functions. The remaining functions are more specialized and we will discuss one of them next.

A theorem of algebra states that an algebraic extension L of a field K of finite index can be expressed as $L = K(u)$, where u is referred to as a primitive element. As a concrete example, the field $\mathbf{Q}(2^{1/4}, i)$ that we used above is expressible as $\mathbf{Q}(u)$ for some u. To find the primitive element u and its minimal polynomial, the function Primfield() can be used. Primfield() can accept two arguments, the extension L and the base field K (the default is $\mathbf{Q}$). Both fields are specified as sets of RootOf(), and, of course, it is necessary that K be a subfield of L, meaning the second argument must be a subset of the first. We will apply Primfield() to find a primitive element for $\mathbf{Q}(2^{1/4}, i)$:

```
>alias(xi=RootOf(x^2+1));
```

$$I, \ xi$$

```
>alias(eta=RootOf(x^4-2));
```

$$I, \ xi, \ eta$$

```
>evala(Primfield({xi,eta}));
```

```
[[%1 = xi + eta],
```

$$[xi = -\ 5/24\ \%1^7\ -\ \frac{127}{24}\ \%1\ -\ 5/24\ \%1^3\ -\ \frac{19}{24}\ \%1^5\ ,$$

$$eta = \frac{151}{24}\ \%1\ +\ 5/24\ \%1^7\ +\ 5/24\ \%1^3\ +\ \frac{19}{24}\ \%1^5\ ]]$$

$$\%1\ :=\ RootOf(4\ \_Z^6\ +\ 2\ \_Z^4\ +\ 28\ \_Z^2\ +\ \_Z^8\ +\ 1)$$

The output from `Primfield()` consists of a list containing two lists. The first list contains an equation whose left side is the primitive element and whose right side is the representation of the primitive element in terms of the generators used to define the extension L. In this instance, the primitive element is just the sum of the generators. The second list contains equations exhibiting the generators in terms of the primitive element. The variable abbreviated `%1` is the minimal polynomial of u.

We can check that $\mathbf{Q}(u)$ does generate the splitting field for $x^4 - 2$ as follows:

```
>alias(u=%1);
```

$$I,\ u$$

```
>factor(x^4-2,u);
```

$$1/331776\ (24\ x\ -\ 151\ u\ -\ 5\ u^3\ -\ 19\ u^5\ -\ 5\ u^7)$$

$$(24\ x\ +\ 29\ +\ 13\ u^2\ +\ 5\ u^4\ +\ u^6)$$

$$(24\ x\ +\ 151\ u\ +\ 5\ u^3\ +\ 19\ u^5\ +\ 5\ u^7)$$

$$(24\ x\ -\ 29\ -\ 13\ u^2\ -\ 5\ u^4\ -\ u^6)$$

According to the first result from `Primfield()`, we can take for u any number of the form $\pm 2^{1/4} \pm I$. Picking one of these and substituting gives a factorization in terms of radicals:

```
>simplify(subs(u=-2^(1/4)+I,"));
```

$$
\begin{array}{cccc}
1/4 & 1/4 & 1/4 & 1/4 \\
(x + 2 \quad) \ (x - 2 \quad) \ (x - I \ 2 \quad) \ (x + I \ 2 \quad)
\end{array}
$$

Note that `Primfield()`, unlike most other `evala()` functions, will not accept radicals as the definition of the field. Because of this, it was necessary to explicitly write `RootOf(x^2+1)` for the complex number i, since `I` is an `alias()` to the radical $(-1)^{1/2}$.

On the subject of splitting fields, you can find the splitting field of a polynomial directly using the `readlib()` defined command `split()`:

```
>readlib(split):
>split(x^4-2,x,'ext');
```

$$
\begin{array}{ccc}
& 2 & 4 \quad 2 \\
(x + \text{RootOf}(\_Z & + \text{RootOf}(\_Z & - 2) \ ))
\end{array}
$$

$$
\begin{array}{ccc}
& 2 & 4 \quad 2 \\
(x - \text{RootOf}(\_Z & + \text{RootOf}(\ Z & - 2) \ ))
\end{array}
$$

$$
\begin{array}{cc}
4 & 4 \\
(x - \text{RootOf}(\_Z & - 2)) \ (x + \text{RootOf}(\_Z & - 2))
\end{array}
$$

```
>ext;
```

$$
\begin{array}{cccc}
4 & 2 & 4 \quad 2 \\
\{\text{RootOf}(\_Z & - 2), \ \text{RootOf}(\_Z & + \text{RootOf}(\_Z & - 2) \ )\}
\end{array}
$$

Maple's representation of the splitting field is returned in the third (optional) variable. You can check that the field extension returned here is equal to $\mathbf{Q}(u)$, where u is the primitive element found earlier.

Multivariate polynomials are handled in a fashion similar to their univariate counterparts:

```
>factor(x^3-y^3);
```

$$(x - y) (x^2 + x y + y^2)$$

```
>factor(x^3-y^3,RootOf(z^2+3));
```

$$1/4 (2 x + y + RootOf(\_Z^2 + 3) y)$$

$$(2 x + y - RootOf(\_Z^2 + 3) y) (x - y)$$

As we mentioned at the end of the previous subsection, in order to have a well-defined extension of **Q**, roots appended should be of an irreducible polynomial. Normally, `evala()` will check that the specified `RootOf()` expressions do correspond to such polynomials and, for extensions involving more than one `RootOf()`, that the roots are independent.

Roots dependent on parameters

We saw earlier that the equations defining a root may contain parameters, as in the following illustration:

```
>RootOf(x^2+b*x+c,x);
```

$$RootOf(\_Z^2 + b \_Z + c)$$

It is useful to know that the derivatives of the roots with respect to the parameters can be obtained without actually having explicit formulas for the roots. Here is an example:

```
>alias(xi=RootOf(x^2+b*x+c,x));
```

$$I, xi$$

```
>diff(xi,b);
```

$$- \frac{xi}{2\ xi\ +\ b}$$

```
>diff(xi,b,c);
```

$$\frac{1}{(2\ xi\ +\ b)^2}\ -\ 2\ \frac{xi}{(2\ xi\ +\ b)^3}$$

Similarly, `series()` will compute expansions of the root in terms of the parameters.

```
>series(xi,b=1,3);
```

$$RootOf(\_Z^2\ +\ \_Z\ +\ c)$$

$$-\ \frac{RootOf(\_Z^2\ +\ \_Z\ +\ c)\ +\ 2\ c}{4\ c\ -\ 1}\ (b\ -\ 1)$$

$$-\ \frac{c\ (2\ RootOf(\_Z^2\ +\ \_Z\ +\ c)\ +\ 1)}{(4\ c\ -\ 1)^2}\ (b\ -\ 1)^2$$

$$+\ O((b\ -\ 1)^3)$$

These are often used to calculate the derivatives and series expansions of eigenvalues of square matrices with respect to parameters appearing in the definition of the matrix.

7.2 Finite fields

This section illustrates the main techniques available in Maple for defining and computing in finite fields. The two subsections are

- Representing Finite Fields
- Computing in Finite Fields

Representing finite fields

In this subsection, we will show how finite fields can be formed and represented in Maple. We begin by recalling that a finite field has p^k elements where p is a prime and k a positive integer. When $k = 1$, the field is just $\mathbf{Z}_p$, which can be represented as the set $\{0, 1, 2, \ldots, p-1\}$ with addition and multiplication performed mod p. If $k > 1$, it is usual to express an element of the field as a polynomial of degree $k-1$ in $\mathbf{Z}_p[\xi]$, where ξ is a primitive element (a root of an irreducible polynomial of degree k over $\mathbf{Z}_p$).

How can we find a suitable irreducible polynomial of degree k? For a first approach, we can make use of the fact that in any finite field of prime characteristic p, the polynomial $x^p - x - a$ is either irreducible or factors completely. It follows that we can construct the field having p^p elements provided we are able to choose a appropriately. For example, if $p = 7$ we can choose $a = 1$:

```
>p := 7;
```

$$p := 7$$

```
>Factor(x^p x-1) mod p;
```

$$x^7 + 6 x + 6$$

We will have more to say about the syntax of this expression in the following subsection. For now, we will just say that mod is an infix operator that causes evaluation of its left inert argument Factor(), modulo its right argument p. From this result, we can obtain the required factorization:

```
>alias(xi=RootOf("));
```

$$I,\ xi$$

```
>Factor(x^p-x-1,xi) mod p;
```

$$(x + 6\ xi + 1)\ (x + 6\ xi)\ (x + 6\ xi + 5)\ (x + 6\ xi + 6)$$
$$(x + 6\ xi + 2)\ (x + 6\ xi + 3)\ (x + 6\ xi + 4)$$

The polynomial splits in $\mathbf{Z}_p[\xi]$, and $\mathbf{Z}_p[\xi]$ represents the field having $823543 = 7^7$ elements. For a more general approach, we can use the readlib() defined function GF() (Galois field). Given a prime p and integer k, GF() can be used to obtain an irreducible polynomial of degree k over $\mathbf{Z}_p$. We illustrate the steps in the following example, where $p = 11$ and $k = 4$:

```
>readlib(GF):
>F := GF(11,4):
>q := F[extension];
```

$$q := 10000000500000007$$

```
>q := F[ConvertOut](q);
```

$$q :- \ ?^4 \ + 5\ ?^2 \ + 7$$

```
>q := subs('?'=x,q);
```

$$q := x^4 \ + 5\ x^2 \ + 7$$

```
>Factor(q) mod 11;
```

$$x^4 \ + 5\ x^2 \ + 7$$

Here is an explanation of this somewhat cryptic output: the function call GF(p,k) returns a Maple table in F (there is an extensive discussion of tables in Section 10.3). The table entry indexed by [extension] contains a representation of an irreducible polynomial of degree k. The entry indexed by [ConvertOut] contains a function that converts the representation of the polynomial to the usual format. This function must be applied to the numerical representation in the way shown. The final result is the polynomial $x^4 + 5x^2 + 7$, which is irreducible over $\mathbf{Z}_{11}$, and the field with $14641 = 11^4$ elements can be represented as $\mathbf{Z}_{11}[\xi]$, where $\xi = \texttt{RootOf}(x^4 + 5*x^2 + 7)$.

Computing in finite fields

The basic technique for computing in finite fields is to set up an expression using inert functions and then to evaluate it mod p. For example, to factor the polynomial $p(x) = x^2 + x + 1$ over $\mathbf{Z}_3$, the inert function $\texttt{Factor()}$ is used:

```
>Factor(x^2+x+1) mod 3;
```

$$(x + 2)^2$$

For finite fields, the infix function mod plays the same role as $\texttt{evala()}$ for algebraic number fields. In the above example, $\texttt{Factor()}$ is inert; it was mod that caused the evaluation. From the help file for mod, here is a list of inert functions that it recognizes:

Berlekamp	Content	Det	Discrim	DistDeg
Divide	Eval	Expand	Factor	Factors
Frobenius	Gausselim	Gaussjord	Gcd	Gcdex
GetAlgExt	Hermite	Interp	Inverse	Issimilar
Lcm	Linsolve	Normal	Nullspace	Power
Powmod	Prem	Prime	Primitive	ProbSplit
Randpoly	Ratrecon	Rem	Resultant	RootOf
Roots	Smith	Sprem	Sqrfree	

In addition to many standard functions, we see from this list that mod recognizes some linear algebra functions. For instance, the Gauss–Jordan elimination function is recognized. To illustrate the use of this function, here is a computation of the solution of a 2×2 system of equations in the field containing nine elements:

```
>with(linalg):
>alias(xi=RootOf(x^2+1)):
>A := matrix([[xi+1,2*xi+2,1],[2*xi+1,0,2]]);
```

$$A := \begin{bmatrix} xi + 1 & 2\,xi + 2 & 1 \\ 2\,xi + 1 & 0 & 2 \end{bmatrix}$$

```
>Gaussjord(A) mod 3;
```

$$
\begin{array}{ccc}
[\ 1 & 0 & xi + 1 \ ] \\
[& & \ ] \\
[\ 0 & 1 & 2 \ ]
\end{array}
$$

To further illustrate the use of the inert functions for computing in finite fields, we will show some calculations centered around the first six cyclotomic polynomials in $\mathbf{Z}_5$. The nth cyclotomic polynomial is defined as the product of linear factors $(x - \xi)$, where ξ ranges over the distinct primitive nth roots of unity. These polynomials may be computed recursively by the formula

$$
g_n(x) = \frac{x^n - 1}{\displaystyle\prod_{m|n, \ m<n} g_m(x)}
$$

The degrees of the cyclotomic polynomials can be found using the Euler totient function, $\phi(n)$, which counts the number of integers in the interval $[1, n]$ that are relatively prime to n. This function is part of the number theory package numtheory[]. The degrees of the first six polynomials are then:

```
>numtheory[phi](i) mod 5 $i-1..6;
```

$$1, \ 1, \ 2, \ 2, \ 4, \ 2$$

To compute the polynomials, we will use a few programming constructs, which are explained in detail in Chapter 10:

```
>for n from 1 to 6 do
    g.n:=x^n-1;
    for m from 1 to n-1 do
      if type(n/m,integer) then g.n:=g.n/g.m fi;
    od;
    g.n:=Normal(g.n) mod 5;
 od:
```

Normal() is used here to remove common factors. The next command displays the polynomials using the dollar operator (Why do you think the forward quotes are needed?):

```
>'g.i' $i=1..6;
```

$$x + 4, \quad x + 1, \quad x^2 + x + 1, \quad x^2 + 1,$$

$$x^4 + x^3 + x^2 + x + 1, \quad x^2 + 4x + 1$$

and their degrees are as expected.

The degree of g_n determines the number of primitive nth roots of unity in $\mathbf{Z}_5$, and they can be found by factoring g_n. For example:

```
>alias(xi=RootOf(g6)):
>Factor(g6,xi) mod 5;
```

$$(x + xi + 4) \ (x + 4 \ xi)$$

which means that the two primitive 6th roots of unity in $\mathbf{Z}_5$ are `xi` and `1-xi= -(xi+4)`. The sequence of all 6th roots of unity is given by the powers of these primitive roots:

```
>seq(Power(xi,n) mod 5,n=1..6);
```

$$xi, \quad xi + 4, \quad 4, \quad 4 \ xi, \quad 4 \ xi + 1, \quad 1$$

As a check:

```
>map(x->Power(x,6) mod 5,["]);
```

$$[1, \ 1, \ 1, \ 1, \ 1, \ 1]$$

Similarly:

```
>seq(Power(1-xi,n) mod 5,n=1..6);
```

$$4 \ xi + 1, \quad 4 \ xi, \quad 4, \quad xi + 4, \quad xi, \quad 1$$

Finally, while `xi+4` is a 6th root of unity, it is not primitive, as the following calculation shows:

```
>seq(Power(xi+4,n) mod 5,n=1..6);
```

$$xi + 4, \ 4 \ xi, \ 1, \ xi + 4, \ 4 \ xi, \ 1$$

The function `GF()` that we mentioned above contains some alternative ways for performing calculations in finite fields. For example, simple operations such as addition and subtraction are implemented as prefix functions. Generally, we have found the infix notation easier to use.

7.3 Polynomial rings

Once you know how to compute in fields of algebraic numbers and finite fields, it is relatively straightforward to compute in the polynomial rings $K[x]$ and in their quotient fields $K(x)$, where K is an algebraic number or finite field. Since the techniques for working with polynomials over the algebraic numbers or finite fields are similar (one just uses `evala()` or `mod`, respectively) we will combine the discussion of the two. The subsections below cover

- Basic Arithmetic
- Polynomial Ring Operations
- Linear Algebra

Basic arithmetic

Given an algebraic number field or finite field K and two polynomials in $K[x]$ (or $K[x, y, \ldots]$), their sum, difference, and product can be computed in the usual fashion. A judicious use of `collect()`, `simplify()`, and `mod` can then convert the result into the standard form of a sum of products of coefficients in K and powers of x (or $x, y, \ldots$). Here are a few illustrations:

```
>alias(xi=RootOf(x^3+2)):
>f:=(xi^2+1)*x^2+(2*xi+1)*x+(xi^2+xi+3):
>g:=(2*xi^2+xi-2)*x+xi:
>fpg:=collect(f+g,x,simplify);

fpg :=
```

$$(xi^2 + 1) \ x^2 + (3 \ xi - 1 + 2 \ xi^2) \ x + 2 \ xi^2 + 3 + xi$$

```
>fg:=collect(expand(f*g),x,simplify);
```

$$fg := (-3\ xi - 4)\ x^3 + (-2\ xi^2 + 4\ xi - 12)\ x^2$$

$$+ (-12 - 2\ xi + 7\ xi^2)\ x + xi^2 + 3\ xi - 2$$

```
>fg mod 7;
```

$$(4\ xi + 3)\ x^3 + (5\ xi^2 + 4\ xi + 2)\ x^2 + (2 + 5\ xi)\ x$$

$$+ xi^2 + 3\ xi + 5$$

The `Normal()` command is provided for doing calculations in the field of quotients $K(x)$. `Normal()` will write an expression involving sums and quotients of polynomials in the form "numerator/denominator," where the numerator and denominator are relatively prime. Unlike the `normal()` command, the inert version `Normal()` does not automatically factor the numerator and denominator. To illustrate:

```
>alias(xi=RootOf(x^2-2)):
>f:=x^4+(-xi+3)*x^3+(-2*xi+4)*x^2+(3-2*xi)*x-xi+1:
>g:=x^4+2*x^3+(3*xi-5)*x^2+(-14+9*xi)*x+6*xi-8:
>evala(Normal(f/g+g/f));
```

$$(2\ x^4 + 2\ x^3 + 2\ xi\ x^3 - 3\ x^2 + 4\ x^2\ xi + 10\ x^2 - 8\ xi\ x$$

$$+ 25 - 16\ xi)\ /\ (x^4 + x^3 + xi\ x^3 - 3\ x^2$$

$$/$$

$$+ 3\ x^2\ xi - 4\ x + 3\ xi\ x - 4 + 2\ xi)$$

The quotient can be factored as follows:

```
>evala(Factor(numer(")))/evala(Factor(denom(")));
```

```
                                                           3
       (- 16 xi + 25 + 2 (5 - 4 xi) x + 2 (1 + xi) x

                                   2       4
            + 2 (2 xi - 3/2) x  + 2 x )

                 /    2
                 /  ((x  + x + 1) (x + xi - 2) (x + 2))
                 /
```

The same example can be computed in the extension of $\mathbf{Z}_3$:

```
>Normal(f/g+g/f) mod 3;
```

```
                        2
              2 x  + 2 xi x + 2 xi + 1
              ------------------------
                   2
              x  + xi x + 2 + 2 xi
>(Factor(numer(")) mod 3)/(Factor(denom(")) mod 3);
```

```
                          2
            (x + RootOf(_Z  + 1) + 2) (x + 1)
        2 ---------------------------------
                             2
            (x + 2) (x + RootOf(_Z  + 1) + 1)
```

The RootOf() expressions appear in this form because $xi = \mathrm{RootOf}(x^2 - 2) \equiv \mathrm{RootOf}(x^2 + 1)$ mod 3.

Ring operations

Many of the standard ring operations such as greatest common divisor, Gcd(), and remainder after division, Rem(), are recognized by both evala() and mod; we will illustrate a few of these functions below. Note, however, that the two evaluators are not completely parallel; for instance, mod will compute the least-common multiple, using Lcm(), whereas evala() will not. Here are some illustrations:

```
>alias(xi=RootOf(x^2-2)):
>f:=x^4+(-xi+3)*x^3+(-2*xi+4)*x^2+(3-2*xi)*x-xi+1:
>g:=x^4+2*x^3+(3*xi-5)*x^2+(-14+9*xi)*x+6*xi-8:
>evala(Gcd(f,g));
```

$$x^2 + 2x - x\,xi + 1 - xi$$

```
>Gcd(f,g) mod 3;
```

$$x^3 + 2x^2\,xi + x^2 + 2x + xi + 2$$

Similarly, we can calculate quotients and remainders:

```
>alias(xi=RootOf(x^2-2)):
>f:=x^4+(-xi+3)*x^3+(-2*xi+4)*x^2+(3-2*xi)*x-xi+1:
>evala(Quo(f,x+2,x,'r'));
```

$$x^3 + x^2 - x^2\,xi + 2x - 1 - 2\,xi$$

```
>r;
```

$$3 + 3\,xi$$

```
>Quo(f,x+2,x,'r') mod 3;
```

$$x^3 + (2\,xi + 1)\,x^2 + 2x + xi + 2$$

```
>r;
```

$$0$$

```
>evala(Divide(f,x-xi+1));
```

$$true$$

```
>evala(Divide(f,x+2));
```

$$false$$

```
>Divide(f,x+2) mod 3;
```

$$true$$

Linear algebra

Many of the commands in the linear algebra package will work for vectors and matrices defined over the field $\mathbf{Q}(x, y, \ldots)$ or $\mathbf{Q}(I, x, y, \ldots)$, where $I = (-1)^{1/2}$ but not directly with algebraic numbers. However, you can perform algebraic number computations with the linear algebra functions by setting indeterminates to be roots of various polynomials and then using `simplify()` and/or `mod` on the result. This provides a way to perform linear algebra in polynomial rings over algebraic number fields. To illustrate this, we will calculate a determinant:

```
>with(linalg):
>alias(xi=RootOf(x^3+2)):
>A := matrix([[xi*x+1,(2*xi^2+1)*x+x+xi],
              [x+xi^2,(2-xi)*x+1-xi]]);
```

```
         [                         2                    ]
         [ xi x + 1   (2 xi  + 1) x + x + xi ]
    A := [                                             ]
         [          2                                  ]
         [  x + xi        (2 - xi) x + 1 - xi  ]
```

```
>detA := det(A);
```

```
              2          2 2         2
>detA := 2 xi x   - 3 xi  x   - 3 xi  x + 2 x + 1 - xi
              4          2              3
         - 2 xi  x - 2 x  - xi x - xi
```

```
>detA := collect(simplify(detA),x);
```

```
detA :=
```

$$(2\ xi^2 - 3\ xi^2 - 2)\ x^2 + (-3\ xi^2 + 2 + 3\ xi)\ x + 3 - xi$$

For matrix-valued quantities, it is necessary to map simplify() onto the result. Here we square the matrix defined above:

```
>Asq:=evalm(A^2):
>Asq:=map(xx->collect(simplify(xx),x),Asq);
```

```
Asq :=
```

$$[(2 + 3\ xi^2)\ x^2 + (2\ xi^2 - xi)\ x - 1,$$
$$(4\ xi^2 + 4)\ x^2 + (4\ xi^2 + 8)\ x - xi^2 + 2\ xi]$$

$$[2\ x^2 + (2 + 2\ xi^2 - xi)\ x + 2\ xi^2 + 2,$$

$$(3\ xi^2 + 6 - 4\ xi)\ x^2 + (4 + 4\ xi^2 - 9\ xi)\ x + xi^2$$

$$- 1 - 2\ xi]$$

We saw earlier that some linear algebra functions have inert forms that mod recognizes. Det() is one of these. Thus, for instance, we can obtain:

```
>Det(A) mod 7;
```

$$(4\ xi^2 + 2\ xi + 5)\ x^2 + (4\ xi^2 + 3\ xi + 2)\ x + 6\ xi + 3$$

However, there is no inert form of evalm(), and consequently there seems to be no direct way to square A mod p. An indirect way to do this is as follows (with p=7 for illustration):

```
>Asq := evalm(A^2):
>Asq := map(xx->collect(simplify(xx) mod 7,x),Asq);

Asq :=
```

$$[(2 + 3\ \text{xi}^2)\ x^2 + (2\ \text{xi}^2 + 6\ \text{xi})\ x + 6,$$

$$(4\ \text{xi}^2 + 4)\ x^2 + (4\ \text{xi}^2 + 1)\ x + 6\ \text{xi}^2 + 2\ \text{xi}]$$

$$[2\ x^2 + (2 + 2\ \text{xi}^2 + 6\ \text{xi})\ x + 2\ \text{xi}^{2s} + 2,$$

$$(6 + 3\ \text{xi}^2 + 3\ \text{xi})\ x^2 + (4 + 4\ \text{xi}^2 + 5\ \text{xi})\ x + \text{xi}^2$$

$$+ 6 + 5\ \text{xi}]$$

By defining matrices with ratios of elements from $\mathbf{Q}(\xi)[x]$, similar techniques can be used to compute in the field of quotients $\mathbf{Q}(\xi)(x)$ and the fields $\mathbf{Z}_p(\xi)(x)$.

7.4 Reference section

DEFINITION OF AND EVALUATION IN FIELD EXTENSION

allvaues	Determines all possible values of a RootOf()
evala	Evaluator over algebraic extensions of $\mathbf{Q}$
GF()	Finite field package (readlib function)
mod	Evaluator over algebraic extensions of $\mathbf{Z}_p$
RootOf	Defines a root of an equation (typically a polynomial)
split	Calculates the splitting field of a polynomial (readlib function)

FUNCTIONS THAT RECOGNIZE RootOf()

alias diff simplify
evalf
series

SOME INERT FUNCTIONS RECOGNIZED BY `evala()` AND `mod()`

Factor	Factorize an expression
Det	Determinant of a matrix (mod only)
Divide	Test to see if one expression divides another
Gaussjord	Eliminate a matrix to Gauss–Jordan form (mod only)
Gcd	Greatest common divisor of a set of polynomials
Normal	Convert an expression to a vulgar fraction
Power	Raise an expression to a power
Primfield	Calculate a primitive element of a field extension
Quo	Quotient of two expressions
Rem	Remainder after division of one expression by another

8 Useful utilities

Maple has several kinds of functions that can be thought of as utilities, including mathematical utilities and utilities that assist interaction with the host computer system. In this chapter, we will discuss these functions.

The first section discusses importing and exporting data. This is a broad topic that includes exporting Maple results to other programs and importing the results of other programs into Maple for additional processing. This form of data exchange is done through files that usually must be precisely formatted. How such formatting is done is discussed in Section 8.1.

In Section 8.2, we will look at utilities that are associated with Maple's interaction with the host system and with the operation of Maple itself. This covers a number of disparate topics, including running external programs from inside Maple, obtaining information about system resources, and getting Maple to tell you what is going on in a computation.

Section 8.3 shows how to use Maple's language-conversion utilities. These functions are used to convert Maple output to a form suitable for input to other programs. There are four converters, and they produce output that can be read by C and Fortran compilers – that is, C and Fortran code – and output that can be read by the typesetting languages TeX (through LaTeX) and the UNIX equation typesetting facility called "eqn." Section 8.4 covers utilities for producing randomized entities such as random numbers and polynomials. We will discuss the form of Maple's primary (quasi) random-number generator and a number of functions built around it.

Sections 8.5–8.6 cover Maple's sorting utility and the numerous options available using the `convert(,)` function. We have used `convert(,)` on several occasions; here, we will give a comprehensive list of what options are available and a breakdown by category. Many useful functions are available as options to `convert(,)` as we will see.

8.1   Reading and writing files

In this section, we cover techniques for reading and writing files from inside Maple. A major use for these techniques is sharing data between Maple and other programs. For instance, you could use Maple to plot data from another source, or you could use fast numerical software to invert a large Maple-generated matrix. Another use for files is saving and reading Maple assignments from a Maple session. The topics for this section are

- Writing and Reading Files with `writedata()` and `readdata()`
- About Files
- Formatted Input and Output
- Saving and Reading Maple Results

Writing and reading files with `writedata()` and `readdata()`

A basic function for writing files (especially numerical files) from inside Maple is called `writedata()`. This function can write sets, lists, lists of lists, and matrices. In its simplest form, `writedata()` opens a specified file, performs the desired writing operation on the file, and then closes the file. For example, in the next two commands we will create a small matrix and write it to a file:

```
> A:=evalm(0.1*linalg[randmatrix](3,4));
```

$$
A := \begin{bmatrix} 4.5 & -.8 & -9.3 & 9.2 \\ 4.3 & -6.2 & 7.7 & 6.6 \\ 5.4 & -.5 & 9.9 & -6.1 \end{bmatrix}
$$

```
> writedata(wtest,A);
```

Here is a snapshot of `wtest`:

```
4.500000        -.800000       -9.300000        9.200000
4.300000       -6.200000        7.700000        6.600000
5.400000        -.500000        9.900000       -6.100000
```

If the named file does not exist it will be created, if it exists it will be overwritten, and in both cases it will be closed at the end of the write operation. Using the word `terminal` as the file name will cause the output to be written to the screen.

The default type for `writedata()` is float. To have data written as integers you specify the word `integer` as a third argument. In this case, data will be converted to the nearest integer. The third argument can be also specified as `float`, `string`, or a list containing the three types. The list argument allows you to write lists of mixed numerical and string data. Floats are represented using six decimal places or, for very small or large numbers, exponential notation. This format is preprogrammed into `writedata()` and cannot be changed by options. To write more digits or to use alternative formatting, see the Formatted Input and Output subsection below.

The `writedata()` function can handle only the types already mentioned. It will not write sequences of numbers for example. However, if you want to write data that is not integer, float, or string it is possible to add a fourth argument consisting of a procedure that can produce the desired formatted output.

The `writedata()` function has a counterpart for reading numerical files called `readdata()`. This function reads a specified number of columns from a file. It will open the file, read the requested data, and then close the file. Data may be specified as either float or integer. When reading floating point data, `readdata()` will read a maximum of `Digits` of the decimal digits of the data. To illustrate the use of this function, we will use the following data file, which is called `rtest`:

```
1.0000000000   1.4142135620   1.7320508080
2.0000000000   2.8284271240   3.4641016160
3.0000000000   4.2426406860   5.1961524240
```

The data in this file has ten decimal digits and currently `Digits` is set to 10. If you call `readdata()` with just the file name, the following is what happens:

```
> readdata(rtest);
```

```
                [1.0000000000, 2.0000000000, 3.0000000000]
```

As you see, the first column has been read and placed in a list. To obtain more columns, the required number is used as the second argument:

```
> readdata(rtest,3);
```

```
          [[1.000000000, 1.414213562, 1.732050808],
            [2.000000000, 2.828427124, 3.464101616],
            [3.000000000, 4.242640686, 5.196152424]]
```

and the result is a list of row lists. The optional third argument to `readdata()` is float or integer. As you can see from above, float is the default.

The advantage of `writedata()` and `readdata()` is that Maple handles the associated file opening and closing operations automatically. Next we will see how to perform these operations manually.

About files

Maple has a number of commands for opening and closing different kinds of files and for reading and writing formatted data with them. A full list of the file manipulation commands is in the SEE ALSO part of `?iolist`, and additional pointers are in `?files`. Unless you are doing some fairly intensive work involving files, you will not have to deal with most of these functions. However, you may well find it useful to be able to read and write files in ways not supported by `writedata()` and `readdata()`. The following subsection will show you how this can be accomplished.

The general topic of files is system dependent to some extent. For instance, UNIX does not distinguish between binary and text files, whereas MS-DOS treats the two kinds of files in different ways. Maple handles this by ignoring unneeded descriptors in file commands. Below, we will mention system-dependent matters only if it seems essential.

To open a file, there are the commands `fopen()` and `open()`. These are analogous to the eponymous C commands and refer to opening what are called buffered and unbuffered files, respectively. Roughly speaking, the difference lies in the mode of transfer of data between disk and memory. The advantage of the buffered type is speed of transfer. Data is transferred in blocks of a specific size that is set by, and convenient for, the operating system. Unbuffered files however, can transfer small amounts of data without using a whole block. Unless you are doing heavy file input and output, you may not notice much difference between the two modes. We will use buffered files in our examples. When you arc done using a file you should close it. The closing commands for buffered and unbuffered files are `fclose()` and `close()`, respectively.

Formatted input and output

After the file is opened, you need to get data in and out of it. For this you use functions such as `fprintf()`, `writeline()`, `fscanf()`, and `readline()`. The functions `fprintf()` and `fscanf()` resemble the C functions of the same name. They can contain formatting information specifying such things as the number of decimal digits to be written or read.

First, we will discuss some details of how formatting commands are embedded in `fprintf()` and its relative `printf()`. The `printf()` function has the same capabilities as `fprint()` and we will use it to explain the formatting rules. The difference between the functions is just that `fprintf()` writes to a named file, whereas `printf()` writes to the screen (or current output stream).

Using `printf()`, you can specify different kinds of numerical output in scientific notation, including octal and hexadecimal integers as well as floating-point numbers. Also, there are specifications for characters and strings and for pointers. The `printf()` function can also imitate `lprint()` output. The next example illustrates some of these capabilities:

```
>printf('%6s Does %d = %f %c \n','     ',1729,1729,'?');
         Does 1729 = 1729.000000 ?
```

The `printf()` function takes two major arguments, a format specification and a sequence of expressions to be formatted. As usual, the expressions will be evaluated before formatting. The format specification (a string, notice) contains format codes that fix the formatting of each expression. Each code starts with a percent symbol and can be followed with several optional symbols. For instance, the first symbol may be a field width, as in the first format code above, or a letter as in the other codes above. A letter specifies the kind of formatting to be applied to the corresponding expression. In the example, `s` stands for string formatting, `d` stands for (decimal or base 10) integer formatting, `f` stands for fixed decimal point formatting, and `c` stands for (single) character formatting.

The example above shows that you can include text in the format specification and have it copied into the output exactly as written, which makes it easy to include unchanging material that would otherwise have to be incorporated as separate strings. The symbol "`\n`" causes a new line to be inserted after the other output. This is a standard C convention. Another way to insert a new line is to follow the `printf()` function with a call to `lprint()` with no arguments.

Here is another illustration of some floating-point formatting:

```
>printf('\n     %10.8e  %10.8g %10.8g\n',evalf(Pi),
        evalf(Pi),1729);

     3.14159265e+000    3.1415927         1729
```

This time the format specification begins by inserting a new line and some space. The first code is a standard scientific notation format, in this case a field of width ten with eight figures after the decimal point. An uppercase `E` can be used in place of `e`. The remaining `g` (or `G`) code is the most flexible numerical conversion because Maple chooses `d`, `f`, or `e` codes according to whether the data is an integer or a float of certain size.

The code for producing `lprint()` output is a. For instance:

```
>A:=[sin(x),sin(x^2),sin(x^3)];
```

$$A := [\sin(x), \sin(x^2), \sin(x^3)]$$

```
>lprint(A);
[sin(x), sin(x^2), sin(x^3)]
```

```
>printf('%a \n',A);
[sin(x), sin(x^2), sin(x^3)]
```

The two outputs are the same, as they should be.

The `printf()` function will display a hardware-dependent maximum number of significant digits, typically sixteen. Further, there are several additional format codes (for example, to format numbers in different bases) and some additional options, mainly for precisely aligning output in columns.

So much for formatted output. What about formatted input? Below, we will see that Maple can read external files line by line, interpreting each line as a string. These strings may contain both numerical and alphabetic substrings. The substrings can be extracted and formatted and put in a list using the function `sscanf()`. As with `printf()`, `sscanf()` has a fairly large number of options. Here, we will cover only the most often used aspects of this function.

The `sscanf()` function takes two main arguments; the string to be scanned and a sequence of format codes. Each format code starts with a percent symbol. If this symbol is followed by an asterisk, the next field is discarded without formatting. In the example that follows, the result should consist of the numerical data in the string and the text should be omitted:

```
> st:='Line 4: Value at (-1.2,2.2) is .921E-3';

      st := Line 4: Value at (-1.2,2.2) is .921E-3
```

```
> sscanf(st,'%*s %d: %*s %*s (%e,%f) %*s %g');

            [4, -1.2, 2.2, .000921]
```

The format code s places the characters that follow it, up to but not including the first space, in a string. In the first format code above, the * causes this field to be ignored. A space follows the s format. This space is significant: It will be matched to the space following the word "Line" in st. The next code, d, stands for a signed or unsigned decimal integer, and again, the following ":" is matched to the same character in st. The parentheses are similarly matched. The e, f, and g codes are equivalent and format their fields as floating-point numbers (Maple floats). The fields may or may not have a decimal point, a sign, or an exponent as in the example. Again, there is a hardware-dependent restriction on the number of significant digits appearing in a numerical conversion; in the example above it is sixteen.

There are some additional codes for sscanf() that format octal and hexadecimal numbers as decimal numbers and a format for pointers. There are also codes that scan up to the first character not in a list (see the example in the following subsection) and a code that counts the number of characters scanned. Finally, there is a code for a single-character scan and one for presenting a string to Maple for parsing.

Now we will illustrate a method for formatted file input and output. First we will create a small file; here are the commands for this step:

```
>   fw:=fopen(weather,WRITE);
```

$$fw := 3$$

```
> fprintf(weather,'Date      Low      High\n'):
> fprintf(fw,'6-15       48.5       70.4\n'):
> fprintf(fw,'6-16       49.0       66.8\n'):
> fprintf(fw,'6-17       42.9       67.2\n'):
> fprintf(fw,'6-18       44.2       69.9\n'):
> fclose(fw);
```

The first command opens the file for writing. The file will be created if it does not yet exist and will be overwritten if it does exist. The value of the command is an integer that can be used subsequently to refer to the file, as we did here. The data is created using a formatted writing operation. In this case, we entered the data as strings. Here is a snapshot of this file as it exists in our system:

```
Date        Low        High
6-15        48.5       70.4
6-16        49.0       66.8
6-17        42.9       67.2
6-18        44.2       69.9
```

We created this file using Maple statements, but in principle it could have been made by an unknown method.

Suppose that you wanted to compute the average low temperature from this file. Using `readdata()` is not the way to input the file because of the nonnumeric characters it contains. Instead we will use `readline()` to read the lines of the file and `sscanf()` to extract the needed data. The `readline()` function automatically opens the file so it is unnecessary to use `fopen()`.

```
>readline(weather);
```

```
              Date          Low          High
```

In this case, we have no further need for this line.

Now we can create a sequence containing the elements in the second column:

```
> seq(op(1,sscanf(readline(weather),'%*s%*[ ]%f')),
      j=1..4);
```

```
              48.5, 49.0, 42.9, 44.2
```

Notice how the `*[ ]` format is used to skip an unknown number of blanks in the input line. This format reads a field up to the first character it finds that is not in the list. In the above example, the field is read up to the first nonblank character, and the blanks are discarded. This lets you get away with knowing a bit less about the input file's structure. Note also that the last field was not read.

It would have been easy enough to average the entries directly, but it is clearer to form it in a separate step:

```
>sum("['j']",'j'=1..4)/4;
```

```
              46.15000000
```

This is the average low temperature. To find the high-temperature average, you can use a similar approach.

When `readline()` has read the last line of a file, a further call returns the number 0 and closes the file. This allows to you to work with files of unknown length by testing for this zero after each `readline()`.

The `readline()` function can read a maximum of 499 characters in a single call. If a line contains more characters than this, it can be read in consecutive calls. At least five files can be open simultaneously for use by `readline()`.

Related functions are `writeto()` and `appendto()`. These functions cause the output stream to be redirected to a named file. Formatted output can be placed in the file with `printf()`.

Saving and reading Maple results

The main utilities for saving and reading Maple results are `save` and `read`, which are used to save results from the current session and read them back into the current or a later session.

The `save` utility has two forms. The first form is as follows:

```
>save 'results':
```

or:

```
>save 'results.m':
```

In both cases, all assignments in the current session are saved. The ".m" extension denotes that the file is to be saved in an internal Maple format. Without the extension, the file is created in a character (ASCII) format using `lprint()`. An advantage of .m files is speed of saving and retreiving. A disadvantage is that they are designed to be read by Maple, not by people.

When all the assignments in a session are saved to a file without an .m extension, the file may contain a fair amount of extraneous information. The .m extension causes such information to be hidden.

Files without the .m extension are suitable for selective saving. For this, the second form of `save` is used in which there is a name, or sequence of names separated by commas, before the filename.

Here are some illustrations for `save` and `read`. First, we will generate some data in a new session:

```
>p:=linalg[hilbert](3);
```

$$
p := \begin{bmatrix} 1 & 1/2 & 1/3 \\ 1/2 & 1/3 & 1/4 \\ 1/3 & 1/4 & 1/5 \end{bmatrix}
$$

```
>q:='hello';
```

$$q := hello$$

```
>r:=x->x^2;
```

$$r := x -> x^2$$

Now we will save the whole session containing the three results and separately save the individual results:

```
>save 'all.m';
>save p,q,r,'some';
```

The string quotes are not strictly necessary in the second case but do no harm. They are essential when the .m extension is used.

Now we will read the data back into this session. Before doing so, we will clear all the current definitions from the session with the restart utility. This is equivalent to starting a new session:

```
>restart;
>read some;
```

$$p := \begin{bmatrix} 1 & 1/2 & 1/3 \\ 1/2 & 1/3 & 1/4 \\ 1/3 & 1/4 & 1/5 \end{bmatrix}$$

$$q := hello$$

$$r := x -> x^2$$

These assignments are now current in the session. For example:

```
>q;
```

$$hello$$

Using `read all.m` merely returns `NULL`, but the variables are nevertheless available in the session. For example, after another `restart` we obtain the following:

```
>read 'all.m';
>eval(r);
```

$$x \to x^2$$

Note that using `save` with a filename creates a file and destroys any existing file of the same name. This means that you have to save multiple results in the same call to `save` and later results in a new file.

The `read` function has no way to select named items (a matrix for example) from a saved file; you have to save individual results in their own files. Note also that many interfaces contain a menu command for saving an entire session verbatim. Also, the `writeto()` and `appendto()` functions can be useful for saving results to files.

8.2   System-related utilities

This section covers functions that provide information about and control of Maple's state and environment. The topics are

- Restarting a Session
- Running External Programs from Maple
- Resource Utilities
- Initialization Files
- Name Utilities
- Information Utilities

Restarting a session

A function we have used already and that everyone should know about is `restart`. The `restart` function simply restarts your Maple session from scratch, including reading the initialization files (see below). All existing assignments and local settings will be lost. It is nearly equivalent to quitting the current session and starting a new one, except that following `restart`, the available memory may not be quite as large as it would be if the session was started from the system level. In addition, the interface may not be reinitialized. The `restart` function is used without parentheses and does not take arguments. It cannot be used inside a procedure.

Running external programs from Maple

To run an external program from a Maple session, for example a compiled C, BASIC, or Fortran program, there is a function called `system()`. The external program's name is the argument to `system()`. To illustrate this, we will run a small executable (compiled) file called "weather.exe" that creates and writes a table of data:

```
>system('weather.exe');
```

$$0$$

The 0 is a status code informing you that execution has occurred. However, on some host systems the file you want to execute must be in the same directory as Maple. If it is in some other directory, `system()` may still return the 0 status code even though no execution has taken place; therefore, an independent check is advisable.

System resource utilities

For timing computations, Maple has a function called `time()`. This returns the current number of seconds that have been spent actually computing (CPU time) since the start of the session. To time a calculation, you call `time()` at the start and finish of the computation and subtract the results. No argument is necessary. We have used `time()` in Inverting Matrices in Section 4.2 and in Using Floating-Point Hardware in Section 5.7.

Another way to obtain timing information is through `showtime()`. This function also provides a figure for the amount of memory used in a calculation and automatically labels each result generated in a session. The labels can be used to refer to the results at later points in the session. The `showtime()` function must first be loaded using `readlib()`. Here is an illustration for `showtime()`:

```
> readlib(showtime):
> on;

O1 := with(linalg):
Warning, new definition for norm
Warning, new definition for trace
Warning, new definition for transpose
time = 0.15, bytes = 176074
O2 := randmatrix(10,10):
time = 0.06, bytes = 49778
O3 := charpoly(O2,x):
```

```
time = 1.66, bytes = 1402366
O4 := subs(x=O2,O3):
time = 0.01, bytes = 3826
O5 := iszero(evalm(O4));
```

$$true$$

```
time = 5.70, bytes = 4828546
O6 := off;
```

Events listed as taking zero seconds actually took less than one second. The labels for the results are O1, O2, and so on and remain valid until the off command is issued. Note that the uppercase letter "O", not zero, is used in the labels. The time and memory results are the same as would be obtained from the status indicator that is (optionally) visible on most interfaces. The showtime() function keeps a record of these resources. In this example, no names were assigned other than the labels, but there is no reason for not naming results in the regular way if that is desired. Also of interest is the fact that only a single ditto works when showtime() is active, so you can refer only to the last result using ditto notation.

There is a close relative of showtime() called history() that works in a similar way except that no time and memory results are reported. Only the labeling feature remains. A measure of the size of any expression can be obtained by using the expression as an argument to the function length().

A general function for obtaining and setting system-level parameters is called kernelopts(). With this function, you can find the version number of Maple, obtain information about the amounts of time and space allocated and used, find statistics on garbage collection (reclaiming unused memory), and other useful facts. Some of the options can be reset and others cannot. An option that cannot be reset is the maximum value of Digits. On our system this value is

```
> kernelopts(maxdigits);
```

$$524280$$

Initialization files

When Maple starts up, it reads files that initialize the Maple session. By inserting Maple commands into these files, you can automatically customize your Maple sessions. For instance, you can tailor the screen display width to fit a document you are writing or load files or packages that must always be present in your sessions.

Maple allows you to create a file with a specific system-dependent name (maple.ini in the MS Windows directory, .mapleinit in some UNIX systems) in your current or home directory that Maple will read at start-up time. You place your initialization commands in this file, which can be created with a text editor. A very simple initialization file might look like the following:

```
interface(screenwidth=55,prompt='>'):
with(linalg):
```

These two commands will be run before the main session starts. Such commands must be placed in the correctly named (including directory) initialization file for your system. Note the use of colons to suppress output, although you still cannot suppress the "New definition of" output that occurs when `linalg[]` is loaded.

There are other initialization files that set things such as graphics modes and default fonts. These files can be modified if necessary, although it is unwise to attempt changes unless you know what you are doing.

Name utilities

The function `unames()` provides a list of all names that are available in the current session but that have no value other than their own name. In addition to user-defined names, this function returns many names, including error messages, used by the system. A related function is `anames()`. This function provides a list of names that currently have a value other than their own name. The `anames()` function can take a type as an argument. In that case, it returns only assigned names of that type; however, even in such a case, many system names can appear in the result. For instance, `anames(procedure)` returns a list of all names currently assigned to procedures, including Maple's own assignments. To find out if a particular name is assigned, you use it as the argument to `assigned()`. The argument will be evaluated to a name only before being passed to `assigned()`. Full evaluation is not applied in this case.

Information utilities

There are some facilities for obtaining information about Maple commands and how they are operating. Two of the most useful are `infolevel[]` and `printlevel`, which cause Maple to write information to the screen about its progress with a computation. First, we will discuss the table called `infolevel[]` (tables in general are discussed in Section 10.3). An argument (or index) in this table is the name of a function, and the corresponding table entry is an information level represented by an integer from 1 to 5. Level 1 represents the least information and level 5 represents the most. When you make an entry in `infolevel[]`, every time the function is invoked information about its progress is reported, up to the specified level. Here is an example of how this works. We will use the procedure `rsolve()` for illustration:

```
>infolevel[rsolve]:=5;
>rsolve(f(n)=f(2*n)+1,f(n));
 rsolve:    solving single equation recurrence
 rsolve/single/process:
 evaluating divide and conquer recurrence
 rsolve/dc:   using default boundary condition
              0 at n = 1
                                    ln(n)
                        f(1) - -----
                                    ln(2)
```

The first statement sets the appropriate table entry. Then we ask for the solution of a recurrence equation. A short description of the steps being taken is given before the result is printed. Normally, only the final result would be printed but `infolevel[]` causes the additional information to be shown. Assigning the table entry `infolevel[all]` an integer value from 1 to 5 will cause every function to reveal its information at the assigned level.

The main drawback to `infolevel[]` is that what it reports is what the author of the function tells it to report. Unfortunately, that is often nothing at all. However, there is another way to inspect Maple's progress through a computation, and that is with a variable called `printlevel`. Although this causes a different kind of information to be printed, it is still useful. The next example shows what `printlevel` does with the above application of `rsolve()`:

```
>infolevel[rsolve]:=1;

                    infolevel[rsolve] := 1

>printlevel:=5;

                    printlevel := 5

>rsolve(f(n)=f(2*n)+1,f(n));
{--> enter rsolve, args = f(n) = f(2*n)+1, f(n)
         rsolve/single := readlib('rsolve/single')
```

```
   rsolve/system := readlib('rsolve/system')

 rsolve/makeproc := readlib('rsolve/makeproc')

  rsolve/ztrans := readlib('rsolve/ztrans')

          f_names := {f(n)}

        v_names := {n}
      f_names := {f(2 n), f(n)}

          f_names := {f}

     reqns := {f(n) = f(2 n) + 1}

unexp :=

  sin, sinh, cos, cosh, tan, tanh, csc, sec, cot, exp

     reqns := {f(n) = f(2 n) + 1}

<-- exit rsolve (now at top level) = f(1)-ln(n)/ln(2)}

                      ln(n)
           f(1) - -----
                      ln(2)
```

The first step sets the value of `infolevel[rsolve]` to a minimal value, where only the most essential things are reported. The second step sets `printlevel`. The `printlevel` function can be set to any integer value, including negative values, which effectively inhibit any printing of results. Larger values cause increasingly detailed reports. In this example, anything less than five gives no additional information. At our value of `printlevel`, we see which procedures are loaded and what assignments are made. Higher values would reveal additional features of the solution process. There is additional coverage of `printlevel` in Section 11.4.

The example above shows how high enough settings of `printlevel` reveal system information, whereas higher settings for `infolevel[]` produce additional messages from the function's author.

8.3 Language-conversion utilities

This section covers some Maple functions for converting Maple results to other computer languages. Currently supported languages are C, Fortran, and the typesetting languages eqn (a UNIX/troff utility) and LaTeX (strictly, not a language but a set of TeX macros). The topics are

- C and Fortran
- LaTeX and eqn

C and Fortran

The C and Fortran utilities (called `C()` and `fortran()`) are particularly useful in the common situation where you want to program long formulas produced by Maple. However, these functions can also produce loops and branches from Maple statements, and they are able to convert Maple procedures that do not contain excessively complicated constructions (such as `package[function](argument)`) to C functions or Fortran subroutines. If you do have a complex Maple code that you think can be translated into C, you may need to know a fair amount about C to make the C version work as it is meant to.

Here, we will discuss the `C()` function. The `fortran()` function is used in a similar way. Both `C()` and `fortran()` must be loaded with `readlib()` before they can be used.

It is in the nature of things that realistic applications of `C()`, say, are too long to print here, so we will have to use a simplified example. We will compute an integral and then produce the C code for it:

```
> ii := int(x^2*(x^2+3)^(3/2),x);
```

$$ii := 1/6\ x\ (x\ + 3)\ ^{5/2}\ ^2\ - 1/8\ x\ (x\ + 3)\ ^{3/2}\ ^2$$

$$- 9/16\ x\ (x\ + 3)\ ^{1/2}\ ^2\ - \frac{27}{16}\ arcsinh(1/3\ 3\ ^{1/2}\ x)$$

The next command produces the required code:

```
> readlib(C)(ii);
      t0 = x*sqrt(pow(x*x+3.0,5.0))/
           6-x*sqrt(pow(x*x+3.0,3.0))/8-9.0/16.0*x*
  sqrt(x*x+3.0)-27.0/16.0*arcsinh(sqrt(3.0)*x/3);
```

As you see, the formula is assigned to the variable t0. Variables t0, t1, t2, and so on are the names Maple uses when it needs to make assignments in C and Fortran. The code produced in this example is not efficient. There is an option to C() that avoids the redundant calculations:

```
> C(ii,optimized);
        t1 = x*x;
        t2 = t1+3.0;
        t3 = t2*t2;
        t4 = sqrt(t2);
        t10 = sqrt(3.0);
        t13 = x*t4*t3/6-x*t4*t2/8-9.0/16.0*x*t4-27.0/
              16.0*arcsinh(t10*x/3);
```

You can direct the C() output to a file. You add the option filename='Ccode' or whatever the file name actually is. You could also use save() or writeto()/appendto() for this. The fortran() function is used in a similar way to C().

There are options available for producing ansi C (instead of the default K&R C that differs mainly in the use of function prototypes) and for specifying the precision of constants and data.

LaTeX and eqn

Now we will discuss the typesetting utilities. For illustration, we will use the latex() function for converting expressions to the LaTeX format. The eqn() function is used in a similar way. Among the useful features of latex() are its ability to produce greek letters from Maple variables with the same name, its knowledge of Maple functions such as Int(), Limit(), and Sum(), and its ability to format matrices. Here are some examples to illustrate these points:

```
>sum(1/i,i=1..n);
```

$$Psi(n + 1) + gamma$$

```
>latex(");
\Psi(n+1)+\gamma
```

Note the correct conversion of the greek letters to the LaTeX format. Inert forms of functions should be used to prevent evaluation, as in the next example:

```
>Limit(sqrt(x^2+x)-sqrt(x^2+1),x=infinity);
```

```
                        2     1/2       2     1/2
      Limit            (x  + x)     -  (x  + 1)
      x -> infinity
```

```
>latex(");
\lim _{x\rightarrow \infty }\sqrt {x^{2}+x}
     -\sqrt {x^{2}+1}
```

Note the correct LaTeX formatting of the limit function and the conversion of infinity. Here is a simple example of array formatting:

```
>q:= (d)->randpoly(x,degree=d);
```

```
      q := d -> randpoly(x, degree = d)
```

```
>a:=array([[q(2),q(1)],[q(1),q(2)],[q(0),q(0)]]);
```

```
           [          2                                   ]
           [ - 61 x  - 23 x - 37         31 x - 34        ]
           [                                              ]
      a := [                             2                ]
           [      - 42 x + 88        - 76 x  - 65 x + 25  ]
           [                                              ]
           [          28                    -61           ]
```

```
>latex(");
\left [\begin {array}{cc} -61\,x^{2}-23\,x-37&31\,x-3\
4\\88-42\,x&-76\,
x^{2}-65\,x+25\\28&-61\end {array}\right ]
```

This is what LaTeX produces from this output:

$$\begin{bmatrix} -61\,x^2 - 23\,x - 37 & 31\,x - 34 \\ 88 - 42\,x & -76\,x^2 - 65\,x + 25 \\ 28 & -61 \end{bmatrix}$$

These basic examples demonstrate the use of `latex()`. In more complex situations, you may have to make adjustments to `latex()` output, but they are usually minor compared to the work of formatting from scratch.

As with `C()` and `fortran()`, `latex()` output can be directed to a file by using an optional file name; you can also use `save()` and `writeto()`/`appendto()` for a similar purpose.

8.4 Random numbers and other items

In this section, we will discuss Maple's facilities for producing random numbers and other random objects. The topics are

- About `rand()`
- Uniformly Distributed Integers
- Other Random Numbers and Distributions
- Other Random Objects

About `rand()`

The source of Maple's random numbers is a function called `rand()`. The `rand()` function is a linear congruence generator: It produces a sequence of "random" numbers with the formula:

$$x_{n+1} = (cx_n) \bmod m, \quad n = 1, 2, \ldots$$

Maple uses the values $c = 427419669081$ and $m = 999999999989$. Here, m is the modulus of the generator. To start the sequence, x_0 (the seed) must be prescribed. Unless told otherwise, Maple takes $x_0 = 1$.

The numbers c and m are carefully chosen so that the sequence produced by the generator is as long as possible before it produces a repetition of an earlier number. This length is in fact $m - 1$, so that the formula will produce almost a trillion numbers before it cycles. Except for special cases, each number produced by the formula will be a twelve-digit integer. For most purposes, these random numbers will be too large and will require scaling. We will discuss scaling below.

To change the seed, you assign a value to a global variable called _seed. To "restart" the random sequence you can reassign _seed. As an example, the next calculation computes three random numbers from the default seed 1, then three from another seed:

```
>seq(rand(),i=1..3);
```

```
427419669081, 321110693270, 343633073697
```

```
>_seed:=4129639439;
```

$$\_seed := 4129639439$$

```
>seq(rand(),i=1..3);
```

$$460642465901, \ 227010660743, \ 699534623606$$

Resetting seed to its default value (or any other value) restarts rand():

```
>_seed:=1;
```

$$\_seed := 1$$

```
>seq(rand(),i=1..3);
```

$$427419669081, \ 321110693270, \ 343633073697$$

When used in this direct way, rand() takes no arguments.

Uniformly distributed integers

The rand() function is also used to obtain uniformly distributed random integers lying in an integer range. The integer range is included as an argument to rand(). Because of this, Maple returns not a random number, but an entire procedure that, when called, returns random numbers in the required range. This procedure will be printed on your screen, and you will be able to see the modulus and the multiplier mentioned above. Here is an example in which Maple returns a generator for the interval [1, 52]:

```
> gen:=rand(1..52);

gen := proc()
        local t;
        global _seed;
          _seed := irem(427419669081*_seed,999999999989);
          t := _seed;
          irem(t,52)+1
        end
```

The gen() function returns random integers in the interval [1, 52]. It is used without arguments similarly to the way rand() was used without arguments above. For example, the following uses gen() to generate five random integers:

```
>seq(gen(),i=1..5);
```

$$42, \ 43, \ 18, \ 8, \ 29$$

The global variable _seed has the same significance as earlier, and it can be changed at any time.

Floating-point random numbers can be obtained by scaling the output from rand(). For example, here is a way to generate three-digit random numbers in $(-1, 1)$:

```
> g:=evalf(rand(-999..999)/10^3,1):
> seq(g(),i=1..5);
```

$$-.245, \ .079, \ .747, \ .477, \ -.535$$

The second argument to evalf() is chosen to ensure that three digits and no more are printed. Setting it to the more reasonable value of three actually produces five printed digits, of which the last two are zero. Inspection of the procedure in the two cases will reveal the reason for this.

Generators for random numbers from a variety of other distributions are contained in the statistics package stats[], which is covered in Chapter 9.

Other random objects

The rand() function is also used to obtain other random objects in Maple. These include randvector() and randmatrix() (in linalg[]) for random vectors and matrices. In both cases, you can include as an argument an equation giving the name of a function for the random numbers. Other functions using rand() are Randpoly() for random polynomials, Randprime() for random polynomials over finite fields, and combinat[randpart](), combinat[randcomb](), and combinat[randperm]() for random partitions, random combinations, and random permutations, respectively. You can generate random points on lines or circles with geometry[randpoint](), pick a random element from a group with group[RandElement](), and pick a random Boolean expression with logic[randbool]().

8.5 Sorting

Sorting of lists and sorting of polynomials by degree is done with the function
`sort()`. To sort a list, the list is used as the first argument to `sort()`. For example:

```
>sort([z,2,1,a]);
```

$$[1, \ 2, \ a, \ z]$$

Numbers appear in increasing order followed by alphabetic entries in alphabetic
order.

Sorting according to other criteria is done by including a Boolean-valued function
as the second argument to `sort()`. Here is an example that sorts complex numbers
in decreasing order according to their modulus (absolute value):

```
>g:=(z1,z2)->evalb(evalf(abs(z1))>evalf(abs(z2)));
```

```
g := (z1,z2) -> evalb(evalf(abs(z2)) < evalf(abs(z1)))
```

```
>sort([1+2*I,1-I,4],g);
```

$$[4, \ 1 + 2 \ I, \ 1 - I]$$

The floating-point evaluation in `g( , )` is used to evaluate the radicals that usually
appear in the modulus expressions.

Boolean functions will be needed for sorting more complex entities such as lists
of lists because `sort()` assumes that an input list is simple. Computations will
often return a polynomial that is not arranged in decreasing or increasing powers.
The `sort()` function can be used to obtain a decreasing power ordering for the
terms. For instance:

```
>e:=expand((x^2-1)*(2-x^3));
```

$$2 x^2 \ - x^5 \ - 2 + x^3$$

```
>sort(e);
```

$$- x^5 \ + x^3 \ + 2 x^2 \ - 2$$

Note that this overwrites the initial `e`, which is lost.

There is more choice for ordering the terms with multivariate polynomials. The default is ordering by total degree, meaning by the sums of the powers of the terms. To illustrate, here is a general polynomial of degree three:

```
>e:=randpoly([x,y],degree=3,terms=10);
```

$$e := -86 + 23\ x - 84\ x^2 + 19\ x^3 - 50\ y + 88\ x\ y$$

$$-53\ x^2\ y + 85\ y^2 + 49\ y^3 + 78\ x^2\ y^2$$

This is a complete cubic polynomial in x and y; it contains all possible terms whose total degree is three or less. Now we will sort it in decreasing powers of total degree and so that terms of any particular degree are arranged in decreasing powers of x:

```
>sort(e,[x,y]);
```

$$19\ x^3 + 78\ x^2\ y - 53\ x^2\ y + 49\ y^3 - 84\ x^2 + 88\ x\ y$$

$$+ 85\ y^2 + 23\ x - 50\ y - 86$$

The second argument specifies the order of powers of a given total degree. The same rules are applied recursively when there are more variables.

The alternative ordering available in sort() is called pure lexicographic. In this approach, the terms are listed as a decreasing-degree polynomial in the first variable whose coefficients are similar polynomials in the remaining variables. An example will show how the terms are constructed:

```
>e:=randpoly([x,y],degree=3,terms=10);
```

$$e := -66 - 32\ x + 78\ x^2 + 39\ x^3 + 94\ y + 68\ x\ y$$

$$- 17\ x^2\ y - 98\ y^2 - 36\ y^3 + 40\ x^2\ y^2$$

```
>sort(e,[x,y],plex);
```

$$39 x^3 + 40 x^2 y + 78 x^2 - 17 x y^2 + 68 x y - 32 x$$
$$- 36 y^3 - 98 y^2 + 94 y - 66$$

The coefficient of x^j is a decreasing-degree polynomial in y. For more variables, the same rules are applied recursively. Note the use of the "`plex`" option to obtain this ordering.

8.6 Reference section for `convert()`

A glance at the help file for `convert()` will show the variety of things that you can use `convert()` to do. Around fifty conversions are possible. Some of them are almost trivial, while others require fairly elaborate functions. This section contains a breakdown by category of the conversions.

Numerical conversions cover base conversions (such as decimal to binary), angle conversions (radians to degrees), number type conversions (such as rational to float), and a function for converting weights and measures to the equivalent metric values.

Function conversions are often used in simplifying and rewriting expressions. The conversions include things such as trigonometrics to exponentials and factorials to GAMMA.

Polynomial, rational function, and series conversions transfer between these functions and between `RootOf` expressions and radicals. A major function in this category creates partial fraction forms for rational functions.

Data structure conversions switch types between tables, lists, sets, and matrices (not all possibilities are catered).

Miscellaneous conversions are few in number. They include things such as converting file names to system file formats and converting names to strings. Also in this category is a (sometimes indispensable) function that converts expressions involving `diff` to a form using `D` and vice versa.

The following is a list of the available conversions. The names given are used as the second argument to `convert(,)`. In some cases, `convert()` takes additional arguments, but they will be third or higher in the argument list. Please check the online help system for full details about the arguments for particular cases.

NUMERICAL CONVERSIONS

base	radix → radix
binary	decimal → binary
confrac	number → continued fraction

`decimal`	binary, hex, octal → decimal
`degrees`	radians → degrees
`double`	Maple double → vendor's format
`float`	call to `evalf()`
`fraction`	float → rational
`hex`	decimal → hexadecimal
`metric`	to metric weights and measures
`octal`	decimal → octal
`polar`	Cartesian complex number → polar form
`radians`	degrees → radians
`rational/fraction`	float → rational (synonymous with fraction)

FUNCTIONAL CONVERSIONS

`binomial`	GAMMA → binomials
`exp`	trigonometrics → exponentials
`expln`	to exponentials and logarithms
`expsincos`	trigonometrics to exponentials, sines, and cosines
`factorial`	GAMMA and binomials → factorials
`GAMMA`	factorials and binomials → GAMMA
`hypergeom`	summations → hypergeometrics
`ln`	arctrigonometrics → logarithms
`sincos`	trigonometrics and hyperbolics → sin(h) and cos(h)
`tan`	trigonometrics to tangents (of half angles usually)
`trig`	exponentials → sin(h) and cos(h)

POLYNOMIAL SERIES AND RATIONAL CONVERSIONS

`fullparfrac`	more general than `parfrac`
`horner`	to nested form
`parfrac`	to partial fractions
`polynom`	series → polynomial
`radical`	`RootOf` → radicals
`ratpoly`	to rational function
`RootOf`	radicals → `RootOf`
`series`	polynomial → series
`sqfree`	to square free form

DATA STRUCTURE CONVERSIONS

`abs/signum`	between these forms
`and/or`	sets and lists to this form

`array`	table, list, array $\rightarrow$ array
`int`	transform $\rightarrow$ explicit integral
`eqnlist`	table, list, array $\rightarrow$ list of equations
`list`	table, etc. $\rightarrow$ list
`listlist`	array $\rightarrow$ list of lists
`matrix`	array, list of lists $\rightarrow$ matrix
`multiset`	table, list, expression $\rightarrow$ multiset
`set`	table, list, expression $\rightarrow$ set
`vector`	list, array $\rightarrow$ vector

MISCELLANEOUS CONVERSIONS

`*`	all operands $\rightarrow$ *
`+`	all operands $\rightarrow$ +
`D`	diff $\rightarrow$ D
`diff`	D $\rightarrow$ diff
`equality`	order relations $\rightarrow$ =
`lessequal`	order relations $\rightarrow$ <=
`lessthan`	order relations $\rightarrow$ <
`mod2`	reduce expression mod 2
`name/string`	expression $\rightarrow$ string or name

8.7 Reference section

This section summarizes the commands discussed in the text and a few other relevant functions.

INPUT AND OUTPUT

`appendto`	Add to existing file
`close,fclose`	Close an open file
`fopen,open`	Open a file for READ or WRITE
`lprint`	Maple's line print command
`print`	Maple's pretty print command
`printf,fprintf`	Formatted print command
`read`	Read results written with save
`readdata`	Read columnar data file
`readline`	Read a line from a file
`save`	Save Maple results to a file
`sscanf,fscanf`	Dissect a string
`writeto`	Create and write to a file (overwrites)

RANDOM OBJECTS

_seed	Global variable for seeding rand()
combinat[randperm]	Random permutation
combinat[randcomb]	Random combination
combinat[randpart]	Random partition
geometry[randpoint]	Random point
group[RandElement]	Random group element
linalg[randmatrix]	Random matrix
linalg[randvector]	Random vector
logic[randbool]	Random Boolean expression
rand	Basic random-number generator
randpoly	Random polynomial
Randpoly	Random polynomial over a finite field
Randprime	Random monic irreducible polynomial over a finite field

LANGUAGE UTILITIES

C	Convert to C code
eqn	Convert to eqn format
fortran	Convert to Fortran code
latex	Convert to LaTeX format

SYSTEM UTILITIES

kernelopts	Obtain information on the kernel
history	Label all results
length	Length of an expression
restart	Start a new session
showtime	Show system rcsources for each result
system	Run an external program
time	Number of CPU seconds so far
addressof	Obtain pointer for an expression
assemble	Form aggregrate from addresses
disassemble	Find component addresses of aggregate
dismantle	Internal representation of object
pointto	Obtain pointer to expression

NAME UTILITIES

anames	List assigned names
assigned	Test a name for assignment
unames	List unassigned names

INFORMATION UTILITIES

`help,?`	General help utility
`infolevel`	Show built in messages (if any)
`printlevel`	Trace through a computation

OTHER UTILITIES

`sort`	Sort lists or polynomials

9 What's in the packages?

A package in Maple is a collection of functions organized around a specific theme or topic. Because a package is simply a Maple table of procedures, anybody with the necessary skills (covered in Chapters 10 through 12 in this book) can create packages and distribute them to other users. Maple users worldwide have created a large number of packages that can often be obtained electronically from central sites.

In addition to users' packages, Maple comes equipped with a collection of approximately thirty standard packages, and we will review the contents of most of these in this chapter. The total number of functions in the standard packages is of the order of many hundreds, so we will not attempt to explain each function in detail. Rather, for each standard package that we cover, we will briefly describe its contents and give examples to illustrate its use. We hope that this approach will help you avoid the (all to) common error of writing procedures that merely duplicate Maple's existing abilities.

Even among the standard packages, some are intended for specialized tasks and assume advanced knowledge on the part of the user. We have not attempted to discuss the mathematics of these advanced packages, only what they can do and how they can be used.

Probably, the most basic packages in Maple are `linalg[]` and `plots[]`. These packages were discussed in detail in Chapters 4 and 6, respectively, and there is no further coverage here. Other standard packages that receive no additional coverage in this chapter are `DEtools()`, `inttrans()`, `LREtools`, `plottools[]`, and `sumtools()`.

The `process[]` package is system dependent. It contains functions and utilities for creating and controlling UNIX processes, which is a specialized topic that is not discussed in this chapter.

9.1 Calculus and operations research

The following topics are discussed in this section:

- Elementary Calculus with `student[]`
- Linear Programming with `simplex[]`

Elementary calculus with `student[]`

The `student[]` package contains functions that are mainly useful in a calculus and precalculus teaching environment. These functions allow operations to be performed in a step-by-step fashion and are useful for demonstrating simple manipulations. The functions in `student[]` can be categorized as: (1) integration functions (`Lineint()`, `Doubleint()`, `Tripleint()`, `changevar()`, `intparts()`, `integrand()`); (2) numerical integration functions (`trapezoid()`, `simpson()`, `leftsum()`, `rightsum()`, `middlesum()`); (3) manipulation functions (`completesquare()`, `isolate()`, `equate()`, `powsubs()`); (4) calculation functions (`extrema()`, `minimize()`, `maximize()`, `slope()`, `midpoint()`, `distance()`, `intercept()`); (5) graphics functions (`leftbox()`, `rightbox()`, `middlebox()`, `showtangent()`; and (6) system-related functions (`value()`, `makeproc()`). The integration functions are described very well by their titles. The capitalized functions are inert and are evaluated using the special evaluator `value()`, which is a part of the package. For example:

```
>r:=-infinity..infinity;
```

$$r := - \text{ infinity } .. \text{ infinity}$$

```
>value(Doubleint(exp(-x^2-y^2),x=r,y=r));
```

```
                          Pi
```

The `leftsum()` function for numerical integration produces the rectangle rule approximation for rectangles whose height is the function value at the left endpoints of the subintervals (see the example below). The `rightsum()` and `middlesum()` functions produce corresponding approximations based at the centers and right endpoints of the subintervals. Of the manipulation functions, `isolate()` is useful for isolating specified terms onto one side of an equation and `equate()` forms a set of equations from a list or set of expressions. The function `powsubs()` is analogous to `subs()` except that it is able to substitute for algebraic terms in an expression, as opposed to substitution for the operands of an expression that `subs()` performs. The calculation functions can find extrema (possibly constrained) and perform basic calculations for linear functions. The `makeproc()` function produces a procedure from an (algebraic) expression. The graphics functions show rectangular approxi-

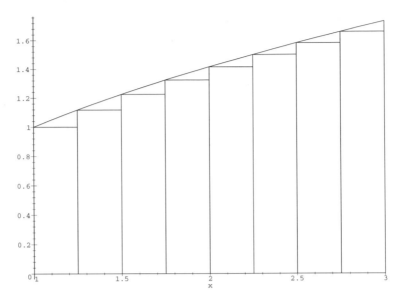

Figure 9.1: Example of leftbox()

mations to functions and can simultaneously graph a function and its tangent line at a point. Here is an illustration of leftbox() using eight subintervals in the interval [1, 3] (see Figure 9.1):

```
>leftbox(sqrt(x),x=1..3,8);
```

The area covered by the rectangles is obtained from:

```
>evalf(leftsum(sqrt(x),x=1..3,8));
```

$$2.704829825$$

Linear programming with simplex[]

For linear programming and related topics, Maple provides the simplex[] package. In addition to being able to solve general linear programs (using minimize(), maximize(), and dual()), simplex[] allows you to access the separate functions used in the solution algorithm (basis(), feasible(), pivot(), pivoteqn(), pivotvar(), ratio(), setup(), and standardize()). Using these functions, you can perform step-by-step solutions, much as you would in a hand calculation although without the arithmetic labor. There are some additional

utilities (`cterm()`, `define_zero()`, `stdle()`, and `display()`) and a function
for computing the convex hull of a set of points (`convexhull()`). To illustrate the
`minimize()` function, we will solve the following linear programming problem:
Minimize z subject to the inequalities

$$-z \leq ax_i + b - y_i \leq z, \quad i = 1, 2, 3,$$

where the points (x_i, y_i) are taken as (0,0), (1,1.25), (2.25,2). The solution to this
problem is in fact the best straight-line fit to the three points, in the sense of having the
least maximum absolute residual. You do not have to write the problem in standard
form to use `minimize()` because Maple does it automatically. Here is the problem
setup and its result:

```
>ineq1:={z+b>=0,z+a+b>=1.25,z+2.25*a+b>=2};

ineq1 :=

    {0 <= z + b, 1.25 <= z + a + b, 2 <= z + 2.25 a + b}

>ineq2:={z-b>=0,z-a-b>=-1.25,z-2.25*a-b>=-2};

ineq2 :=

    {0 <= z - b, -1.25 <= z - a - b, -2 <= z - 2.25 a - b}

>minimize(z,ineq1 union ineq2);

    {z = .1805555556, a = .8888888889, b = .1805555556}
```

In this case, there are no nonnegativity constraints in the problem formulation. If
there is a nonnegativity requirement for all of the variables, it can be incorporated
as an optional third argument.

9.2 Graphs and combinatorics

The following topics will be discussed in this section:

- Graph Theory with `networks[]`

- Combinatorics with `combinat[]`
- The `combstruct[]` Package

Graph theory with `networks[]`

The `networks[]` package is a fairly comprehensive collection of functions for creating graphs and networks and performing calculations such as extracting subgraphs (for example, spanning trees), computing polynomials (chromatic, Tutte, and others), and performing network optimizations such as finding minimum flows. The `networks[]` package contains many functions for defining and creating graphs. Below, we will illustrate the process of representing a graph for use with the functions in `networks[]`. Here we will discuss the built-in graphs (`complete()`, `petersen()`, `cube()`, `random()`, `tetrahedron()`, `dodecahedron()`, `icosahedron()`, and `cycle()`) and some of the functions for forming new graphs from old (`addedge()`, `addvertex()`, `gunion()`, `connect()`, `induce()`, `shrink()`, `gsimp()`, `complement()`, and others).

For obtaining subgraphs and subsets of edges and vertices of existing graphs, there are functions such as `spantree()`, `djspantree()`, `mincut()`, `cycle base()`, `shortpathtree()`, `path()`, `allpairs()`, `neighbors()`, `arrivals()`, `departures()`, and others. In addition, there is `flow()` for finding the maximum flow in a network and `isplane()` for testing planarity. Numerical properties of graphs are obtained from the functions `counttrees()`, `countcuts()`, `girth()`, `diameter()`, `mindegree()`, `maxdegree()`, `connectivity()`, `rank()`, and others. Matrices and polynomials associated with graphs may be obtained from the functions `incidence()`, `adjacency()`, `charpoly()`, `chrompoly()`, `acycpoly()`, `spanpoly()`, `rankpoly()`, `tuttepoly()`, and others. Graphs can be displayed geometrically (`draw()`) or by properties (`show()`). To show the data structure involved in a GRAPH object, we will set up a graph with one edge and two vertices and look at the corresponding structure. The next three commands set up the graph called G1:

```
> with(networks):
> new(G1):
> addvertex(1,2,G1);
```

$$1, \ 2$$

```
> addedge([1,2],G1);
```

$$e1$$

The function show() is used to obtain the structure:

```
>show(G1);

            table([
                _Edges = {e1}
                _Head = table([
                            e1 = 2
                        ])
                _Econnectivity = _Econnectivity
                _Bicomponents = _Bicomponents
                _Status = {DIRECTED}
                _Tail = table([
                            e1 = 1
                        ])
                _Ends = table([
                            e1 = {1, 2}
                        ])
                _EdgeIndex = table(symmetric,[
                                (1, 2) = {e1}
                            ])
                _Vweight = table(sparse,[])
                _Neighbors = table([
                                1 = {2}
                                2 = {1}
                            ])
                _Eweight = table([
                            e1 = 1
                        ])
                _Countcuts = _Countcuts
                _Counttrees = _Counttrees
                _Vertices = {1, 2}
                _Emaxname = 1
            ])
```

The information is mostly self-explanatory and is recorded in a Maple table with several variables and subtables. The values of the variables can be set by calls to functions. For instance, the trees can be counted as follows:

```
>counttrees(G1);
```

$$1$$

and if you now inspect the structure you will find that _Countrees has indeed been set to 1.

Here is another example of a setting up a graph:

```
>new(G2):
>addvertex(1,2,3,4,5,6,G2);
```

$$1, \ 2, \ 3, \ 4, \ 5, \ 6$$

```
>addedge([1,2],G2);
```

$$e1$$

```
>addedge(Cycle(2,5,6),G2);
```

$$e2, \ e3, \ e4$$

```
>connect({2,5},{3,4},G2);
```

$$e5, \ e6, \ e7, \ e8$$

Here, the graph is set up with a cycle and all vertices in the set 2, 5 are connected to all vertices in the set 3, 4. The graph is planar:

```
>isplanar(G2);
```

$$true$$

and can be drawn as shown in Figure 9.2:

```
>draw(G2);
```

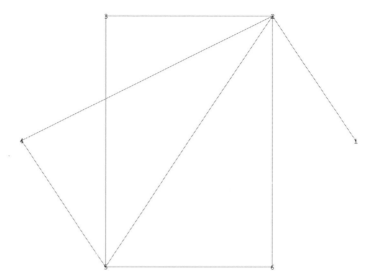

Figure 9.2: Plotting a planar graph

As a final illustration, we will obtain a random undirected graph and compute its characteristic and chromatic polynomials. The random graph is defined by choosing edges with probability 1/2 from the complete graph of order 4:

```
>G3:=random(4):
>charpoly(G3,x);
```

$$x^4 - x^2$$

```
>chrompoly(G3,x);
```

$$x^3 (-1 + x)$$

Combinatorics with `combinat[]`

A very useful package, which we used earlier to produce random permutations and combinations, is `combinat[]`. The main uses for `combinat[]` are (1) to produce numbers of combinatorial interest (`bell`, `stirling`, `fibonacci`); (2) to create and count permutations and combinations of sets (permute, numbperm, rand-perm, randcomb, subsets, powerset); and (3) to create and count compositions and partitions of integers (partition, composition, firstpart, nextpart, prevpart, lastpart, conjpart, numbcomp, numbpart, vectoint, int-tovec, ncodepart, decodepart). The combinat[] package can also compute the character table for a symmetric group (character, Chi) and produce the Gray code ordering of the *n*-bit numbers (graycode). The last function orders the numbers containing *n* or less significant bits so that successive numbers differ in just a single bit position. Here is an illustration with $n = 4$:

```
>combinat[graycode](4);
```

    [0, 1, 3, 2, 6, 7, 5, 4, 12, 13, 15, 14, 10, 11, 9, 8]

To see the binary form, we map onto the list as follows:

```
>map(convert,",binary);
```

    [0, 1, 11, 10, 110, 111, 101, 100, 1100, 1101, 1111,
        1110, 1010, 1011, 1001, 1000]

A composition of a positive integer is a way of writing it as a sum of smaller positive integers. To illustrate, here are the compositions of 6 with three members:

```
>combinat[composition](6,3);
```

    {[4, 1, 1], [1, 4, 1], [3, 2, 1], [2, 3, 1],
        [3, 1, 2], [2, 2, 2], [1, 3, 2], [1, 2, 3],
        [2, 1, 3], [1, 1, 4]}

Something that we do not want to list are the compositions of length 5 of 22, and here is the reason:

```
>combinat[numbcomp](22,5);
```

                             5985

The number of partitions of *n* grows rapidly as *n* increases. Why not use combinat[] and plot[] to display just how rapidly? As a final example, here is a way to make a shuffled deck of cards of two suits with five cards in each suit:

```
>d:=combinat[randperm](10);

          d := [8, 1, 5, 4, 10, 2, 6, 7, 9, 3]

>p:=x->[iquo(x,6),x-iquo(x,6)*5];

          p := x -> [iquo(x, 6), x - 5 iquo(x, 6)]

>map(p,d);

    [[1, 3], [0, 1], [0, 5], [0, 4], [1, 5], [0, 2],
        [1, 1], [1, 2], [1, 4], [0, 3]]
```

The suits are labeled 0 and 1. With a similar method, you could easily make a fifty-two card deck using nonnumerical symbols for the picture cards.

The `combstruct[]` package

This is a package for specialized work in combinatorics. It allows you to construct certain kinds of random combinatorial objects and perform counts on them. The file `?combstruct` has additional information.

9.3   Finance and statistics

The topics in this section are

- Taking Care of Business with `finance[]`
- The Statistics Package `stats[]`

Taking care of business with `finance[]`

The finance package contains functions for computing present and future values (annuity(), cashflows(), futurevalue(), growingannuity(), growing-perpetuity(), levelcoupon(), perpetuity(), presentvalue()), loans (amortization(), effectiverate()), bonds (yieldtomaturity()), and pricing options (blackscholes()).

To illustrate the use of this package, suppose that starting one month from now you will receive $1000 per month for two years from Aunt Millie's estate. Because you would rather have a lump sum to put toward your new yacht, you want to sell your inheritance. How much is it worth if interest rates hold steady at 7%? Stated otherwise, what is the present value of your asset? The `annuity()` function is designed to answer such questions. First, we need to compute the equivalent monthly interest rate, which is obtained by solving the equation $(1 + x)^{12} = 1.07$. Here is the calculation:

```
> i:=fsolve((1+x)^12=1.07,x,0..0.01);
```

$$i := .005654145387$$

The range is included to pick off the desired root of the equation. Now we apply `annuity()` with the amount, the interest rate, and the number of payments as arguments. The result is

```
> annuity(1000,i,24);
```

$$22383.80070$$

which is the present value of your inheritance. As an extra suprise, Aunt Millie also left you an option to buy 1000 shares of the BigGreen corporation at $80 a share six months from now. The current price of the shares is $101. How much can you sell the option for? To answer this question, you need to know a certain stochastic "volatility" measure for the stock. Your broker tells you that it is 0.28 for this stock (based on historical data). Now you fire up Maple and compute:

```
> evalf(blackscholes(101,80,.07,6/12,0.28));
```

$$24.45807854$$

The third argument is the interest rate and the fourth is the time to expiration. The answer given is the per-share value of the option. The next and last step is to be grateful to your generous relative.

The statistics package `stats[]`

The statistics package, `stats[]`, is one of the larger packages. It is divided into six subpackages that can be individually loaded. The functions in `stats[]` can be classed into four sets. The first set of functions are for descriptive statistics. There are around forty of these, so we will not attempt to list them individually. However, they are all included in two subpackages called `transform[]` and `describe[]`. The second set of functions is associated with statistical distributions and enables particular values of distributions to be calculated. The relevant subpackages here are `stateval[]` and `random[]`. The third set of functions are for data fitting and graphics and are in the subpackages `fit[]` and `statplots[]`. The fourth set of functions are in `anova[]` and are used for performing analysis of variance calculations. We will summarize the contents of each subpackage in the following paragraphs.

Unlike earlier packages, the `stats[]` package is not a table of procedures. In fact, `stats[]` itself is a procedure. This is unimportant unless you want to read the code of the functions in the package. If you wish to do so, you may have to work through a heirerachy of procedures to get to the procedure you want to read.

The `transform[]` package contains functions for transforming data between different representations. For instance, it contains functions for tallying data into classes (`tally()`, `tallyinto()`), for performing various counts of the data (`frequency()`, `cumulativefrequency()`), and for restructuring data (`classmark()`, `split()`, `statvalue()`). In addition, there are utilities for sorting (`statsort()`) and `map()`-style functions tailored for statistical data (`apply()`, `multiapply()`). Another function (`moving()`) can compute moving averages of serial data.

The `describe[]` package contains functions for computing various numbers associated with statistical data. There are a number of functions for computing measures of central tendencies of data (`mean()`, `geometricmean()`, `harmonicmean()`, `median()`, `mode()`) and functions for computing measures of spread (`standarddeviation()`, `variance()`, `covariance()`, `range()`, `percentile()`, `quartile()`) and other characteristics such as moments, skewness and kurtosis (`moment()`, `skewness()`, `kurtosis()`). This list is by no means exhaustive.

The second class of functions are associated with specific probability distributions. There are two subpackages associated with these functions, the first being `statevalf[]`. The `statevalf[]` subpackage is best thought of as an evaluator for probability distributions, of which Maple knows the following:

```
Discrete distributions:
binomiald, discreteuniform, empirical, hypergeometric,
                negativebinomial, poisson
```

and

```
Continuous distributions:
beta, cauchy, chisquare, exponential, fratio, gamma,
laplaced, logistic, lognormal, normald, students,
                uniform, weibull.
```

The parameters required to specify particular distributions may be found in the help file ?distribution. The statevalf[] subpackage uses two arguments. The first argument specifies the form in which the distribution is to be evaluated. For instance, continuous distributions take one of three forms: pdf for the probability density function, cdf for the cumulative density function, and icdf for the inverse cumulative density function. There are corresponding functions for the discrete distributions. The second argument to stateval[] is the name of the distribution from one of the above lists. Arguments to the distribution (its parameters) are added as separate arguments in the manner illustrated below.

The second subpackage associated with distributions is for generating random numbers. Random numbers can be generated for any of the distributions mentioned above. Generally, random numbers from a specific distribution are obtained by transforming the output from a uniform generator using the inverse cumulative density function of the distribution. The uniform generator can be the standard one supplied with Maple or you can supply your own. You can choose to have a generator returned as a function or a specified quantity of random numbers. In addition to the general method for obtaining random numbers, efficient custom generators are also supplied for some distributions.

The third set of functions in the subpackages fit[] and statplots[] perform linear least squares fitting (leastsquares()) and make several plots of statistical interest such as histograms and scatter plots (histogram(), scatterplot()).

There are three functions in the subpackage anova[]. The functions perform one- and two-way analyses of variance and are oneway(), twoway(), and twowayreplicated().

Data is presented to stats[] in one or more *statistical lists*. A statistical list is just a regular Maple list containing any number of entries of the following types: (1) a number, range, or symbolic quantity; (2) the keyword missing (indicating the absence of a datum); and (3) an entry of the form Weight(value, weight), where value denotes an item of type (1) above and weight denotes a numerical value.

Data can be read from files using stats[importdata]. Now we illustrate a few of the many functions in stats[]. Here is a statistical list containing alphabetic text:

```
>d:=[i,s,a,w,e,s,a,u,s,i,t,t,i,n,g,o,n,a,s,e,e,s,a,w]:
```

To count the frequency of the letters, we can use transform[tally,d] or the following:

```
>with(stats):
>with(transform):
```

```
>tally(d);
```

```
[Weight(w, 2), Weight(s, 5), Weight(e, 3),
    Weight(t, 2), u, g, o, Weight(i, 3), Weight(a, 4),
    Weight(n, 2)]
```

This result is another statistical list containing the required information. The following is a statistical list with a variety of entries:

```
>d2:=[1.2,-1.3,1.25..1.35,missing,Weight(-1..1,4)];
```

```
d2 :=
```

```
[1.2, -1.3, 1.25 .. 1.35, missing, Weight(-1 .. 1, 4)]
```

There are two numerical entries followed by a range, a missing item, and a weighted range. For most numerical computations, ranges in statistical lists are replaced by their classmarks (midpoints). For instance, if we ask for the mean of the above list, the third entry is taken as 1.3 and the last as 0 repeated four times:

```
>with(describe):
>mean(d2);
```

```
                    .1714285715
```

To illustrate the second class of functions, here is a computation of the 99% confidence limit of the standardized normal distribution:

```
>with(statevalf):
>icdf[normald[0,1]](.995);
```

```
                    2.575829304
```

and here is a check on the result:

```
>q:=";
```

```
            q := 2.575829304
```

```
>cdf[normald[0,1]](q)-cdf[normald[0,1]](-q);
```

$$.9900000000$$

These functions could also be accessed in the form `statevalf[icdf,normald[0,1]]`, for example.

To obtain a random-number generator for random numbers from the standardized normal distribution, one possible syntax is the following (assuming that `stats[]` has been loaded):

```
>with(random):
>g:=normald[0,1](generator,uniform,inverse):
```

The generator can now be used without specifying arguments:

```
>g();
```

$$1.175839568$$

```
>g();
```

$$-.5633641309$$

A longer form of this definition would be `random[normald[0,1]]` followed by the arguments. It avoids the `with(random)` command. The arguments can be modified to obtain alternative forms of the results. The first argument may be replaced by an integer, in which case that number of random numbers will be produced directly. The second argument can be used to specify another source for the random numbers that will be transformed. The third argument can ensure the use of certain custom generators that exist only for special distributions (the option is `auto`).

9.4 Algebra and logic

Topics discussed in this section are

- Groups and `group[]`
- Bases from `grobner[]`
- Boolean Algebra Using `logic[]`
- The `Domains[]` Package

Groups and `group[]`

The procedures in this package are used to define and manipulate groups. Maple has two ways to represent groups. Finite groups can be represented as subgroups of a permutation group (recall that any finite group is isomorphic to such a subgroup) and are referred to as `permgroups` in the help files. As usual, permutations of n variables are represented as injective mappings from the set $\{1, 2, \ldots n\}$ onto itself. Finitely generated groups are represented using (words of) generators and relations, and are referred to as `grelgroup` groups. Typically, functions in the group package work with either `permgroups` or `grelgroups`. Note that there are relatively few algorithms for manipulating groups defined by generators and relations so that most of the functions in this package pertain to `permgroups`.

A `permgroup` is an unevaluated call to the procedure `permgroup()`. The `permgroup()` procedure simply checks its arguments and returns unevaluated. As an example, the dihedral group of order six, D_6, can be represented as

```
> with(group):
> D6 := permgroup(6,{[[1,2,3,4,5,6]],[[2,6],[3,5]]});

D6 := permgroup(6, {[[1, 2, 3, 4, 5, 6]],
                    [[2, 6], [3, 5]]})
```

The first argument to `permgroup()` gives the degree (the size of the set on which the permutations act), and the second argument is a set of generators for the group. The generators are expressed as disjoint cycles expressed as a list of lists. For example, the permutation `[[2,6],[3,5]]` maps 1, 2, 3, 4, 5, 6, 7, 8 to 1, 6, 5, 4, 3, 2. The generators may be named as in `b=[[2,6],[3,5]]`. A product of permutations, `a &* b`, is interpreted as the composition `(a &* b)(i) = a(b(i))`. The functions that work with permgroups are

DerivedS	LCS	NormalClosure	RandElement	Sylow
areconjugate	center	centralizer	core	cosets
cosrep	derived	groupmember	grouporder	inter
invperm	isabelian	isnormal	issubgroup	
mulperms	normalizer	orbit		

Most of the function names are self-explanatory. For example, `center()` returns the center of the group and `Sylow()` will calculate the Sylow subgroups. As an illustration, we calculate the order of the group D_6 defined above, and find one of its Sylow subgroups:

```
> grouporder(D6);
```

$$12$$

```
> Sylow(D6,2);
```

```
permgroup(6, {[[1, 5], [2, 4]], [[1, 2], [3, 6],
          [4, 5]]})
```

```
> grouporder(");
```

$$4$$

When the group package is loaded, `type()` recognizes `disjcyc` (disjoint cycle) as its second argument and `convert()` recognizes both `disjcyc` and `permlist` for converting between permutations expressed as lists (images of permutations) and disjoint cycle notation.

A `grelgroup` is represented as an unevaluated call to `grelgroup()`. For example, the fundamental group of the complement of the trefoil knot in three space has three generators, say a, b, and c, and relations ba=cb, cb=ac, and ac=ba. This group is then represented by:

```
> g :=
grelgroup({a,b,c},{[b,a,1/b,1/c],[c,b,1/c,1/a],
          [a,c,1/a,1/b]});
```

```
g := grelgroup({a, b, c},
```

```
  {[b, a, 1/b, 1/c], [c, b, 1/c, 1/a], [a, c, 1/a, 1/b]}
```

As indicated above, each relation is represented as a list in which inverses are expressed as reciprocals. The functions that work with `grelgroups` are

RandElement	cosets	cosrep	grouporder
isnormal	permrep	pres	

Clearly most of these commands will work only when Maple can determine that the group is in fact finite. Subgroups of `grelgroups` are constructed using the function `subgrel()`, which takes as a first argument generators for the subgroup and as a

second argument a grelgroup. The command pres() will return a grelgroup
representation of a subgrel().

Bases from grobner[]

The main function in this package is gbasis(), which determines a Gröbner basis
for a set of (multivariate) polynomials, that is, a basis for the ideal generated by the
given set of polynomials. Recall that such a basis is not canonical, so a choice of representation is involved. The default choice is to order polynomials based upon their
total degree (for example, $x^2y^2 > x^2y$ where $>$ indicates an ordering) and for monomials of the same degree, to specify an ordering of the indeterminates. For example,
if we specify [y,x], indicating that $y > x$, then $x^2y^2 > x^3y$ (pure lexiographical
ordering can also be specified). A simple example illustrates these principles:

```
> with(grobner):
> gbasis([x^2*y,x^2-y^2-1],[y,x]);
```

$$[x^2 y, -x^2 + y^2 + 1, x^4 - x^2]$$

```
> gbasis([x^2*y,x^2-y^2-1],[x,y]);
```

$$[x^2 - y^2 - 1, y^3 + y]$$

In the first example, $-y^2$ is the leading monomial of $x^2 - y^2 - 1$ (because $y > x$)
and in the second, x^2 is the leading monomial. These choices affect the selection
of the basis because a Gröbner basis not only generates the ideal generated by the
given polynomials, but the leading monomials of a Gröbner basis also generate all
of leading monomials of the ideal. The function leadmon() returns the leading
monomial and its coefficient:

```
> leadmon(x^2-y^2-1,[y,x]);
```

$$[-1, y^2]$$

```
> leadmon(x^2-y^2-1,[x,y]);
```

$$[1, x^2]$$

The most obvious application of Gröbner bases is to find the common zeros of a collection of polynomials. Instead of working with the (possibly large) collection, it suffices to find the common zeros of the basis elements. The `solvable()` function determines if a collection of polynomials has a common root, and `finite()` determines if there are a finite number of roots:

```
> solvable([x^2-y^2-1,x^2*y]);
```

$$true$$

```
> finite([x^2-y^2-1,x^2*y]);
```

$$true$$

The `gsolve()` function will set up a "minimal" set of equations, whose solutions are the common roots of the collection of polynomials:

```
> gsolve([x^2-y^2-1,x^2*y]);
```

$$[[x, y^2 + 1], [x - 1, y], [x + 1, y]]$$

Upon converting the lists of equations to sets, `solve()` will compute the solutions:

```
> map(convert,",set):
> map(solve,",{x,y});
```

$$[\{x = 0, y = RootOf(\_Z^2 + 1)\}, \{x = 1, y = 0\},$$
$$\{x = -1, y = 0\}]$$

If a univariate polynomial $p(x_i)$ is contained in an ideal, its roots will contain all possible x_i values of "roots of the ideal" (points at which every polynomial in the ideal vanishes). The function `finduni()` attempts to find the smallest such univaritate polynomial in a given indeterminate. Note that the existence of such a polynomial is guaranteed only when there are a finite number of roots (which can be verified with `finite()`), and `finduni()` expects to find this situation as the following example demonstrates:

```
> finduni(x,[x^2-y^2-1,x^2*y]);
```

$$x^4 - x^2$$

```
> finduni(y,[x^2-y^2-1,x^2*y]);
```

$$y^3 + y$$

In the above examples, the only variables appearing were the indeterminates x and y. If other names are present, the indeterminates must be specified, as in

```
> finite([a*x^2-y^2-b,x^2*y],[x,y]);
```

$$true$$

```
> finduni(x,[a*x^2-y^2-b,x^2*y],[x,y]);
```

$$- b x^2 + x^4 a$$

Gröbner bases are also used by `simplify()` to reduce expressions. Recall that if it is known that x is a root of a polynomial $p(x)$, then the division algorithm guarantees that any polynomial $P(x)$ can be written as $P(x) = q(x)p(x) + r(x) = r(x)$, where the degree of $r(x)$ is less than that of $p(x)$ (in the language of algebra, $r(x)$ generates the same coset as $P(x)$ in the ring $F[x]/p(x)F[x]$). A similar method can be used to simplify multivariate polynomials. Given a collection of multivariate polynomials, any one can be reduced to a simpler form through "quotienting out" by polynomials in a Gröbner basis (this is where the properties satisfied by the leading monomials of a Gröbner basis, mentioned above, are useful). The command `normalf()` will preform such a reduction.

```
> F := gbasis([x^2*y,x^2-y^2-1],[y,x]);
```

$$F := [x^2 y, - x^2 + y^2 + 1, x^4 - x^2]$$

```
> p := 10*x^4*y^3 - 7*x^4*y + 8*x*y^3 + 4:
> normalf(p,F,[y,x]);
```

$$- 8 \; x \; y \; + \; 4$$

The `normalf()` function expects its second argument to be a Gröbner basis with the ordering specified in the third argument. This is identical to specifying side relations in `simplify()` as demonstrated here:

```
> simplify(p,{0=x^2-y^2-1,0=x^2*y},[y,x]);
```

$$- 8 \; x \; y \; + \; 4$$

To illustrate some of the issues that can arise, we return to an example from Chapter 2:

```
> simplify(a2*b3-a3*b2,{a1*b3-a3*b1,a1*b2-a2*b1});
```

$$a2 \; b3 \; - \; a3 \; b2$$

The two side relations imply `a1*(a2 b3 - a3 b2)` vanishes, and Maple can verify this:

```
> simplify(a1*(a2*b3-a3*b2),{a1*b3-a3*b1,a1*b2-a2*b1});
```

$$0$$

The reason for the differing results can be seen in the Gröbner basis for the two side relations as in:

```
> gbasis([a1*b3-a3*b1,a1*b2-a2*b1],[a1,a2,a3,b1,b2,b3]);
```

$$[- \; a1 \; b3 \; + \; a3 \; b1, \; - \; a1 \; b2 \; + \; a2 \; b1,$$
$$- \; a1 \; a2 \; b3 \; + \; a1 \; a3 \; b2]$$

The last element of the basis is clearly the product of `a1` with the expression to be simplified. In this context, `a1` is considered to be an indeterminate in the polynomial ring **Q**`[a1,a2,a3,b1,b2,b3]` and so is not invertible. Contrast this with the following basis generated in the ring **Q**`[a2,a3,b1,b2,b3]`:

```
> F := gbasis([a1*b3-a3*b1,a1*b2-a2*b1],
              [a2,a3,b1,b2,b3]);
```

$$F \; := \; [- \; a1 \; b3 \; + \; a3 \; b1, \; - \; a1 \; b2 \; + \; a2 \; b1,$$
$$- \; a2 \; b3 \; + \; a3 \; b2]$$

When a Maple name appears in a polynomial that is not an indeterminate, it is assumed to be a nonzero coefficient from the base field, **Q**, and so is invertible. Simplification with the new basis now gives

```
> normalf(a2*b3-a3*b2,F,[a2,a3,b1,b2,b3]);
```

$$0$$

A similar effect can be acheived by using a third argument to `simplify()`. Here is the modified `simplify()` command:

```
> simplify(a2*b3-a3*b2,{a1*b3-a3*b1,a1*b2-a2*b1},
          [a2,a3,b1,b2,b3]);
```

Boolean algebra using `logic[]`

The `logic[]` package contains functions for manipulating and testing Boolean expressions. Expressions are created using variables and the operators `&and`, `&or`, `&not`, `&iff`, `&implies`, `&nor`, `&nand`, and `&xor`. These expressions can then bc placcd in canonical forms (`canon()`) or converted to alternative representations (`convertMOD2()`, `convertfrominert()`, `converttoinert()`) and simplified (`bsimp()`, `distrib()`, `environ()`). Expressions can be tested for equality, for tautology, or dualized, and the values rendering them true can, if possible, be obtained (`bequal()`, `tautology()`, `dual()`, `satisfy()`). There is also a function for producing random Boolean expressions.

As a first example, we will check one of de Morgan's laws:

```
>bequal(&not(a &or b),&not(a) &and &not(b));
```

$$true$$

As another example, we will create a random Boolean expression over three symbols, reduce it to the mod 2 canonical form, then find a valuation of the symbols:

```
>randbool({a,b,c});
```

```
    &or(&and(&not a, &not b, &not c),
        &and(b, &not a, &not c), &and(a, b, &not c),
        &and(b, c, &not a))
```

```
>canon(",{a,b},MOD2);
```

$$1 + c + b c + a b + a + a c$$

```
>satisfy(");
```

$$\{a = false, b = false, c = false\}$$

The Domains[] package

This package provides a toolbox of rather technical routines for coding certain algebraic algorithms in Maple. To illustrate the reason for this, we note that Maple has four different functions to calculate the Smith normal form of a matrix. The linalg[] package contains ismith() and smith() for integer and polynomial matrices, respectively. The inert function Smith() is evaluated using mod() to calculate the Smith normal form with modular arithmetic, and GIsmith() works over the ring of Gaussian integers. In each case, the same algorithm could be used; the only difference is in the type of arithmetic. The Domains[] package provides a programming environment in which a single Smith routine would exist. A user would supply a "ring descriptor" to implement the form of arithmetic required. In this environment, the Smith normal form of a matrix over any ring (more specifically, principal ideal domain) could be computed.

9.5   Number theory

The following topics and packages are discussed in this section:

- Number Theory with numtheory[]
- Gaussian Integers with GaussInt[]
- The p-adic Numbers with padic[]

Number theory with numtheory[]

The numtheory[] package contains over fifty functions, which can be grouped into six categories. The functions in the first category enable you to factor integers (ifactor(), ifactors(), factorEQ(), sq2factor(), factorset(), issqrfree()) and to compute and count their divisors (divisors(), phi(), invphi(), sigma(), tau(), bigomega()). The functions factorEQ() and sq2factor() allow you to factor over extensions of the integers containing square roots. Also in this category are pprimroot() and primroot() for calculating generators of the group of integers relatively prime to a given integer and mcombine() for solving two simultaneous congruences.

In the next category are functions for working with prime numbers. You can obtain primes by several methods (nextprime(), prevprime(), ithprime(), `mersenne()`, `safeprime()`) and test for primality (`isprime()`). The function `fermat()` returns the Fermat numbers and information currently known about their primality.

The next category contains functions for powers, roots, and logarithms. While it is rare for an integer to have an integer root or logarithm in the traditional sense, these quantities often exist in modular arithmetic, and Maple provides a number of functions for computing them (`imagunit()`, `index()`, `mlog()`, `mobius()`, `mroot()`, `msqrt()`, `nthpow()`, `order()`, `rootsunity()`).

For Diophantine equations and approximations, there are functions for solving in both the integers and p-adic numbers. These are `isolve()`, `kronecker()`, `minkowski()`, `nearestp()` `sum2sqr()`, and `thue()`.

There are some functions for geneating and picking parts of continued fractions: they are `cfrac()`, `cfracpol()`, `nthconver()`, `nthdenom()`, and `nthnumer()`.

In the miscellaneous category are the functions `bernoulli()`, `euler()`, `jacobi()`, and `legendre()` for computing special numbers and polynomials. Cylcotomic polynomials are computed by `cyclotomic()`, and the number of irreducible polynomials over a given finite field is returned by `mipolys()`. Finally, `lambda()` is Carmichael's lambda function, which computes the order of a particular cyclic group.

To illustrate a few of the above commands, we will verify that Maple's random-number generator `rand()` has the maximum possible period. The `rand()` function generates numbers according to the formula $x_{n+1} = ax_n \bmod p$, where $a = 427419669081$ and $p = 999999999989$, as illustrated by:

```
> rand(1..5);


proc()
local t;
global _seed;
    _seed := irem(427419669081*_seed,999999999989);
    t := _seed;
    irem(t,5)+1
end
```

and the initial value x_0 is taken to be unity.

We can readily verify that the number p is prime:

```
> isprime(999999999989);
```

$$true$$

and in this situation, the `rand()` will cycle through all of the numbers in the range $1 \le p \le p - 1$ before repeating, provided $a \not\equiv 0 \bmod p$ and $a^{(p-1)/q} \not\equiv 1 \bmod p$ for all primes q dividing $p - 1$. We verify that $a = 427419669081$ and $p = 999999999989$ satisfy these conditions. The first condition is easy to check:

```
> a := 427419669081:
> p := 999999999989:
> a mod p;
```

$$427419669081$$

To verify the second condition we use `ifactors()` to extract the prime factors of $p - 1$:

```
> with(numtheory):
Warning, new definition for F
Warning, new definition for order
> ifactors(p-1);
```

$$[1, [[2, 2], [11, 1], [124847, 1], [182041, 1]]]$$

```
> qq := seq(q[1],q="[2]);
```

$$qq := 2, 11, 124847, 182041$$

Here, `ifactors()` produces a list containing the sign of its argument and a list containing the factors and their multiplicities. It is now elementary to verify that $a^{(p-1)/q} \not\equiv 1 \bmod p$:

```
> seq(a^((p-1)/q) mod p, q=qq);
Error, integer too large in context
> seq(a &^ ((p-1)/q) mod p, q=qq);
```

$$999999999988, 650085006945, 400585256072, 808879095496$$

Clearly none of these numbers is one, so Maple's random-number generator has period $p - 1 = 999999999988$. The last evaluation provides a nice illustration of the need for the inert form of ^.

Gaussian integers with `GaussInt[]`

The Gaussian integers are the subset (ring) of complex numbers lying on the integer lattice. The `Gaussint[]` package is a collection of routines for doing arithmetic and basic ring operations on the Gaussian integers. To a great extent, these functions are counterparts of functions in the prime numbers and factoring parts of the number theory package. One exception is `GIbasis()`, which will return `true` or `false` depending upon whether or not its two arguments are generators for the ring.

Here are some simple illustrations for `Gaussint[]`. The integer 29 is prime in the ring of integers; however, it factors over the Gaussian integers:

```
> GIprime(29);
```

$$false$$

```
> GIfactor(29);
```

$$(- 5 - 2 I) (- 5 + 2 I)$$

When factoring a Gaussian integer, there is a choice of representation because each factor could be multiplied by a power of `I`. The help file for `GIfactor()` explains Maple's choice. The functions `GInormal()` and `GIunitnormal()` handle alternative forms.

The function `GInorm()` returns the norm of a Gaussian integer, that is, the square of the Euclidean distance from the origin, and `GIsieve()` returns a list containing the Gaussian integers in the first octant having norm less than a given integer. `GInearest()` returns the Gaussian integer nearest to a complex number, and `GIsqrt()` returns the Gaussian integer nearest to the square root of its argument.

Univariate and multivariate factorization of polynomials over the Gaussian integers are done with `GIroots()` and `GIfacpoly()`, respectively. As an example, we factor the polynomial, which is irreducible over the integers:

```
> p := x^2 - 6*x + 25:
> factor(p);
```

$$x^2 - 6 x + 25$$

```
> GIroots(p);
```

$$[[3 + 4 I, 1], [3 - 4 I, 1]]$$

The two functions `GIhermite()` and `GIsmith()` reduce matrices to echelon and Smith form, respectively.

The p-adic numbers with `padic[]`

The p-adic numbers (where p is a prime integer) are similar to real numbers in that they are obtained as a completion of the rational numbers. The p-adic norm of a rational number a/b (with a and b relatively prime) is small if a large power of the prime divides the numerator a. Any p-adic number can be expressed as a formal series of the form

$$a = \sum_{k=-m}^{\infty} a_i p^i$$

where the coefficients satisfy $0 \le a_i \le p - 1$. The integers and certain rational numbers are naturally represented as finite sums. The functions in `padic[]` can perform exact arithmetic with p-adic numbers that have finite representations and can calculate approximations of various p-analytic functions. The p-analytic functions are defined by the same power series as their complex analogs. The only difference is that convergence is determined by the p-adic norm.

The norm of a p-adic number is found using `valuep()`, and for a rational number, it will always be a power of the prime p. This power is computed by (the negative of) `ordp()`. To illustrate:

```
> valuep(50/17,5);
```

$$5^{-2}$$

```
> ordp(50/17,5);
```

$$2$$

```
> valuep(50/2125,5);
```

$$5$$

```
> ordp(50/2125,5);
```

$$-1$$

The evaluator `evalp()` will convert a rational number to the standard representation as in:

```
> evalp(50/2125,5);

   -1                    2       3       4       5       7       8
  5   + 1 + 3 5 + 2 5 + 3 5 + 4 5 + 2 5 + 4 5 + O(5 )

> lprint(");
PADIC([5, -1, [1, 1, 3, 2, 3, 4, 2, 0, 4, 3]])
> Digitsp;

                              10
```

The first line in this example shows the truncated series representation for the rational number 50/2125, and the second line illustrates how Maple represents the truncated series as an unevaluated call to the function `PADIC()`. The global variable `Digitsp` controls how many terms are retained in the series. The function `ratvaluep()` sums the truncated series representing a p-adic number.

Maple will compute approximations of p-adic versions of all the standard trigonometric and exponential functions. A listing of these functions is given in `?padic[functions]`. The function names are formed by appending a `p` to their real counterparts. The following example illustrates the errors involved with the truncation of the series:

```
> sinp(50/17,5);

    2     3       4       5       6       7       8       9
   5  + 5  + 3 5 + 2 5 + 2 5 + 2 5 + 2 5 + 2 5
               10        12
           + 3 5   + O(5  )

> arcsinp(");

    2     3       4       5       6       7       8       10
   5  + 5  + 3 5 + 2 5 + 3 5 + 4 5 + 2 5 + 4 5
               11
           + O(5   )

> valuep("-50/17);

                            -12
                          5
```

Observe that when calling `sinp()` with a rational number, it was necessary to specify the prime $p = 5$; however, when calling `arcsinp()` and `valuep()`, this was unnecessary because the argument was a Maple p-adic number that contains the prime. The function `sqrtp()` will calculate (an approximation of the) square root of a p-adic number if it exists:

```
> sqrtp(6,5);
```

$$1 + 3 \cdot 5 + 4 \cdot 5^3 + 2 \cdot 5^4 + 5^5 + 2 \cdot 5^6 + 3 \cdot 5^7 + 5^8 + O(5^9)$$

```
> sqrtp(7,5);
```

$$\mathrm{FAIL}$$

As illustrated by this example, `FAIL` is returned whenever the series for a particular analytic function fails to converge for the specified value. The function `rootp()` factors polynomials in over the p-adic numbers. For example, all fourth roots of unity are contained in the 5-adic numbers:

```
> rootp(x^4-1,5);
```

$$1,$$

$$3 + 3 \cdot 5 + 2 \cdot 5^2 + 3 \cdot 5^3 + 5^4 + 2 \cdot 5^6 + 5^7 + 4 \cdot 5^8 + O(5^9),$$

$$2 + 5 + 2 \cdot 5^2 + 5^3 + 3 \cdot 5^4 + 4 \cdot 5^5 + 2 \cdot 5^6 + 3 \cdot 5^7 + O(5^9),$$

$$4 + 4 \cdot 5 + 4 \cdot 5^2 + 4 \cdot 5^3 + 4 \cdot 5^4 + 4 \cdot 5^5 + 4 \cdot 5^6 + 4 \cdot 5^7 + 4 \cdot 5^8 + O(5^9)$$

9.6 Approximations and polynomials

The following topics are discussed in this section:

- Generating Orthogonal Polynomials with `orthopoly[]`
- The Formal Power Series Package `powseries[]`
- Numerical Approximations from `numapprox[]`

Generating orthogonal polynomials with `orthopoly[]`

The `orthopoly[]` package has six functions that return orthogonal polynomials. The polynomials are first- and second-kind Chebyshev (`T()` and `U()`), Legendre (`P()`), Laguerre (`L()`), Hermite (`H()`), and the Gegenbauer (ultraspherical) polynomials (`G()`). As an example, here is the third Laguerre polynomial:

```
>L(3,x);
```

$$1 - 3\ x + 3/2\ x^2 - 1/6\ x^3$$

and here is an orthogonality check:

```
>int(exp(-x)*L(3,x)*L(4,x),x=0..infinity);
```

$$0$$

The formal power series package `powseries[]`

The `powseries[]` package contains functions for manipulating formal power series. A series is defined by giving a formula for its coefficients, together with specific individual values if that is needed (`powcreate()`). The standard operations of addition and subtraction, multiplication, multiplicative inversion and quotients, composition and reversion, exponentiation and taking logarithms, differentiation and integration, and truncation are permitted (`add()`, `subtract()`, `multiply()`, `multconst()`, `negative()`, `inverse()`, `quotient()`, `compose()`, `reversion()`, `powexp()`, `powerlog()`, `powerdiff()`, `powerint()`, `tpsform()`, and `powpoly()`). There is also an evaluator that can evaluate combinations of many of these operations (`evalpow()`) and a function for producing power series solutions of ordinary differential equations (`powsolve()`). To illustrate a few points about `powsubs[]`, we will define a formal power series, differentiate it, look at the coefficient of z^5 in the derivative, and print the first few terms of the derivative series:

```
>powcreate(w(n)=2^(n-1),w(0)=0);
```

The previous command defines the general term of the series and specifies a special value for the initial term:

```
>wd:=powdiff(w);
```

```
wd := proc(powparm)  ... end
```

Note that the result of the differentiation is in the form of a procedure that is evaluated in the manner shown next:

```
>wd(5);
```

$$192$$

To see the general term in the series, you do the following:

```
>wd(_k);
```

$$(\_k + 1)\ w(\_k + 1)$$

and to view several terms of the series:

```
>tpsform(wd,z,6);
```

$$1 + 4\ z + 12\ z^2 + 32\ z^3 + 80\ z^4 + 192\ z^5 + O(z^6)$$

You may run into trouble if you attempt to reassign the terms of an existing series due to Maple "remembering" past results. If this happens you can use read-lib(forget) before remaking the series (see the information on remember tables in Chapter 11 for an explanation of why this is necessary).

Numerical approximations from numapprox[]

The numapprox[] package contains functions used in approximation theory. There are several types of polynomial and rational functions expansion (taylor(), laurent(), chebyshev(), chebpade()), functions associated with min-max approximations – approximations of least maximum absolute errors – (minimax(), remez(), infnorm()), and two functions for rearranging rational functions for efficient evaluation (confracform(), hornerform()). We already illustrated minimax() in Section 5.8 and the laurent() function, which is a restricted version of the series() function mentioned in Section 3.4. For a different kind of illustration, we will rearrange a polynomial in nested form suitable for numerical evaluation. The rearrangement is done by hornerform():

```
>orthopoly[P](5,x)/orthopoly[P](6,x);
```

$$\frac{63/8\ x^5 - 35/4\ x^3 + 15/8\ x}{\frac{231}{16}\ x^6 - \frac{315}{16}\ x^4 + \frac{105}{16}\ x^2 - 5/16}$$

```
>numapprox[hornerform](");
```

$$
\cfrac{(15/8 + (- 35/4 + 63/8\ x^2)\ x^2)\ x^2}{- 5/16 + \left(\cfrac{105}{16} + \left(- \cfrac{315}{16} + \cfrac{231}{16}\ x^2\right)\ x^2\right)\ x^2}
$$

9.7   Geometry Maple-style with `geometry[]`

The `geometry[]` package contains functions for two-dimensional Euclidean geometry. Using this package, you can do things such as define lines, circles, and triangles and then perform geometric computations on them. For example, you can test properties (`IsEquilateral()`, `IsRight()`, `AreSimilar()`, `Are-Tangent()`, and more) and make additional constructions (`circumcircle()`, `centroid()`, `Eulercircle()`, `inversion()`).

To illustrate how geometry is used, we first define a point C, which becomes the center of a circle of radius 2, and we then inspect the data object that represents the circle:

```
>point(C,0,1);
```

$$
C
$$

```
>coordinates(C);
```

$$
[0,\ 1]
$$

```
>circle(Z,[C,2]);
```

$$
Z
$$

```
> detail(Z);
    name of the object: Z
    form of the object: circle2d
    name of the center: C
    coordinates of the center: [0, 1]
    radius of the circle: 2
    assume that the name of the horizonal and vertical
                  axis are _x and _y
    equation of the circle: _x^2-3+_y^2-2*_y = 0
```

The `detail()` function is interesting in that it is implemented using at-tributes `()`. For instance, look at the following:

```
> attributes(Z);
          table([
                geom2d/coeffs = [1, 0, 1, 0, -2, -3]
                geom2d/form = circle2d
                geom2d/centercoord = [0, 1]
                geom2d/centername = C
                geom2d/radius = 2
          ])
```

This example says that information about `Z` has been set by associating `Z` with the above table using the `setattribute()` function. Stated otherwise, the `details()` function provides an interface to the `attributes()` of `Z`.

Individual properties of an object may be accessed by the method illustrated next. First, we will compute the tangent to the circle through $(3, 0)$, which is a matter of a simple call to `tangentpc()` (`tgt` is our name for the tangent line):

```
>tangentpc(tgt,point(A,sqrt(3),0),Z);

                              tgt

> Equation(tgt);
enter name of the horizontal axis >
> x;
enter name of the vertical axis >
> y;
                        1/2
          - 3 + 3      x - y = 0
```

9.8   The Lie-symmetry package `liesymm[]`

Similarity solutions of some (systems of) ordinary and partial differential equations can be found by looking for transformations that leave the underlying equation(s) invariant. We illustrate part of this process using Burger's equation:

$$u_t(x, t) + u(x, t)u_x(x, t) = \mu u_{xx}(x, t)$$

```
> with(liesymm):
```

```
> burger := Diff(u(x,t),t) + u
> (x,t)*Diff(u(x,t),x) = mu * Diff(u(x,t),x,x);
```

$$\text{burger} := \left(\frac{d}{dt}\, u(x,\ t)\right) + u(x,\ t)\ \left(\frac{d}{dx}\, u(x,\ t)\right) = $$

$$\text{mu Diff}(u(x,\ t),\ x,\ x)$$

Note that the partial derivatives are defined using the inert `Diff()` function.

The Lie group formalism seeks a one-parameter group of transformations of the form

$$X(x, t, u; \epsilon) = x + \xi(x, t, u)\epsilon + O(\epsilon^2)$$
$$T(x, t, u; \epsilon) = t + \tau(x, t, u)\epsilon + O(\epsilon^2)$$
$$U(x, t, u; \epsilon) = u + \phi(x, t, u)\epsilon + O(\epsilon^2).$$

Substituting this change of variables into the equation and equating coefficients of ϵ results in an overdetermined system of linear partial differential equations for ξ, τ, and ϕ. The command `liesymm[determine]` can be used to find these equations:

```
> eqns := determine([burger],V,[u(x,t)],U):
```

We suppressed the rather lengthy output, and used the command `latex(eqns)` (covered in Chapter 8) to produce a readable result:

$$\left\{ \frac{\partial^2}{\partial u \partial x} V3(x, t, u) = \frac{\frac{\partial^2}{\partial x^2} V1(x, t, u)}{2}, \quad \frac{\partial}{\partial x} V1(x, t, u) = \frac{\frac{\partial}{\partial t} V2(x, t, u)}{2}, \right.$$

$$\frac{\partial^2}{\partial u^2} V3(x, t, u) = 2 \frac{\partial^2}{\partial u \partial x} V1(x, t, u),$$

$$\frac{\partial}{\partial t} V1(x, t, u) = \frac{\left(\frac{\partial}{\partial t} V2(x, t, u)\right) u}{2} + V3(x, t, u), \quad \frac{\partial^2}{\partial x^2} V3(x, t, u) = 0,$$

$$\frac{\partial}{\partial x} V2(x, t, u) = 0, \quad \frac{\partial^2}{\partial u \partial x} V2(x, t, u) = 0, \quad \frac{\partial}{\partial u} V2(x, t, u) = 0,$$

$$\frac{\partial}{\partial u} V1(x, t, u) = 0, \quad \frac{\partial}{\partial x} V3(x, t, u) = -\frac{\frac{\partial}{\partial t} V3(x, t, u)}{u},$$

$$\left. \frac{\partial^2}{\partial x^2} V2(x, t, u) = 0, \quad \frac{\partial^2}{\partial u^2} V2(x, t, u) = 0, \quad \frac{\partial^2}{\partial u^2} V1(x, t, u) = 0 \right\}$$

In the above, $V1$, $V2$, and $V3$ are identified with ξ, τ, and ϕ, respectively. The general solution of this set of equations is

$$V1 = axt + bt - cx + e, \qquad V2 = at^2 - 2ct + d,$$
$$V3 = ax + b + (-at + c)u,$$

where a, b, c, d, and e are arbitrary constants. Maple can verify this solution:

```
> soln := V1(x,t,u)=a*x*t+b*t-c*x+e,
          V2(x,t,u)=a*t^2-2*c*t+d
> , V3(x,t,u)=a*x+b + (-a*t+c)*u:


> map(expand@value, subs(soln,eqns));


    {0 = 0, a t - c = a t - c, a = a, a x + b = a x + b}
```

(the solution of linear overdetermined systems of equations like this can be simplified using ideas from Gröbner bases).

9.9 Miscellaneous packages

In this section, the topics discussed are

- Differential Forms with `difforms[]`
- The `NPspinor[]` and `totorder[]` Packages

Differential forms with `difforms[]`

The differential forms package `difforms[]` contains functions for manipulating differential forms. There are functions for evaluating wedge products and for exterior differentiation (`&^()`, `d()`). In addition to these, there are functions for simplification and a number of utilities for such things as finding the degree and parity of a form, finding parts of a form, and miscellaneous type checks (`simpform()`, `wdegree()`, `parity()`, `formpart()`, `scalarpart()`, `typescalar`, `typeform`, `typeconst`, `mixpar()`). Before a form is recognized by these functions, it must be defined using `defform()`. The command that follows defines two forms to each be of type scalar:

```
>with(difforms):
>defform(x=0,y=0);
```

The above returns NULL. Next we compute the exterior derivative of a form in these scalars:

```
>q:=d(x*y);
```

$$q := y \; d(x) \; + \; x \; d(y)$$

and note that, as it should be, the second exterior derivative is zero:

```
>d(q);
```

$$0$$

Differentiating another form and wedging it with the first gives the following:

```
>r:=d(x*y^2);
```

$$r := y^2 \; d(x) \; + \; 2 \; x \; y \; d(y)$$

```
>&^(q,r);
```

$$y^2 \; x \; (d(x) \; \&^\wedge \; d(y))$$

The previous result shows how differentials can be represented in the `difforms[]` package.

The `NPspinor[]` and `totorder[]` packages

The `NPspinor[]` package supercedes the `np[]` package, both of which are used for Newman–Penrose calculations in special relativity. This is a relatively specialized topic, which we will not discuss here. Finally, we mention the package `totorder[]` that assigns an order to a collection of Maple names.

10 Looping, branching, and data structures

As preparation for writing procedures, this brief chapter covers the main features for program flow control and for structuring data with Maple. Some of this material has already been covered in previous chapters. Here, we will collect together and amplify that material, and we will also introduce some new tools for structuring data.

The first section of the chapter is about setting up repetition statements and the associated decision structures. Included in the discussion are Boolean expressions, selection statements, and loop constructions. The second section reviews expression sequences and their role in defining lists and sets. The third section contains a systematic treatment of the Maple data structure and type called a table.

10.1 Loops and branches

This section covers selection and repetition statements in Maple. Selection statements are statements that select from a number of actions based on a Boolean test. We discussed selection statements in the Conditional Statements subsection, in Section 2.6, in connection with arrow functions, and we will review that material below. Repetition statements correspond to the usual "do," "for," and "while" loops encountered in most other programming languages. In this section, the subsections are

- Boolean Expressions
- Selection Statements
- Looping Constructs

Boolean expressions

Boolean expressions are used in selection statements for flow control in programs. In this subsection, we will review the main aspects of Boolean expressions and their evaluation. Generally, a Boolean expression can be evaluated to one of the Boolean constants `true` or `false` or, in some cases a special "don't know" value called `FAIL`.

Boolean expressions are formed using relational and logical operators. The relational operators are <, <=, >, >=, =, and <>. The logical operators are `and`, `or`, and `not`. Note that Maple automatically converts > and >= relations to < and <= relations as in

```
>2>=1;
```

$$1 <= 2$$

Relations are not automatically evaluated as Boolean; to do so would conflict with the method used to represent equations and inequalities. However, automatic evaluation does take place in the expression following the `if` and `elif` keywords used in selection statements (see below) and also if an expression contains any of the logical operators.

In Boolean expressions the = sign can be thought of as extending Fortran's ".EQ." and C's double equals "==". In Maple, Boolean evaluation applied to = tests whether two expressions are identical in the sense of their internal representation. This means that expressions that are mathematically identical such as 1 and 1.0 may be not (=:)

```
>evalb(1=1.0);
```

```
false
```

Boolean expressions are often constructed using the algebraic operators +, -, *, and / in association with the operators mentioned above. A well-defined system of precedences exists for operators. The highest-precedence operator is the decimal point and the lowest is the assignment symbol (type `?operators[precedence]` for the complete table). The arithmetic operators have a higher precedence than the logical operators. This means that in an expression where both appear, if there are no parentheses indicating otherwise, arithmetic operators are evaluated before logical operators. For example, 3<2+3 has the same Boolean value as 3<(2+3) so that the parentheses in the second form are redundant. However, liberal use of parentheses is the way to avoid precedence errors.

Using `evalb()`, any Boolean expression can be evaluated to one of the results `true`, `false`, or `FAIL`. Whereas `FAIL` is somewhat similar to an unevaluated return, it differs in that it is a logical value that can be combined with other logical values using the logical operators `and`, `or`, and `not`. The truth tables for these combinations can be found as follows:

```
>x:=FAIL: y:=true:
```

```
>evalb(x or y);
```

$$true$$

```
>evalb(x and y);
```

$$FAIL$$

and so on.

The logical operators and and or evaluate their right operands only if it is necessary, considering the result of the evaluation of the left operand. For example, the expression a and b is considered to be false, if a is found to be false, and in that case b will not be evaluated.

Selection statements

The general form of the selection statement is the following:

```
if <expr> then <statseq>
elif <expr> then <statseq>
elif <expr> then <statseq>

        . . .

else <statseq>
fi
```

The Maple "keywords" are if, elif, else, and fi; <expr> stands for expressions that will be evaluated as Boolean, and <statseq> stands for statement sequences that will be executed if the associated Boolean is true. The keyword elif stands for "else if." The elif <expr> then <statseq> part can be repeated any number of times or may be absent, as may the else <statseq> part. The fi keyword must always be present to match the if. The expressions <expr> appearing in the selection statement are automatically evaluated as Boolean expressions. If you (inadvertently) attempt to use a non-Boolean expression, Maple will inform you. In this connection, a common error involving a non-Boolean expression occurs when a variable that is used in a relation has no assigned value as in

```
>if i>2 then i fi;
Error, cannot evaluate boolean
```

This occurs simply because i has no assigned value and cannot be compared with the number 2. However, evalb() returns unevaluated in this situation.

Maple has no "case" statement corresponding to C's "switch." The selection statement is used instead.

Looping constructs

Loops in Maple are set up using repetition statements. There are two possible formats for repetition statements. The first is as follows:

```
for <name> from <expr> by <expr> to <expr> while <expr>
do <statseq>
od
```

Any of the keywords and their associated expressions may be absent except for do and od. For instance, here is a way to obtain the 10th prime number using just one of the optional keywords:

```
>p:=0:
>to 10 do p:=nextprime(p) od:
>p;
```

$$29$$

Actually, it would be quicker to type the expression ithprime(10) for this result, but that is beside the point. This example also illustrates that the expressions following from and by are assumed to be equal to 1 if omitted.

When the keyword while is present, the expression following it is evaluated as Boolean and execution of the loop proceeds if the result is true. To illustrate, here is a way to print a list of the prime numbers that are less than ten:

```
>p:=10:
>while p>2 do p:=prevprime(p) od;
```

$$p := 7$$

$$p := 5$$

$$p := 3$$

$$p := 2$$

It is possible for all of the keywords to appear in a single statement. The example that follows does this in a backward search to find the position of a specific item in a list:

```
>l:=[John, Paul, George, Ringo];
```

$$l := [John, Paul, George, Ringo]$$

```
>for i from 4 to 1 by -1 while l[i]<>George do od;
>i;
```

$$3$$

Note that the value of the loop counter is available outside the loop. In addition, even though in this example there are no statements between do and od, these keywords may not be omitted.

The second repetition statement has the form

```
for <name> in <expr> while <expr> do <statseq> od
```

The while keyword is optional. We will illustrate the use of this repetition by counting the number of times an entry appears in a list. The first step is to make some data; this will be a list of randomly chosen integers, either 1 or 2. We will then count how many 2s are in the list.

```
>u:=rand(1..2):
>l:=[seq(u(),i=1..6)];
```

$$l := [2, 1, 2, 2, 2, 1]$$

```
>ct:=0:
>for k in l do if k=2 then ct:=ct+1 fi od;
>ct;
```

$$4$$

The for part could be written less concisely as for k from 1 to nops(l) and correspondingly, the conditional would be written as if op(k,l)=2 then ct:=ct+1 fi. The point of the for–in loop is to avoid the relatively clumsy use of nops() and op(). Incidentally, this counting task could be done more quickly with convert(l,multiset).

Maple offers two ways to alter the flow in a repetition statement. The first uses the keyword `break`. When `break` is encountered in a repetition statement, control is transferred out of the (innermost) loop in which it occurs to the first statement following the loop. This is similar to the use of the same keyword in C. Values of variables used in the exited loop are still available. The second way to alter the flow uses the keyword `next`. When `next` is encountered, control is transferred to the beginning of the loop in which it occurs. This can be useful when you want to work over a subset of a data structure such as a list. To illustrate, the example below finds the smallest positive element in a list:

```
>u:=rand(-10..20):
>l:=[seq(u(),i=1..10)];
```

$$l := [10, 17, -3, -3, -10, -9, 13, 15, 11, 16]$$

```
>m:=20:
>for i in l do if i<=0 then next else m:=min(m,i) fi od;
>m;
```

$$10$$

Maple does not have any labeling facility for statements, and it does not have a "go to" statement.

This is a good point at which to recall that it is more efficient to form expression sequences with `seq()` than with `for` loops. The reason is that within the `for` loop, the sequence has to be built by joining new elements one by one, whereas `seq()` is programmed to avoid the intermediate steps. To illustrate this point, we will build an expression sequence of integers in a `for` loop:

```
>e:=NULL:
>for i to 5 do e:=e,i od;
```

$$e := 1$$

$$e := 1, 2$$

$$e := 1, 2, 3$$

$$e := 1, 2, 3, 4$$

$$e := 1, 2, 3, 4, 5$$

Initializing e (even to NULL) is essential to avoid a stack overflow error. The `seq()` function does not form the auxiliary expression sequences:

```
>e:=seq(i,i=1..5);
```

$$e := 1, 2, 3, 4, 5$$

This is likely to be an issue only if you are dealing with large or complex expression sequences.

Recall from Section 1.3, Working with Structured Data that there is also a for–in type construction for use with `seq()`.

10.2   Expression sequences, sets, and lists

In Working with Structured Data in Section 1.3, we discussed the role of expression sequences and other expressions made from them. We will review this material here.

An expression sequence is formed by separating ordinary expressions by zero or more commas. Such sequences form the building blocks for other Maple entities including sets and lists. To form a set, you enclose an expression sequence in braces, and to form a list, you enclose it in square brackets.

In forming a set from an expression sequence, remember that duplicates will be removed and that the order of the remaining expressions may vary. There are times when this may be inconvenient. For instance, `solve()` returns the solution to a system of equations as a set of equations for the variables (remember you can convert these to assignments with `assign()`). Because the variables are in a set, it is not possible to predict the order in which they will appear. If the order matters, you have to do a bit more work, for instance, with `sort()`. To find the number of members in a set, you use the function `nops()`. The individual entries are found using `op()`. Remember that for the same arguments, `op()` for a set may return different results on different occasions. Here is a small reminder of these points:

```
>e:=a,b,a,z;
```

$$e := a, b, a, z$$

```
>s:={e};
```

$$s := \{a, b, z\}$$

```
>nops(s);
```

3

```
>op(s);
```

$$a, \ b, \ z$$

```
>op(1..2,s);
```

$$a, \ b$$

```
>op(2,s);
```

$$b$$

A more convenient method for accessing individual elements or ranges of elements is through selection using square brackets. For the previous two results, this is done as follows:

```
> s[2];
```

$$b$$

```
> s[1..2];
```

$$\{a, \ b\}$$

You cannot assign new entries to a set. However, the set theoretical functions union, intersect, and so forth are available for adding new entries and other manipulations.

Working with lists is in many ways similar to working with sets except that order is preserved and duplicates are not removed. The functions op() and nops() also work in a way similar to sets.

A potentially confusing point concerns expression sequences themselves. The functions nops() and op() cannot take an expression sequence with multiple entries as an argument. The reason is simple: nops(), for example, takes a single argument, but because of the way procedure arguments are interpreted, a general expression sequence is interpreted as multiple arguments by nops() and rejected. To find the length of an expression sequence, it is easiest to wrap list brackets around it and then apply nops(). Individual entries may be obtained by applying op() to the wrapped sequence and also by selection from the sequence itself. For instance, the earlier expression sequence e gives the following results:

```
>e;
```

$$a, \ b, \ a, \ z$$

```
>nops(e);
Error,
wrong number (or type) of parameters in function nops;
>nops([e]);
```

$$4$$

```
>op(1,e);
Error,
wrong number (or type) of parameters in function op;
>op(1,[e]);
```

$$a$$

```
>e[2];
```

$$b$$

In the next section we will discuss another and more flexible (but less efficient) way to work with structured data.

10.3 Tables and arrays

Among the various data structures in Maple, the table structure is the most general. Among other things, tables are used to represent arrays as well as to encapsulate functions in packages. In this section, we will cover the definition and use of tables and arrays. The topics are

- Definition and Creation of Tables
- Evaluation of Tables
- Parts of Tables
- Copying and Renaming Tables
- Arrays

Definition and creation of tables

A table can be created explicitly or implicitly. The explicit method uses an assignment of the form illustrated next:

```
>Curves:=table();
```

$$Curves := table([])$$

In this assignment, we have set up a table called `Curves`. The table is currently empty, as indicated by Maple's response. Table entries can be specified by assignments such as

```
>Curves:=table([Cardioid='plot([1+cos(t),t,t=0..2*Pi],
>coords=polar)']);

Curves :=

table([
    Cardioid = plot(

        [1 + cos(t), t, t = 0 .. 2 Pi],
          coords = polar) ])
```

This table has a single entry, which is a command to plot a cardioid. The plot statement is quoted because we want the table entry to be the plot statement itself, not its result. The index of this entry is `Cardioid`. In this case, the entry is a single equation in a list. To obtain a plot of a cardioid we have only to type (output suppressed here):

```
>Curves[Cardioid]:
```

Generally, any number of equations can appear in a list of table entries. The left side of each equation is the index for the entry, and the right side is the corresponding entry. If any index is omitted, Maple indexes all the entries numerically starting from one. The effect of this is to make the equations themselves the table entries. The example that follows illustrates this point:

```
>Gender:=table([Joe=man,Zoe=woman,Gail]);

            Gender := table([
                         1 = (Joe = man)
                         2 = (Zoe = woman)
                         3 = Gail
                    ])
```

Now the indices are the integers 1, 2, and 3. If the final entry is an equation or is omitted, the left sides of the equations would become the indices.

Entries can be added to a table by assignment as follows:

```
>Curves[HyperbolicSpiral]:='plot([cos(t)/t,sin(t)/t,
>t=1..10])';
```

$$Curves[HyperbolicSpiral] :=$$

$$plot([\frac{cos(t)}{t}, \frac{sin(t)}{t}, t = 1 .. 10])$$

Existing entries can be reassigned in a similar way.

For the example below, we will add two more functions to our `Curves` table:

```
>Curves[Folium]:='plots[implicitplot]
>(x^3+y^3-3*x*y, x=-2..2,y=-2..2)';
```

$$Curves[Folium] := plots[implicitplot]($$

$$x^3 + y^3 - 3 x y, x = -2 .. 2, y = -2 .. 2)$$

```
>Curves[ArchimedesSpiral]:='plot([t/5,t,t=0..2*Pi],
>coords=polar)';
```

$$Curves[ArchimedesSpiral] :=$$

$$plot([1/5 t, t, t = 0 .. 2 Pi], coords = polar)$$

Anticipating some points from the next subsection, we may ask: What happens if you attempt to use a nonexistent table value? The answer is that the index will be evaluated and returned as the index of the last name in the overall evaluation chain. The last name will most often be the name of the table, so that the result will be similar to the input. For example, `Curves` has no entry for `Clothoid` so not much happens when we ask for it:

```
>Curves[Clothoid];
```

$$Curves[Clothoid]$$

Note that if you want to save Curves to a file, you should add another level of quotes to the plot commands to allow for the evaluation associated with the read command.

Now we will discuss the implicit method of table creation. In the above assignment to Curves[Folium], the table Curves already exists and we merely added an entry. The implicit method simply amounts to this: If a table assignment is made to a table that does not exist, the table will be automatically created and the entry inserted. Here is an example:

```
>Trig[arg1]:=sin;
```

$$Trig[arg1] := sin$$

Assuming that no table with the name Trig currently exists, this assignment creates one and assigns the value sin to the index arg1. If the table already exists, the corresponding entry will be created or overwritten.

Evaluation of tables

By now we are familiar with the idea that most expressions are subject to full evaluation. However, tables are one of the few (but important) exceptions to this rule. To illustrate, if we attempt to inspect the Gender table in the previous section, the following is what results:

```
>Gender;
```

$$Gender$$

Contrary to appearance, the Gender table does still exist. The result is an illustration of the fact that tables follow last name evaluation rules: If the end product of an evaluation process is a table structure (not just a table entry), then the result of the evaluation is defined to be not the table structure but the last name encountered in the evaluation process. Normally, that will be the name of the table structure as in the illustration above.

To evaluate a table, you use the evaluator eval(). For Gender, this gives the expected result:

```
>eval(Gender);
```

```
table([
        1 = (Joe = man)
        2 = (Zoe = woman)
        3 = Gail
    ])
```

We will use `eval()` to show that table structures can be nested. Here, for illustration, is a table defined implicitly:

```
>Diet[Friday][Lunch]:=cookies;
```

$$Diet[Friday][Lunch] := cookies$$

This is a new table, but because it is implicitly created, Maple does not produce the same details as when a table is explicitly created. The `eval()` function reveals the structure:

```
>eval(Diet);
```

```
table([
    Friday = table([
                Lunch = cookies
             ])
])
```

`Friday` is an index into the table `Diet`. `Lunch` is an index into the table `Diet[Friday]`. Note carefully that the above evaluation is not asserting that `Friday` is a table. All it says is that `Friday` is an index (the left side of the equation) and that the corresponding entry is the table shown on the right side of the equation. You can check these statements with `type( ,table)` tests. To assign another entry to `Diet[Friday]`, you would do the following:

```
>Diet[Friday][Breakfast]:=pancakes;
```

$$Diet[Friday][Breakfast] := pancakes$$

```
>eval(Diet);
```

```
table([
    Friday = table([
                Lunch = cookies
                Breakfast = pancakes
             ])
])
```

Parts of tables

Two useful functions for inspecting tables are `indices()` and `entries()`. These are straightforward to use. To see the indices of `Curves`, for instance, we do the following:

```
>indices(Curves);
```

```
    [Cardioid], [Folium], [ArchimedesSpiral],
        [HyperbolicSpiral]
```

and to see the entries of `Diet`,

```
>entries(Diet);
```

```
    [table([                    ]
            Lunch = cookies
            Breakfast = pancakes
        ])
```

A table can have an indexing function. This is a procedure, which may be user supplied, and all access requests for the table entries must pass through it. The default indexing function is `NULL`, implying that access to the table entries is unconstrained. For a general table argument, the `nops()` function returns the value 2. The first operand is the indexing function's name and the second is the list of equations making up the table. To illustrate on `Gender`,

```
>op(1,eval(Gender));
>op(2,eval(Gender));
```

```
    [1 = (Joe = man), 2 = (Zoe = woman), 3 = Gail]
```

The first evaluation returns `NULL`. In the second evaluation, use of `eval()` ensures that the entries of the table are returned.

Copying and renaming tables

Suppose you wanted to make a new table from `Curves` containing only the spirals. You might try something like the following:

```
>Spirals:=Curves;
```

```
            Spirals := Curves
```

```
>Spirals[Cardioid]:='Spirals[Cardioid]';

            Spirals[Cardioid] := Spirals[Cardioid]

>Spirals[Folium]:='Spirals[Folium]';

            Spirals[Folium] := Spirals[Folium]
```

The idea is to make a copy of the original table and then unassign the unwanted entries. The problem with this approach is revealed below:

```
>eval(Curves);

table([
    ArchimedesSpiral =
        plot([1/5 t, t, t = 0 .. 2 Pi], coords = polar)
    HyperbolicSpiral =

                cos(t)   sin(t)
        plot([------, ------, t = 1 .. 10])
                  t        t

])
```

As you see, the changes have been made to Curves and the other two original entries of Curves have been lost. This behavior is special to tables. The important point is that copies of tables are not made unless explicitly requested. Consequently, the name Spirals became identified with the name Curves when we made the assignment above and the single table (eval(Curves)) can be referred to by either name. Changing Spirals or Curves merely changes one table that in effect, has acquired two names.

The way to make a copy of a table is through the copy() function that is provided for this purpose. After restoring Curves from a file, we can set up the Spirals table as follows (outputs suppressed):

```
>Spirals:=copy(Curves):
>Spiral[Cardioid]:='Spiral[Cardioid]':
>Spiral[Folium]:='Spiral[Folium]':
```

Now Curves remains intact and Spirals is as wanted. In this instance, it would be more efficient to copy the two spiral definitions (suitably enclosed in forward quotes) directly to a new table, relying on implicit creation. However for large tables, using copy() is often the quickest way to make a modified copy.

Arrays

An array is a specialization of the table structure to the case where indices are given by zero or more integer ranges. Array references are checked to see that the referenced element is within the bounds established in the ranges, if any. Usually at least one range will be present, but that is not necessarily so. For instance, a function might signal an error condition by returning an array with no range argument.

As we already know, an array is created by a command such as the following, which sets up a 4 × 5 array with two assigned entries:

```
>a:=array(-3..0,4..9,[(-2,7)=sin(x)/x,(0,4)=tan(x)/x]):
```

The lengthy output is suppressed. Note that the entries after the ranges follow the standard pattern for tables, that is, a list of equations. The entries can be any Maple expressions. Entries can be assigned and changed in the same way as for any table. Last name evaluation rules apply, and eval() is used to obtain evaluation of an array. The copy() function is needed to make a copy of an array just as for other tables.

The function nops() applied to an array gives the result 3 instead of 2 as for a regular table. The first operand gives the indexing function as before, the second gives the ranges in the form of an expression sequence, and the third gives the equations defining the entries. The indices() and entries() functions give the indices for which assignments or entries have been made.

It is useful to note that space for array entries is not allocated until the entries are defined. This means that there is no memory penalty for defining large arrays. The illustration below demonstrates this point:

```
>a:=array(0..1):
>length(eval(a));
```

$$263$$

```
>a:=array(0..1000000):
>length(eval(a));
```

$$269$$

```
>for i from 0 to 10 do a[i]:=x^i od:
>length(eval(a));
```

$$394$$

```
>for i from 0 to 100 do a[i]:=x^i od:
>length(eval(a));
```

$$1565$$

```
>for i from 0 to 1000 do a[i]:=x^i od:
>length(eval(a));
```

$$10877$$

10.4   Reference section

REPETITION STATEMENTS

`for <name>`		
	`from <expr>`	Defaults to 1
	`by <expr>`	Defaults to 1
	`to <expr>`	
	`while <expr>`	`<expr>` is evaluated as Boolean
	`do <statseq> od`	Mandatory
`for <name>`		
	`in <expr>`	Do over the operands of `<expr>`
	`while <expr>`	`<expr>` is evaluated as Boolean
	`do <statseq> od`	Mandatory

SELECTION STATEMENTS

`if <expr> then <statseq>`	`<expr>` is evaluated as Boolean
`elif <expr> then <statseq>`	
`elif <expr> then <statseq>`	
. . .	
`else <statseq>`	
`fi`	Mandatory

TABLES AND ARRAYS

`table`	Creates a table explicitly
`<name>[<name>]`	Creates a table implicitly
`indices`	Gives the indices of a table
`entries`	Gives the entries of a table
`copy`	Must be used for copying a table
`array`	Table with range indexes of the form $m..n$

11 Introducing Maple programming

This chapter provides an introduction to Maple programming. Although in many ways programming in Maple is similar to, say, C programming, there are some significant differences. Among other things, this chapter explains these differences and their consequences.

The first section covers a number of basic definitions and operations for procedures, including returning results and checking arguments. The second section covers the very important ideas of evaluation and scope. It is here that many of the unusual features of Maple programming emerge. The third section covers various options available with procedures. The fourth section discusses debugging and how to read Maple procedures in the library. The fifth section explains how to turn a set of procedures into a package. The chapter concludes with a reference section.

11.1 Introducing procedures

This section covers the following topics:

- The Simplest Procedures
- The General Form of a Procedure
- Returning Results from Procedures
- The Variables `nargs`, `args`, and `procname()`
- Type Checking and Procedure Arguments

The simplest procedures

As we illustrate in this subsection, some programming tasks can be performed using only the general syntax for procedures. Later subsections cover cases in which arguments have to be assigned and local variables are needed. As an example of a simple procedure, we will print out data in a specific format. The procedure `niceP()`

below prints two numbers described by some text:

```
>niceP:=proc(x,y)
>    printf('     Value of x = %6.4f: Value of y =
            %6.4f',x,y);
>    lprint()
>end;
```

The `niceP()` procedure illustrates the usual format for defining a procedure, which is to assign its name to the word `proc` followed by an expression sequence (maybe empty) enclosed in parentheses. In the case of `niceP()`, the expression sequence contains the two entries `x` and `y`. The assignment of the name to the procedure is followed by commands that make up the body of the procedure, which in turn, are terminated by the (mandatory) keyword `end`. Note that no semicolon or colon is needed before `end` or after `proc()`.

You invoke the procedure, as with any Maple function, by using its name with appropriate arguments:

```
>niceP(1.1,298.45);
```

```
       Value of x = 1.1000:   Value of y = 298.4500
```

The effect of evaluating the procedure (through the invocation) is to cause its statements to be executed. As we will see below, the result returned by a procedure is the last evaluation before the procedure finishes. The example above is somewhat deceptive in that respect because the last result is NULL (the value of `lprint()`). The result you see is printed as a side effect of `printf()`.

The parameters `x` and `y` are local to the procedure and have no value outside it. The general question of the "visibility" of variables in procedures is discussed in Scope Rules in Section 11.2 below.

More complicated procedures will usually have local variables, arguments to be assigned in the procedure, and, possibly, additional procedures embedded in them. To write such procedures, you need a greater knowledge of how evaluation works in the procedure context and of how variable values are treated in embedded procedures. These and other topics are covered in the Section 11.2 below.

General form of a procedure

Every procedure has the structure shown below:

```
proc(<nameseq>)
    local <nameseq>
    global <nameseq>
    options <nameseq>
    description <string>
    <statseq>
end;
```

The `local`, `global`, `description`, and `options` keywords may be absent. In each case, `<nameseq>` denotes a (possibly empty) sequence of names separated by commas and the `<statseq>` denotes a (possibly empty) sequence of Maple statements separated by semicolons or by colons. The body of the procedure is the text between `proc` and `end`. It is not required that a procedure be laid out line by line. It can be written in a continuous line, provided the appropriate separators (for example, semicolons and spaces) are present.

One way to write a procedure is through an arrow function. When you input the arrow function, Maple automatically writes a procedure to represent it. For example, here is an arrow function and the corresponding procedure to compute the absolute value of a number:

```
>g:=x-> if x>0 then x else -x fi;
```

```
g := proc(x)
        options operator,arrow;
            if 0 < x then x else -x fi
        end
```

Maple creates a procedure for the arrow function. This procedure has the single parameter x and uses the options shown. Note that the procedure has been assigned to the name g and recall that to use the arrow function you evaluate, for instance, g(-3.2).

A procedure does not have to be named. A common situation occurs with the `map()` function. The example that follows illustrates the principle involved:

```
>map(x->if x>0 then x else -x fi, [-1,2,3,-3]);
```

$$[1, 2, 3, 3]$$

Any procedure could replace the arrow function here.

Given that a Maple procedure is running inside a Maple session (the "global environment"), what are the rules about global and local variables? For instance, suppose you have a variable w in the global environment (a global variable) with the value 1, say, and the name w appears in the body of a procedure. When the procedure is invoked, how is the evaluation of w performed? The answer depends on how w appears in the procedure. First, if w appears in the name sequence of the `local` keyword, then the w of the procedure (a local variable) is a different entity from the global variable of the same name. Inside the procedure, the local variable can be freely manipulated without affecting the global variable; outside the procedure it has no existence. Second, if w appears on the left side of an assignment statement or as a loop index or as a `seq()` index it is automatically treated as `local` and Maple will warn you of this. In all other cases, the variable is assumed to be global. For w, this means that the value 1 will be substituted wherever w appears in the procedure (see below). Maple will issue a warning when it is assuming that a variable is global and issue an error message if you try to use a local variable in the argument list of a procedure. Probably, we do not need to remind you that good programming practice requires explicit `local` or `global` declarations for all variables.

Like tables, procedures are subject to last name evaluation rules. To see the full procedure, you use `eval()` with the procedure name as argument. Individual parts of procedures such as the `option` sequence can be obtained using `op(i,eval())`, where giving i an integer value from 1 to 6 shows the argument sequence, the locals, the options, the remember table (discussed below), the description string, and the globals, respectively.

Returning results from procedures

How do you control the information that is returned from a procedure? There are several methods. The examples above illustrate the most basic method: the value of a procedure is defined to be the value of its last evaluated expression. In the following example, there are three possible last evaluations:

```
>ex1:=proc(x)
>          if type(x,numeric) then
>             if x>0 then x*ln(x)
>             elif x=0 then 0
>             else 'Negative argument not allowed'
>             fi
>          else
>            'Non numeric argument'
>          fi
>      end:
>ex1(2);
```

$$2 \ln(2)$$

```
>ex1(x);
```

Non numeric argument

An elementary error that sometimes occurs in this context is illustrated in the following variation of `ex1()`:

```
>ex2:=proc(x)
>         if type(x,numeric) then
>             if x>0 then x*ln(x)
>             elif x=0 then 0
>             else 'Negative argument not allowed'
>             fi
>        fi;
>             'Non numeric argument'
>        end:
>ex2(2);
```

Non numeric argument

Can you see what happened?

Another method for returning results from a procedure uses a function called `RETURN()`. This function takes an expression sequence, maybe empty, for its argument. The expression sequence represents the results of the computation. To illustrate, here is a procedure that tests to see if a given list contains all identical entries and if so, returns the common value:

```
>isconst:=proc(l)
>             if nops(l)<=1 then RETURN('procname(args)')
>             else
>                 if nops({op(l)})=1 then RETURN(true,l[1])
>                 else
>                     false
>                 fi
>             fi
>            end:
>isconst([3,3,3]);
```

true, 3

The first use of `RETURN()` in this procedure is a special technique to create an unevaluated return. This refers to a situation in which no detectable error has occurred,

yet the computation could not be carried out for some reason. You use RETURN()
with the special string 'procname(args)' as shown. Here is what it produces:

```
>isconst([Joe]);
```

$$isconst([Joe])$$

Note that RETURN() is a Maple function and must be used with parentheses even if
there is no result to return. (Incidentally, a quick way to check for identical elements
in a list is to convert() it to a set.)

Another function that causes a return from a procedure is called ERROR(). This
procedure is used in a similar way to RETURN() to exit from the procedure and
provide information. Here is an example showing what ERROR() actually produces:

```
>ex := proc() ERROR('Don't call me') end:
```

```
>ex();
Error, (in ex) Don't call me
```

When the ERROR() function is encountered, control is returned to the global environment and the argument expression sequence is printed along with the other
information shown. You have probably seem similar messages many times and now
you know how they are generated!

The other method for returning results of functions is through their arguments. We
will cover this in the Evaluation Rules for Arguments subsection below because this
method depends on knowing some facts about how evaluation works in connection
with procedures.

The variables nargs, args, and procname

Three useful variables that are available in all procedures are nargs, args, and
procname. The first two give information about the arguments of the invocation.
The nargs variable is the number of actual arguments in the invocation. The args
variable is an expression sequence containing the arguments. Subsequences of args
are selected using ranges or numerical arguments. For instance, the ith argument is
called args[i]. The args and nargs variables are often used in procedures that
have optional arguments. Here is an illustration for these functions:

```
> p:=proc(a,b,c,d) local i;RETURN(nargs,[seq(i,i=args)])
  end:
> p(1,2,3,5);
```

$$4, \ [1, \ 2, \ 3, \ 5]$$

This procedure simply returns the number of its input arguments and a list of the input arguments. In the above example, the number of input arguments may be more or less than four; a correct result will still be obtained. Related to this is the possibility of using an empty argument list as in the modified version of the procedure p() given next:

```
> q:=proc() local i;RETURN(nargs,[seq(i,i=args)]) end:
> q(1,{x},[y],sin(u),a);
```

$$5, \ [1, \ \{x\}, \ [y], \ \sin(u), \ a]$$

If you plan to use such a technique, you may need to check the types of the input arguments inside the procedure. Type checking is covered in the following subsection.

Incidentally, it is advisable to allow Maple to have exclusive use of the name args inside procedures. Naming your own variables args can cause errors.

The procname variable gives access to the name of the procedure, assuming it has one. An application was given earlier in connection with unevaluated returns.

Type checking and procedure arguments

In this subsection, we will discuss methods for checking the types of incoming arguments in procedures. Recall that a type in Maple is a property of a variable that can be checked using the function type().

Unlike most procedural languages, Maple does not require explicit type declarations for variables. In fact, it could be difficult to enforce types on variables in a program that is as versatile as Maple. However, there are occasions when it is essential to know the type of a variable, for instance, when procedure arguments can be of different types at different invocations. On such occasions, it may be necessary to do a thorough analysis of the types occurring in an expression. Maple contains a set of tools for performing this analysis. Here, we will discuss the methods for checking incoming data types in procedures.

We will begin with a brief discussion of types. Maple recognizes a great variety of basic types. A few relatively familiar ones are algebraic, numeric, string, list, polynom, function, matrix, range, and so forth. A complete list of the standard types can be found under ?type. When the type() function signifies that an entity is indeed of a specific type, we say that the entity matches that particular type. Many expressions will match more than one type. For example sin(x) matches both algebraic and function. Beyond this, it is easy to imagine combinations of types; a simple example would be a list of numerics. You can easily see that the number of possible combinations of types is too large for each to be listed individually. Instead,

Maple provides an easy way to form type combinations that can then be checked by type(). The resulting type combinations are called structured types. The easiest way to understand structured types is to look at a few examples, and that is what we will do now.

A simple example of a structured type is the one for a list of numeric types, which is list(numeric). In general, parentheses used in this way tell type() to check that the subexpressions of the list or other type (assuming it is matched) consist of the type in the parentheses. Parentheses can also be nested. Here is an example using nested parentheses:

```
>type(sin([1,2,3]),function(list(numeric)));
```

$$true$$

Note that this is purely a pattern-matching operation: The expression sin([1,2,3]) has no practical significance. That there is no attempt to check that an expression "makes sense" is a general feature of structured types. This is not surprising because it is type() that does the work. When any of several types are acceptable as the result of a type test, the test can be done by including the types in set braces. For instance, you may wish to know if some data is either a list of numbers or a list of such lists. In that case, you could make the test in the way illustrated next:

```
>t:={list(numeric),list(list(numeric))};
```

$$t := \{list(numeric), \ list(list(numeric))\}$$

```
>type([1,2],t);
```

$$true$$

```
>type([[12],[3,4]],t);
```

$$true$$

A similar approach can be used to check the structure of relations. The structured type appearing in the next example is an equation (the official name for an equation is the = sign) between the types name and range:

```
>e:=x=1.4..2;
```

$$e := x = 1.4 \ .. \ 2$$

```
>type(e,name=range);
```

$$true$$

The same expression can be tested in more detail as follows:

```
>type(e,name=float..integer);
```

```
                              true
```

In addition to relations, you can check the structure of logical and arithmetical expressions. For arithmetical expressions, the types `'+'`, `'*'`, and `'^'` are most useful. Note that to check infix addition of objects, you use the `&+` form of addition as in

```
>type(sin(x)+sin(y),algebraic &+ algebraic);
```

```
                              true
```

For infix multiplication you use `&*`.

To check the names and arguments of functions, there are several options depending on exactly what you want to do. To check that an expression is a function with specific argument types, there is a structured type called `anyfunc()`, which works as follows:

```
>type(F(10,1..4),anyfunc(numeric,range));
```

```
                              true
```

This is another example of pattern matching by `type()` as there is no currently defined function `F()`. To check for a specific instance of a function, the structured type is `specfunc()`. Here is an example for `specfunc()`:

```
>type(F(1.4,10),specfunc(numeric,F));
```

```
                              true
```

The `specfunc()` type takes just two arguments, a type and the function to be tested for. To check the arguments of a specific function in more detail, you can use the following test:

```
>type(F(10,1..4),F(integer,range));
```

```
                              true
```

Observe in the last case that, unlike the previous examples, the second argument does not start out with a type name.

Although there is far more that could be said about types and type testing, the above will be sufficient to explain the role of types in connection with argument passing.

To illustrate type checking of arguments, our first example is a procedure called eB() that returns an arrow function consisting of the input arrow function with its two arguments exchanged. The eB procedure will check that its input argument is a procedure that has just two name arguments. To make the first check, we use a technique that permits the type test to be placed in the parameter list. The idea is to put a double colon followed by the type (which may be structured) immediately after the parameter to be checked. In eB, we want to check for a procedure so that is the type name placed after the parameter. In this approach, the type() function is called implicitly. The second test is in the procedure body. Using a structured type, it tests that the list of arguments of the input procedure contains just a pair of names. Here is the resulting procedure:

```
>eB:=proc(f::procedure)
>local e;
>e:=op(1,op(f));
>if not type([e],[name,name]) then ERROR fi;
>unapply(f(e[1],e[2]),e[2],e[1])
>     end:
```

It would have been better to test for an incoming arrow function, not a general procedure. We leave that as an exercise. Now we define an arrow function to test eB:

```
>w:=(P,Q)->P*sin(Q);
```

$$w := (P,Q) \rightarrow P \sin(Q)$$

The result of the invocation is then

```
>eB(w);
```

$$(Q,P) \rightarrow P \sin(Q)$$

As a more complex example, here is a recursive procedure called sL() that takes either one or two arguments and returns different results accordingly. This function can return either the sum or the mean of a list of numerical quantities or the sum or mean of a list of such lists presented as the first argument. If a second argument is present, the mean is returned. The `sL()` function has a structured type test in the parameter list and a structured type test in the body that is used to decide whether a recursive call to `sL()` is needed to sum an element of a list of lists. Here is the procedure:

```
sL:=proc(a::{list(numeric),list(list(numeric))},m)
    global s;
    local i,s1;
    if not type(a,list(numeric)) then
       sL([seq(convert(op(i,a),'+'),i = 1 .. nops(a))])
    else s := convert(a,'+')
    fi;

    if nargs = 1 then s
    else s1 := s; sL(map(nops,[op(a)])); m := s1/s
    fi
end:
```

and here are the results of two simple invocations:

```
>sL([[1,2,3],[3,2,1]],'m');
```

$$2$$

```
>sL([[1,2,3],[3,2,1]]);
```

$$12$$

We will use this procedure later to illustrate debugging using `printlevel`.

11.2 Evaluation rules and scope

This section covers the aspects of Maple programming that seem to cause the most difficulties. We will illustrate the common pitfalls and how to avoid them. The topics are

- Evaluation Rules for Arguments
- Evaluation Rule for Local Variables
- Scope Rules

Evaluation rules for arguments

In the previous section, there was a hint of the differences between standard procedural languages and Maple in the way variable values in procedures may be taken from the global environment. In fact, there are other differences as we will see in this section. These differences are not trivial from the standpoint of standard language programming.

We will begin with evaluation. Initially, evaluation enters the arena through the arguments or parameters of the procedure. There are two kinds of parameters. *Formal parameters* refers to the names in the <nameseq> of the proc(). The idea is that formal parameters refer to the names themselves, which are static entities, rather than their associated expressions, which can vary with different applications (invocations) of the procedure. In the context of a specific application of a procedure, when the names are replaced by other expressions, the term *actual parameters* is used. Formal parameters are informally referred to as parameters and actual parameters are often called arguments.

The first key point about procedures and evaluation is this: When you invoke a procedure, the formal parameters are evaluated in the standard way and the resulting arguments are then "substituted" wherever they occur in that particular procedure. Moreover, no further evaluation of the arguments will occur. This can lead to seemingly strange behavior. For instance, look at the next evaluation:

```
>q:=1: q:=q+1;
```

$$q := 2$$

Nothing unusual here. Now suppose you try to put essentially the same computation into a procedure like the following:

```
>a:=proc(p) p:=p+1 end:
```

Invoking the procedure gives an error:

```
>a(1);
Error, (in a) Illegal use of a formal parameter
```

The explanation is that Maple attempted to substitute the value of p, in this case the number 1, to the left side of the assignment. Because you cannot assign to a number, the message is generated. The replacement on the left side exemplifies the substitution technique in that the arguments are substituted in each occurrence of the parameter in the procedure body, whether on the left or right side of an assignment or somewhere else. (Substitution, in the sense used above, is a basic operation in the "λ–calculus." The λ–calculus is a branch of mathematical logic that provides a foundation for certain aspects of programming languages.)

The examples above imply that you cannot directly change the values of an argument (except a name) in a procedure. Usually, it will be necessary to make a copy of the argument and change that. Here is a modified version of a() that shows how this works:

```
>a:=proc(p) local q; q:=p; q+1 end:
>a(1);
```

$$2$$

In this particular case, you can obtain a result by omitting the $p := $ in the original procedure, but such opportunities are rare in realistic situations.

You can change table entries even if the table is an argument. The example that follows illustrates this point:

```
>t:=table([(1)=sin,(2)=cos,(3)=sin/cos]):
>b:=proc(t) t[3]:=tan end;
    b := proc(t) t[3] := tan end
>b(t);
```

$$tan$$

The explanation is that t is a table and evaluates only to a name, which can be assigned. If you examine t now, you will see that its third argument has indeed changed. Table entries can be assigned as often as you wish in a single invocation of a procedure.

Here is a further illustration of how substitution can be deceptive:

```
>c:=proc(x) x:=1; x end;
    c := proc(x) x := 1; x end
>c(z);
```

$$z$$

The explanation of this result is that after substituting z in place of x in the procedure body, the procedure is executed. The value of the procedure is the last encountered evaluation, which is simply the name z.

To illustrate some additional techniques that can be useful in connection with substitution, the next procedure is meant to return the sequence of operands in an expression:

```
> opex:=proc(xp,n) local i; n:=nops(xp);
  seq(op(i,xp), i=1..n) end:
> opex(x*y+sin(x),'n');
Error, (in opex) unable to execute seq
```

In this instance, n is a name that is intended to return the number of operands in the expression. It is quoted in the invocation to ensure that it really does evaluate to a name and not to some value it may have had in the current session. This computation has produced the error shown because in attempting to evaluate the range argument in seq(), the argument n is encountered. However, because the arguments were initially substituted into the body of the procedure, it is merely the name n, which has no meaning as a range index. To correct the procedure, you can use a local variable or use eval() to force an evaluation of the offending name. Here is how the first method works:

```
> opex:=proc(xp,n) local m,i; m:=nops(xp);
  n:=m;seq(op(i,xp),i=1..m) end;
```

```
opex := proc(xp,n)
        local m,i;
            m := nops(xp);
            n := m; seq(op(i,xp),i = 1 .. m)
        end
```

which gives the result

```
> opex(x*y+sin(x),'n');
```

$$x\ y,\ sin(x)$$

Evaluating n gives

```
>n;
```

                    2

The other approach, using eval(), is illustrated below:

```
>opex:=proc(xp,n) local i; n:=nops(xp);
 seq(op(i,xp), >i=1..eval(n)) end;


opex := proc(xp,n)
    local i;
        n := nops(xp); seq(op(i,xp),i = 1 .. eval(n))
    end


>opex(x*y+sin(y),'n');
```

$$x \; y, \; \sin(x)$$

We emphasize that to pass a result out of a procedure, you input a name argument. After the desired result is obtained in the procedure, you assign the name to it.

There is a faster way to write `opex()` using the for–in approach in `seq()`:

```
>opex:=proc(xp,n) local i; n:=nops(xp); seq(i,i=xp) end:
```

This works just as well as the previous version shown above.

Evaluation rule for local variables

In addition to procedure arguments, local variables are also subject to a special evaluation rule. This rule is simply that evaluation is carried out only to the first level of the expression tree. Here is an example that illustrates the effect:

```
> d:=proc() local x,y; x:=y; y:=1; x end:
> d();
```

$$y$$

This procedure resembles the procedure `c()` above. However, because `d()` has no parameters, the explanation for the result shown is different. Because x is local, it is evaluated to just one level. In the first assignment, it is just a name that is then used for the variable y. The final evaluation ends at the first level. Another level of evaluation is needed to evaluate y and therefore x to 1, but it is not performed.

Another example that illustrates the one-level evaluation of local variables is given in the procedure below. This procedure provides a (not very sensible) way to regurgitate the entries in a list:

```
>v:=proc(x,l) local t; t:=x; seq(t,x=1) end;
```

```
Warning, 'x' in call to 'seq' is not local
v := proc(x,l) local t; t := x; seq(t,x = 1) end
```

```
>v('x',[1,2,3]);
```

$$x, \ x, \ x$$

This is not the expected result. To understand the problem, here is a version that works:

```
>v := proc(x,l) local t; t := x; seq(eval(t),x = 1) end:
Warning, 'x' in call to 'seq' is not local
```

```
>v('x',[1,2,3]);
```

$$1, \ 2, \ 3$$

In the first case, the local variable t in seq() is subject to one-level evaluation on each element of the list, and this evaluation yields x. In the second case, full evaluation of the local variable occurs.

Scope rules

A difference between Maple and C or Fortran is that Maple permits nested procedures, which raises the important question of the scope of variables appearing in such procedures. Briefly, this is the issue of interpreting the values of nonlocal variables in procedures. An example will reveal the problem. Here is a procedure that calls on a nested procedure to effect a multiplication by a nonlocal variable:

```
> s:=proc(x) local t; t:=proc(u) u*x; end;t(x) end:
```

The procedure s() has the single formal parameter x. Its body consists of another procedure t(), which itself has the formal parameter u, together with an invocation of t() with the actual parameter x (the value of the formal parameter).

In this example, the question of scope concerns the value of x in the expression u*x appearing in t(). If you haven't already done so, it would be a good idea to predict the result of a call such as s(2). Most people expect a result of 4 from this call, but that is not what happens, and the reason goes straight to the heart of the scoping issue. Here is the result of the call:

```
>s(2);
```

$$2\ x$$

Can this be right? Didn't we set x to 2? The answers are: yes and no, at least in Maple 5.4.

If you did predict a value of 4 for s(2), it is because you reasonably assumed that the value of x in t() would be taken from the environment containing the procedure body, in this case the function s(). This way of obtaining values for nonlocal variables is called lexical (or static) scoping, but it is not the way Maple operates. Maple uses another form of scoping, more like what is called dynamic scoping, in which nonlocal variables are evaluated at the global level. This is the reason for the result produced above. At the global level, there is no value for x other than its name so that is what appears in the result. In other words, the two x's appearing in the procedure s() are unrelated. To make this explicit, change the name of the global variable and repeat the invocation:

```
> s:=proc(x) local t; t:=proc(u) u*xx; end;t(x) end:
> s(2);
```

$$2\ xx$$

If we now (randomly) assign xx at the global level and evaluate s() again, we obtain:

```
>xx:=int(tan(x),x);
```

$$xx := -\ ln(cos(x))$$

```
>s(2);
```

$$-\ 2\ ln(cos(x))$$

Regardless of whether the variable in t() is called x or xx, it is always evaluated at the global level.

While Maple's approach to scoping may seem unusual, it is actually very easy to understand (at least in principle). In a nutshell, variables in a procedure are evaluated in one of just three ways: (1) As arguments to the specific procedure; (2) as local variables to the procedure; or (3) as global variables.

In the first of these, the word "specific" is included to rule out the possibility of an argument being carried forward, just as in the example above the argument x was not carried into t(). Most scoping problems can be solved by careful examination of the values of variables considering the three alternatives above. Realizing that you have a scoping problem is usually harder than solving the actual problem.

It is important to understand that arrow functions are themselves procedures and are subject to the scoping rules above. This is easy to overlook and sometimes causes apparently baffling errors. For example, suppose you wanted a procedure that normalized a vector by its first component, assumed to be nonzero. Here is an apparently reasonable approach and its result:

```
>m:=proc(a) map(z->z/a[1],a) end:
>m([3,6,9]);
```

```
         3      6      9
       [----, ----, ----]
        a[1]   a[1]   a[1]
```

Not quite what we wanted. Trying to use eval(a[1]) does not help and neither do several other tricks. This is a scoping problem. To see why, note that the procedure is equivalent to the following:

```
>n:=proc(a) local d; d:=proc(z) z/a[1] end;
 map(d,a) end;
```

```
n := proc(a)
       local d;
            d := proc(z) z/a[1] end; map(d,a)
     end
```

As a check:

```
>n([3,6,9]);
```

```
         3      6      9
       [----, ----, ----]
        a[1]   a[1]   a[1]
```

The problem is that in `d()`, the value `a[1]` has just its name as its value in the global environment. A remedy is to pass the desired value as an argument to the inner procedure. Here is the resulting procedure:

```
>n:=proc(a) local d; d:=proc(z,b) z/b end;
>map(d,a,a[1]) end;

n := proc(a)
        local d;
            d := proc(z,b) z/b end; map(d,a,a[1])
        end

>n([3,6,9]);
```

$$[1, \ 2, \ 3]$$

Remember that when you `map()` a procedure, you include additional arguments as the third argument to `map()` as illustrated above.

11.3   Procedure options

This section covers the options that can be used with procedures. There are two subsections:

* The `remember` Option
* Other Procedure Options

The `remember` option

It sometimes pays to keep a record of the results computed by a procedure. A time-worn example is using recursive procedures to evaluate recurrence relations, the Fibonacci recurrence being the common test case. The Fibonacci numbers f_n satisfy

$$f_0 = 0, \qquad f_1 = 1, \qquad f_n = f_{n-1} + f_{n-2}, \quad n = 2, 3, \ldots$$

A recursive procedure to evaluate these numbers is then:

```
>f:=proc(n) if n<2 then n else f(n-1)+f(n-2) fi; end:
```

To compute, for example, f(5), the values of f(4) and f(3) must be computed. However, in computing f(4) a further copy of f(3) will be computed, etc. For larger values of n, the number of these redundant evaluations is so great that the number of additions used grows exponentially with n (in fact to find f(n) takes $f_{n+1}+1$ additions, which is $O(\gamma^n)$, where $\gamma = (1+\sqrt{5})/2$. This should be compared with the "procedural" approach shown below:

```
>fp:=proc(n,a) for i from 2 to n do
>a[i]:=a[i-1]+a[i-2] od; end:
```

This time, once the initial two entries are placed in the table a, the calculation takes just $n-1$ additions. Other procedural approaches take a similar amount of work.

The redundant evaluations inherent in the recursive procedure can be avoided by using a remember table. As its name suggests, this is simply a table containing the results of procedure invocations. In the case of f() above, at each invocation Maple looks in the remember table for the current argument, and if it is present, the corresponding value of f() is returned. Redundant evaluations of f() are avoided and the evaluation of f(n) takes a number of additions that increase linearly with n.

To attach a remember table to a procedure, you include option remember; or options remember;. For the Fibonacci example, this results in

```
>f:=proc(n) option remember;
>if n<2 then n else f(n-1)+f(n-2) fi;
>end;


f := proc(n)
       options remember;
          if n < 2 then n else f(n-1)+f(n-2) fi
     end
```

Here is a moderately large Fibonacci number that is quickly computed using this function:

```
>f(100);
```

$$354224848179261915075$$

It is not recommended that you try this without the remember option!

Entries to remember tables can be assigned without invoking the procedure. For instance, we could rewrite the f() procedure without the conditional by assigning the initial conditions directly to the `remember` table before executing the procedure. While this is not a particularly good technique, it does illustrate the point under consideration. The new procedure is then

```
>g:=proc(n) option remember;
>g(n-1)+g(n-2);
>end;
```

```
g := proc(n) options remember; g(n-1)+g(n-2) end
```

Now we make the assignments to the `remember` table. Note that such assignments do not cause the procedure to be invoked. The values given are directly assigned to the table without any invocation:

```
>g(0):=0; g(1):=1;
```

$$g(0) := 0$$
$$g(1) := 1$$

Invoking the procedure gives the expected result:

```
>g(100);
```

$$354224848179261915075$$

While the code for `g()` is shorter, it is all too easy to forget to assign the initial conditions, which leads to an unending recursion. For that reason, the approach using `f()` is better. However, there are situations where direct assignment to a `remember` table is preferable to the alternatives.

What happens if you assign a nonexistent procedure name in the above way? Interestingly, Maple makes an appropriate procedure. Here is an illustration of what happens (there is initially no procedure in existence with the name `1()`):

```
>1(4):=12;
```

$$1(4) := 12$$

```
>type(1,procedure);
```

$$true$$

```
>eval(1);
```

```
proc() options remember; 'procname(args)' end
```

As we know from the Returning Results from Procedures subsection, `1()` will
return unevaluated except on the argument 4. This technique is useful in contexts
other than procedure writing. There was an example in The D Operator subsection
in Section 3.2.

It can be important to know whether a procedure is remembering its results. We
met a case in `evalf(Eigenvects())` in Chapter 5 where the eigensystem of a
matrix was remembered. Then, inputting a different matrix with the same name as
a previous one produced the eigensystem of the original matrix! If a procedure has
a `remember` table, it is the fourth operand of the procedure's first operand. Using
this to obtain the current remember table of `1()`, we find:

```
>op(4,op(1,1));
```

$$table([$$
$$4 = 12$$
$$])$$

The same result can be obtained from `op(4,eval(1))`. If there is no remember
table, the operand will be NULL.

To remove the entries from a `remember` table, there is the `readlib` function
`forget()`. Applying this to `1()` we obtain:

```
>readlib(forget):
>forget(1);
>op(4,op(1,1));
```

$$table([])$$

The `remember` table is now empty, but it still exists. The `forget()` function also
has options that allow selective deletion of results from the `remember` table. To
remove the `remember` table itself, you have to delete the option from the procedure.

Other procedure options

The option `operator` defines the procedure as a Maple item called a *functional
operator*. Examples of these operators are arrow functions and the D function for differentiation. The option `arrow` is used with `operator` to signify the corresponding
kinds of function. There is an illustration for `arrow` in the procedure `g()` near the
beginning of The General Form of a Procedure subsection above.

The option `builtin` indicates that a procedure is one of Maple's inner procedures. This option is printed when you attempt to inspect one of these procedures

(see Reading Maple's Procedures below). Ordinarily, this option has no function in a user-written procedure. The option `system`, if present, allows garbage collection to be applied to the `remember` table of the procedure. Otherwise, the `remember` table of the procedure will not have garbage collection applied to it.

The `trace` option is a debugging facility that is mentioned at the end of the following subsection.

11.4 Debugging procedures

In this section, we will cover some techniques for debugging Maple procedures. The subsections are

- Debugging with `printlevel`
- Using Maple's Debugger

Debugging with `printlevel`

One of the main debugging tools in Maple is a facility called `printlevel`. The `printlevel` facility produces a detailed accounting of the execution of a procedure, including procedure calls with their arguments, subcomputations, and results. You can control the depth of the debugging by setting `printlevel` appropriately. To illustrate the use of `printlevel`, we will apply it to the procedure `sL()` used earlier, which computes the sum or mean of the entries in a list or list of lists of numerical quantities. Once again, here is a listing of this procedure:

```
>eval(sL);

proc(a::{list(numeric),list(list(numeric))},m)
    global s;
    local i,s1;
    if not type(a,list(numeric)) then
        sL( [seq(convert(op(i,a),'+'),
            i = 1 .. nops(a))] )
    else s := convert(a,'+')
    fi;
    if nargs = 1 then s
    else s1 := s; sL(map(nops,[op(a)])); m := s1/s
    fi
end
```

The default value of `printlevel` is 1. In that case, procedures print what is coded into them. As the value of `printlevel` is increased, additional information is printed. This information is highly useful for debugging purposes. Here is what happens with a small value of `printlevel`:

```
>printlevel:=5;
```
$$printlevel := 5$$

```
>sL([[1,2,3],[4,5,6]],'m');
{--> enter sL, args = [[1, 2, 3], [4, 5, 6]], m
<-- exit sL (now at top level) = 7/2}
```
$$7/2$$

The initial entry is recorded with the arguments, followed by the final exit and the exit value. To see more information we will increase `printlevel` to 10:

```
>printlevel:=10;
```
$$printlevel := 10$$

```
>sL([[1,2,3],[4,5,6]],'m');
{--> enter sL, args = [[1, 2, 3], [4, 5, 6]], m
```
$$21$$
$$s1 := 21$$
$$6$$
$$m := 7/2$$
```
<-- exit sL (now at top level) = 7/2}
```
$$7/2$$

This time more intermediate results are printed, although the recursive invocations of the procedure are not recorded. To see them, we move to a still higher value of `printlevel`:

```
>printlevel:=15;
```
$$printlevel := 15$$

```
>sL([[1,2,3],[4,5,6]],'m');
 {--> enter sL, args = [[1, 2, 3], [4, 5, 6]], m
 {--> enter sL, args = [6, 15]
                            s := 21

                        21

 <-- exit sL (now in sL) = 21}
                    21

                    s1 := 21

 {--> enter sL, args = [3, 3]
                        s := 6

                    6

 <-- exit sL (now in sL) = 6}

                    m := 7/2

 <-- exit sL (now at top level) = 7/2}
                7/2
```

This example shows that there were three invocations of sL() and prints the intermediate results and final results of each argument. At this stage, we have obtained all the information about the workings of sL(), excluding what is relevant to Maple's internal working. Further increases in the value of printlevel yield no additional information.

You can usually predict what will be printed at a given setting of printlevel by applying two rules: (1) an evaluation will have its result printed if the "notional" value of printlevel is 5 or greater for a procedure and 2 or greater otherwise; (2) each entry to a procedure reduces the "notional" value of printlevel by 5 and each entry to a loop or conditional reduces the current level by 1. The notional value of printlevel is an artifact that allows us to state the rules in a concise way. The actual value of printlevel does not change. It is important to emphasize this because printlevel is a Maple global variable that may appear within a procedure.

These rules can be applied to the example of sL(). For instance, with printlevel set to 10, the notional level reduces to 4 for the recursive invocation. At that stage, the notional value becomes −1 and further printing does not occur until the recursive invocation is completed. A setting of 15 is sufficient to permit printing of all the intermediate results.

If a high value of `printlevel` is set in the main session, some unexpected consequences can ensue. For instance, if you look at a help page you will discover that you have invoked a function called "help" that has arguments and that may invoke other procedures in the form of help files. Unwanted information can also appear when you invoke utilities such as the Maple editor, which is supplied with DOS systems.

The `printlevel` facility can be assigned inside procedures. By assigning different values in different procedures, you can control the amount of information produced by each one. An alternative approach is to use a function called `trace()`. This function takes as argument(s) the procedure(s) to be traced. Only the named procedures are subjected to tracing. In addition to the arguments and results of the specified procedure, tracing provides the result of each of its statements' execution. Beyond this, there is no control over the `trace()` output. The function `untrace()` is used to remove the effect of `trace()`. As an alternative to the `trace()` function, the `trace` option can be set in the procedure with a similar effect.

Using Maple's debugger

Beyond `printlevel`, Maple provides a standard type of debugger that allows you to set breakpoints and examine the values of variables. We will illustrate the use of these facilities with the procedure that follows. This procedure selects an item at random from a multiset (a set with repeated entries) given as a list whose entries represent the number of elements of each type. Here is the main procedure (`pick()`) and its subprocedure (`whch()`):

```
pick:=proc(u)
    local i,m,nt,n,t:
    n:=nops(u): nt:=convert(u,'+'):
    m:=rand(1..nt):
    t:=whch(u,m()):
    printf('Random object has type %d\n', t):
end:

whch:=proc(U,M)
    local i,ps;
    ps:=U[1]: for i from 1 to nops(U) do
        if M<=ps then RETURN(i) fi:
        ps:=ps+U[i+1]:
    od:
end:
```

These were created in a text editor and read into the Maple session using the read()
command.

The first function counts the number of list entries and adds them. Then a random
integer is used to select one of the items. Finally, the second function is called to
find out which type of object has been selected (that is, from which list position it
originates). You can think of the list as a box containing colored balls, where a list
entry gives the number of balls of a particular color. The goal of the function is to
pick a ball at random.

The debugger (for help use ?debugger) is not a single function. It is a collection
of functions for numbering the lines in a function, setting lines at which execution is
suspended, restarting execution, and so on. The idea is that with execution suspended,
you can evaluate expressions to find out what is happening in the code. We will
illustrate the main functions using pick(). To begin, we will number the lines as
follows:

```
> showstat(pick);

pick := proc(u)
local i, m, nt, n, t;
   1    n := nops(u);
   2    nt := convert(u,'+');
   3    m := rand(1 .. nt);
   4    t := whch(u,m());
   5    printf('Random object has type %d\n',t)
end
```

We will also number the lines of whch() by a separate call to showstat(). At
this stage the program executes in the usual way as the following shows:

```
> pick([2,4,6,8]);
Random object has type 1
```

Now we will invoke the debugger by setting a "breakpoint" on the first line of the
code. The following uses the function stopat():

```
> stopat(pick,1);
```

```
                          [pick]
```

To see what has happened, we will print out lines 1 and 2 of pick():

```
> showstat(pick,1..2);

pick := proc(u)
local i, m, nt, n, t;
   1*    n := nops(u);
   2     nt := convert(u,'+');
       ...
end
```

The asterisk means that a breakpoint has been set. When we execute the procedure, it will be suspended at this point. Any line number can be a breakpoint.

Next, we invoke the procedure with the same argument as before:

```
> pick([2,4,6,8]);

pick:
   1*    n := nops(u);
```

The first line after the command is the value of the last executed expression and the second is the next expression to be evaluated. The prompt has changed to >DBG, meaning that we are executing under control of the debugger. There are several ways to work through a program that differ in the amount of detail they reveal. For instance, to "step through" the program without looking at the lines of functions it calls, you use next as follows:

```
DBG> next
4
pick:
   2     nt := convert(u,'+');

DBG> next
20
pick:
   3     m := rand(1 .. nt);
```

Notice the evaluation results shown in each case. We "stepped over" the functions of lines 1 and 2. To continue:

```
DBG> next
proc () local t; global _seed;
_seed := irem(427419669081*_seed,999999999989);
t := _seed; irem(t,20)+1 end
pick:
   4     t := whch(u,m());
```

Here we see the procedure produced as the value of the call to `rand()`. As a check on our position, we can print five statements around our current point with `list`:

```
DBG> list

pick := proc(u)
local i, m, nt, n, t;
    1*    n := nops(u);
    2     nt := convert(u,'+');
    3     m := rand(1 .. nt);
    4 !   t := whch(u,m());
    5     printf('Random object has type %d\n',t)
end
```

Next we will set a breakpoint in `whch()` and go to it:

```
DBG> stopat(whch,1)
[pick, whch]
pick:
    4    t := whch(u,m());

DBG> cont
whch:
    1*    ps := U[1];
```

The `cont` command takes you to the next breakpoint. Let's check the values of the incoming M argument:

```
DBG> M
2
whch:
    1*    ps := U[1];
```

That seems correct, so lets go back to `pick()`:

```
DBG> return
1
pick:
    5    printf('Random object has type %d\n',t)
```

So far, we have stepped over the various functions in our path. To conclude, we will "step into" a function, in this case `printf()`:

```
DBG> step
printf:
    1      fprintf(default,args);

DBG>
fprintf:
    1      iolib(9,args)
```

We could continue (pressing *return* or *enter* each time to repeat the last command) to see the additional details of how `printf()` is implemented, but instead we will end our minidebugging session here:

```
DBG> done
>
```

You can also use `quit` or `stop` to end debugging.

11.5 Reading Maple's procedures

An outstanding feature of Maple is the accessibility of the code for library functions. Around ninety-five percent of the Maple system can be read. This is feasible because most functions in the Maple system are themselves written in the Maple language. The excluded part is the lowest level of Maple, the kernel.

Reading a procedure is simple in principle. First, you have to set an interface variable called `verboseproc`. This variable may be set to 0, 1, 2, or 3. To see procedures in their entirety, use the value 3. Then, making sure the procedure of interest is loaded, you evaluate or print it. As a simple illustration, here is the Maple code for the function `vectdim()`, which returns the size of a vector:

```
>interface(verboseproc=3);
```

This returns NULL.

```
>with(linalg):
Warning, new definition for norm
Warning, new definition for trace
Warning, new definition for transpose
```

```
> eval(vectdim);
proc(A)
options 'Copyright 1990 by the University of Waterloo';
    if nargs <> 1 then
        ERROR('wrong number of arguments') fi;
    if type(A,'list') then RETURN(nops(A)) fi;
    if not type(A,'array') then
        ERROR('expecting a vector') fi;
    if type(A,name) then [op(2,eval(A))]
        else [op(2,A)] fi;
    if nops(") <> 1 then ERROR('expecting a vector') fi;
    if op(1,"[1]) = 1 then op(2,"[1])
    else ERROR('vector dimensions must be
                indexed from 1')
    fi
end
```

Few procedures are as easy to follow as this one. For instance, take a look at dsolve(). This is a function with many different options and algorithms depending on the form of the input data. Nevertheless, given sufficient patience even functions as complex as dsolve() can be broken down into their parts and examined.

The result of verboseproc=3 differs from that of verboseproc=2 only by the presence of the current remember table; the two results will be identical most of the time.

If a procedure is not readable, it will show the option builtin and a numerical identification code as illustrated next:

```
>eval(sort);

proc() options builtin; 148 end
```

Efficient sorting algorithms work with pointers to the data being sorted so it is natural for sort() to be builtin.

11.6 Encapsulating procedures

When you have collected a number of procedures for a project, it is natural to encapsulate them in some way. In this section, we will look at how procedures can be encapsulated in a package and how to make online help pages for the functions and the package. The topics are

- User Packages and Libraries
- Making Help Pages

User packages and libraries

A package is merely a table of procedures. The notation for the package function `linalg[vector]`, for example, refers to the function `vector()` as an index into the table `linalg[]`. Armed with this knowledge, it is easy to write your own package. For example, the next few assignments set up a package called `PwrPak[]` containing three functions:

```
>PwrPak[zero]:=proc(x) 1 end;

PwrPak[zero] := proc(x) 1 end

>PwrPak[one]:=proc(x) x end:
>PwrPak[two]:=proc(x) x^2 end:
```

The table could also have been set up by assigning the table's entries to the procedures' names. Here is a procedure that will be added that way:

```
th:=proc(x) x^3 end;
```

and here is the way to add it:

```
>PwrPak[three]:=eval(th);

PwrPak[three] := proc(x) x^3 end
```

Notice the (necessary) use of `eval()`.

The package can be saved to a file using `save()`. On reading the file back in with `read()`, the procedures can be used in the "long form," using the package name as illustrated next:

```
>PwrPak[three](sin(z));
```

$$sin(z)^3$$

To avoid using the package name when invoking a procedure, the package must first be loaded using the `with()` function. For that to work, Maple must be told the location of the package in a specific way. The preferred method uses a variable called `libname`. This variable is already used at start-up to tell Maple where to find the library in the file system of the host computer, but it is also used to provide search paths for user libraries and packages. To find the current value of `libname`, you proceed as for any other variable. One system gives the following result:

```
>libname;
```

$$../lib$$

This is the name of the directory where the Maple library is resident. We will be modifying the value of `libname` below, but first we want to illustrate the need for caution. Briefly, you can make the Maple library inaccessible if you inadvertently omit its location. For example, in the next assignment, `libname` is assigned to the name containing a single blank:

```
>libname:=' ';
```

$$libname :=$$

and now when we try to use a Maple function we get a message:

```
>int(x,x);
Error, could not find int in the library
```

Quite possibly, it will be necessary to restart Maple if you get such a message.

Now we will change `libname` to incorporate a directory called`/mapl src ce`, where `PwrPak.m` has been saved with the standard `.m` extension. This extension must be used for the following steps to work. Here are the steps that modify `libname`:

```
>oldlibname:=libname;
```

$$oldlibname := ../lib$$

```
>libname:=libname,'/maplsrce';
```

$$libname := ../lib, /maplsrce$$

The first assignment is a safety measure so we can restore `libname` in case problems arise (although this would not restore `int()` in the above example). The second assignment makes `libname` into an expression sequence with two members. Additional files can be incorporated if necessary. Now the `with()` function can be used to load `PwrPak`:

```
>with(PwrPak);
```

$$[one, \ three, \ two, \ zero]$$

and the routines can be used with the short form names, as in

```
>two(exp(x));
```

$$exp(x)^2$$

Other libraries and files can be made accessible in a similar way except that the command `readlib()` is used in place of `with()`, which is used only for packages. Normally, the suitably modified `libname` variable would be assigned in the .ini (initialization) file to avoid the potentially hazardous technique of changing library locations in midsession.

Making help pages

When you type `?topic` for information on `topic`, Maple puts up a special interface-dependent window or screen area containing the information in a standardized format. You can make similar help pages for your own functions using the function `TEXT()`. Saving the result of `TEXT()` to the name help, text, or topic, will cause the text to be printed in response to `?topic`. More generally, the result of `TEXT()` can be assigned to any variable and it will be displayed in a window when the variable is evaluated. Here is an example:

```
>msg:=TEXT('1. First line of text',
           '2. Second line of text');

msg :=

  TEXT(1. First line of text, 2. Second line of text)
```

The text material is enclosed in string quotes separated by commas. Each string will start on a new line in the output. To force a new line to appear use a blank string ' '. Typing `msg;` will cause the above text to be printed in two lines on your screen in the usual window for help pages. Among the conventional headings on a regular help page are FUNCTION:, CALLING SEQUENCE:, SYNOPSIS:, and SEE ALSO. Each of these is a separate string. The text belonging to each heading is entered as a string.

Now let's say we want to add some help files to the `PwrPak` package we used above. The most straightforward thing to do is to make the help variables (the names help, text, or topic) part of the package itself. This requires making additions to the package. To show the method, we will make a (pretend) help page for the package and one for the function called `one()`. First the package must be loaded, and we will use `read()` for this:

```
>read 'c:/maplev2/bin/packs/PwrPak.m';
```

Now it is simply a matter of explicitly setting new table entries:

```
>PwrPak['help/text/PwrPak']:=TEXT('HELP FOR PwrPak'):
```

```
     PwrPak[help/text/PwrPak] := TEXT(HELP FOR PwrPak)
```

```
>PwrPak['help/text/one']:=TEXT('HELP FOR PwrPak[one]');
```

```
     PwrPak[help/text/one] := TEXT(HELP FOR PwrPak[one])
```

After saving to PwrPak.m and reloading using `with()`, we obtain

```
>with(PwrPak);
```

```
[help/text/PwrPak, help/text/one, one, three, two, zero]
```

and help can be obtained from `?PwrPak` and from `?one`.

The method just discussed has the disadvantage that the help data must be typed directly into the Maple session. There is also a function called `makehelp()` that allows the help data to be read in from a file. Please see `?makehelp` for more information.

11.7 Reference section

Here is a summary of the main points relating to the procedures covered in this chapter. The *Maple Language Reference Manual* is the main source for additional information on procedures.

General form of a procedure

```
proc<nameseq>
    local<nameseq>
    global<nameseq>
    options<nameseq>
    <statseq>
end
```

Options

```
remember, operator arrow, builtin, system, trace
```

Returning results

- Last evaluated result is returned
- RETURN()
- RETURN('procname(args)')
- ERROR('message here')

Argument functions

```
nargs,args
```

Argument type checking

```
proc(name::type,...,name::type)
```

Evaluation rules

(1) For arguments: Arguments are evaluated and substituted in the procedure body. No further evaluation takes place.

(2) For local variables: Variables declared local are evaluated to the first level of the expression tree only. For deeper evaluation use eval().

Scope rules

Variables can be interpreted in one of just three ways: (1) As arguments to the specific procedure; (2) as local variables to the procedure; and (3) as global variables.

Debugging aids

Assign printlevel to a high value. Set the trace option in the procedure. Invoke the debugger.

Packages of user procedures

Assign functions to be table entries to make the package. To use `with()`, add the filename containing the package to `libname`. Help pages are made with `TEXT()`.

EXERCISES

1. Write a procedure to evaluate the function ϵ_{ijk} defined by

$$\epsilon_{ijk} = \begin{cases} 1 & \text{if } (i, j, k) \text{ is an even permutation of } (1,2,3) \\ -1 & \text{if } (i, j, k) \text{ is an odd permutation of } (1,2,3) \\ 0 & \text{if } (i, j, k) \text{ is not a permutation of } (1,2,3) \end{cases}$$

   Use your procedure to verify the formula $(a \times b)_i = \sum_{j,k=1}^{3} \epsilon_{ijk} a_j b_k$ for three-dimensional vectors.

2. Write a procedure `rm(f,name)` that removes the entry `name` from the remember table of the procedure `f`.

3. Write a procedure that accepts an expression of the form $a_1 x_1 + a_2 x_2 + \cdots + a_n x_n$, where a_i are numerical values, and returns the list $[a_1, a_2, \ldots, a_n]$.

4. Tridiagonal Matrices: A tridiagonal matrix A is one with the property that $A_{ij} = 0$ if $|i - j| > 1$. Tridiagonal matrices can usually be factored into a product of lower and upper bidiagonal matrices L and U, where U has a unit diagonal and the same superdiagonal as A. Write a function whose input arguments consist of the three diagonals of A and that returns the lower and main diagonals of L.

5. Given a set S, write a recursive procedure to list all subsets of S.

6. A single step of a "bubble sort" of a numerical array finds the largest element of the array and exchanges it with the last element of the array. Write two procedures, one recursive and one nonrecursive, to bubble sort a one-dimensional array of numbers. Which procedure runs faster?

7. The following exercise illustrates a use for type checking in symbolic programming. Write a procedure `newton()` so that entering the command:

   ```
   > newton(x0,f);
   ```

   will return the root of the function $f(x)$ found by Newton's method with an initial guess x_0. Your procedure should produce either a root or an appropriate message for each of the following calls:

   ```
   f := x -> cos(x) - sqrt(x);
   newton(0.6,f);

   a := 'a';
   f := x -> cos(x) - sqrt(x);
   ```

```
newton(a,f);
newton(0.6,a);
newton(0.6,f,a);

f := proc(x) 5; end;
newton(0.6,f);

a := 'a';
f := x -> cos(x) - a * sqrt(x);
newton(0.6,f);

f := x -> x*x + 2;
newton(0.6,f);
```

12 Programming examples

This chapter contains some example programs that demonstrate a variety of programming techniques.

The first program takes a Maple expression for its input and prints out a representation of the corresponding Maple expression tree. This program provides an elementary illustration of recursive programming.

Recursive programming is also used in the second program, which is a simplifier for three-dimensional vector identities involving dot and cross products. This program is capable of doing most homework problems that require proofs of vector identities. It can also serve to illustrate a basic principle of the operation of simplification programs.

The third program illustrates some aspects of graphics programming. This program is able to draw various fractals and "plants" in the style of A. Lindenmayer.

The fourth program solves the frequently occurring and rather tedious problem of making finite-difference formulas for derivatives and obtaining the accuracy of given formulas. This is not difficult (at least not in one dimension), but it does provide a useful exercise in programming symbolic manipulations.

The fifth program involves more numerical computation than the others. It implements an algorithm of Donald Knuth's for testing the quality of the output from a class of random-number generators (of which `rand()` is one). Knuth's test requires computations with large integers and is a natural example for Maple.

12.1 Printing Maple expression trees

As the first programming example, we will show how to write a program to print the expression trees that Maple uses for its internal representation of expressions (see Section 1.2). Here is an example of the output from such a program for the expression `(a+2*b)*c*d`:

```
>tree((a+2*b)*c*d,0);
(a+2*b)*c*d, Type[*]
  a+2*b, Type[+]
    a, Type[string]
    2*b, Type[*]
       2, Type[integer]
       b, Type[string]
  c, Type[string]
  d, Type[string]
```

The level of indentation indicates the depth in the tree, so that the original expression is of type * and has three branches with leaves, `a+2*b`, `c`, and `d`; `a+2*b` is of type + with two branches; and so on.

Such a tree is a candidate for recursion; each call to the procedure prints the current leaf and, while not at a terminal leaf, calls itself to continue. Because we want to progressively indent the printout with descent down the tree, we keep track of the depth of recursion by passing the procedure an integer, which is incrementally changed with each subsequent call. In the example above, this integer is the second argument. Setting it to higher values simply indents the whole of the output farther to the right. On the basis of these considerations, here is our first attempt at a program:

```
tree := proc(expr,level::integer)
        local i;
            for i to level do  printf('%s','  ') od;
            printf('%a, Type[%s]\n',expr,whattype(expr));

            if 1 < nops(expr) then
                 map(tree,[op(expr)],level+1)
            fi;
            RETURN()
        end
```

The first two lines print the input expression and its type. If this expression has subexpressions, then `if` calls `tree()` to print them also. The empty `RETURN()` statement simply hides unwanted results returned from the `map()` or `printf()` commands.

The `tree()` function is quite satisfactory for many expressions. For example:

```
> tree((5/7)*x + 2.5*y - z,1);
  5/7*x+2.5*y-z, Type[+]
     5/7*x, Type[*]
        5/7, Type[fraction]
           5, Type[integer]
           7, Type[integer]
        x, Type[string]
     2.5*y, Type[*]
        2.5, Type[float]
           25, Type[integer]
           -1, Type[integer]
        y, Type[string]
     -z, Type[*]
        -1, Type[integer]
        z, Type[string]
```

This shows, among other things, how Maple stores floats as the product of an integer raised to an integer power of 10 and that subtractions are additions of a product involving -1.

A little experimentation shows that expressions involving functions or procedures don't always print out as expected. Here are three examples:

```
> tree(x->x^2+5,1);
  proc (x) options operator, arrow; x^2+5 end,
     Type[procedure]
     x, Type[string]
     operator, Type[string]
     arrow, Type[string]

> g := x -> x^2+5;
                              2
                 g := x -> x  + 5
> tree(g,1);
  g, Type[string]

> tree(f(7*x+5),1);
  f(7*x+5), Type[function]
```

In the first example, the procedure was printed out along with the procedure's operands. The additional output is redundant. In contrast, there is a shortage of output when a procedure is assigned to a variable as shown in the second example. The third example involves an unevaluated function (which has only one operand), and in this case, we would like the expression tree of the argument to be printed also. These details can be fixed with the following modifications to the procedure:

```
tree := proc(expr,level::integer)
    local i;
        for i to level do  printf('%s','  ') od;
        printf('%a, Type[%s]\n',expr,whattype(expr));

        if type(expr,procedure) then
            if type(expr,string) then
                tree(op(expr),level+1) fi
        elif 1 < nops(expr) or type(expr,function) then
            map(tree,[op(expr)],level+1)
        fi;
        RETURN()
    end
```

As you can see, the program now checks for type `procedure`. If the expression is also of type `string`, then its operand (the procedure) is printed; otherwise the procedure's operands are not printed. The problem with function input is cured by checking for type `function`, and mapping `tree()` onto its operand (the argument). Repeating the above examples now gives satisfactory results:

```
> tree(x->x^2+5,1);
  proc (x) options operator, arrow; x^2+5 end,
      Type[procedure]
```

```
> g := x -> x^2+5;
                            2
               g := x -> x  + 5
```

```
> tree(g,1);
  g, Type[string]
     proc (x) options operator, arrow; x^2+5 end,
          Type[procedure]
```

```
> tree(f(7*x+5),1);
  f(7*x+5), Type[function]
    7*x+5, Type[+]
      7*x, Type[*]
        7, Type[integer]
        x, Type[string]
      5, Type[integer]
```

We conclude with an example containing a few more Maple types:

```
> tree('int(sin(x^2)*x+5,x=0..1)',1);
  int(sin(x^2)*x+5,x = 0 .. 1), Type[function]
    sin(x^2)*x+5, Type[+]
      sin(x^2)*x, Type[*]
        sin(x^2), Type[function]
          x^2, Type[^]
            x, Type[string]
            2, Type[integer]
        x, Type[string]
      5, Type[integer]
    x = 0 .. 1, Type[=]
      x, Type[string]
      0 .. 1, Type[..]
        0, Type[integer]
        1, Type[integer]
```

12.2 Vector identities and simplification

Our next example uses recursion to simplify symbolic expressions containing dot and cross products of three-dimensional vectors. The techniques used in this section are also used inside Maple for performing simplifications.

We want the simplifier to be able to verify the kind of vector identities that are encountered in an introductory vector algebra course. For instance, we want to be able to check formulas such as

$$a \times (b \times c) + b \times (c \times a) + c \times (a \times b) = 0$$

and

$$(a \times b) \cdot (c \times d) = \det \begin{bmatrix} a \cdot c & b \cdot c \\ a \cdot d & b \cdot d \end{bmatrix} = a \cdot c \, b \cdot d - b \cdot c \, a \cdot d$$

To illustrate how this may be done, we will develop two functions, `dot()` and `cross()`, which will automatically perform certain vector simplifications on symbolic data.

We will code `dot()` to recognize the following identities:

1. $a \cdot (b + c) = a \cdot b + a \cdot c$
2. $(a + b) \cdot c = a \cdot c + b \cdot c$
3. $a \cdot b + b \cdot a = 2a \cdot b$
4. $a \cdot (xb) = (xa) \cdot b = x(a \cdot b)$
5. $(a \times b) \cdot (c \times d) = a \cdot b \times (c \times d)$
6. $a \cdot (a \times b) = a \cdot (b \times a) = (a \times b) \cdot a = (b \times a) \cdot a = 0$

In the above, we have assumed that a, b, etc., are three-dimensional vectors and that x is constant.

Here is the code for the function dot:

```
dot:=proc(a,b)
    if type(a,'+') then map(dot,a,b)
    elif type(b,'+') then map(dot,b,a)
    elif a <> b and sort([a,b])[1]=b then dot(b,a)
    elif type(a,'*') then cons(a)*dot(a/cons(a),b)
    elif type(b,'*') then cons(b)*dot(a,b/cons(b))
    elif type(a,specfunc(algebraic,cross)) and
       type(b,specfunc(algebraic,cross))
       then dot(op(1,a),cross(op(2,a),b))
    elif (type(a,name) and type(b,'cross'(name,name)))
       and (a=op(1,b) or a=op(2,b)) then 0
    elif (type(b,name) and type(a,'cross'(name,name)))
       and (b=op(1,a) or b=op(2,a)) then 0
    else 'dot'(a,b)
    fi
end;
```

The idea behind the code is quite straightforward: The body of the procedure is essentially an `if` statement set up to identify each of the known situations that we can simplify. The procedure checks for each situation in the order listed above. The distribution of dot products over addition is accomplished with the `map()` command. Maple's automatic simplification facility will always simplify `dot(a,b)+dot(a,b)` to `2dot(a,b)`. Then to ensure that `dot(a,b)` + `dot(b,a)` is simplified to the same result, it is sufficient to have `dot()` sort its arguments into some specific order independent of the order in which the arguments are passed. This is accomplished using sort(). Note that it is necessary to check that the arguments a and b are distinct in order to prevent an infinite recursion. The function cons(), given below, extracts numeric constants from a product and is used in the manner shown to remove constants appearing inside the dot product (cons also recognizes that a dot() product is a scalar that can be factored out). The simplification of the dot product of two cross products uses specfunc() to see if the two arguments a and b are cross products (cross() will further simplify the result to a pair of dot products). Type checking is also used to see if one argument is a cross product and the other argument is one of the factors in the cross product so that the dot product is zero. The simplifications are applied recursively until no more simplifications are possible with the given rules. If none of these simplifications is applicable, dot() simply returns unevaluated.

The corresponding set of simplifications for the cross product are the following:

1. $a \times a = 0$
2. $a \times (b + c) = a \times b + a \times c$
3. $(a + b) \times c = a \times c + b \times c$
4. $a \times (xb) = (xa) \times b = x(a \times b)$
5. $a \times b - b \times a = 2a \times b$
6. $a \times (b \times c) = (a \cdot c)b - (a \cdot b)c$
7. $(a \times b) \times c = (a \cdot c)b - (b \cdot c)a$

The code for cross is very similar to that of dot():

```
cross:=proc(a,b)
   if a=b then 0
   elif type(a,'+') then map(cross,a,b)
   elif type(b,'+') then (-1)*map(cross,b,a)
   elif type(a,'*') then cons(a)*cross(a/cons(a),b)
   elif type(b,'*') then cons(b)*cross(a,b/cons(b))
   elif sort([a,b])[1]=b then (-1)*cross(b,a)
   elif type(b,specfunc(algebraic,cross)) then
      dot(op(2,b),a)*op(1,b) - dot(op(1,b),a)*op(2,b)
   elif type(a,specfunc(algebraic,cross)) then
      -dot(op(1,a),b)*op(2,a) + dot(op(2,a),b)*op(1,a)
   else 'cross'(a,b)
   fi
end;
```

The remaining function is `cons()`. This is used to remove constants from dot and cross products:

```
cons := proc(a)
  if not type(a,'*') then ERROR('argument not a
                                 product');
  elif type(op(1,a),numeric) or
       type(op(1,a),specfunc(algebraic,dot))
     then RETURN(op(1,a));
  else ERROR('illegal product');
  fi;
end;
```

Note that Maple sorts products so that any numeric present is the first operand. It is important to check that the argument to `cons()` does contain a numeric or a `dot()` to avoid meaningless simplifications like `dot(a,b/c) = b dot(a,1/c)`, where presumably `c` was intended to be a constant. Note that an expression like `b/5` is represented in Maple as the product `(1/5) b` so that `dot(a,b/5)` will simplify to `(1/5) dot(a,b)`.

We now demonstrate the operation of `dot()` and `cross()` in verifying some well-known vector identities. An elementary identity is $(a-b) \times (a+b) = 2(a \times b)$:

```
> cross(a-b,a+b);
```

$$2 \ cross(a, \ b)$$

Here is a check of the identities discussed at the beginning of this section:

```
> cross(a,cross(b,c)) + cross(b,cross(c,a))
    + cross(c,cross(a,b));
```

$$0$$

and

```
> dot(cross(a,b),cross(c,d));
```

$$dot(b, \ d) \ dot(a, \ c) - dot(b, \ c) \ dot(a, \ d)$$

12.3 Fractals, graphics, and L-systems

The book *Lindenmayer Systems, Fractals and Plants*[1] discusses elementary algorithms for generating some surprisingly realistic images of plants, complete with flowers, leaves, and branches. While a complete implementation of these ideas would carry us far afield, we will show how to use Maple to produce some aesthetically pleasing images. The basic algorithm consists of two steps. The first step generates a string of characters according to a prescribed procedure, and the second step interprets this string as a graphic image. As an elementary example, consider the string of characters f+f+f+f. If the character f is interpreted as a command to draw a line segment of unit length in the current direction, and the character + is interpreted as a command to increment the current direction by an angle of 90 degrees, then the above string will correspond to a square. This formulation is sometimes referred to as turtle graphics, the idea being that the string of characters is fed to a trained turtle with a two-character vocabulary and a pen tied to its tail.

One way of producing intricate strings is to start with a seed string and to specify a rewrite rule. For example, letting the seed be f+f+f+f as above, a simple rewrite rule is f←ff+f+f+f+f+f-f, meaning that every f in the seed is replaced by the string on the right-hand side of the arrow. In the above, the character – indicates that the current direction should be changed by a decrement of 90 degrees. This rule can then be applied recursively to obtain a long and intricate string.

These ideas are rather easy to implement in a Maple procedure. The arguments to the procedure are the seed, expressed as a list, a rewrite rule, and the number of times that the rule is to be applied. Note that the symbols + and – are always considered binary operations in Maple, so to avoid having to put string quotes around every + and – symbol, we simply use the symbol p for plus and m for minus.

```
tg := proc(seed::list,rule::procedure,level::integer)
    local i,plant,pts,tt,xx,yy;

        plant := seed;
        for i to level do  plant := map(rule,plant) od;
        xx := 0;
        yy := 0;
        tt := 1/2*Pi;
        pts := [xx,yy];

        for i in plant do
```

[1] P. Prusinkiewicz and J. Hanan, Springer Verlag, Lecture Notes in Biomathematics, 1989.

```
       if   i = p then tt := tt+1/2*Pi
       elif i = m then tt := tt-1/2*Pi
       elif i = f then
             xx := xx+cos(tt);
             yy := yy+sin(tt);
             pts := pts,[xx,yy]
       fi
   od;

       plot([pts],axes = NONE,scaling = CONSTRAINED)
end
```

The first loop in the procedure applies the rule to the seed the specified number of times, then the second loop generates the sequence of points. We illustrate the operation of this routine with the example detailed above (see Figure 12.1):

```
>rule := x -> subs(f=(f,f,p,f,p,f,p,f,p,f,p,f,m,f),x):
>tg([f,p,f,p,f,p,f],rule,3);
```

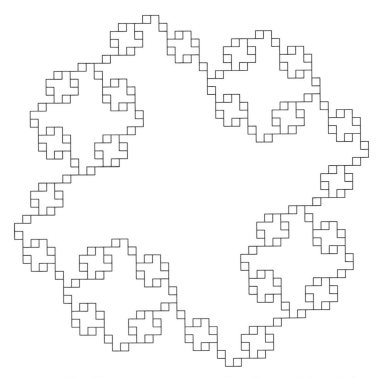

Figure 12.1: Seed: f+f+f+f, f←ff+f+f+f+f+f−f, level=3

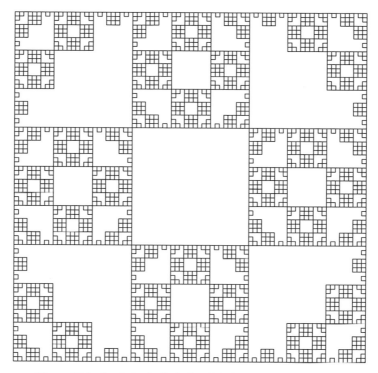

Figure 12.2: Seed: `f+f+f+f, f←ff+f+f+f+ff, level=4`

Another example is (see Figure 12.2).

```
>rule := x -> subs(f=(f,f,p,f,p,f,p,f,p,f,f),x):
>tg([f,p,f,p,f,p,f],rule,4);
```

By introducing other symbols into the rewrite rules, other patterns can be generated. For example, letting the seed be `xf` with rewrite rules:

```
x←x+yf++yf-fx--fxfx-yf+        y←-fx+yfyf++yf+fx--fx-y,
```

and letting `+/-` signify an increment/decrement of 60 degrees in the direction, the pattern in Figure 12.3 is produced:

```
>rule := z -> subs({x=(x,p,y,f,p,p,y,f,m,f,x,m,m,f,
                    x,f,x,m,y,f,p),
>y=(m,f,x,p,y,f,y,f,p,p,y,f,p,f,x,m,m,f,x,m,y)},  z):

>tg([x,f],rule,4,Pi/3);
```

Figure 12.3: Seed: `xf, x←x+yf++yf-fx--fxfx-yf+, y← -fx +yfyf ++yf+fx--fx-y,` `level=4`, $\theta = 60°$

Note that the extra symbols are ignored when producing the graph (that is, the turtle's vocabulary has not been enlarged) and that we have anticipated one of the modifications below, where the increment/decrement angle is now passed as the fourth argument instead of being hard coded as $\pi/2$.

Although the above algorithm can produce images of fractals, it is too simple to produce anything that resembles a plant. A first step toward that goal is to enhance the vocabulary of the turtle by the symbols [and]. A left bracket will require the turtle to push the current position and orientation onto a stack, and a right bracket will require the turtle to pop the stack and return to the popped position and orientation (without drawing a line). For example, a typical rewrite rule may be `f←ff+[+f-f-f]-[-f+f+f]` (see Figure 12.4).

To implement this, it is necessary to construct a last-in-first-out (LIFO) stack. We simulate this using a Maple list as indicated in the following code; also, because the left and right brackets have special meanings in Maple, we use the symbols `l` and `r` for the left and right brackets, respectively:

```
tg := proc(seed::list,rule::procedure,level::integer,
          theta::realcons)
  local i,lst,plant,pts,stack,tt,xx,yy,xyt;

  plant := seed;
  for i from 1 to level do plant := map(rule,plant) od;

  xx := 0;
  yy := 0;
  tt := Pi/2;
  lst := NULL;
  stack := [];
  pts := [xx,yy];

  for i in plant
    do
    if  i = p then tt := tt + theta;
    elif i = m then tt := tt - theta;
    elif i = l then stack := [[xx,yy,tt],op(stack)];
    elif i = r then
      if nops(stack) < 1 then ERROR('Stack Problem.');
        fi;
      xyt := stack[1];
      stack := subsop(1=NULL,stack);
      xx   := xyt[1];
      yy   := xyt[2];
      tt   := xyt[3];
      lst := lst,[pts];
      pts := [xx,yy];
    elif i = f then
      xx := xx + cos(tt);
      yy := yy + sin(tt);
      pts := pts,[xx,yy];
    fi;
    od:

  plot({lst,[pts]},axes=NONE,scaling=CONSTRAINED);
end;
```

Figure 12.4: Seed: f, f←ff+[+f-f-f]-[-f
+f+f], level= 4, θ = 22.5°

In the above example, the increment/decrement angle is now passed as an argument, and `lst` becomes a sequence of lists, each list containing a connected portion of the figure. The push operation for the stack simply appends the current location and direction onto the beginning of a list, and the pop operation extracts the first element of the list and then removes it using `subsop()`.

The Maple code used to produce Figure 12.4 is

```
>rr := x -> subs(f=(f,f,p,l,p,f,m,f,m,f,r,m,l,m,
                    f,p,f,p,f,r),x):
>tg([f],rr,4,Pi/8);
```

A less bushy plant is generated from seed f and rewrite rule f←f[+f]f[-f]f with `level=5` and θ = 25.7° (see Figure 12.5):

```
>rr := x -> subs(f=(f,l,p,f,r,f,l,m,f,r,f),x):
>tg([f],rr,5,Pi/7);
```

Two other interesting examples (which we leave as exercises) are (1) seed=x x←f-[[x]+x]+f[+fx]-x, f←ff, level=5, and θ = 22.5°; and (2) seed=y, y←yfx[+y][-y], x←x[-fff][+fff]fx, level=6, and θ = 25.7°. One final example, shown in Figure 12.6, has seed aaaa and has rewrite rules a←x+x+x+x+x+x+, x←[f+f+f+f[---x-y]+++++f++++++++f-f-f-f], y←[f+f+f+f[---y]+++++f++++++++f-f-f-f], level=5 and increment/

Figure 12.5: Seed: f, f←f[+f]f[-f]f,
level=5, $\theta = 25.7°$

decrement angle of $\theta = 15°$. The Maple code is

```
>rr := t -> subs({a=(x,p,x,p,x,p,x,p,x,p,x,p),
>x=(1,f,p,f,p,f,p,f,1,m,m,m,x,m,y,r,p,p,p,p,p,f,
    p,p,p,p,p,p,p,p,f,m,f,m,f,m,f,r),
>y=(1,f,p,f,p,f,p,f,1,m,m,m,y,r,p,p,p,p,p,f,p,p,
    p,p,p,p,p,p,f,m,f,m,f,m,f,r)},
>t):


>tg([a,a,a,a],rr,5,Pi/12);
```

12.4 Finite-difference formulas

When constructing finite-difference schemes, it is common to be given a collection of grid points $\{x_j\}_{j=1}^J$ and weights $\{w_j\}_{j=1}^J$, and to be asked what derivative the weighted sum $\sum_{j=1}^J w_j f(x_j)$ approximates at a given point t. A related question is how to find the weights that will give the most accurate approximation of a particular derivative, given a set of points. In this section, we develop a Maple procedure to answer these questions for one-dimensional difference stencils.

Figure 12.6: Seed: aaaa, a←x+x+x+x+x+x+, x←[f+f+f+f [--
-x-y]+++++f+++++++++f-f-f-f], y←[f+f+f+f[---y]+++
++f+++++++++f-f-f-f], level=5, $\theta = 15°$

The first question is answered by expanding each of the terms $f(x_j)$ as a Taylor series.

$$\sum_{j=1}^{J} w_j f(x_j) = \sum_{j=1}^{J} \left(\sum_{k=0}^{\infty} f^{(k)}(t) \frac{(x_j - t)^j}{k!} \right)$$

$$= \sum_{k=0}^{\infty} \left(\frac{1}{k!} \sum_{j=1}^{J} w_j (x_j - t)^k \right) f^{(k)}(t).$$

If a finite-difference expression approximates the lth derivative, the coefficients in the bracket in the last sum should vanish for $k = 0, 1, \ldots l - 1$; moreover, the accuracy is determined by the first nonzero coefficient after the lth. The same Taylor series expansion can also be used to answer the second question. If the weights are chosen to get the most accurate approximation of the lth derivative, we should chose them to render as many of the coefficients zero as possible except for the lth, which should be unity. Inspection of the coefficients shows that they are linear in the weights, so the

maximum number of terms that we can specify is J. This means that we should solve
the linear system of equations $Aw = b$, where w is the vector of weights, b is a vector
containing zeros in every position except for the lth, which contains a one, and the
coefficients of the matrix are given by $A_{kj} = (x_j - t)^k/k!$, where $k = 0 \ldots J - 1$
and $j = 1 \ldots J$. When the points are all distinct, this matrix is nonsingular, so the
approximation of a specified derivative does exist.

   To implement these ideas, we give below a Maple procedure that accepts three
arguments. These are a list of points x, the point t about which the expansions are
made, and a third argument, a3, which is either a list containing a set of weights
or an integer. In the first case, the procedure determines which derivative is being
approximated and the accuracy of the approximation, and in the second case, the
procedure calculates the weights necessary to approximate the derivative whose
order is given by the integer. Here is the procedure:

```
fd:=proc(x::list,t,a3::{list,integer})
  local e,j,J,k,q,sig,w;
  J:=nops(x);

  sig:=proc(x,w,t,k)  # Form coefficient for degree k
    local j;
      if k = 0 then
        sum(w[j],j=1..nops(x));
      else
        sum(w[j]*(x[j]-t)^k,j=1..nops(x))/k!;
      fi;
  end;

  if type(a3,integer) then
        # Solve the linear equations.
    if J <= a3 then ERROR('Not enough points') fi;
    w := array(1..J);
    q := [seq(sig(x,w,t,k),k=0..J-1)];
    q := subsop(a3+1=q[a3+1]-1,q);
    solve({op(q)},{seq(w[j],j=1..J)});
    assign(");
  else
    w := a3;
  fi;
```

```
k := 'k';
e:=sum(sig(x,w,t,k)*D^k,k=J..J+1);
    # Error terms (first 2)

if type(a3,integer) then        # Output section
  eval(w)+e;
else
  expand(sum('sig(x,w,t,k)'*D^k,k=0..J-1)+e);
fi
end;
```

The local procedure sig() computes the coefficients of the kth derivative in the Taylor expansion of the finite-difference stencil. A little care is required both in the definition and use of sig(). First, the if statement is necessary to avoid problems with terms like 0^0, which are clearly undefined. Second, it is necessary to delay evaluation of sig() in the third to last line, as the following example shows:

```
> sig := proc(x,w,t,k)
    local j;
        if k = 0 then sum(w[j],j = 1 .. nops(x))
        else sum(w[j]*(x[j]-t)^k,j = 1 .. nops(x))/k!
        fi
    end:

> sig([-1,0,1],[-1,2,-1],0,k);
```

$$- \frac{(-1)^k - 1}{k!}$$

```
> subs(k=0,");
```

$$-2$$

```
> sig([-1,0,1],[-1,2,-1],0,0);
```

$$0$$

Of course this problem could be avoided by returning `sig()` unevaluated unless `k` is of type numeric. Note too that we did not use the linear algebra package to solve the system of linear equations. At first glance, it appears easier to set up the matrix of coefficients with a statement like the following:

```
> A := matrix(J,J,(k,j)->(x[j]-t)^(k-1)/(k-1)!);
```

However, this results in a scoping problem. Remember that at the time of execution, the the formal argument `x` no longer exists in `fd()` because the value of the actual argument is substituted in its place. However, the argument is not substituted for `x` in the arrow procedure; indeed, `x` is considered a global variable inside the arrow procedure. As a consequence, it was just as easy to use Maple's `solve()` command as it was to coerce the correct values into a matrix and use the linear algebra package.

We illustrate the use of `fd()` by constructing approximations of the second derivative. We first find the weights for the second derivative on three points and then verify that the other half of the code works by specifying the computed weights as the third argument:

```
> fd([-h,0,h],0,2);
```

$$\left[\frac{1}{h^2}, \ -\frac{2}{h^2}, \ \frac{1}{h^2} \right] + 1/12 \ h^2 \ D^4$$

```
> fd([-h,0,h],0,[1/h^2,-2/h^2,1/h^2]);
```

$$D^2 + 1/12 \ h^2 \ D^4$$

As a further illustration, an approximation of the second derivative on five mesh points is shown below:

```
> fd([-2*h,-h,0,h,2*h],0,2);
```

$$\left[-\frac{1}{12 \ h^2}, \ \frac{4}{3 \ h^2}, \ -\frac{5}{2 \ h^2}, \ \frac{4}{3 \ h^2}, \ -\frac{1}{12 \ h^2} \right] - 1/90 \ h^4 \ D^6$$

12.5 Testing random numbers

One of the most common techniques for constructing (apparently) random numbers is to use a linear congruence; given a seed x_0 as an initial value, successive numbers are computed as $x_{n+1} = (ax_n + c) \bmod m$, where a, c, and m are specified. Typically $m = 2^w$, where w is the word size of the computer being used. D. Knuth gives a detailed analysis of these sequences in his book *The Art of Computer Programming*.[2] For example, in order for the sequence to cycle through all possible values before repeating, Knuth shows that it is necessary to have c relatively prime to m, $(a - 1)$ divisible by every prime that divides m, and that $(a - 1)$ be a multiple of 4 if m is a multiple of 4. Knuth also discusses various tests that check the randomness of a sequence. One of these tests is distinguished from the others in that all good linear congruential generators currently known pass this test, and all bad ones actually fail it. This test is called the *spectral test*, and we provide a Maple implementation in this section.

Given a linear congruential generator $s(x) = (ax + c) \bmod m$ that has period m, we consider the collection of all t vectors in the unit cell of the form $(1/m)[x, s(x), s(s(x)), \ldots (s @ @ (t-1))(x)]$ for various modest values of t, where x is an integer in the range $(0 \le x < m)$. The spectral test then takes collections of equispaced parallel $(t-1)$ dimensional hyperplanes that pass through each of the above points and defines the quantity v_t to be the reciprocal of the maximum possible distance between the planes of such a collection. The idea behind this test is that if the sequence of points is indeed random, then the collection of vectors should not lie in a small number of hyperplanes, so that v_t should in some sense be large. A brief discussion of how large v_t should be is given with the examples at the end of this section.

Knuth shows that $v_t^2 = \min\{x^T Q x \mid x \ne 0, \ x \in \mathbf{Z}^t\}$ where $\mathbf{Z}^t$ is the set of t-vectors with integer coordinates, and the matrix Q is given by $Q = U^T U$ with

$$
U = \begin{bmatrix}
m & -a & -a^2 & \cdots & -a^{t-1} \\
 & 1 & & & \\
 & & 1 & & \\
 & & & \ddots & \\
 & & & & 1
\end{bmatrix}
$$

The integers in the top row of the form a^i can be all computed mod m without altering the minimum of $f(x) \equiv x^T Q x$.

In order to find the minimum value of f, Knuth first establishes bounds on the sizes of the components of the vector x that minimizes f. The argument is this:

---

[2] Addison–Wesley, Computer Science and Information Processing Series, 1987.

Noting that $f(y) = \|Uy\|^2$, where $\|z\| = \sqrt{z_1^2 + \ldots + z_t^2}$ is the Euclidean length of a vector, the Cauchy Schwarz inequality states that:

$$|y \cdot Ux|^2 \le \|y\|^2 \|Ux\|^2 = \|y\|^2 f(x)$$

If y is chosen to be the kth row of U^{-1}, then the left-hand side becomes x_k^2, so that a bound on each component of the minimizing vector is given by:

$$x_k^2 \le \|v^{(k)}\|^2 f(x) \le \|v^{(k)}\|^2 f(y)$$

where y is any nonzero integer vector and $v^{(k)}$ is the kth row of U^{-1}.

It follows (at least in principle) that the minimum value of f, and so of v_t, can be found by an exhaustive search over all integer vectors whose components satisfy the bounds computed above. Unfortunately, these bounds may be quite large (remember that m is typically the largest integer the computer can store in a word), so this strategy is not usually practical. To improve the situation, Knuth uses a special technique to reduce the bounds found above. To explain this, we begin by recalling that a unimodular matrix is a matrix M with integer entries having a unit determinant (so that M^{-1} is also unimodular). Multiplication by a unimodular matrix maps the set of integer-valued vectors onto itself. It follows that the functions $f(y) = y^T Q y$ and $\tilde{f}(y) = y^T M^T Q M y$ will have the same minimum value over the set of nonzero integer-valued vectors. Note that if $Q = U^T U$, then $M^T Q M = (UM)^T (UM)$, so that $\tilde{f}$ has the same structure as f. Because the bounds for the components of the minimizing vector depend on $V = U^{-1}$, the expectation is that with a good choice of the matrix M, they can be reduced when U is replaced by UM.

The unimodular matrices M are chosen to have the following form:

$$M = \begin{bmatrix} 1 & & & & \\ & \ddots & & & \\ q_t & \cdots & 1 & \cdots & q_t \\ & & & \ddots & \\ & & & & 1 \end{bmatrix}, \qquad M^{-1} = \begin{bmatrix} 1 & & & & \\ & \ddots & & & \\ -q_1 & \cdots & 1 & \cdots & -q_t \\ & & & \ddots & \\ & & & & 1 \end{bmatrix}$$

The integers q_j in the ith row are chosen to be those closest to $u^{(i)} \cdot u^{(j)} / u^{(i)} \cdot u^{(i)}$ in order to reduce the bounds on the components as much as possible, where $u^{(k)}$ is the kth column of U. Because $Q = U^T U$, these dot products can be computed by $u^{(i)} \cdot u^{(j)} / u^{(i)} \cdot u^{(i)} = Q_{ij} / Q_{ii}$ (similarly, $\|v^{(k)}\|^2 = R_{kk}$ where $R = Q^{-1}$). This process can be repeated for each row, i, of the matrix and then iterated until no reduction in the bounds results. At this point, an exhaustive search can be done to locate the minima.

We now implement these ideas in Maple. The code is broken down into several procedures. First, here is the main procedure:

```
SpecTest:=proc(m,a,t)
   local R,Q,M,Minv,x,i,j,ntest,newtest,f;
   with(linalg);
   Q:=matrix(t,t): R:=matrix(t,t); M:=matrix(t,t);

   init(t,Q,R,m,a);

   f:=min(seq(Q[j,j],j=1..t));
   x:=[seq(floor(sqrt(f*R[j,j])/m),j=1..t)];
   ntest := product(2*x['j']+1,'j'=1..t);

   do:
     for i to t do
       M:=Unimod(Q,i,t); Minv:=inverse(M);
       Q:=multiply(transpose(M),Q,M);
       R:=multiply(Minv,R,transpose(Minv));
     od:

     f:=min(f,seq(Q[j,j],j=1..t));
     x:=[seq(floor(sqrt(f*R[j,j])/m),j=1..t)];
     newtest := product(2*x['j']+1,'j'=1..t);
     if ntest <= newtest then break; fi;
     ntest := newtest;
   od;


   f:=search(t,x,Q,f);
   print('Exhaustive search checks ',newtest,' points,
          nu^2 = ',f);
 end;
```

After setting up the local variables and defining the matrices Q, R, and M, the procedure init() is called to initialize Q, and $R = m^2 Q^{-1}$; this normalization guarantees that R is an integer matrix. The variable f records the smallest value of $f(x) = x^T Q x$ currently known and is initialized to the minimum diagonal entry of Q. The variable ntest records the number of function evaluations that would be required for an exhaustive search and is computed as a suitable product of the latest bounds. After this initialization, the loop to reduce the search space is entered. Every pass through this loop computes the unimodular matrix corresponding to each column, updates Q and R appropriately, and then checks to see if the search space has been reduced. If the size of the search space is no longer reduced by this process, the loop is terminated and the exhaustive search routine, `search()`, is called.

The service routines `init()` and `Unimod()` are rather straightforward:

```
init:=proc(t,Q,R,m,a)
   local k,A,Id;
    A:=matrix(t,1,1);
    Id:=array(identity,1..t,1..t);

    for k to t-1 do A[k+1,1]:=mods(a*A[k,1],m); od;
    A[1,1]:=m;
    Q:=evalm(Id + A &* transpose(A));
    Q[1,1]:=Q[1,1]-1;
    R:=scalarmul(inverse(Q),m^2);
end;
```

Except for the $[1,1]$ entry, the matrix Q is the sum of an identity matrix and a rank-one matrix containing various powers of a and is computed as such:

```
Unimod:=proc(Q,i,t)
   local j,q,ei,Id;
   Id:=array(identity,1..t,1..t);
   ei:=array(sparse,1..t,1..1,{(i,1)=1});
   q:=matrix(1,t,[seq(-floor(Q[i,j]/Q[i,i]+1/2),j=1..t)]);
   q[1,i] := 0;
   evalm(Id + ei &* q);
end;
```

The unimodular matrices are the sum of an identity matrix and the rank-one matrix $e_i q^T$, where q is the vector of coefficients chosen to reduce the size of the search space, and e_i is the ith unit vector. It is tempting to initialize q by

```
q := matrix(1,t,(k,j)->floor(Q[i,j]/Q[i,i]+1/2));
```

but this results in a scoping error because inside the arrow procedure Q and i are considered global variables.

The following code is used to do the exhaustive search for the minimum:

```
search:=proc(t,x,Q,f)
  local j,k,y,ff;
  y:=vector(t,0); ff:=f;
  do;
    j := 0;
    for k from t to 1 by -1 do
      y[k]:=y[k]+1;

      if y[k]<=x[k] then
          for j from k+1 to t do y[j]:=-x[j] od;
          ff:=min(ff,multiply(transpose(y),Q,y));
      else
          if k=1 then RETURN(ff) fi;
      fi;

    if j <> 0 then break fi;
    od;
  od;
end;
```

The idea behind this piece of code is to consider each integer-valued vector in the search space as a t-digit "number", $y_1 y_2 \ldots y_t$, where the ith digit lies in the range $-x_i \le y_i \le x_i$, x_i being the bound computed previously for this component. Generically, the statement y[k]:=y[k]+1; will have k=t, so it increases the number by increments of one, and the loop for j from k+1 ... will do nothing except assign a nonzero value to j. When k is not t, the statement y[k]:=y[k]+1; incrementally inreases a higher-order digit, so all of the lower-order digits are set to their minimum values by the loop for j from k+1 .... Notice that this algorithm only checks the vectors whose first nonzero entry is positive (that is, numbers whose most significant digit is positive), which is sufficient because $f(x) = f(-x)$.

We now demonstrate the operation of SpecTest() with a few examples taken from Knuth's book:

```
> m := 2^35: a := 3141592653:
> seq(SpecTest(m,a,t),t=2..6);
Error, (in SpecTest) cannot evaluate boolean
```

`SpecTest()` uses **Maple**'s `floor()` function in several places with arguments involving products and quotients of rather large numbers. This function attempts to find the greatest integer less than its argument by evaluating the argument using floating-point arithmetic. The `floor()` function checks to see if roundoff error with the current setting of `Digits` could lead to erroneous answers and will return unevaluated if this is the case (see `?floor`). If this happens within `SpecTest()`, an `if` statement usually fails, causing the `cannot evaluate boolean` message. This is cured by setting `Digits` to a larger value:

```
> Digits := 30:
> m := 2^35: a := 3141592653:
> seq(SpecTest(m,a,t),t=2..6);
   Exhaustive search checks,3, points, nu^2 =, 2997222016
   Exhaustive search checks,3, points, nu^2 =, 1026050
   Exhaustive search checks,3, points, nu^2 =, 27822
   Exhaustive search checks,3, points, nu^2 =, 1118
   Exhaustive search checks,27, points, nu^2 =, 1118
```

Another example is

```
>m := 10^10: a := 4219755981:
>seq(SpecTest(m,a,t),t-2..6);
  Exhaustive search checks,9, points, nu^2 =, 10721093248
  Exhaustive search checks,9, points, nu^2 =, 2595578
  Exhaustive search checks,3, points, nu^2 =, 49362
  Exhaustive search checks,1323, points, nu^2 =, 5868
  Exhaustive search checks,3, points, nu^2 =, 820
```

To decide whether a generator passes or flunks the spectral test, Knuth recommends computing the numbers

$$\mu_t = \frac{\pi^{t/2} v_t^t}{(t/2)! m},$$

and suggests that a generator "passes" the spectral test if $\mu_t > 0.1$ for $2 \le t \le 6$ and "passes with flying colors" if $\mu_t > 1$ for each such value of t. Accordingly, we compute this quantity and have `SpecTest()` return it by adding the line

```
RETURN( evalf(sqrt(Pi*f)^t/(m*GAMMA(1+t/2)),5) );
```

prior to the end; statement. (Incidentally, upper bounds for μ_t are 3.63, 5.92, 9.87, 14.89, and 23.87 for $t = 2, 3, 4, 5$, and 6, respectively.)

We can now rate the various generators. For example:

```
> m := 2^35: a := 3141592653:
> seq(SpecTest(m,a,t),t=2..6);
  Exhaustive search checks,3, points, nu^2 =, 2997222016
  Exhaustive search checks,3, points, nu^2 =, 1026050
  Exhaustive search checks,3, points, nu^2 =, 27822
  Exhaustive search checks,3, points, nu^2 =, 1118
  Exhaustive search checks,27, points, nu^2 =, 1118

     .27404, .12671, .11117, .0064025, .21018

>m := 10^10: a := 4219755981:
>seq(SpecTest(m,a,t),t=2..6);
 Exhaustive search checks,9, points, nu^2 =, 10721093248
 Exhaustive search checks,9, points, nu^2 =, 2595578
 Exhaustive search checks,3, points, nu^2 =, 49362
 Exhaustive search checks,1323, points, nu^2 =, 5868
 Exhaustive search checks,3, points, nu^2 =, 820

       3.3681, 1.7516, 1.2024, 1.3885, .28494
```

The first pair flunk the spectral test, and although the second pair pass, they don't do so with flying colors.

How does Maple's generator (rand()) do on the spectral test? The rand() function generates sequences using the formula $x_{n+1} = ax_n \bmod m$ as you can see from the next result:

```
> rand(1..50);

proc()
local t;
global _seed;
    _seed := irem(427419669081*_seed,999999999989);
    t := _seed;
    irem(t,50)+1
end
```

The examples in Section 9.5 on the `numtheory[]` package verified that this generator does have maximal period ($m − 1$), so that the spectral test is applicable. Here is the result from `SpecTest()`:

```
>Digits := 30:
>seq(SpecTest(999999999989,427419669081,t),t=2..6);


Exhaustive search checks,3, points, nu^2 =,651722379493
Exhaustive search checks,3, points, nu^2 =, 68362993
Exhaustive search checks,3, points, nu^2 =, 595862
Exhaustive search checks,9, points, nu^2 =, 51070
Exhaustive search checks,9, points, nu^2 =, 6635


        2.0474, 2.3676, 1.7522, 3.1026, 1.5095
```

This computation shows that Maple's random-number generator passes the spectral test with flying colors. Of course it not necessary to set m to be a machine-word size (that is, power of two) when computing in Maple, so the authors of Maple's random-number generator had the luxury of selecting m solely to give good random numbers. (For machines with a 64-bit word size, the pair $m = 2^{64}$ and $a = 6364136223846793005$ give a good generator.)

EXERCISES

The exercises given below can be generalized in many different ways and we encourage you to experiment.

1. The `tree()` procedure presented in Section 12.1 produces the following uninformative result for the expression tree of an array:

```
> a := array(1..4);


        a := array(1 .. 4, [])


> tree(a,0);
a Type[string]
```

Modify `tree()` to produce a more detailed tree structure for arrays. Repeat this exercise for tables.

2. Write a program to expand bilinear forms according to the following rules:
   (a) `[ax,y]` `=` `a[x,y]` (where a denotes a possibly complex numerical constant)

(b) $[x, ay] = \bar{a}[x,y]$ ($\bar{a}$ denotes a complex conjugate).

(c) $[x+y,z] = [x,z]+[y,z]$

(d) $[x,y+z] = [x,y]+[x,z]$

(e) $[[u,v]x,y] = [u,v][x,y]$

(f) $[x,[u,v]y] = [v,u][x,y]$

The rules are those of the Hermitian inner product for complex vectors.

3. Modify the graphics procedure in Section 12.3 to put a square flower on the end of the branches of the trees the given in the text. A square flower can be constructed, for example, from the string f+f+f+f, where the + signifies a ninety-degree rotation. The size of the flower should vary inversely with branch depth to simulate the stage of development.

4. Write a procedure in the spirit of Section 12.4 to analyze and synthesize two-dimensional finite-difference stencils.

5. Calculus of Variations: Given the functional

$$I(y) = \int_a^b F(x, y(x), y'(x))\,dx$$

and boundary condition $y(a) = \alpha$ for scalar-valued functions y, write a procedure that returns the corresponding Euler equation and natural boundary condition in a form suitable for input to dsolve().

6. The merge sort algorithm sorts an array of numbers using the following recursive algorithm.

- Sort the first half of the array.

- Sort the second half of the array.

- Merge the two sublists together to produce a sorted list.

The first two steps are preformed recursively.

For sufficiently large arrays, this algorithm is more efficient than the bubble sort algorithm given in Exercise 6 in Chapter 11. Write a program to implement the merge sort and use it to estimate the size of the array for which the merge sort becomes more efficient than the bubble sort.

7. Tower of Hanoi: You are given three lists, the first of which contains the integers $1, \ldots, N$ in order; the other two are empty. A single step consists of moving the last integer from the end of one list to the end of another list. At all times the lists must contain increasing sequences. The following algorithm shows how to move all of the integers from the first list to the third list.

- If there is only one number in the list, move it.

- Otherwise, move the top $n-1$ numbers from the first to the middle list using the last list for temporary storage.

- Move the remaining number to the last list.
- Move the top $n - 1$ numbers from the middle list to the third list using the first list for temporary storage.

Recursion enters at the second and fourth steps. Write a Maple procedure to implement this algorithm. If you are feeling sufficiently energetic, produce a visual animation of the motion of the integers between the lists.

Index